Transforming Corporate Governance in East Asia

Edited by
**Hideki Kanda, Kon-Sik Kim
and Curtis J. Milhaupt**

Routledge
Taylor & Francis Group

LONDON AND NEW YORK

First published 2008
by Routledge
2 Park Square, Milton Park, Abingdon, Oxon OX14 4RN

Simultaneously published in the USA and Canada
by Routledge
270 Madison Ave, New York, NY 10016

Routledge is an imprint of the Taylor & Francis Group, an informa business

© 2008 Editorial selection and matter, edited by Hideki Kanda, Kon-Sik Kim
and Curtis J. Milhaupt. Individual chapters, the contributors.

Typeset in Times New Roman by
Taylor & Francis Books
Printed and bound in Great Britain by
CPI Antony Rowe, Chippenham, Wiltshire

British Library Cataloguing in Publication Data
A catalogue record for this book is available from the British Library

Library of Congress Cataloging-in-Publication Data
Transforming corporate governance in East Asia / edited by Hideki Kanda,
    Kon-Sik Kim, Curtis J. Milhaupt.
        p. cm.
    1. Corporate governance–Law and legislation–East Asia.
    2. Corporation law–East Asia. I. Kanda, Hideki, 1953– II. Kim,
    Kon-sik, 1955– III. Milhaupt, Curtis J., 1962–
    KNC309.T73 2008
346.5'0664–dc22   2007052730

ISBN 978-0-415-45099-7 (hbk)
ISBN 978-0-203-93120-2 (ebk)

Transforming Corporate Governance in East Asia

Over the past ten years, the corporate governance environment in East Asia has undergone a significant transformation. The Asian Financial crisis, together with Japan's long economic malaise, undermined confidence in the corporate structures, governance practices, and regulatory oversight of firms in the region. Since that time, each of the countries in the region has been a hotbed of legislative, judicial, and market activity in the realm of corporate governance.

This book takes stock of the most important recent corporate governance changes in the region and the challenges still to be overcome. The contributors pursue this objective, not by describing laundry lists of legal reforms and problems, but by focused in-depth legal analysis on specific issues facing the separate systems in the wake of—sometimes in spite of—the voluminous reforms and market changes of the past decade. Written by the leading corporate law scholars and policy advisors in East Asia and some of the most renowned scholars of comparative corporate governance in the United States, the papers are methodologically united in their careful attention to the impact, and limitations, of legal reforms on corporate governance in East Asia today.

This volume will be of interest to legal scholars, economists, political scientists and sociologists interested in comparative corporate governance, Asian law and Asian economics

Hideki Kanda is Professor of Law at the University of Tokyo and Director of its Center of Excellence in Business Law.

Kon-Sik Kim is Professor of Law at Seoul National University and Director of its Center for Financial Law.

Curtis J. Milhaupt is Fuyo Professor of Japanese Law; Albert E. Cinelli Enterprise Professor of Law; and Director of the Center for Japanese Legal Studies at Columbia Law School.

Contents

Illustrations

Figure

Tables

Contributors

Donald C. Clarke is a Professor of Law at the George Washington University Law School, where his primary field of research and publication is Chinese law. He has testified before Congress on the Chinese legal system and is a member of the Council on Foreign Relations.

Tomotaka Fujita is Professor of Law at the University of Tokyo. He is the co-director of the University's Center of Excellence in Business Law.

Ronald J. Gilson is the Mark & Eva Stern Professor of Law and Business at Columbia Law School, and the Charles J. Meyers Professor of Law and Business at Stanford Law School. He is a fellow of the American Academy of Arts and Sciences and of the European Corporate Governance Institute.

Nicholas C. Howson is an Assistant Professor of Law at the University of Michigan Law School. Prior to entering academia, he was a partner of the international law firm Paul, Weiss, Rifkind, Wharton & Garrison, where he served as managing partner of the firm's China practice and Beijing office. He has advised on the drafting of Chinese corporate and securities legislation.

Hideki Kanda is Professor of Law at the University of Tokyo and Co-Director of its Center of Excellence in Business Law. He is deeply involved in corporate, securities, and financial law reform in Japan, and served as the Chair of the Corporate Value Study Group, which provided advice to the Japanese government on hostile takeover policy.

Hwa-Jin Kim is Associate Professor of Law and Business at Seoul National University College of Law. He has advised the Office of the President of Korea and is a member of the Specialist Chapter of the National Economic Advisory Council to the President of Korea.

Kon-Sik Kim is Professor of Law at Seoul National University and Director of its Center for Financial Law. He has advised the Korean government on legal reform and has served as an independent director of several major Korean firms.

Michael Klausner is the Nancy and Charles Munger Professor of Business and Professor of Law at Stanford Law School. Prior to entering academia, he was a White House Fellow, practicing lawyer, and law clerk to Justice William Brennon.

Lawrence S. Liu is Executive Vice President and Chief Strategy Officer of China Development Holding, President of China Development Industrial Bank, and adjunct professor at the Soochow University Graduate School of Law and National Taiwan University Graduate School of Management, in Taipei. He is a permanent core member of the OECD Asian Corporate Governance Roundtable.

Curtis J. Milhaupt is the Fuyo Professor of Japanese Law and the Albert E. Cinelli Enterprise Professor of Law at Columbia Law School. He has organized major corporate governance projects for non-governmental organizations and was a member of an international project team on the institutional consequences of Korean unification.

Kenichi Osugi is Professor of Law at Chuo University in Tokyo. An expert on mergers and acquisitions, defensive tactics, and securities regulation, he was a member of the Corporate Value Study Group, which provided advice and recommendations to the Japanese government on hostile takeover policy.

Yuan-Chi (Carol) Pang is a J.D. candidate at Yale Law School. She holds an LL.M. from National Taiwan University.

Ok-Rial Song is Assistant Professor of Law at Seoul National University College of Law. Formerly, he worked as an attorney for Kim & Chang, a major Korean law firm, and participated in several governmental projects on corporate governance reform of *chaebol* firms.

Xin Tang is Associate Professor of Law at Tsinghua University in Beijing. He has worked as an attorney, arbitrator, and independent director in China, and serves on a panel of expert advisors to the China Securities Regulatory Commission.

Wen-Yeu (Wallace) Wang is Professor of Law and Director of the Center for Corporate and Financial Law at the College of Law, National Taiwan University. He was a Commissioner of the Taiwan Fair Trade Commission from 2004 to 2006, and practiced law in Taipei and New York prior to entering academia.

Introduction

The (uneven, incomplete, and unpredictable) transformation of corporate governance in East Asia

Curtis J. Milhaupt

A decade ago, who could have predicted that a book on corporate governance[1] in East Asia would contain essays on hostile takeovers in Japan and Korea, a call for class action securities litigation in China, or analyses of shareholder litigation against the managers of Korea's flagship conglomerates? Yet readers will find these essays and much more that is novel between the covers of this book. As the title of this volume declares, the corporate governance environment in East Asia has undergone a significant transformation. The Asian financial crisis, together with Japan's long economic malaise, undermined confidence in the corporate structures, governance practices, and regulatory oversight of firms in the region. Although China escaped the direct effects of the Asian financial crisis, policy makers there took note of the consequences of weak corporate governance institutions for domestic economies. Since that time, each of the countries in the region has been a hotbed of legislative, judicial, and market activity in the realm of corporate governance.

Begin with legislative activity. China has already replaced the original corporate and securities laws enacted at the outset of its economic reform process. In Tokyo and Seoul, corporate and securities reforms have been enacted at a feverish pace since the late 1990s. Among the most salient of these legislative reforms, shareholders' rights were bolstered, rules on takeovers were streamlined, and the liability regime for corporate directors was made more shareholder friendly. Board composition changed as a result of mandatory independent director requirements in Korea, China, and Taiwan. In Japan, firms were given an option to switch to U.S.-style committee structure for the board (see Gilson and Milhaupt 2005).

Throughout the region, courts became players in corporate governance essentially for the first time. The phenomenon is most apparent in Japan and Korea, and the judicial decisions generated over the past ten years by shareholder derivative litigation and hostile takeover attempts are analyzed in depth by several authors in this volume. Even in China, pressure built to permit shareholders to sue corporate issuers and their managers for securities fraud. Although to date, Chinese courts are far from effective vehicles for investor protection, it seems significant simply that the judiciary has become engaged in corporate governance issues.

Simultaneous with these legal developments, market conditions and corporate practices have changed in important ways. Stable shareholding patterns weakened in Japan (though they seem to be on the rise again[2]), foreign portfolio ownership grew substantially, particularly in Korea and Japan, and institutional investors became more active in their pursuit of higher financial returns on their investments. Incidents of firm-level shareholder activism vis-à-vis management are on the rise in each country. Hostile takeover bids and other aggressive takeover tactics—once literally unheard of in the region—have become relatively routine (if still controversial) events.

Against this backdrop of legal and market activity, China's rising economic influence has added several new dimensions to the corporate governance environment in East Asia. The emergence of publicly held Chinese firms, and their listing on overseas stock exchanges, has highlighted serious corporate governance issues in the world's fastest growing major economy. The flap over CNOOC's bid for Unocal in 2005 is only the first of what promises to be a host of controversies over Chinese financing and governance practices as the country's firms expand their investments and operations internationally. Moreover, to the extent that domestic institutional quality affects firm and country competitiveness, China's rise has lent a strategic imperative to improving economic institutions and governance practices across the region.

Thus, in many important dimensions, there has been a transformation of corporate governance in East Asia over the past decade. One objective of the essays in this volume is to take stock of these developments. The authors pursue this objective, not by making laundry lists of legislative reforms, but by focusing in-depth legal analysis on specific issues facing the national systems in the wake of—sometimes in spite of—the voluminous reforms and market changes of the past decade. Thematically, the chapters focus on takeovers, managerial liability, the governance problems endemic to controlling minority shareholder structures, and legal enforcement mechanisms.

Despite this "transformation," however, big challenges remain throughout the region. Activist (particularly foreign) investors in Korea and Japan have faced stubborn resistance to the introduction of practices identified with "Western" (or more specifically "American") capitalism. Hostile takeover attempts, though no longer unprecedented, are still viewed with considerable suspicion, and a complete policy and legal framework for takeovers is not yet in place in any East Asian country. Many Chinese listed companies are beset with corporate governance problems resulting from heavy state involvement in their management and financing, as well as inadequate monitoring and enforcement structures at both the firm and state level. Taiwanese firms face the problems inherent in any controlling family ownership structure—potential exploitation of minority shareholders—yet corporate governance reforms in Taiwan over the past decade have often been swayed by larger political dynamics related to its unique and precarious geopolitical situation (see the essay by Lawrence S. Liu in this volume). Xenophobia, while certainly not unique to East Asia, has colored perceptions of the legislative and market reforms catalogued above. In Korea, for example, attempts to reform the *chaebol* family conglomerates are often cast in the media as foreign-inspired attempts to kill the goose that has laid the golden egg of Korean prosperity. Japanese courts recently threw the proverbial book at two maverick players in the takeover market for securities law violations—Takafumi Horie, who created a huge stir in Japan when his firm, Livedoor, launched an unsolicited tender offer for Nippon Broadcasting Corporation (chronicled in this volume by Kenichi Osugi) and Yoshiaki Murakami, head of a buyout fund convicted of insider trading in connection with the tender offer. Though both men are Japanese, the controversy surrounding their activities stems in large measure from the perception that they adopted distinctively un-Japanese business practices in the pursuit of profit. The possibility that both men were selectively prosecuted and sentenced cannot be ruled out.

Thus, the volume not only discusses the most important corporate governance changes in the region, it also highlights the challenges still to be overcome. Written by the leading corporate law scholars and policy advisors in East Asia and some of the most renowned scholars of comparative corporate governance in the United States, the papers are united in their careful attention to the *impact*—and *limitations*—of legal reforms on corporate governance in East Asia today. The essays in this book grapple deeply with the way legal rules (whether in the hands of legislators, judges, or investors) are formed and enforced, how they influence market behavior, and the limits of legal solutions to Asia's corporate governance problems. Readers of this volume will not only be quickly brought up to speed on the current "state of play" in corporate Japan, Korea, China, and Taiwan, but also made privy to analysis of key issues facing each of these systems by the region's leading scholars and policy advisors.

Yet this is not intended as a book written solely *by* lawyers *for* lawyers. "Governance" has become a central policy and research theme around the world. How countries transform their economic institutions, how firms restructure, and the larger linkages between economic governance, political accountability, and competitiveness are questions occupying scholars and policy analysts well outside the confines of the law. Indeed, as suggested above, the quality and adaptability of a country's economic institutions seems to have taken on regional and perhaps even geopolitical significance in today's global markets.[3] Not only is the topic of interest to those outside the law, but a close reading of this volume shows that legal scholars themselves do not have a uniform view of law's role in corporate governance. Several authors in this volume treat law as relatively autonomous. That is, they limit their focus to statutes, court cases, and legal enforcement mechanisms, analyzing the operation of law solely according to its own internal mechanisms. By contrast, other authors devote far less attention to legal detail and focus instead on the interaction of law with other processes, be they political, social, or market oriented. Donald Clarke, in his essay, goes even further and focuses exclusively on non-legal institutions needed to complement China's weak legal infrastructure for corporate governance. Neither the law-centric approach nor the more holistic approach is necessarily the "correct" way to approach these issues. Much can be learned, for example, through close analysis of court cases—an approach pursued to excellent effect by Kon-Sik Kim, Kenichi Osugi, Nicolas Howson, and a number of other contributors to this volume. At the same time, the contributions by authors such as Clarke, Ronald Gilson and Michael Klausner rightly emphasize that law's effectiveness both affects and depends upon a wide range of non-legal forces which shape human behavior and organizational structures. One unique aspect of this volume's exploration of the topic is this mixture of careful, lawyerly analysis with broader-gauged focuses on surrounding institutional settings.

Common themes

Several themes emerge out of these essays, and these themes provide guideposts for evaluating the future trajectory of corporate governance reform in East Asia. One common theme is the distinction between legislation and enforcement. While the authors (particularly of the essays on Taiwan) identify some specific areas of needed legislative improvement, taken together these essays suggest that the corporate and securities laws in the region—at a formal level—are now of high quality. Indeed, several authors explicitly make the point that their country's corporate law is essentially indistinguishable from that of the United States and other developed western countries. Even if, as the influential law and finance literature suggests, legal protections for investors are crucial to stock market development and dispersed shareholding structures (see La Porta *et al.* 1997; 1998), there is little reason to believe that today serious legislative shortcomings are holding back corporate governance improvements in East Asia. Thus, if legal obstacles to good corporate governance remain, they remain largely outside the statute books. Of course, this is to be expected. Even major legislative reforms of the sort witnessed throughout post-financial crisis Asia are rarely adequate to change behavior in the absence of effective enforcement practices.

This problem is not unique to East Asia, and it has become a truism in the literature that "law on the books" matters far less than "law as enforced." What it may mean for the East Asian systems, however, is that the hardest work still lies ahead. Given political obstacles and the law of unintended consequences, amending statutes to achieve a policy result is not itself a particularly easy task, as the essays in this volume by Tomotaka Fujita and Ok-Rial Song attest. But improving enforcement is typically even more difficult, because it requires resource allocation, regulatory competence, consensus on enforcement priorities, and sometimes even the creation of entirely new institutions or practices.

The precise natures of the enforcement problems confronting the corporate governance systems examined here differ substantially, of course, particularly given the dramatic stage-of-development differences among these systems. But many contributors to this volume, regardless of the system they are examining, focus on the role of the judiciary as a critical, but still underdeveloped, enforcement mechanism in corporate governance. A number of the essays that follow raise serious questions about whether the courts in the various East Asian systems are up to the task of serving as effective enforcers of corporate and securities laws. Skepticism about judicial competence arises either from an author's macro-level analysis of judicial structure, training, and politics, or from a micro-analysis of judicial reasoning in specific cases. It is worth emphasizing again that no judiciary in the region, regardless of stage of economic and institutional development, seems immune from questions of this type. Thus, these essays suggest that judicial competence in deciding corporate and securities cases is a bellwether of corporate governance improvements throughout the region.

Another common theme is the ongoing problem posed by controlling minority shareholder structures, particularly in the Korean and Taiwanese contexts. This problem has defined the two corporate governance regimes since their inception, and despite a heightened awareness of the detrimental impact such structures can pose for investors and capital market development, addressing the problem remains a daunting challenge. The reasons why economically inefficient controlling shareholder structures persist are now well understood as a theoretical matter. (See Bebchuk and Roe 1999, Gilson 2006 and Wang and Pang in this volume.) The question raised by the contributors to this volume is whether legal or market forces are better suited to make headway against these obstacles. Readers will not find a uniform response to this question between the covers of this book. That is not surprising, given the knottiness of the issues involved. If one *were* to hazard a prediction on the basis of these essays, the safest would be that policy makers and academics will still be struggling to find ways of mitigating the problems of controlling shareholder structures a decade from now.

The contributions to this volume also subtly underscore an irony that merits greater attention: Many of the essays highlight the impact of global capital markets, particularly an influx of foreign investors, on domestic corporate governance regimes.[4] Yet China's economic ascendancy underscores the continuing role of the state in corporate governance, almost twenty years after the collapse of the socialist regimes of Eastern Europe. Not only must scholars and policy makers find new ways to understand corporate governance problems in an economy heavily populated by state-owned enterprises (SOEs), a crucial task unto itself; beyond Chinese SOEs is an emerging category of firms that might be called "state-influenced enterprises." Consider corporate governance in an Asian country not examined in this volume, Singapore. A major shareholder of many publicly listed firms in Singapore is Temasek Holdings, a state investment vehicle. Today, many governments are examining the Temasek model as a means of more effectively investing their foreign exchange reserves and maintaining state influence over important distributional issues in corporate governance, such as employment stability. We may need a new conceptual apparatus to fully understand the corporate governance problems and priorities of state-owned and state-influenced enterprises. Although that is a task for future scholarship,[5] this book implicitly suggests the importance of new thinking about these issues, particularly as scholars grapple with "Asian" corporate governance problems.

Organization and chapter summaries

The book is divided into four parts—three containing country- (or in the case of mainland China/Taiwan, system-) specific analyses, and one containing more thematic analysis and commentary.

Part I: Japan

Tomotaka Fujita, "Transformation of the management liability regime in Japan in the wake of the 1993 revision." Fujita examines the swing of the pendulum with regard to managerial liability following a (seemingly minor) revision of the procedures for bringing shareholder derivative suits in 1993. In a fascinating analysis, Fujita shows how and why the scope of the liability regime has swung back and forth in the hands of legislators, judges, and corporate lobbyists. His conclusion that "the magnitude of the 1993 revision has been considerably mitigated" will surprise and educate even careful observers of Japanese corporate governance.

Kenichi Osugi, "Transplanting poison pills in foreign soil: Japan's experiment." In this essay, a member of an influential advisory committee to the government provides an insider's analysis of Japan's new rules for hostile takeover defenses. Osugi trenchantly analyzes the rise of U.S.-inspired "poison pill" defenses in the Japanese market, and provides a unique political economy perspective on the development of hostile takeovers in Japan from his vantage point on the advisory committee. Osugi carefully analyzes recent judicial decisions on the validity of takeover defenses under the new Japanese legal regime.

Hideki Kanda, "What shapes corporate law in Japan?" There is a long-standing debate in the United States about the role of jurisdictional competition in the creation of corporate law. To the extent that commentators have ever brought Japan into this debate, they have assumed that competition does not play a role in the creation of corporate law in Japan due to its unitary governmental structure. Kanda argues that, in fact, Japanese corporate law has been shaped by competitive influences, but those influences have come from the securities law. He advances and illustrates the provocative argument that for large Japanese companies today, the securities law is more important than the corporate law.[6]

Collectively, these three essays in this part provide striking evidence of change in Japanese corporate governance. Their focus is on the courts, the market for corporate control, and political-economy influences on legislation—topics that would not have registered a heartbeat in Japan's corporate governance debate a decade ago. Equally significant is what is *not* discussed—or even mentioned—in these chapters: the main bank system, bureaucratic guidance of economic players, and stable, long-term relationships among firms in corporate groups. .

Part II: Korea

The defining characteristic of Korean corporate organization and governance both pre- and post- Asian financial crisis is the *chaebol* structure—family-controlled conglomerates that dominate the Korean economy. In the background of all three essays on Korea is the continuing struggle to address the *"chaebol* problem" of controlling minority-shareholder exploitation of public minority shareholders.

Hwa-Jin Kim, "A tale of three companies: the emerging market for corporate control in Korea." Kim argues that the market for corporate control transcends cultural boundaries and is an essential component of good corporate governance in any system. His essay analyzes the current state of the market for corporate control in Korea by examining three recent, high-profile judicial decisions and related regulations involving takeover attempts or other activist shareholder challenges to management of the *chaebol*. All three cases show how Korea is struggling to adapt in the wake of an important post-Asian financial crisis development—the rise of foreign ownership of listed Korean firms. Kim asserts that in order for the market for corporate control to function effectively in Korea, legal duties and liabilities of directors must be developed beyond their current state under Korean corporate law.

Ok-Rial Song, "Improving corporate governance through litigation: derivative suits and class actions in Korea." In contrast to Hwa-Jin Kim, Song begins with the premise that the market for corporate control and other market constraints on managers are unlikely to be made functional in Korea. Thus, legal mechanisms are needed. In this provocative paper, Song argues that, despite a host of legal reforms that brought Korean corporate law up to international standards, Korean corporate governance will not improve significantly unless a "lawyer-driven legal market" similar to the U.S. model—replete with incentives to bring class action suits and derivative litigation—is developed in Korea.

Kon-Sik Kim, "The role of judges in corporate governance: the Korean experience." Through careful analysis of recent lawsuits brought by shareholders against executives of the *chaebol*, Kim shows that Korean judges display a striking schizophrenia in their rulings. At times they are highly formalistic in their interpretation of the corporate law; at other times they freely depart from the text of the code to make results-oriented decisions. Kim discusses several possible explanations for this behavior, including the possibility that Korean judges are finding ways to rule in favor of successful business structures seen to be under attack by short-term profit-minded foreign investors.

Part III: Greater China (The Mainland and Taiwan)

Xin Tang, "Protection of minority shareholders in China: a task for both legislation and enforcement." Tang provides a detailed overview of recent corporate and securities law reforms that have significantly improved the *formal* environment for corporate governance in China. Tang then discusses possible strategies to improve enforcement capabilities, without which, he sensibly argues, the legislative improvements will have little effect on corporate governance. In particular, Tang argues that China is ready for a class action suit mechanism for corporate and securities fraud.

Donald Clarke, "The role of non-legal institutions in Chinese corporate governance." A complement to Tang's contribution, this essay emphasizes the *limitations* inherent in China's formal corporate governance institutions, and carefully examines the potential of non-legal institutions to improve shareholder protections and managerial accountability in China. Clarke's appraisal of the contemporary Chinese corporate governance environment may not inspire optimism, but it does provide a trenchant road map for institutional improvement in China.

Nicholas Howson, "The doctrine that dared not speak its name: Anglo-American fiduciary duties in China's company law and case law intimations of prior convergence." Through extensive case analysis, Howson shows that, conventional wisdom about China's "civil law origins" notwithstanding, Chinese judges have developed "Anglo-American" fiduciary doctrines to decide corporate cases. This is significant, because some scholars have pointed to the critical role of judges in applying fiduciary duties as an important component of investor protections in the United States (see, e.g. Coffee 1989). If Howson's analysis is accurate, the Chinese courts may have greater capacity to provide investor protections than is commonly assumed.

Lawrence S. Liu, "The Politics of Corporate Governance in Taiwan." Liu examines the unique political context in which corporate law and governance reform takes place in Taiwan. He highlights numerous political-economy reasons why, despite meaningful legal reforms over the past decade, a robust environment for good corporate governance has been slow to develop in Taiwan.

Wen-Yeu Wang and Yuan-Chi Pang, "An analytical framework for controlling minority shareholders and its application to Taiwan." Wang and Pang provide a framework for understanding the circumstances giving rise to controlling minority-shareholder structures. Using that framework and carefully parsing key provisions of Taiwan's corporate law, they conclude that the controlling minority-shareholder structures that pervade Taiwanese corporate governance are likely the result of poor legal protections for investors rather than of a value-enhancing monitoring strategy. Their analysis shows how difficult is it remedy controlling-shareholder abuses through legislation.

Part IV: Analysis and commentary

The final part of the book contains two essays offering non-country-specific analyses of important facets of Asian corporate governance.

Ronald Gilson, "Controlling family shareholders in Asia: anchoring relational exchange." In this essay, Gilson explores one of the most puzzling features of corporate structures in East Asia: Why do we observe minority shareholders at all, given the potential for exploitation posed by controlling-family ownership structures? Provocatively, Gilson suggests that in a weak legal environment for contract enforcement, a firm's treatment of minority shareholders may serve as a device to signal the firm's reliability to trade partners and creditors. Thus, minority shareholders are the "canary in the coal mine," indicating whether it is safe to do business with a firm even in the absence of a strong legal system.

Michael Klausner, "The uncertain promise of shareholder suits in Asian corporate governance." Klausner notes that shareholder suits figure prominently in corporate governance reform in Asia, and Asian reform advocates continue to seek liberalized shareholder access to courts. At the same time in the U.S., many argue that the costs of shareholder suits exceed their benefit, and that in reality the risk of liability is insignificant (e.g. Black *et al.* 2006). Klausner does not claim that shareholder suits cannot be beneficial additions to Korean, Chinese, and Japanese corporate governance regimes. But he cautions that two questions should be addressed as reformers pursue their agendas: Will the shareholder suits operate in these countries differently from how they operate in the U.S.? If not, does the absence of other governance mechanisms justify the introduction of shareholder suits even with their flaws?

Conclusion

So the transformation of corporate governance in East Asia is uneven—despite some powerful forces driving reform in all systems, each is simultaneously responding to locally entrenched interests, domestic politics, and distinctive institutional cultures that shape change in unique ways. The transformation is incomplete—not only with respect to enforcement, but also more fundamentally in the sense that a widely shared consensus on the proper role of the corporation in society remains elusive. The dramatic economic events in East Asia over the past decade upended many stable expectations about how economic actors and their regulators should behave. Yet, not surprisingly, legal and market change have been insufficient to completely alter long-standing mindsets about big issues such as the purpose of the corporation and the proper relationship between the firm and its various stakeholders. Complicating matters even further, China's rapid economic growth has taken place in a heavily state-interventionist form of capitalism without many of the legal and organizational features commonly deemed essential in the conventional wisdom. For all of these reasons, the transformation of corporate governance in East Asia remains unpredictable. Readers of this volume will not find a crystal ball with which to predict future developments, but they will find a useful map for understanding, if only imperfectly, where we now stand and the general direction in which institutional reforms are leading.

Notes

1 Corporate governance refers essentially to the distribution of rights and responsibilities among different participants in the corporation, most prominently the shareholders and directors, and the structures that promote fulfillment of corporate objectives and compliance with legal requirements. See, e.g. OECD "Principles of Corporate Governance" 2004.
2 "Cross-Shareholding Sees First Rise Since '90s," *Kyodo News*, September 2, 2007.
3 Lest anyone think this claim is overwrought, consider the angst-laden report of the so-called Paulson Committee on the Sarbanes-Oxley Act's possible impact on the competitiveness of the U.S. capital markets, particularly vis-à-vis London, which operates under a regime of considerably less regulatory intensity. Committee on Capital Market Regulation 2006.
4 For other perspectives on this issue, see Milhaupt 2003.
5 The discussion in this paragraph anticipates work I am undertaking with Ronald Gilson.
6 A similar claim has been made with respect to the situation in the United States. See Thompson and Sale 2003.

References

Bebchuk, Lucian, and Mark Roe (1999) "A Theory of Path Dependence in Corporate Governance and Ownership," *Stanford Law Review* 52: 127–170.
Black, Bernard, Brian Cheffins and Michael Klausner (2006) "Outside Director Liability," *Stanford Law Review* 58: 1055–1158.
Coffee, John C. Jr. (1989) "The Mandatory/Enabling Balance in Corporate Law: An Essay on the Judicial Role," *Columbia Law Review* 89: 1618–1691.
Committee on Capital Market Regulation (2006) Available at www.capmktsreg.org/pdfs/11.30Committee_Interim_ReportREV2.pdf.
Gilson, Ronald (2006) "Controlling Shareholders in Corporate Governance: Complicating the Comparative Taxonomy," *Harvard Law Review* 116: 1641–1678.
Gilson, Ronald and Curtis J. Milhaupt (2005) "Choice as Regulatory Reform: The Case of Japanese Corporate Governance," *American Journal of Comparative Law* 53: 343–377.
La Porta, Rafael, Florencio Lopez-de-Silanes, Andrei Shleifer, and Robert W. Vishny (1997) "Legal Determinants of External Finance," *Journal of Finance* LII (3):1131–1150.

—— (1998) "Law and Finance," *Journal of Political Economy* 106 (6): 1113–1155.

Milhaupt, Curtis (2003) *Global Markets, Domestic Institutions: Corporate Law and Governance in a New Era of Cross-Border Deals* (New York: Columbia University Press)

Organization for Economic Cooperation and Development (OECD) (2004) "Principles of Corporate Governance", available at www.oecd.org.

Thompson, Robert and Hillary Sale (2003) "Securities Fraud as Corporate Governance: Reflections upon Federalism," *Vanderbilt Law Review* 56: 859–910.

Part I
Japan

1 Transformation of the management liability regime in Japan in the wake of the 1993 revision

Tomotaka Fujita

Introduction

Few would disagree that the reform of the derivative action system in 1993 was one of the most influential events in the history of the Japanese corporate governance regime. The shareholders' derivative action, which had been dormant since its introduction in 1950, was suddenly activated. No other revision has been more criticized by the business community. Few revisions have been more controversial in academic circles.

It was, however, a little enigmatic as to why this reform took place at all. It has been well recognized in recent economic literature that corporate governance systems in each state are full of "complementarities."[1] When a system is marked by strong and widespread complementarities, it may be difficult to change. Changing only a few of the system components, rather than a fully coordinated move of the whole system, may have negative effects.[2] Although economic analyses often focus on complementarities among non-legal elements or between legal and non-legal elements of the corporate governance system, they also exist between legal rules. Kanda and Fujita (1998), for example, argued that complementarities among legal rules are the key to understanding the variety and the evolution of the corporate law in each country. Their argument puts forward the following predictions:

1 The legal rules are stable where strong complementarities exist among them. Even if a specific rule looks inefficient, it does not easily disappear under these conditions.
2 Legal rules are unstable where strong complementarities do not exist. Numerous corporate law reforms in post-war Japan have occurred in areas where relatively weak complementarities exist.
3 Even where strong complementarities exist, change could occur if an extraordinary force simultaneously changes a set of rules as a whole. Such changes would take place within an unusual political environment—Japanese corporate reform following World War II, under the direction of GHQ, is a notable example.

Although Kanda and Fujita (1998) observe that the development of Japanese corporate law has basically followed the pattern suggested above, the 1993 Revision of the Commercial Code, which includes the reform of derivative actions, was a notable exception for their hypothesis.[3] The 1993 Revision took place in an area where one of the strongest complementarities exists, and a single but significant rule was changed without changing any rules which could have correlations. It was, and still is, difficult to understand how such a phenomenon could ever occur.[4]

However, the story did not end there. The management liability regime under Japanese corporate law has experienced continuing change since 1993. It is a little unfortunate that much corporate governance literature focuses on the 1993 reform in an isolated manner and simply ignores the subsequent changes. This article traces the aftermath of the 1993 Revision.

The article begins with the 1993 Revision of derivative actions. While the Revision is relatively well known,[5] a brief explanation here may be helpful. Empirical studies of the reform are also reviewed. The article then goes on to examine the further developments of procedural rules for derivative action. They can be regarded as a direct response to the 1993 Revision. The reform of the exoneration procedure for management liability, another direct response to the revision follows. Finally, we will see the changes in substantive rules on management liability.

The 1993 Revision as an unexpected shock

Derivative actions under Japanese law: before the 1993 Revision

Derivative actions were incorporated into Japanese corporate law by way of the 1950 Revision, together with other elements of the American system, including the board system and authorized capital. The number of derivative actions, however, was surprisingly modest until the 1990s.[6] Although the small number of derivative actions has sometimes been erroneously attributed to the general anti-litigation sentiment among the Japanese people,[7] the litigation fee became recognized as the real determining factor.

Under the Japanese litigation system, plaintiffs must pay the litigation fee upon filing a lawsuit,[8] and the fee is calculated based on the "amount of the claim" (Article 3 of the Law on the Fee of Civil Lawsuits). It was thought, in court practice, that the "amount of the claim" in a derivative action was the amount of the management's alleged liabilities to the company, and not the economic benefit of the plaintiff (i.e., individual shareholders) should they win. This meant that shareholders had first to pay large sums of money, before they could file a derivative action claim for substantial damages.[9] Although this interpretation was later decided by the Supreme Court to be incorrect,[10] the court practice had been a grave obstacle to derivative action in Japan for many years.

The 1993 Revision as an unexpected shock

The 1993 Revision of the Commercial Code effectively set a ceiling for the litigation fee.[11] The revised Article 267(4) of the Commercial Code provides that derivative actions "shall be deemed to be lawsuits with respect to non-property claims for the calculation of the amount of the claim." The amount of non-property claims was, pursuant to Article 4(2) of the Law on the Fee of Civil Lawsuits, deemed to be JPY950,000 and the litigation fee was fixed at JPY8,200, regardless of the amount of alleged liability.

Although a similar proposal had been advocated by some academics,[12] it was a little surprising that such a reform had been achieved so easily and without resistance from industry. Whatever the reason driving the Revision, it was effective enough, and the number of derivative actions has risen considerably since 1993.[13]

Numbers of derivative suits pending at district and high courts

Date	District courts	High courts	Total
31 December 1993	76	10	86
31 December 1994	129	10	139
31 December 1995	148	14	162
31 December 1996	150	13	163
31 December 1997	172	15	187
31 December 1998	186	14	200
31 December 1999	202	18	220
31 December 2000	187	20	20
31 December 2001	166	23	189
31 December 2002	141	NA	NA
31 December 2003	150	NA	NA
31 December 2004	126	NA	NA
31 December 2005	102	NA	NA

The economic impact of the Revision

Introduction

Was the reform good news for corporate governance in Japan? Has the performance of Japanese companies improved due to increased pressure from shareholders? Proponents of the unique governance system of Japanese firms might argue that the high costs of litigation had effectively suppressed shareholder activism and had also protected the unique system ("J-model") under which management is relatively independent of the shareholders' interests.[14] From this point of view, the 1993 Revision had a seriously detrimental impact. On the other hand, a recent series of empirical studies assert that firms show more excellent performance in those legal systems with greater shareholders' rights.[15] It might be argued that the reform, in the long run, would improve the performance of Japanese firms.

The answers to these questions are inconclusive. This is in part because a long recession of the Japanese economy followed the 1993 Revision and the macro-economic influence made the impact of the revision somewhat untraceable. If data on the impact on firms' performance in general is not available, one must focus on other kinds of data.

The effect of the filing of derivative actions

A line of literature studies the impact of the filing of derivative action after the 1993 revision and suggests that litigation simply destroys the value of firms. West (2001) and Fukuda (2000) using the method of "event study," have found there has been a very small—perhaps even a slightly negative—impact on the return of a company's stock due to the filing of derivative suits. The results seem plausible when one takes into account the low probability of successful suits and the limited amounts recoverable in such cases. Studies in the United States had already shown similar findings.[16]

However, the decline of the company's value at the beginning of a derivative action, at least in theory, does not necessarily mean that such litigation should always be avoided. The principal should, in some cases, enforce the agent's liability—even when the enforcement itself is not cost-effective—in order to give an optimal incentive to the agent.[17] This is a phenomenon that economic literature calls "dynamic inconsistency," where an optimal *ex post* action does not offer the optimal *ex ante* incentive.[18] A derivative action may be such an example.

The effect of the 1993 Revision on the stock price of firms whose managements were sued

Is the incentive effect of possible derivative action plausible? Although critics of the derivative actions may assert that the disciplinary effect is illusory, there has been no empirical study that supports the assertion. Hirose and Yanagawa (2002) tried to measure the disciplinary effects of the enhanced probability of derivative action. They analyzed the reaction of stock prices of the Nikkei 225 Companies to the 1993 Revision. Their analysis found that the share prices of those firms whose directors were sued by derivative action shortly after the Revision showed a negative response to the 1993 Revision, as compared to those of other firms. In addition, they compared (1) those firms whose directors lost a derivative action after the Revision and (2) those firms whose directors won. It was confirmed that the former showed a relatively deeper drop in their stock price. From these findings, they conclude that the Revision enhanced the disciplinary effect on management misbehavior.

Although the increased probability of the derivative action, in theory, could (1) cause the company increased expected costs resulting from the litigation and (2) enhance the disciplinary effect on managements' future behavior, Hirose and Yanagawa (2002) interpret the negative reaction of the firms' stock prices to be a proxy of the increased probability of subsequent derivative actions.[19] The reason is as follows: It is most likely that the derivative actions analyzed in the article are related to management behavior prior to the 1993 Revision—which, of course, was not influenced by the change. Therefore, one can safely assume that the different reaction of stock price between those firms whose managements were sued after the revision and other firms reflects the increased probability of litigation and related costs to the company.

If shareholders' derivative actions work correctly (i.e., if derivative actions are more likely to be brought against those who would be held responsible in the final decision), the stock market would expect the 1993 Revision to raise the probability of litigation against those companies whose directors acted improperly before the Revision more sharply than others, and the stock prices of such companies would drop accordingly. This was exactly the result that Hirose and Yanagawa (2002) found in their study. Therefore, Hirose and Yanagawa (2002) conclude that the stock market anticipated that the directors who were expected to be held responsible in the final decision were more likely to be sued than others, and in this sense the 1993 Revision enhanced the monitoring function over misbehavior on the part of management.

Several reservations should be appended to the above conclusion. First, even if the Revision enhanced the monitoring function and thereby improved the firms' performances, as Hirose and Yanagawa (2002) argue, the effect might not outweigh the expected cost of wasteful litigations. Second, the conclusion was drawn on the hypothesis that those directors who lost a derivative action had "misbehaved" prior to the Revision. This assumption relies upon an optimistic view that the substantive rules on management liability under Japanese corporate law are correctly imposed on behaviors that need to be deterred, and that the court does not err in applying those rules. As is shown in the latter part of this article, the substantive rules on management liability changed significantly after the 1993 Revision, and this casts a strong doubt upon the assumption that the rules at that time were optimal.

Summary

The number of derivative actions increased dramatically after the 1993 Revision. The Revision attracted the attention of corporate law researchers, who tried to measure its economic impact. For the reasons explained in this section, the result was ambiguous. What is worse, there is another factor that makes the conclusion even more indeterminate. Although commentators have focused on the increased number of derivative actions, this cannot constitute a complete evaluation of the 1993 Revision. It is not merely the number of litigations that the Revision caused; rather, considerable and subsequent transformations have occurred in the management liability regime in the wake of the Revision.[20] The following sections trace those changes.

Transformation in procedural rules on derivative actions

Abusive use of derivative actions

Soon after the 1993 Revision, many lawyers recognized the necessity of properly regulating worthless litigations. Although the possibility for the "abusive use" of derivative actions had often been mentioned (or even exaggerated) prior to the 1993 Revision, the nature of the problem of possibly worthless derivative actions was not well understood until recently.

The possibility of abusive litigations is not a phenomenon unique to derivative actions and it is, to some extent, unavoidable for any judicial procedure. However, it is worth noting that "abusive litigation" has a unique feature in the context of derivative actions as compared to ordinary litigation. "Abusive litigation" ordinarily means an unreasonable filing of an action by the plaintiff, with intent to harass the defendant or to acquire unjustified benefits from litigation at the expense of the defendant. The main concern with worthless derivative actions is not the harm to the defendant; rather, it is the interest of the shareholders as a whole that is at stake. In other words, the problem lies not in the conflict between the plaintiff and the defendant, but in conflict among potential plaintiffs (i.e., shareholders). This is why the derivative action needs additional consideration compared to ordinary "abusive litigations."[21]

Corporate law should offer a mechanism by which to achieve an optimal level of enforcement for management liability. If the incumbent management were to have exclusive discretion to dismiss derivative actions, the enforcement level would become too low; this is the very reason why derivative actions exist. However, if an individual shareholder has unlimited discretion for enforcement, the decision made by each shareholder does not necessarily maximize the interest of the shareholders as a whole; they may simply behave irrationally, or they may have a private interest in bringing about a lawsuit that is not compatible with the interests of other shareholders. Indeed, it was reported that a substantial portion of the increased number of derivative actions were motivated by something other than shareholder wealth maximization.[22]

The issue is further aggravated by the fact that Japanese law was not equipped with mechanisms to deter the problems. For instance, unlike U.S. law,[23] Japanese procedural law does not require that the plaintiff of the derivative action "fairly and adequately" represent the interests of shareholders. There is no "special litigation committee" system such as exists under the U.S. law whose decision to dismiss the derivative action is more or less respected by the court.[24] It was argued that a certain mechanism should be incorporated into Japanese corporate law to correct decisions by an individual shareholder. How can this be achieved? We shall see the courts' efforts in the following section.

Court order to post a bond: current court practice

Court practice after the 1993 Revision

To regulate worthless litigations, the courts began shortly after the 1993 Revision to rely on the order for posting a bond by the plaintiff. Articles 267(6) and (7) of the Japanese Commercial Code provide that a court shall, upon the request of the defendant, order the plaintiff of the derivative action to post a bond as security when the defendant establishes a *prima facie* case that the derivative action was filed in "bad faith" (Article 106(2)). Defendants of a derivative action almost always seek the said bond, and the order is often, if not always, granted.

Current prevailing court practice dictates that the court should order the bond in cases where (1) the plaintiff would be most likely to lose on the merits, but he nevertheless dares to bring an action recognizing the likely results; and (2) the plaintiff filed the litigation with the purpose of obtaining unlawful gain from the litigation.[25] The majority of cases have relied on the first of these two criteria when ordering the bond posting.[26] These requirements are derived from the Supreme Court decision[27] that set forth the criterion where a malicious civil litigation constitutes a tort to the defendant. The assumption is that a court order to post bond against the plaintiff is to secure the defendant's potential claim against the plaintiff for filing a wrongful lawsuit.[28]

Although this criterion is based on the ensuring adequate financial security for the defendants' (managements') claim against the plaintiff (a shareholder), it appears that the court, in reality, considers whether the derivative action in question serves shareholders' interests, rather than whether it constitutes wrongful litigation (i.e. a tort) against the defendant.[29] In other words, the court order for bond posting has served as a substitute for the requirement of "fair and adequate" representation in the United States.

A proposal in the 2005 Revision

Many commentators observe that the courts' practice of issuing bond orders has worked well within its limit.[30] Empirical research has found a positive reaction on the share price when the order is issued.[31] The result could be interpreted that the court order has effectively excluded worthless litigations. The system is retained in new Corporate Code of 2005 (Article 847 (7) and (8)).

On the other hand, there appears to be a discrepancy between the form and substance in this practice because the court order, by nature, is designed for the protection of the defendant; it is not intended to circumvent worthless litigations that are not compatible with the shareholders' interests.[32] This results in limitations to court orders. The court order, for example, cannot prevent litigations where the plaintiff has a considerable chance of winning, because litigation by a winning plaintiff usually does not constitute a tort. However, the continuation of such litigation, even if the plaintiff has a high probability of winning, may not be wise in terms of benefits to the shareholders as a whole, considering litigation costs, the judgment proof status of the defendant, possible damage to the reputation of the company, and other circumstances. A court order to post a bond cannot remedy the interest of shareholders in this situation.

A proposed Revision in 2005 intended a more straightforward solution. The Revision confers upon the court the power to dismiss an action when the continuation of such an action leads to unreasonable costs or damage to the company. The proposed revision would have denied a derivative action where: (1) the purpose of the litigation is either to derive benefits for the plaintiff or other person, or to damage the company; or (2) it is, with adequate certainty, expected that the litigation would cause serious damage to the interest of the company, would impose an excessive cost to the company, or the like (Proposed Corporate Code Article 847(1)). The first limitation refers to a general limitation for abusive litigation, and it is not unique to derivative actions. The second can be understood as a Japanese version of the "fair and adequate" representation requirement for the plaintiff of derivative actions.[33] If the proposal had been adopted, the courts could have considered explicitly whether the litigation was good for the company (i.e., shareholders as a whole), rather than whether it was a wrongful action for the defendant.

During the discussion in the Diet, the second limitation was deleted from the final bill as part of a packaged deal between political parties. It was argued that while the new Corporate Code marked considerable "deregulation," it was necessary not to lose the monitoring function of the derivative action against the management. Although it was ultimately not adopted in the 2005 Revision for political reasons, it is worth noting that the necessity for the circumvention of worthless derivative actions was recognized in the discussion of the Legislative Council of the Ministry of Justice.

Company intervention in derivative action for the benefit of the directors

Introduction

Shareholders are required to demand that the company enforce management liability before they file a derivative action (Article 267(1)–(3) of the Commercial Code, Article 847(1), (3) and (4) of the Corporate Code 2005). Once the company rejects the shareholders' demand and the derivative action is subsequently filed, the board is likely to try to persuade the court that its decision not to sue the management was correct, and to challenge the shareholders' decision to sue. Such a challenge takes the form of company intervention in (or participation in) the derivative action.

Can a company intervene in the derivative action for the benefit of directors—and if so, to what extent? The rule was not clear until recently, and lower court cases were divided.[34] There are two different issues to be addressed regarding this: (1) does the company have standing in such an intervention; and (2) does the structure of the derivative action impose any restriction if the board decides to intervene?[35]

A Supreme Court decision in 2001

A Japanese Supreme Court decision of 2001 answered the first question in the affirmative under certain limited circumstances.[36] Following the decision, the 2001 Revision responded to the second question, providing a detailed procedure by which a company could take part in the litigation process and assist the defendant directors.[37] Although not without limitation,[38] boards were authorized to challenge shareholders' claims as being inadequately grounded.

The 2005 Revision

The 2005 Revision took another step. It provides that the company *always* has standing in an intervention for the benefit of one party of the derivative action (Article 849(1) of Corporate Code). Limitations set forth by the Supreme Court were removed. Now, the defendant management can always enjoy the legal assistance of the company if the necessary procedures are followed.

Summary

Changes to procedural rules relating to derivative actions are a direct result of the 1993 Revision. While few insist that the law should revert to the situation before 1993, we have seen a certain degree of swing-back of the legal pendulum following the 1993 Revision. We can safely say that all the changes following the 1993 Revision are based on the assumption that the individual shareholder's judgment to sue is often not necessarily to the benefit of shareholders as a whole. The optimistic idealism of law enforcement by private parties—which underpins the 1993 Revision—has been overturned in a short period of time.

Transformation in procedural rules for exonerating management liability

Procedure for exonerating management liability

In the foregoing, we examined the reforms of procedural rules for derivative actions. They are, in essence, reforms that expand the role of the courts in managing litigation. While people in the business community certainly welcomed the reforms, they were not totally satisfied with them. The judgments by the court, they claimed, might not always be trustworthy. Therefore, following the 1993 Revision, the business community repeatedly demanded that the requirement for the exoneration of management liability be relaxed. The Japan Federation of Economic Organizations (Keidanren), for example, published "Urgent Recommendations Concerning Corporate Governance" (September 16, 1997), which highlights the new system for exonerating management liability. The demand reached its height when one court decision ordered JPY80 billion in compensation—a surprisingly high amount by Japanese standards—against the directors of Daiwa Bank.[39] Although the case was finally settled at a fairly modest amount (JPY250 million), the business community emphasized the danger of relying solely on the discretion of the court in managing derivative action. The decision was not completely supported even by academics, who are usually unsympathetic to management.[40] Politicians were quick to respond to these concerns, and that action resulted in the 2001 Revision, which we shall examine next.

The 2001 Revision

Simplified procedures for exonerating management liability

Prior to the 2001 Revision, management liability could be exonerated only by unanimous consent of the shareholders (Article 266(5) of the Commercial Code). The rule, in effect, made it impossible to exonerate management liability for a public corporation.

The 2001 Revision introduced an important exception to that rule:

1 management liability can be exempted by shareholders' super-majority voting (Article 266(7))
2 management liability can be exempted by the board's decision, when authorized by the certificate of incorporation (Article 266(12)), and
3 the liability of outside directors can be exempted by contract between a company and a director, when authorized by the certificate of incorporation (Article 266(19)).

There are several limitations to the special exoneration procedure.[41] First, the rule does not allow for total exoneration. The liability cannot be reduced below

1 six years' remuneration for representative directors
2 two years' remuneration for "outside" directors, or
3 four years' remuneration for others.

Exoneration beyond this limitation still requires the unanimous consent of shareholders. Second, the rule applies neither in cases of gross negligence on the part of the directors, nor in cases of liability arising out of unlawful distribution to shareholders, for self-dealing, and for several other cases (Articles 266(7), (12) and (19). See also, Article 266(17) and (18)). Industry continues to protest the limitations.[42]

Procedure for settlement of derivative actions

The 2001 Revision also provided for the procedure by which to settle the litigation (Articles 268(5)–(7)). Before the Revision, there was controversy as to whether the plaintiff of the derivative action could settle, because a settlement, by its very nature, always includes an element of the exoneration of liability and the unanimous consent required for it.[43] The revision, requiring certain procedures of the company, authorized settlement.

Effects of the 2001 Revision

Although the new exoneration procedure sounds like good news for management, cynics may observe that the change driven by the 2001 Revision is rather illusory, and it works only as a "tranquilizer" for management rather than a real legal defense. First, the reduction of liability does not apply to cases where management acted with "gross negligence." Given the fact that the business judgment rule protects directors well (see the 2005 Revision, below), there are relatively few cases where courts impose liability on management without evidence of "gross negligence," and the procedure for reducing liability applies mainly to cases where management is not liable at all. Second, the requirement for the reduction of liability is fairly cumbersome. When the reduction of management liability is approved at the shareholders' meeting or by the board, "the facts constituting the cause of the liability and the amount of damage for which the director is liable" should be disclosed (Articles 266(8)(i) and 266(16) of the Commercial Code, Article 425(2), 426(3) of Corporate Code 2005). The "facts constituting the cause" are usually specified in the formal judicial proceedings; therefore, exoneration would ordinarily occur during the trial in the court of appeals, after management has been held liable in the first instance. Third, the reduction of liability by the board's decision is allowed only in cases where such "reduction is especially necessary in light of the facts constituting the cause of director's liability, the status of the performance of its duties, and other circumstances" (Article 266(12), Article 426(1) of Corporate Code). These may be the primary reasons why relatively few corporations amend their certificate of incorporation to enable the board to reduce management liability.[44]

Some suggest that the 2001 Revision could have a more complicated effect if we take the psychological aspects of the judges into account. The more modest the penalty, they argue, the more easily courts find a sentence of guilty. It is sometimes claimed that the courts now find it easier to find breaches of fiduciary duty than before. Unlike under the U.S. legal system, Japanese judges have little discretion as to the amount of liability when the management is held liable. The defendant is fully responsible for the whole of the damages, as far as the court recognizes "reasonable causation"[45] between the breaches of management's duty and the damage to the company. The amount of liability for the derivative action would be extremely huge in most cases, and the court involved has no means to discount it. Thus, before the 2001 Revision, the judges had to ask themselves, "Did this director behave so badly that he should go bankrupt?" Now, following the 2001 Revision, judges ask themselves, "Did this director behave badly enough to relinquish several years of salary?"

However, since no empirical evidence has been shown either way, we must conclude that the overall effect of the new procedure still remains untested.

The 2005 Revision

The 2001 Revision on exoneration and settlement procedures was maintained in the 2005 Revision with the following amendment: Special exoneration procedures in the 2001 Revision did not apply to the director's liability arising out of unlawful dividends or other distribution of corporate assets to shareholders, property transfer to a shareholder in relation to its exercise of right, loan to any other directors, or self-dealing (Article 266 (1)(i)-(iv) of the Commercial Code). The 2005 Revision expanded the scope of exoneration procedure in the above situations with narrow exceptions.[46]

Summary

The new procedure of exonerating management liability is another direct result of the 1993 Revision. Although the Revision is, as suggested, a double-edged sword and the real economic impact is not as clear as it appears, many commentators see the reform as a swing-back of the 1993 Revision.

Transformation of substantive rules regarding the basis of liability

Changing the substantive rules on management liability

One can see the reforms on procedural rules of derivative actions and exoneration of management liability as a direct response to the 1993 Revision. In addition to those responses, even more deeply rooted changes have been taking place since the late 1990s. In the following, we first see the recent changes in the statutes and in current case law with respect to the substantive rules on management liability.

Management's strict liability under current law

The most apparent change in substantive rules in recent corporate law reform is the abolition of strict liability in the field of management liability. The Commercial Code traditionally imposed strict liability on management under several circumstances. Among the most important are the following.

Liability arising out of distribution of corporate assets

Japanese corporate law, like corporate law in the rest of the world, restricts the distribution of corporate assets to shareholders based on the figures on the balance sheet. Management is responsible if the company makes an unlawful distribution. What is unique to Japanese law is the nature of the liability for unlawful distribution. If a director submits a proposal for a distribution to the shareholders' meeting beyond the statutory restriction, he is held responsible without regard to his fault for such a submission (Article 266(1)(i) of the Commercial Code). Even if the figure on the balance sheet is incorrect and management reasonably relies on the report of the CPA—who overlooked the incorrect information—there is no excuse. In addition to the director who actually makes the proposal, other directors are also jointly and severally liable, unless they express an objection to the proposal.[47]

Liability arising out of self-dealing

Another example is strict liability resulting from self-dealing. If a director enters into a transaction with a company and the transaction causes damage to the company, he is responsible without regard to personal fault. Like the regulation in the United States, a self-dealing transaction requires approval by the board, but the approval still allows no exempting effect for the directors who trade with the company. The strict liability does not seem too harsh when a director achieves personal gain from the company as a result of the self-dealing in question. The rule, however, seems more questionable in cases where a transaction is between affiliate companies with an interlocking directorate. Directors could be strictly liable for the damage to the company, without regard to their exercise of due diligence in such dealing. In addition, as in the case of unlawful distribution, directors or officers other than those who participated in the transaction are also jointly and severally liable unless they express an objection to the transaction at the time it is approved by the board. A hypothetical case would be helpful to illustrate the point. Assume that the board of parent company A decided upon a bailout for its subsidiary B, and that one of A's board members, X, is a representative director of B. The bailout transaction is self-dealing for X, and he is strictly liable for the result of the transaction. In addition, all of A's board members who authorized X's self-dealing (the bailout) are jointly and severally liable together with X, unless they individually express objections to the board's decision. The rule would often be an unreasonable obstacle to a corporate restructuring.

These rules have been criticized for many years and several recent lower court cases have tried to avoid harsh results, almost ignoring the language and the structure of the Commercial Code; many believe that the decisions went beyond the interpretation of the current statute.[48]

The 2002 and 2005 Revisions

The 2002 Revision took an important step toward the total reform of the basis of management liability. It introduced a new corporate governance system: the Committee System. Although the emphasis is often put on the composition of the board and the committee for the new system, it is also noteworthy that it adopts a different basis of liability for management. For instance, the Revision abolishes the special liability of directors arising out of unlawful distribution.[49] It allows even for the officers who made the proposal of distribution to prove their non-negligence, in order to avoid their liability. The Revision also changes the rules for self-dealing to a fault-based liability.[50]

The proposed 2005 Revision extends the new rule to corporations in general.[51] In short, strict liability has almost disappeared in the area of management liability during recent reform.

One might suspect that those substantive rules were being changed simply because they were inefficient, and that the 1993 Revision had nothing to do with it. This is only partially true. The question is, why are they being changed *at this time*? Although it is true that the rules were criticized even before the 1993 Revision, they had remained intact for more than 50 years. There is no doubt that the 1993 Revision motivated the change.

The rise of the business judgment rule

The concept of the business judgment rule in the United States[52] has been well recognized for many years among Japanese academics. However, there had been few cases that explicitly declared the rule. Since the 1993 Revision, there has been a significant increase in the number of cases that explicitly refer to management's broad discretion in making a business decision.[53] For instance, one of the recent cases[54] states as follows:

> A director's business decisions in relation to a certain business activity are not beyond the permitted scope of his discretion and therefore do not constitute a breach of duties of care or duty loyalty unless there is an important and careless misunderstanding of the factual basis for the decision and the process and substance of the decision making is markedly unreasonable and improper for a corporate manager.[55]

Probably, it was not the substance of the courts' decision that was changed. Even earlier cases did not review the merits of management's business decision. Rather, it was a change in form. Many courts refer explicitly to the business judgment rule, and announce the limited scope of their review of management's decision before they examine the particular cases. Those cases may be best understood as the courts' message to those in the business community who are not satisfied with the case-by-case decisions but seek more explicit guarantees of non-interference in business decisions.

Summary

Substantive rules on management liability have been changed considerably since the late 1990s. Strict liability is disappearing and the courts repeatedly declare the business judgment rule. These changes would mitigate potential risk to which management members are exposed. Although the changes in substantive rules regarding management liability are not direct responses to the 1993 Revision, they should not be regarded as independent movements. Those rules may be reasonable by themselves but it should be noted that they were never introduced in the many revisions before that of 1993.

Conclusions

This article has reviewed the transformation of the management liability regime in Japan since the 1993 Revision. In retrospect, the 1993 Revision marked the beginning of a series of changes in statutory and case law. The 1993 Revision, in itself, results in an increase in the probability of litigation. It has already had ambiguous effects. The Revision may have enhanced the disciplinary effect on management and, at the same time, increased dead-weight loss caused by possible wasteful litigation.

In addition, the 1993 Revision, directly or indirectly, caused subsequent reforms of the management liability regime. One cannot be sure to what extent the potential liability of directors and officers has been significantly enhanced. Although I do not assert that the effect of the 1993 Revision was totally canceled by the subsequent changes, the magnitude of the reform has been considerably mitigated. The evaluation of the 1993 Revision is made even more complicated by the fact that some revisions subsequent to the 1993 Revision also have had ambivalent effects. For instance, the changes in procedural rules on derivative actions may alleviate the cost of wasteful litigation. At the same time, a reform such as unlimited authorization for a company's intervention for the benefit of defendant management could simply aggravate other agency costs.

What does the short history after the 1993 Revision suggest for the theory of corporate law? As was indicated in the introduction, the 1993 Revision changed a single rule in an area of corporate law where one of the strongest complementarities exists, without accompanying simultaneous changes in related rules. As such, the 1993 Revision itself is an exception to the predictions put forward in an earlier article.[56] The subsequent transformation in Japanese corporate governance should give us an additional prediction, that when a change in one of the components of corporate law does take place in an area where strong complementarities exist, subsequent changes in legal rules will follow.

What is the future of the management liability regime in Japan? It appears that the 2005 Revision is not the end of the development, and the transformation is continuing. One can easily imagine that there may be further changes. I would like to mention two important movements at this stage. First, the role of outside directors has become increasingly emphasized in recent corporate law reform. Although Japanese corporate law did not recognize any legal effect of "outside directors" for many years, recent revisions incorporate deregulation coupled with the adoption of outside directors.[57] A board decision approved by a body of outside directors may be upheld more easily by the court in connection with potential management liability. Although current Japanese corporate law does not contain judicial doctrine to provide such an effect,[58] it may be possible that future case law will incorporate such elements found in the United States courts.[59] In fact, several companies voluntarily set up a non-statutory committee that consists of more "independent" professionals in the context of takeover defenses, apparently expecting that its decision would, in effect, exclude the court's review on the merits. Second, there is a movement towards another direction: management's enhanced duty to establish a proper risk management and compliance regime for the company. The duty was recognized in the Daiwa Bank decision[60] and is becoming a major source of litigation.[61] The Corporate Code of 2005 makes an explicit reference to the risk management and compliance regime in connection with the power of the board (Article 362(4)(vi) and 362(5). See also Regulation for Implementation of Corporate Code Article 100). Further, the Financial Products Trading Act requires listed companies to evaluate their compliance regime to the extent it is related to financial information (Article 24-4-4) and managements are responsible for the correctness of the evaluation (Article 24-4-6 and Article 20). Given the ongoing changes in the management liability regime, only future historians can evaluate the significance of the 1993 Revision, which has caused a series of subsequent transformations.

Notes

1 See, for example, Aoki (2001). For formal mathematical treatments of complementarities, see Milgrom and Roberts (1990) and Milgrom and Roberts (1995). For the application of the concept to Japanese firms, see Milgrom and Roberts (1994).
2 Milgrom and Roberts (1995).
3 Kanda and Fujita (1998: 474, footnote 46). The three predictions in Kanda and Fujita (1998) may be supplemented with the following: When a change of part of

the components in corporate law does take place in an area where strong complementarities exist, subsequent changes in legal rules will follow.

4 Motoyoshi Nishikawa, one of the leading actors in the corporate law reform process representing industry, recalls that people in industry regret that they easily accepted decreases in litigation fees without introducing such systems as exoneration of management liability, litigation committees, business judgment rules, requirements for "fair and equitable" representation and D&O insurance. See, Egashira *et al.* (2005), p. 91.

5 See, for example, West (1994) and Milhaupt and West (2004).

6 Milhaupt (2003) reported that Japanese shareholders brought a total of approximately 20 derivative actions during the period of 1950 to 1990.

7 Since changes to the rule regarding the payment of litigation fees dramatically increased the number of litigations, it is now apparent that the costs of litigation—rather than the cultural background—had been the key obstacle.

8 Although the loser of the suit ultimately bears the litigation fee, the initial financial burden is on the plaintiff.

9 For an example of the calculation of a litigation fee, see West (1994).

10 *Asai vs. Iwasaki et al.*, Kosai-Minshu [High Court Reporter] v. 46, p. 20 (Tokyo High Court, 30 May 1993) decided that the litigation fee for the derivative action was JPY8,200. Tokyo High Court thought that a derivative action was a lawsuit with respect to non-property claims and calculated the litigation fee on that basis. An appeal to the Supreme Court was denied (*Asai vs. Iwasaki et al.*, Kinyu-Shoji-Hanrei [Financial & Commercial Cases], v. 1105, p. 15 (Supreme Court, 10 October 2002)).

11 Although it is often asserted that the 1993 Revision changed the rule for litigation fees, the revision simply confirmed the correct interpretation of the previous law in *Asai vs. Iwasaki*, note 10 above.

12 See Takeuchi (1998).

13 The the table shows the numbers of derivative suits pending at district and high courts. I am grateful to Shoji-Homu Co. for the data.

14 Aoki (1990) points out that the relative independence of management has been one of the salient features of Japanese corporate governance.

15 Schleifer and Vishny (1997).

16 Romano (1991).

17 Baird, Gertner and Picker (1994: 117).

18 As seminal works, see Kydland and Prescott (1977) and Barro and Gordon (1983).

19 West (2001) and Fukuda (2000) report a negative impact of filing derivative action on the firm's stock price.

20 See also Kanda (2004), who examines the relationship between the 1993 Revision and subsequent reform of management liability.

21 A commentary by the former Counselor of the Civil Affairs Bureau in the Ministry of Justice demonstrates that a proper understanding of the unique problem of worthless derivative actions was completely lacking (Yoshikai (1996)). (There is always the possibility of abusive litigation in every legal procedure, and it is inappropriate to build a preventive mechanism designed only for abusive litigation against directors.)

22 West (2001).

23 See, Federal Civil Procedure Rules 23.1.

24 The standard of review by the courts to the committee's decision varies among States. Compare the approach of the cases such as *Zapata Corp. vs. Maldonado*, 430 A. 2d 779 (Del. 1981) [Delaware], *Auerbach vs. Bennett*, 47 N.Y.2d 619, 419 N.Y. S. 2d 920, 939 N.E.2d 994 (1979) [New York] and *Alford vs. Shaw*, 320 N.C. 465, 358 S.E.2d 323 (1987) [North Carolina].

25 *Morita* vs. *unidentified respondent*, Tokyo District Court, Hanrei-jiho vol. 1504, p. 121 (22 July 1994).
26 *Morohashi* vs. *Suzuki*, Tokyo High Court, 159 Shiryoban Shoji-homu 193 (30 May 1997); *Taguchi* vs. *Kuji*, Gifu District Court, 155 Shiryoban Shoji-homu 148 (16 January 1997); *Ito* vs. *Suzuki*, Nagoya Distict Court, 1473 Kinyu-homu-jijyo 47 (10 June 1996); *Ito* vs. *Suzuki*, Nagoya High Court, 1531 Hanrei Jiho 134 (7 March 1995).
27 *Hirohara* vs. *Nagano*, 42 Saihan Minshu [Supreme Court Reporter (Civil)] 1 (26 January 1988).
28 As to the "abuse of rights" doctrine that provides the foundation for claims against the plaintiff, see, West (1994), pp 1468–70.
29 Fujita (1998).
30 Kabunushi Daihyo Sosho Seido Kenkyu-kai (2001).
31 West (2001) and Fukuda (2000).
32 See footnotes 22 and 23, and accompanying text.
33 The industry wanted an even more radical solution, namely, a "litigation committee" system (Japan Business Federation (Nippon Keidanren), Proposal for Revision of the Corporations Law: Securing International Competitiveness for Corporations, Respecting the Choices of Corporations, Shareholders, and Other Stakeholders (16 October 2003)). The litigation committee, consisting of a body of independent parties, can decide whether a derivative action should be continued or dismissed for the benefit of the shareholders. The idea is apparently based on a similar practice in the United States (see, Klein and Coffee (2007: 212–213). The idea was rejected during the discussion for the 2005 Revision as being premature.
34 Lower court cases are divided. Those cases that permitted intervention include Tokyo District Court, 30 November 1995, Hanrei-jiho vol. 1556, p. 137; Tokyo High Court, 2 September 1997, Hanrei-Jiho vol. 1633, p.140 and Tokyo District Court, 25 April 2000, Hanrei-jiho vol. 1709, p 3. Those where intervention was denied include Nagoya High Court, 11 July 1996, Hanrei-jiho vol. 1588, p. 145.
35 A system of derivative actions, by nature, is based on the assumption that the judgment of the board on whether to sue cannot be trusted. One might argue that this distrust might affect the judgment of whether the company (i.e., the board) can intervene in the litigation.
36 *Manpyo Co Ltd* vs. *Yamamura*, Saihan Minshu (Supreme Court Reporter [Civil]) vol. 55, p. 30 (30 January 2001) (allowing the company's participation in the derivative action for the benefit of the defendant, where the action was brought claiming that the decision of the board was unlawful).
37 The consent of the statutory auditor is required for the intervention for the benefit of defendant management (Article 268(8)).
38 In *Manpyo Co Ltd* vs. *Yamamura*, the Supreme Court states that the company's participation is possible in such a case where an action was brought claiming that the decision of the board was unlawful. The subsequent lower court cases interpret the requirement set forth by the Supreme Court rather liberally, permitting the participation relatively easily. See, for example, Miyazaki District Court, 1126 Kinyu-shoji-hanrei 30 (18 May 2001); Fukuoka High Court, 1126 Kinyu-shoji-hanrei 25 (25 July 2001); Tokyo District Court, 1790 Hanrei-jiho 156 (21 June 2001).
39 *Kameda* vs. *Abekawa et al.*, Hanrei Jiho vol. 1721, p. 3 (Osaka District Court, 20 September 2000).
40 See, for example, Iwahara (2000a, 2000b).
41 For exoneration beyond the limits—which is a traditional procedure— to take place, the unanimous consent of shareholders is required.
42 The Japan Business Federation (Nippon Keidanren) proposed two years' remuneration as proper limitation for all management (Proposal for Revision of the

Corporations Law: Securing International Competitiveness for Corporations, Respecting the Choices of Corporations, Shareholders, and Other Stakeholders (16 October 2003)).

43 The Tokyo High Court permitted the settlement on 31 March 1994, after the district court held the directors responsible (*Yoshitake* vs. *Totani*, Hanrei Jiho vol. 1480, p. 154 (Tokyo District Court, 21 September 1993)).

44 According to research by the Japan Corporate Auditors' Association in 2004, approximately 15 percent of the listed companies have adopted the amendment.

45 "Reasonable causation" (see Article 416 of the Commercial Code) is a term of art which roughly corresponds with "foreseeability test" for scope of the contractual liability in the U.S. law.

46 Shareholders' unanimous consent is required only for the following cases: (i) to exonerate the liability of the directors or officers who distributed the corporate assets to shareholders beyond the statutory limitation (Article 462(3)), (ii) to exonerate the liability of the directors or officers who transferred the corporate property to a shareholder in relation to its exercise of its right (Article 120(5)), and (iii) to exonerate the liability of directors or officers who entered into self-dealing with the corporation for their own benefit (428(2)). The most important difference with the 2001 Revision is as follows: Taking the unlawful dividends ((1) above) as an example, the 2001 Revision does not allow the exoneration not only for the directors who paid the dividends or who proposed such dividends but also for all directors who supported such dividends at board meetings. In contrast, the 2005 Revision allows the special exoneration for the latter category of directors. Similar distinction applies to the cases of (2) and (3) above.

47 Article 266(3) of the Commercial Code provided that when an act (in this case, the submission of a proposal for distribution to the shareholders' meeting) was based on a board's decision, the directors who voted for the decision were deemed to have performed such an act by themselves.

48 *Sogo* vs. *an unidentified respondent* (Tokyo District Court 8 December 2000), Kinyu-homu-jijyo vol. 1600, p. 94 [denying the liability of outside directors resulting from unlawful distribution]; *Hamasaki* vs. *Usui* (Osaka District Court 30 January 2002); Hanrei Taimuzu vol. 1108, p. 248 [denying the liability of the board members who decided on the bailout to the affiliated companies with interlocking directorates].

49 For officers who submitted the proposal to the board, Article 21-18 of the Law for Special Provisions for the Commercial Code Concerning Audits, etc., of Joint Stock Company (the Special Provisions) provides the fault-based liability with a burden of proof on the officer. Liability of the directors is imposed pursuant to the general duty of care and loyalty (21-17 of the Special Provisions).

50 Article 21-21 of the Special Provisions.

51 It was proposed by the Japan Business Federation (Nippon Keidanren), Proposal for Revision of the Corporations Law: Securing International Competitiveness for Corporations, Respecting the Choices of Corporations, Shareholders, and Other Stakeholders (16 October 2003).

52 A recent formulation is found in American Law Institute (ALI), Principles of Corporate Governance: Analysis and Recommendations (1994), Article 4.01(c).

53 As recent cases, see, *Keihoku Yakult* vs. *unidentified defendant*, Hanrei Jiho vol. 1888, p. 3 (Tokyo District Court 16 December 2004), *Unidentified plaintiff* vs. *Sogo*, Hanrei Jiho vol. 1886, p.112 (Tokyo District Court 28 September 2004), *Unidentified plaintiff* vs. *unidentified defendant*, Hanei Times vol.1167, p. 208 (Osaka District Court July 28, 2004), *Unidentified plaintiff* vs. *unidentified defendant*, Kinyu Shoji Hanrei vol. 1172, p.39 (Tokyo District Court 12 May 2003).

54 *Hongo* vs. *Matsushita*, Hanrei Jiho vol. 1710, p 153 (Osaka District Court 16 May 1999).

55 Although those cases are no doubt influenced, they are different from the business judgment rule in the United States, in that the court does check that the substance of the management's decision is markedly inappropriate or not based on detailed fact findings, even where the court does not find any problem in the decision-making or information-gathering processes. Compare the decision with the ALI's formulation cited in note 52.

56 Kanda and Fujita (1998).

57 For example, when an outside director is appointed, simplified procedure becomes available for several corporate actions that otherwise need board meeting approval. See Corporate Code Article 373(1)(ii). Companies with "Committee Systems" can delegate substantial corporate decisions to officers, while it is a requirement to have three statutory committees, the majority of members of which should be outside directors (Corporate Code 400(3)).

58 See Gilson and Milhaupt (2005).

59 Unfortunately, the definition of the term "outside director," under current law, is too loose to give their approval a function of justifying the management decision. See, Gilson and Milhaupt (2005).

60 See note 39.

61 See, for example, *Kono Taro* vs. *Unidentified defendant*, Hanrei jiho vol. 1892, p. 108 (Osaka District Court 22 December 2004).

Bibliography

Aoki, Masahiko (1990) "Towards an Economic Model of the Japanese Firm," *Journal of Economic Literature* 28: 1–27.

Aoki, Masahiko (2001) *Toward a comparative institutional analysis*, Cambridge, MA: MIT Press.

Baird, Douglas G., Robert H Gertner and Randal C Picker (1994), *Game Theory and the Law*, Cambridge, MA: Harvard University Press.

Barro, Robert J. and David B. Gordon (1983) "A Positive Theory of Monetary Policy in a Natural Rate Model," *Journal of Political Economy* 91: 589–610.

Egashira, Kenjiro, *et al.* (2005) "Kaisei Kaisha-ho Semina (14) [Seminar on Corporate Law Revision]," *Jurist* 1277: 88–113.

Fujita, Tomataka (1998) "Kabunushi-daihyo Sosho no Teiki ga Akui ni Idetamonotoshite Tanpoteikyo-ga Meijirareta Jirei" [The Case Where the Court Orders to Post a Bond as Shareholders' Derivative Action was Filed in Bad Faith]," *Jurist* 1144: 117–20.

Fukuda, Mitsuo (2000) "Kabunushi Daihyo Sosho ha Ko-pore-to Gabanansu no Shudan to Shite Yuko ka [Are Derivative Suits an Efficient Corporate Governance Tool?]," in Hiroshi Kosano & Yuzo Honda (eds) (2000) *Gendai no Kin'yu to Seisaku [Modern Finance and Policy]*.

Gilson, Ronald J. and Curtis J. Milhaupt (2005) "Choice as Regulatory Reform: The Case of Japanese Corporate Governance," *American Journal of Comparative Law* 53: 343–378.

Hirose, Sumio and Noriyuki Yanagawa (2002) "Daihyo-sosho-seido Kaisei no Kigyo-kachi heno Eikyo [The Impact of Reform on Derivative Actions to the Firm Value]," unpublished manuscript.

Iwahara, Shinsaku (2000a) "District Court Decision of Daiwa Bank Derivative Action and the Revision of Shareholders Derivative Action (1)," *Shoji-Homu (Commercial Law Review)* 1576: 4–14.

—— (2000b) "District Court Decision of Daiwa Bank Derivative Action and the Revision of Shareholders Derivative Action (2)," *Shoji-Homu (Commercial Law Review)* 1577: 4–16.

Kabunushi Daihyo Sosho Seido Kenkyu-kai [Study Group on Shareholders' Derivative Action System] (2001) "Kabunusi Daihyo Sosho oyobi Kansayaku Seido ni Kansuru Shoho-tou Kaiseihouan ni taisuru Iken (1) [An Opinion to the Proposed Revision of the Commercial Code Regarding Shareholders' Derivative Action and Corporate Auditor System (1)]," *Shoji-Homu (Commercial Law Review)* 1605: 36–48.

Kanda, Hideki (2004) "Understanding Recent Trends Regarding the Liability of Managers and Directors in Japanese Corporate Law," *Zeitschrift für Japanisches Recht* 17: 29–37.

Kanda, Hideki and Tomotaka Fujita (1998) "Kabushiki kaisha ho no tokushitsu, tayosei, henka [Features, Variety and Evolution of Stock Corporation Statutes]," in Yoshiro Miwa *et al.* (eds) (1998) *Kaisha-ho no keizaigaku [Economics of Corporate Law]*, Tokyo: Tokyo University Press.

Kydland, Finn E. and Edward C. Prescott (1977) "Rules Rather than Discretion: The Inconsistency of Optimal Plans," *Journal of Political Economy* 85: 473–492.

Klein, William A and John C Coffee Jr. (2007) *Business Organization and Finance: Legal and Economic Principles*, 10th edn, New York: Foundation Press.

Milgrom, Paul and John Roberts (1990) "The Economics of Modern Manufacturing: Technology, Strategy and Organization," *American Economic Review* 80: 511–528.

—— (1994) "Complementarities and Systems: Understanding Japanese Economic Organization," *Estudios Economicos* 17: 3–42.

—— (1995) "Complementarities and the Fit: Strategy, Structure, and Organizational Change in Manufacturing," *Journal of Accounting and Economics* 19: 179–208.

Milhaupt, Curtis J.(2003) "A Lost Decade for Japanese Corporate Governance Reform?: What's Changed, What Hasn't, and Why," *Columbia Law and Economics Working Paper* No. 234.

Milhaupt, Curtis J. and Mark D. West (2004) *Economic Organizations and Corporate Governance in Japan: The Impact of Formal and Informal Rules*, London: Oxford University Press.

Romano, Roberta (1991) "The Shareholder Derivative Suit: Litigation without Foundation?," *Journal of Law, Economics and Organization* 7: 55–87.

Schleifer A. and Vishny R.W. (1997) "A survey of corporate governance," *Journal of Finance*, 52: 737–775.

Takeuchi, Akio (1998) "Torishimariyaku-no Sekinin to Daihyo-sosho [The Director's Liability and Derivative Actions]," *Hogaku-kyoshitsu* 99: 6–17.

Tomotaka (1998) "Kabunushi-daihyo Sosho no Teiki ga Akui ni Idetamonotoshite Tanpoteikyo-ga Meijirareta Jirei [The Case Where the Court Orders to Post a Bond as Shareholders' Derivative Action Was Filed in Bad Faith]," *Jurist* 1144: 117–120.

West, Mark (1994) "The Pricing of Shareholder Derivative Actions in Japan and the United States," *Northwestern University Law Review* 88: 1436–1507.

—— (2001) "Why Shareholders Sue: The Evidence from Japan," *Journal of Legal Studies* 30: 351–382.

Yoshikai, Shuichi (1996) *Heisei Gonen-Rokunen Kaisei Shoho [The 1993 and 1994 Revised Commercial Code]*, Tokyo: Shoji-homu Kenkyu-kai.

2 Transplanting poison pills in foreign soil

Japan's experiment

Kenichi Osugi

Theme and structure of this essay

Legal issues related to hostile takeovers and defensive measures are the most topical issue in Japanese corporate law. Until it was broken by several entrepreneurs and active hedge funds, a hostile bid had long been a taboo in the Tokyo market. Although hostile bids have been infrequent since, an increasing number of managers of listed companies in Japan are afraid that the companies they manage will become possible targets of hostile bids.

In fact, the advent of hostile takeovers had been anticipated earlier. About five months before the commencement of Livedoor's attempt to take over NBS in February 2005, the Ministry of Economy, Trade and Industry (METI) in Japan organized a group to study and formulate a proper response to hostile takeovers. The group surveyed the legal frameworks for mergers and acquisitions (M&As) of listed companies in the U.S., U.K., and several other countries in Europe. It concluded that the introduction of the poison pill in Japan would assist Japanese companies in coping with this issue.

This essay illustrates how Japan "imported" the poison pill from the U.S. and shows that the existing legal framework in Japan is compatible with the U.S. poison pill. Further, it also demonstrates that the importation process was strategic and selective rather than purely driven by economic factors. Since a part of the history has already been recorded by Curtis Milhaupt,[1] I shall provide a complementary account from an insider's viewpoint by virtue of being partially involved in the importation process.[2]

For approximately one hundred years, the Commercial Code (CC) and several related statutes[3] had governed businesses that were incorporated in Japan. In 2005, these dispersed rules were restructured under a single new Companies Act (CA)[4] after considerable revision. All the three cases that are analyzed in the penultimate part of this essay applied the old CC; however, this essay occasionally cites the corresponding sections of the new CA as well. As far as the rules applied in the three cases are concerned, the basic rules in the new code are almost the same as those in the old one.

This essay is organized as follows. An overview of the M&A practices, both friendly and hostile, of listed companies in Japan is followed by a brief description of the legal framework with regard to M&As in which it is argued that the Japanese framework is closer to that of the U.S. than to that of European countries. The basic structures of defensive measures, called a "rights plan" (or poison pills), in Japan are then outlined, followed by analysis of three judicial reviews of hostile takeovers and defensive measures that were issued in 2005. The essay concludes by discussing the background and evaluation of the recent transformation of takeover rules in Japan.

M&A practices of listed corporations in Japan

Friendly acquisitions

The CA provides various statutory means for M&As such as mergers, "share exchanges,"[5] "share transfers,"[6] and "company splits,"[7] while the Securities and Exchange Act (SEA)[8] [*Shôken Torihiki Hô*] stipulates the rules for takeover bids (TOBs).[9] These means may be employed either independently or in various combinations.

Often, a friendly merger or other integration of companies is purported by corporate managers of both parties to be a "merger between equals" in order to maintain the pride and morale of the employees of the companies involved in the deal. However, recent revisions of accounting standards have changed this convention, and more and more M&As are distinguishing the involved parties as acquiring and acquired companies. In addition, the number of TOBs, which were rarely used until recently, is showing an increase.

Hostile acquisitions

In this essay, "hostile acquisitions" refers to unsolicited attempts both by business corporations, undertaken to integrate target corporations and operate synergistically with them, and by speculators or arbitragers. In both cases, most acquirers in Japan have relied upon market transactions (trade conducted in stock exchanges) rather than tender offers. In fact, there have been several examples in which a hostile acquirer has successfully obtained a controlling block of shares in the target company and has taken over the management. In some takeover attempts by business corporations, a company has acquired a block of shares in a target company (a listed but relatively small company), and negotiations between the acquirer and the acquired companies have ended in an affiliation between them. There have also been a few instances of takeovers where purportedly "vicious" raiders, financed by dubious sources, successfully bought out a target company, and the latter has been frequently exploited by related-party transactions by the former.

Since 1996, there have been some hostile attempts that have employed tender offers;[10] however, most of them were unsuccessful.

Legal framework

Until 2004

The origin of Japanese corporate law can be traced to German corporate law. Japan and Germany are somewhat similar in several aspects, such as patterns of corporate-management and labor-management relations as well as social norms. In terms of these patterns and norms, differences between Japan and Germany are probably less than those between Japan and the U.S. However, with regard to the legal framework pertaining to M&A activities, existing corporation law and securities regulation in Japan are considerably closer to those of the U.S. than to those of Germany or other EU countries,[11] as is explained below.

A person who attempts to acquire one-third or more of the outstanding shares in a listed company must use either market transactions or tender offers. In other words, an off-exchange offer is not allowed in any attempt to acquire one-third or more of the outstanding shares of a firm. This rule is not the same as that in the EU Directive that prohibits both off-exchange and market transactions in obtaining controlling blocks of shares. Further, rules pertaining to TOBs in Japan do not obligate an acquirer to bid for all outstanding shares or offer an equitable price. Moreover, the Financial Services Agency (FSA) in Japan hesitates to engage in discretionary supervising activities on takeover transactions; however, the Takeover Panel in England is willing to engage in such activities.

On the other hand, company managers in Japan are not entirely barred from formulating defensive measures against hostile acquisitions. Without shareholders' approval, a board of directors can decide on a company's issuance of new shares and (from April 2002 onward) share warrants,[12] and share warrants can be structured as a rights plan, similar to poison pills[13] in the U.S. However, a shareholder may file an injunctive suit in a court when an issuance of shares or share warrants is deemed unfair, and the existence of judicial review provides a balance between an acquirer and a target board.

Specifically, in this regard, courts in Japan have mentioned the "primary purpose test," which initially questions whether the primary purpose of a stock issuance is to raise funds or to maintain managers' control of the company. In most cases, courts have considered the issuances as appropriate because the primary purpose is financial.[14]

Therefore, the legal framework in Japan in 2004 was somewhat similar to that followed in the U.S. around 1980; at that time, the Delaware court had not developed detailed standards to decide on defensive measures against hostile takeovers.

A step toward the American system

In anticipation of a surge in hostile takeovers, the METI set up an unofficial study group (Corporate Value Study Group) in September 2004. The group held eight meetings before it released "Summary Outline of Discussion Points" (*Ronten Kôkai Kosshi*)[15] on 7 March 2005. Just before its release, on 8 February, a well-known battle for Nippon Broadcasting Systems (NBS) broke out between Livedoor (hostile bidder) and Fuji Television Network (an affiliated company with NBS and the white knight in this case). This matter was brought to the courtroom (a summary of this case is provided below). After slight modifications and considerable additions, the Summary Outline was finalized and changed to the Corporate Value Report (*Kigyô Kachi Hôkokusho*),[16] which appeared on 27 May 2005. On the same date, after negotiations and some conflicts between the METI and the Ministry of Justice, the two Ministries jointly released a set of Guidelines.[17] Although the Guidelines were not legally binding, they were regarded as a quasi-safe harbor for formulating defensive measures during "peacetime" (i.e., a time when no contest for corporate control has begun).

The METI Report cited and relied more on Delaware rules such as the *Unocal* and *Revlon* standards, particularly emphasizing the notion of "corporate (enterprise) value," which was purported to distinguish a good hostile bid from a bad one as well as an adequate usage of defensive measures from its abuse. On the other hand, the Joint Guidelines had virtually no trace of Delaware rules and developed native legal thoughts instead. In the beginning, the Guidelines indicated three fundamental principles:

1 adoption, activation, and abolition of the defensive plan shall be made for maintaining or improving the corporate value and eventually shareholders' collective interests
2 a defensive plan shall disclose its purpose, contents, etc. when it is adopted and shall be dependent on the rational will of shareholders, and
3 a defensive plan shall be allowed only when it is necessary and proper to prevent [inadequate] takeovers.

Subsequently, the Guidelines listed various legal structures of rights plans and the legal procedures for adopting them. The Guidelines did not mention what constituted an appropriate standard that would help adjudicate a target board's activation of a defensive plan during a control contest. This was probably because the authority to interpret statutes was vested only with the judiciary. Compared to the Delaware rules, the METI Report and, to a larger extent, the Guidelines, laid greater emphasis on shareholders' power to adopt and/or abolish a defensive plan. Both the Report and the Guidelines recommended that a defensive plan be structured such that an acquirer can redeem the pill with a proxy fight at a shareholders' meeting. In other words, a company adopting a plan should not follow any arrangement, such as that of a staggered board, that would require an acquirer to wait an unduly long time.

In addition to deregulation of share warrants, since 2002, corporate law in Japan has also deregulated rules for classes of shares. Legally, a listed company can issue shares with de facto multiple voting rights as well as shares with veto rights and allocate them to managers or to an employee-ownership plan. However, the Tokyo Stock Exchange (TSE) revised its listing agreement in order to plug the loophole. At first, a tentative regulation was adopted; subsequently, a more comprehensive draft was discussed with market players, and the latest self-regulation came into effect on 8 March 2006. This regulation in principle prohibits listed companies from introducing golden shares or dead-hand poison pills, even when the plan is approved by shareholders. However, the case of Inpex Corporation is an exception. Inpex Corporation, which was incorporated to secure petroleum resources for national interests, went public on 17 November 2004, and on the same date, it issued shares with veto rights to a government institution. Since the TSE is now willing to monitor the abuse of defensive tactics by listed companies, it is not likely that golden shares or other preclusive defensive measures will spread among publicly held corporations in Japan. In contrast, the TSE and other self-regulatory bodies are relatively liberal with regard to more lenient measures such as rights plans, as long as they do not have dead-hand features. This is partly because these measures are considered to be negotiation tools between acquirers and target managers, and thus they are redeemed when a negotiation is over.

Changes in tender offer regulations

As mentioned in note 8, the SEA was thoroughly revised in June 2006, and new rules pertaining to TOB regulations and disclosure of ownership of large blocks of shares (the "five per cent rule") came into effect in December 2006. While the old TOB rule lacked flexibility and thus put unnecessary burden on offerors, particularly hostile acquirers who intended to launch TOBs, the new regulation provides offerors with greater flexibility. Specifically, the new rule eases the restriction on change in offer terms and curtails the list of prohibitions for bidders to withdraw. As a result, a hostile bidder can reduce the minimum number of shares to acquire or rescind the bid, if the defensive tactics by the target company appear to negatively affect the bidder.

Before the revision, one could circumvent the mandatory tender offer rule by acquiring 32 percent of the shares in the target company via an off-exchange transaction and immediately securing another two percent via a market transaction. After the revision, on- and off-market transactions within six months have been combined, and if the combined ratio of shareholding exceeds the one-third threshold, the rule of mandatory tender offer prevails. This implies that the abovementioned route, i.e., that of market transactions, has been banned. Thus, it is expected that, in the future, hostile bidders will rely more on tender offers than on market transactions, which was the case until recently.

Overview of the recent version of rights plans in Japan

Basic structures

There are variations in the structuring of rights plans. Here, I shall explain the most common "pre-warning" type of rights plans. The other types of rights plans are "conditional resolution," "trust-type," and so on.[18]

The reason different types of Japanese pills were developed was that several big law firms in Japan competed against each other for a pill that was attractive to company managers, by attempting to decrease the probability of judicial injunction and the risk of managers owing liabilities to the company and/or its shareholders. Since the case involving Japan Engineering Consultants Co., Ltd. (JEC), wherein the court upheld a pre-warning plan in July 2005, as is shown below in the review of the JEC case, such plans have gained in popularity.

In a pre-warning plan, a company issues a notice requesting a potential bidder to observe a designated procedure when making an offer; such a notice is typically announced at a time when a sign of contest for corporate control is not yet imminent. Generally, a bidder is required to disclose an acquisition plan and submit information, including that related to the post-merger business plan, before he/she can acquire more than a specified percentage of the target's shares (typically 20 percent is stipulated). Further, a bidder is required to provide a specified period of time to the target shareholders to allow them to decide whether or not to tender their shares to the bidder as well as whether or not to allow the target directors to look for other potential bidders (i.e., white knights).

Finally, the announcement of a plan warns that the company may trigger defensive tactics in any of the following scenarios:

1 when the bidder does not abide by the requests mentioned
2 when the offer is structured coercively, such as two-tier tender offers, and thus deprives the shareholders of the freedom of making an investment decision
3 when the target board of directors judges the bidder to be vicious (e.g., who aims to exploit the target company after the acquisition or who indulges in greenmail), or
4 when the acquisition plan is harmful to the target corporation.

Typically, the company will issue share warrants and make a pro rata allocation of them to its existing shareholders without consideration (*Mushô Wariate*, Sec. 277 of CA). The warrants have a discriminatory exercise clause that excludes a hostile bidder from the persons who are qualified to exercise the warrants.[19] The result is similar to poison pills in the U.S.—the ownership of the hostile bidder would be diluted to half or to a one-third level in terms of both monetary benefit and voting power. However, even if a hostile bidder is not allowed to exercise his/her warrants, the bidder may sell them to persons who are deemed friendly to the target management and thus recover monetary damages.

Variety in adopted plans

Even within a pre-warning plan, there is variety when the adopted plans are considered in detail. For instance, there are different ways to introduce the plan or to trigger the pill.

From March 2005 to June 2007, approximately 390 listed companies (about 10 percent of all listed corporations in Japan) introduced rights plans. Among them, 371 plans (87 percent) were of the pre-warning type. Among the 390 companies that adopted some form of a defensive plan, 353 companies (92.7 percent) adopted rights plans with shareholders' approval, whereas others adopted plans only by a resolution of the board of directors.[20] This is probably because the TSE had released a policy that requested listed companies planning to adopt a defensive plan to consult with it in advance (see above).

Altogether 327 companies (85.8 percent) adopted a rights plan that set up an independent committee. Some committees were ad hoc while some others were standing committees. Among them, 138 companies (42.2 percent) had a committee comprising one or more statutory auditor(s) from outside and one or more independent committee member(s) who was/were not director(s) or statutory auditor(s). Independent committees usually comprised attorneys, certified public accountants, college professors, or company managers.[21] Even if a plan set up an independent committee, it provided that the final decision on whether or not to trigger lay with the entire board of directors, with the independent committee functioning only as a consultative body.[22]

A specified triggering event, which provided for the conditions that enable the target board to trigger defensive measures, tended to respond to the procedure in adopting and triggering the plan. A plan that designated a wide range of triggering events, including point (4) mentioned above,[23] was often adopted with shareholders' approval and was accompanied by a committee comprised only of independent members. In addition, the committee is empowered to make independent judgments on whether or not to trigger the plan. In contrast, a plan that had a more limited range of triggering events was usually introduced without shareholders' approval and was not accompanied by an independent committee. This was based on the theory that in the triggering events of points (1) and (2) mentioned above,[24] conflicts of interests between directors and shareholders are not imminent, and therefore a constraint on the directors' discretion by shareholders or independent committees is not essential.

One important variation in the pre-warning type plan is the "judgment of shareholders' meeting." It provides that a board of directors will issue share warrants if a bidder launches a bid for acquisition without observing the prescribed requests and a shareholders' meeting can trigger the plan against an acquirer even when the bidder abides by the required acts. In effect, it implies that the board can trigger the plan only when a bidder launches an acquisition bid without prior notice or disclosure of the acquisition plan or the post-merger business plans; further, it implies that the more subtle issues, such as whether the time and information given by the bidder is sufficient, will not be judged by directors but by shareholders. This is believed to be the most chewable pill, since its misuse by the managers is least probable.

Among the 371 companies that adopted a pre-warning type plan, 340 (91.6 percent) chose a pill that would be triggered by the board of directors, while 31 (8.4 percent) chose the "judgment of shareholders' meeting" type of pill. Among the former, 306 companies set up an independent committee (90.0 percent), whereas only 11 companies of the latter group provided for a committee (35.5 percent).

An evaluation

As described above, the legal framework for M&As in Japan is gravitating toward that of the U.S. rather than toward the U.K. model. However, I believe that in a broader sense, the difference between the U.S. and EU patterns of regulation should not be overemphasized. Instead, it should be noted that both the U.S. and EU patterns share several common functions. For example, the acquisition of blocks of shares should be implemented with tender offers and not with market transactions or off-exchange transactions;[25] in addition, each jurisdiction debates the fine line between what the directors can and cannot do without shareholders' authorization in M&A deals. Further, a rough consensus is reached and continually renewed.

As of 2008, the legal infrastructure in Japan is still in transition. Considering the development of law both by court decisions (as shown below) and by continuous revisions of the SEA (as shown above), it is safe to argue that the legal infrastructure in Japan is steadily gravitating toward the key features found in both the U.S. and U.K.

Judicial review of defensive measures: overview of recent court cases

In 2004, Ronald Gilson expected that in Japan, where independent directors have been uncommon, the court should play an even more important role than the role of U.S.[26] courts in policing defensive measures against hostile takeovers. To examine Gilson's assumption, the recent court cases in Japan are overviewed here. The facts and analysis provided below are simplified and present only one interpretation that can be deduced from the long and complete set of decisions.

The NBS case[27]

Nippon Broadcasting Systems, Inc. (NBS) was a listed company and ran radio stations under a government license. It belonged to a media conglomerate called Fuji-Sankei Group (FSG). Fuji Television Network, Inc. (FTV) was also a listed company and a member of FSG, and it was widely perceived as the main company that led the group. Despite this, NBS held 22.5 percent of FTV's outstanding shares, whereas FTV held only 12.4 percent of the shares of NBS.[28]

On 17 January 2005, Fuji announced a takeover bid for all NBS shares in order to make NBS its subsidiary and simplify the share ownership structure. The board of directors of NBS approved the bid, and thus the deal was considered friendly. However, in the meantime, Livedoor intervened in the deal.

Livedoor was also a listed company running Internet businesses and had become famous in a relatively short time span of two to three years for the acquisition of many IT companies. Livedoor held 5.4 percent of NBS shares, and without revealing its intent in advance to NBS managers, it acquired another 30 percent of shares on the morning of 8 February in a pre-market trading run on the TSE.[29] On that day, Livedoor announced that it had become a 35 percent blockholder in NBS, and this resulted in a serious backlash among NBS managers.

On 23 February, the NBS board decided to issue share warrants amounting to 144 percent of the then outstanding shares if exercised. The board decided to allocate these shares solely to FTV in order to fend off the hostile acquirer. Livedoor filed a complaint in the District Court of Tokyo for a temporary injunction of the issuance of share warrants.

The share warrants used in this case were not as complicated as the average poison pills in the U.S.; they were structured rather simply. They could be redeemed by a resolution of the NBS board. The issuance price (offer price) of the warrants was JPY 336 per share, and the strike price was set at JPY 6,750 per share. It was probable that FTV would exercise the warrants if Livedoor did not give up its takeover bid, while NBS would redeem the warrants and pay FTV the issuance price if Livedoor gave up its attempt. Apart from FTV or NBS having the "option" of exercising or redeeming the pills, the issuance of share warrants was rather similar to the typical defensive measure of issuing a large amount of shares to a friendly subscriber (see above). Thus, the defensive plan in this case was relatively primitive. Moreover, the pills were introduced when a hostile acquirer appeared, and thus the defensive tactics adopted by the FTV-NBS board were distinct from the average pills used in the U.S., which are introduced when there is no dispute regarding corporate control.

Livedoor vs. *NBS* was essentially the first case in which injunctive relief was sought in relation to share warrants. In this case, the court had approximately four weeks' allowance for hearing and deciding the case.

A total of three court decisions[30] were made in relation to the injunctive order against the issuance of warrants by NBS: two decided by the Tokyo District Court, and the third by the Tokyo High Court. All three decisions held that the defensive measures adopted by the NBS board were inappropriate (Sec. 280–39, para. 4 and Sec. 280–10 of CC),[31] and thus the issuance of share warrants was to be enjoined.[32]

The NBS case was extensively reported in major newspapers, and one media company (Nikkei Newspaper) uploaded the entire decision of the first District Court on its website. In fact, the decisions attracted considerable attention partly because the parties involved were well known.

This essay deals with the first decision by the District Court and the last one by the High Court (i.e., it omits the second decision by the District Court) and analyzes them as if they constitute a single case law rather than emphasizing the differences between them.[33]

Both the District and High courts argued that during a contest involving control of a corporation, if corporate managers issue share warrants aimed at lowering the percentage of ownership of a hostile shareholder and maintaining/ensuring the control of friendly shareholders, the issuance of warrants is held as unfair and thus enjoined. However, this is not the case if the issuance has a compelling reason to protect the interests of the entire body of shareholders of the corporation.

According to the decision of the High Court, defensive measures can be allowed when "the hostile acquirer does not intend to run the target company in a sincere manner" and "the target company would suffer unrecoverable harm if it is controlled by the hostile acquirer"; these requirements must be proven by the target company (i.e., the incumbent managers).

Moreover, the High Court presented four scenarios that could have possibly justified an otherwise dubious issuance. The four exceptions were as follows: (i) the acquiring person is a greenmailer trying to increase the share price and requiring the target company or people closely associated with the company to buy back his/her shares at a high price, without aiming to participate in running the business; (ii) the acquirer is attempting a transfer

Table 2.1 Classification of case law by the timing of installment of the pills

	Judicial review during peacetime (the time of adoption)	*Judicial review during control contests*
Plans that are adopted and triggered during control contests	NA	The NBS case (2005)
Plans that are adopted during peacetime and could be triggered later	The Nireco case (2005)	The JEC case (2005)

of the target company's intangible assets such as know-how, secret information, or goodwill resulting from good relations with its customers to the acquiring company; (iii) the acquirer intends to exploit the target's assets as collateral for the acquirer's debt; or (iv) the acquirer aims to dispose of the target's assets to obtain high dividends.[34] However, the order held that the attempt of Livedoor did not qualify under any of these categories and that no other reasons were proved by NBS that would equate its defensive measures with the protection of the interests of all shareholders.

Some experts believe that the decisions of both courts were correct in terms of enjoining the issue of warrants;[35] however, they harbored certain doubts on the legal argument behind the decisions. It is generally pointed out that court decisions in Japan do not often cite precedents and that makes it difficult to understand the relation between decisions and the degree of consistency among them.[36] The four exceptions mentioned above are particularly criticized by the experts.[37]

An observation reveals only a nominal standard called the "primary purpose test" (see above) in traditional case law before the NBS case. Decisions on the NBS case could be interpreted as exhibiting a more substantial standard of a two-step analysis of necessity and appropriateness, which could be a close equivalent of Delaware's *Unocal* standard.[38] The author, however, supposes that the new standard set in the Livedoor case did not intend to change but to elaborate on the previous primary purpose test.

In any case, the decisions in *Livedoor* vs. *NBS* had substantial impact on both the industry and the general public because they ruled in favor of the hostile acquirer, whereas most injunctive decisions in the past had ruled in favor of incumbent managers.

In the aftermath of the ruling, FTV and Livedoor agreed to a settlement that involved the following actions: Livedoor would transfer its shares in NBS to FTV; FTV and Livedoor would form a joint venture; and FTV would invest in Livedoor. However, before this association could obtain fruitful results, the top executives of Livedoor were arrested by the Tokyo District Prosecutors' Office in January 2006 on charges of false disclosure in another M&A transaction. Livedoor was delisted from the TSE in April 2006, and FTV repealed the joint venture. Mr. Takafumi Horie, the then chief executive officer of Livedoor, was sentenced to two years' imprisonment on 16 March 2007.

The Nireco case[39]

The plaintiff was a limited liability company based in the Cayman Islands. Its main business entailed raising capital from investment funds, pension funds, and other institutional investors of the U.S. and Europe, and investing in the shares of listed companies in Japan.

Nireco Corporation, the defendant, was a company listed on the TSE. Its main business involved manufacturing automatic control devices, measurement hardware, and control instruments for printing that applied hydraulic and electronics engineering technologies. Due to its technical capabilities, several foreign investors were interested in its shares; the plaintiff was the eighth-largest shareholder in the company, having obtained 3.2 percent of the shares as of 30 September 2004. The economic press reported that the price-book value ratio of the company was as low as 0.55 in September 2004 and that its ratio of net cash against total assets was relatively high. Further, it stated that its market capitalization was relatively small. Thus, the company was vulnerable to a hostile buyout.

Based on the advice of the attorneys of a large law firm, Nireco developed the first poison pill (called a "rights plan") in Japan and announced the same in March 2006. According to the plan, shareholders would receive two share warrants per share; the warrants were vested with the shareholders on the shareholders' list on the record date of 31 March 2005. Since the warrants were nontransferable, shareholders could sell only their shares after 1 April 2005, and the warrants remained with them even after the transfer of shares. Further, the buyer of Nireco stock could obtain a warrant (Figure 2.1).

Suppose that the share price of Nireco was JPY 1,200 and the strike price of a warrant was JPY 1. A hostile bidder then appeared and therefore the warrants became exercisable. Now, all warrant holders would exercise the warrants they held and the share price would decrease to approximately JPY 400. If the pill were triggered, shareholders holding warrants would not gain or lose; investors who had already sold the shares but held warrants would gain JPY 400 per warrant; on the other hand, shareholders who had bought shares after 31 March and did not obtain a warrant would lose JPY 800 per share.

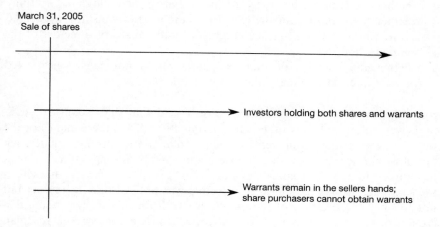

Figure 2.1 Transactions in Nireco shares and their impact on the ownership of warrants.

This appears unjust at first glance. However, the appearance of a hostile acquirer does not necessarily trigger the pill: The pill is exercised only if the independent committee regards the buyout offer by the bidder as inappropriate. Thus, in this case, the pill was not intended to harm the bidder but to enable the Nireco management to negotiate with the bidder and obtain necessary time and information.

In fact, the plan of Nireco entailed the establishing of a special committee initially comprising two outside members and the chief executive officer of the company. According to the plan, the outside members should be attorneys, certified public accountants, or academic experts. However, they did not have to be directors or statutory auditors of the company. Further, although the final decision on whether or not the company should trigger the pill would have to be made by the board of directors, the plan laid down that the board would have to pay serious attention to the recommendation of the committee. Thereafter, Nireco appointed an attorney, an associate professor of a university, and the CEO of the company as the committee's members.

This plan was later (during the court battle) revised so that the committee would consist solely of three outside members. Nireco excluded its CEO from the committee and instead added another attorney.

The plaintiff sought temporary injunctive relief from the court.[40] The Tokyo District Court stipulated the following rule:

> When a contest for corporate control is not imminent in a company, it is allowed to issue share warrants with defensive features only when the issuance is appropriate. Further, whether or not the issuance is appropriate is determined by circumstances such as the following:
>
> 1 whether the issuance has reflected the will of the shareholders' meeting
> 2 whether the condition of the exercise of the warrants installs a mechanism that prevents an arbitrary judgment by the board of directors of the company, and
> 3 whether the issuance of share warrants would not cause unexpected losses to the shareholders other than hostile bidders.

Further, given the relevant facts, the court held that the issuance of warrants was unfair and thus subject to an injunction. Since the issuance of the warrants was neither approved by a shareholders' meeting nor made such that it would expire unless the plan were approved by the subsequent annual meeting in June, the issuance was not deemed to have reflected the will of the shareholders. As the board of directors was obliged only to respect but not to obey the decision of the committee with outside members, the discretion of the board was not deemed to be restricted. Moreover, the plan was considered unfair as it would have caused unexpected losses for the shareholders in Nireco (as shown below). This court ruling was probably intended not only to deal with the particular case but also as a warning that a defensive measure should not be abused.

On the other hand, the Tokyo High Court did not mention the first two elements that the District Court had mentioned. Instead, it focused on the third element. The key facts were as follows. As shown above, an investor who had bought shares of Nireco after 1 April 2005 (practically, the ex-rights date was March 28) would lose two-thirds of the value of the shares he/she held if the company's board of directors declared that the warrants had become exercisable, even if the investor were not the hostile bidder. Further, since the probability of the emergence of a hostile bidder and/or a decision by the company to trigger the pill was rather unclear, the price of Nireco shares fluctuated. The High Court's decision held that as the poison pill would make the Nireco shares rather unstable, they would become an unattractive investment. Thus, the price would be effectively capped. In other words, a shareholder who had bought Nireco shares before the ex-rights date would bear the risk of losing expected capital gains, which was unfair (Sec. 280-39 para. 4 and Sec. 280-10 of CC). In fact, this analysis was presented in the Joint Guidelines of METI and the Ministry of Justice,[41] which were published only a few days before the first decision in this case was made.

The decisions, the Guidelines, and self-regulation by stock exchanges[42] shaped the way in which a defensive plan could be legally structured, and the second generation of Japanese poison pills rapidly converged with the pre-warning type plan discussed earlier. I have the following impressions on this matter. When the Nireco pill was debated, some M&A lawyers in Japan attempted to devise a defensive pill that is not subject to judicial review when triggered. However, more and more lawyers came to believe that the pre-warning plan is more promising because it does not circumvent judicial review when it is triggered, and thus, it is less prone to injunction when adoption of the plan is contested.

The JEC case

Yumeshin Holdings (Yumeshin), the plaintiff, was a listed company and, as the holding company of the Yumeshin group, held shares in companies whose main business was designing architectural drawings and supervising building construction. JEC, the defendant, was also a listed company, and its main business was construction consulting. On 7 July 2005, Yumeshin offered JEC a plan for a business alliance between the two companies and asked JEC to reply by 15 July if the latter was prepared for further discussions on the offer.

As JEC was reluctant to accept the plan, the Yumeshin board decided to launch a tender offer on 19 July 2005, and on 20 July the offer was launched. The tender offer period was set between 20 July and 12 August. In the meantime, between the proposal and the commencement of the TOB, the JEC board introduced the pre-warning type of rights plan on 8 July. The board of directors of JEC triggered the plan on 18 July—a day before

Yumeshin decided on the commencement of the TOB. Yumeshin filed for injunctive relief, but the Tokyo District Court ruled against it.[43]

In this case, the defensive measure adopted was a 5-for-1 stock split (Sec. 218 of CC). In simple terms, suppose that the number of outstanding shares in JSE was 1,000. Further, suppose that, collectively, 50 percent of the shareholders were ready to sell their shares (500 shares in total) to Yumeshin. However, the record date of the register of shareholders for the stock split was fixed as 8 August, which preceded the final date of Yumeshin's tender offer (12 August); further, the effective date of the stock split was 3 October, which was after the closure date of the tender offer. Practically, Yumeshin would find it difficult to acquire via the tender offer 4,000 new shares that would be issued by the stock split. Although 50 percent of the shareholders were ready to sell their shares,[44] Yumeshin would be able to obtain only 500 shares out of the 5,000 outstanding shares (10 percent), whereas 2,000 new shares would be given to the shareholders who had applied for the tender offer. At the same time, this measure would not cause the acquirer to incur monetary damages.

The decision denied the direct or analogous application of Section 280-10 of CC in order to enjoin the stock split at issue.[45] The District Court held as follows:

> In order for the shareholders of the target company to decide properly on whether to tender into the tender offer, the board of directors of the target is allowed to ask the bidder to provide additional information that is more extensive than that required by the TOB regulations, as well as to provide the target shareholders with sufficient time for the consideration of the offer. This interpretation of law does not necessarily contradict the purpose of the TOB regulation. The board of the target is further allowed to take adequate actions for the purpose of securing appropriate information and time.

The court denied injunctive relief, holding that the defensive measure in the case did not fall beyond the line of appropriateness and that the board of directors of the target did not abuse its power.

An analysis suggests that this decision contained a proportionality test, and thus it was closer to the *Unocal* standard. Further, it is to be noted that the decision did not take into account whether or not the bidder violated the pre-warning that the target board had announced. It is evident that a pre-warning announcement does not have legal effects of its own but only prepares a platform for discussion by both acquiring and acquired parties.

Summary

The METI Report adopted an ambivalent stance toward Delaware law. It preferred the U.S. framework to that of the EU countries and cited several

Delaware cases; however, it appealed to the sense of good practice of both (hostile) acquirers and target boards rather than considering judicial review as a key element, which would strike a balance between a bidder and target, and thus enhance corporate economy. Various reactive measures have followed the METI Report, including the Joint Guidelines, self-regulation by TSE, court decisions, and improvement of the structures of defensive plans. Even though these measures did not intentionally imitate Delaware law, they have forged the missing link in the METI Report.

The implantation of a particular foreign legal system often generates a different result from that obtained in its home country. However, I believe that with the recent trials and errors, the legal framework in Japan is increasingly becoming similar to that of the Delaware[46] system. This result can be ascribed to the flexibilities enjoyed by the Japanese legal system and its lawyers. The development of M&A rules in Japan may take a different— and possibly wrong—course in the future. However, even in such a scenario, it is expected that mistakes would be corrected either by the legislature or the judiciary as long as these mistakes were minor and a strong "forum" for discussing complicated policy issues were maintained both inside and outside the courtroom.

Conclusion

In a political-economic context, the METI Report was framed with several motives. First, managers of listed companies in Japan wanted protection from hostile takeovers. Second, public officials at that time desired to achieve a proper balance between requests by managers and the governmental policy supporting foreign direct investment into Japan. Conversely, the idea of "corporate value" (enterprise value) was adopted as a compromise. The reasoning behind this was that "a buyout offer could be frustrated by the target board if it decreased corporate value, but an offer, either friendly or hostile, should not be rejected as long as it increased corporate value" and gathered support from a wide range of channels. This was because the concept of "corporate value" was ambiguous enough to be interpreted either as shareholder interests or as wider interests of the entire body of stakeholders, such as the employees.

The Delaware rules appeared to be more attractive than the EU rules. Some members of the study group who were corporate lawyers opted for the Delaware rules because this promised them a successful poison-pill business, although this business turned out to be less lucrative than it had appeared.[47] Moreover, the adoption of TOB rules such as those in the EU Directive would have led to two obstacles that would have been difficult to overcome—the founding of a supervisory body and the establishing of a neutrality principle. There appeared to be no ministry or self-regulatory body that could assume a supervisory function. Incorporating a neutrality rule into a corporate law or a securities regulation would probably have caused a political backlash. In contrast, the adoption of the Delaware system was a viable option, since it attempted to bridge the gaps in legal rules with judicial decisions and thus did not necessitate a large-scale renovation of the existing institutions or statutory rules.

The abovementioned factors notwithstanding, the Delaware rules were only partially introduced. Most players, such as large law firms, investment banks, M&A advisers, and courts, have acted without a particular will to imitate Delaware, and such behaviors have been related to each other. These ongoing dynamics have assisted in forming a more precise idea of what distinguishes Delaware rules.

As is shown above, the legislature in Japan has played a relatively limited role in the development of M&A rules. Politicians have not been indifferent to this issue. They have evinced considerable interest in the matter. For instance, revisions of TOB rules in 2006 were influenced by one of the ruling parties. However, the essential part of the revisions was elaborated by public officials, practitioners, and academics, and thus, it was only mildly deterrent to hostile takeovers. A persistent argument exists over the framing of an anti-takeover statute; however, the proposals thus far have been generally as tempered as that of Delaware. Anti-takeover statutes, which were first framed in the late 1980s in many states in the U.S., are considerably more inimical to hostile bids.

Thus far, there has not been any serious antagonism between the supporters and opponents of hostile takeovers. Instead, there have been considerable differing opinions both among supporters and opponents.

The manner in which the Delaware courts have proceeded is certainly inefficient: The combination of an ambiguous set of rules (or "standards") and their case-wise application has proved to be costly. However, it does have one merit: It is a realistic approach toward the gradual advancement of M&As.

A dichotomy that distinguishes the shareholder and stakeholder models is evident in the endeavor for a proper model of public corporations. The *Unocal* standard and other components of the Delaware system lie somewhere between the two poles. As such, some observers may consider Japan's reliance on Delaware as an excuse for avoiding the direct influence of a shareholder model as far as possible. There is also another explanation for this phenomenon. In countries where shares in large companies are mostly held by people, either directly or indirectly through institutional investors, the maximization of shareholder value is less likely to deviate from an increase in the national wealth. However, in Japan and many other countries, the pattern of share ownership and distribution does not conform to this construct.[48] Instead, in a previous era, Japan enjoyed economic success by effectively restricting shareholders' voices and encouraging investment in human capital.

Despite the global pressure of convergence to a shareholder model of public corporations,[49] there will remain national differences with regard to means of combining human and capital resources.[50] Even in the U.S., several academic texts have focused on achieving a balance between shareholders and other stakeholders and players;[51] although these works are not necessarily consistent with each other, some of them may provide a more generous assessment of an emerging order in Japan.

It remains to be observed whether the reconciliatory process in Japan functions smoothly. [52]

Notes

1 Milhaupt (2005). See also Jacobs (2006b).
2 The author is a member of the Corporate Value Study Group (*Kigyô Kachi Kenkyû-Kai*) sponsored by METI. See "A step toward the American system" in this essay. The author, however, does not claim that he played a major role in introducing Delaware law; rather, he was a passive spectator at the time the importation occurred.
3 Of the special Acts that dealt with corporate matters, *Yûgen Kaisha Hô* [Limited Liability Corporation Act] and *Kabushiki Kaisha no Kansa tô ni kansuru Shôhô no Tokurei ni kansuru Hôritsu* [Act Regarding Exceptional Rules of the Commercial Code Concerning Auditing, etc., of Stock Corporations] were particularly important.
4 The Companies Act, Law No. 86, July 26, 2005. This new code came into effect on 1 May 2006. With slight revisions, the CC remains in effect as a statute that lists the basic rules for businessmen (*Shônin* in Japanese or *Kaufleute* in German) and business transactions (*Shô-kôi* in Japanese or *Handelsgeschäfte* in German).
   For an overview of the new CA, see http://corporation.rikkyo.ac.jp/en/overview.html (accessed 1 September 2007), which includes a link to a translated text of the Act.
5 The phrase "share exchange" is a literal translation of *Kabushiki Kôkan* (Sec. 2, subpara. 31 of CA). By this method, an acquiring company (A) may convert a target company (T) into A's subsidiary. Company A will issue new shares to T shareholders and, in exchange, will acquire all the outstanding shares of A from them. This method is often used by a parent company to squeeze out minority shareholders from the subsidiary and acquire 100 percent ownership.
6 "Share transfer" is also a literal translation of *Kabushiki Iten* (Sec. 2, subpara. 32 of CA). By this method, an existing company (S) may set up its parent company (P) and become P's subsidiary. P will issue shares to shareholders of S, and in exchange for these shares, P acquires all the outstanding shares of S from its shareholders. This method is often used for the integration of two or more companies, i.e., companies S1 and S2 (often, both are listed companies) jointly set up a holding company P with share transfer, and shareholders in both S1 and S2 acquire shares in P.
7 This is a literal translation of *Kaisha Bunkatsu*. Through a "company split," a splitting company A may transfer all or a part of its rights and obligations to a receiving company B (*Kyûshû Bunkatsu*) (Sec. 2, subpara. 29 of CA) or to a newly formed company C (*Shinsetsu Bunkatsu*) (Sec. 2, subpara. 30 of CA), while B or C issues shares and delivers them to A.
   For further description of the recent renovations of statutory means for M&As, see Bälz (2006).
8 Law No. 25/1948 as amended. For further description of the tender offer rules and practices in Japan, see Kanda (1998: 934–6).

SEA was also thoroughly revised and rewritten in 2006. The revisions were scheduled to gradually come into effect, and the Act was renamed as Financial Instruments and Exchange Act [*Kinyû Shôhin Torihiki Hô*] in September 2007. Several important revisions concerning tender offer rules came into effect in December 2006. See Financial Services Agency, Japan, "New Legislative Framework for Investor Protection—'Financial Instruments and Exchange Law'" (June 2006) www.fsa.go.jp/en/policy/fiel/ (accessed 1 September 2007).

9 In this essay, the phrases "tender offer(s)" and TOB(s) are used interchangeably.

10 Some examples of such attempts since 2005 are as follows: The attempt of Yumeshin Holdings Co., Ltd. to acquire Japan Engineering Consultants Co., Ltd. (July 2005), as discussed in this chapter; Don Quijote Co., Ltd./Origin Toshu Co., Ltd. (February 2006); Oji Paper Co., Ltd./Hokuetsu Paper Mills, Ltd. (August 2006); and Aoki Holdings, Inc./Futata Co., Ltd.(August 2006).

In each of the above cases except that of Aoki/Futata, a white knight appeared and saved the target management.

11 The two different role models of takeover regulation in the U.K. and the U.S. are shown and analyzed by Davies and Hopt (2004: 163–73).

12 The outlook on Japanese law in this essay applies only to stock corporations that do not restrict the transfer of their shares by a provision in their articles of incorporation. In companies that restrict share transfer, a special resolution (with two-thirds of affirmative votes) passed at the shareholders' meeting (which shall satisfy the quorum required by Sec. 309, para. 2 of CA) is needed to decide on stock and warrant issuance. Sec. 199, para. 2 and Sec. 238, para. 2 of CA.

With regard to stock corporations that do not restrict share transfer, a resolution at the shareholders' meeting is required for the issuance of new stock or share warrants only when the issuance price is clearly advantageous to the subscribers of the stock or warrants. In other words, shareholders' approval is not necessary when the price is fair, even if the issuance is large and/or it causes change or transfer of control of the company. To compensate for this lack of shareholders' veto powers, managers are required to make a public announcement of stock/warrants issuance according to CA at least two weeks before the effective date (Sec. 201, para. 3 and Sec. 240, para. 2 of CA). Furthermore, CA gives shareholders the right to file for injunctive relief during this two-week period. Plaintiff shareholders prevail if the issuance is held as either illegal or unfair (Secs. 210 and 247 of CA). Lower courts in Japan, mainly the Tokyo and Osaka District Courts, have used their discretion as to whether or not to enjoin share issuances in dispute.

13 In this essay, the phrases poison pill(s) and rights plan(s) are used interchangeably.

14 In some cases where injunctive relief was rejected, hostile acquirers were supposed to be either greenmailers or other "bad guys." They would probably fall within the first or second categories that the High Court's decision on the Livedoor case outlined as exceptions (see the text accompanying note 34 below), though those cases avoided finding that the acquirer was a greenmailer.

15 The English version of the Summary Outline is available at www.meti.go.jp/english/information/downloadfiles/Corporate%20Value.pdf (accessed 1 September 2007).

16 An English abstract of this report is reprinted in *Zeitschrift für Japanisches Recht*, 21: 137–9 (2006).

17 *Kigyô Kachi, Kabunushi Kyôdô no Rieki no Kakuho mata ha Kôjô no tameno Baishû Bôeisaku ni kansuru Shishin* [Guidelines Regarding Takeover Defense for the Purposes of Protection and Enhancement of Corporate Value and Shareholder's Common Interests]. The English version of the guideline is reprinted in *Zeitschrift für Japanisches Recht*, 21: 143–61 (2005).

18 In a "trust" plan, share warrants are issued to a trust when the plan is intro-duced, and they are purportedly distributed to the shareholders when a hostile bidder appears. On the other hand, "pre-warning" and "conditional resolution" plans are structured such that these plans merely announce cautions when intro-duced, and warrants are issued to the shareholders of the company when a hos-tile bidder appears.

19 Since the plan contains a discriminatory clause, the question of whether or not it violates the principle of equal treatment of shareholders has been debated. Although the equal treatment principle was not codified in the old CC, it was presumed to be the basic principle of a stock corporation. The principle is clearly stated in Sec. 109 of the new CA.

Until quite recently, the discriminatory exercise clause in the plan had been believed to be against the equal treatment principle. The Guidelines, above note 17, however, argue that the clause does not violate the principle. The reason is that the principle only requires a company to treat shareholders equally and fairly according to the content of the shareholders' rights, and the clause does not constitute the content of a shareholders' right.

20 The author was provided with this data by Sumitomo Trust and Banking Co., Ltd.

21 In some cases, committee members are outside directors or statutory auditors (*shagai-kansayaku*), and in other instances, they are neither directors nor statu-tory auditors. Although the CA in Japan has adopted a very loose definition of the outside director and the statutory auditor as given in Sec. 2, subparas. 15 and 16, most companies that adopted rights plans appointed committee members who were apparently more independent than required as per the statutory definition.

22 This is because a legal doctrine does not allow directors to abandon their fidu-ciary duties in order to maximize corporate and shareholder value. At the same time, a rights plan normally prescribes that except in extraordinary circum-stances, the board of directors should do their utmost to respect the committee's judgment.

23 This almost amounts to alleging that the target board is superior to the bidder in terms of running a company.

24 In most plans, the trigger of event (3) above is included because the NBS case, in an *obiter dictum*, held that a board of directors may adopt preventive measures against a hostile acquirer when the bidder is vicious. See review of the NBS case below.

25 In the U.S., in the early 1980s, a dubious practice termed "market sweep" (or street sweep) was prevalent, although it was not necessarily deemed illegal. This phrase refers to the on- and off-market transactions of shares when a tender offer for holders of the same securities was made. However, this practice dissipated, mainly due to the diffusion of poison pills and state anti-takeover statutes in the mid-1980s.

26 Gilson (2004).

27 See also Takahashi (2005: 232–5).

28 Such an upside-down share ownership structure is observed in the cases of some listed companies in Japan, and it is believed that this structure attracts hostile bidders who seek gains from arbitrage. The upside-down ownership structure between FTV and NBS was born of a conflict between the managers and the founding family of FSG that occurred in 1992, wherein the managers successfully ousted the founders.

Since the ruling in this NBS case went against the NBS management, several listed companies with important listed subsidiaries have restructured their share-holding pattern to decrease the risk of being taken over.

29 The trading was carried out through ToSTNeT (Tokyo Stock Exchange Trading Network System) and was *Tachiaigai-Torihiki* (off-floor trading) as well as *Jikangai-Torihiki* (after-hours trading or pre-market trading). See www.tse.or.jp/

rules/tost/index.html (accessed 1 September 2007), which explains the mechanisms of ToSTNeT in Japanese.

Before the revision of the SEA of Japan in 2005, Sec. 27-2, para. 1 of the Act provided that a market transaction of listed securities is not subject to the mandatory tender offer rule. Further, Sec. 2, para. 17 of the SEA implied that after-hours trading on a system that is run by a stock exchange qualified as a market transaction and thus was not subject to the mandatory tender offer rule. Based on this interpretation, the FSA announced that the transaction was not against the then existing SEA sections.

However, certain types of after-hours trading did not operate according to the market mechanism of pricing. Instead, this transaction had several aspects in common with a negotiated transaction outside the stock exchange. Some commentators therefore suspected that the trading by Livedoor was illegal because it was against the spirit of a rule that obligates a tender offer or market dealing when an acquirer tries to obtain one-third or more of the outstanding shares in listed companies.

Shortly after the Livedoor case, the FSA moved to revise the SEA to plug this loophole. As a result, after-hours trading was made subject to mandatory tender offer, and thus it became impossible to acquire more than one-third of the stock in a listed company with after-hours trading. The amendment was approved by the Diet and came into effect in July 2005.

30 *Livedoor* vs. *NBS*, 1173 Hanrei-Taimuzu 143, 1726 Shôji-Hômu 47 (Tokyo District Court, March 11, 2005); *Livedoor* vs. *NBS*, 1726 1173 Hanrei-Taimuzu 140, Shôji-Hômu 51 (Tokyo District Court, March 16, 2005) (confirming the first temporary injunction passed by other judges in the same instance); *NBS* vs. *Livedoor*, 1899 Hanrei-Jihô 56, 1728 Shôji-Hômu 41 (Tokyo High Court, March 23, 2005) (denying the appeal).

31 These old sections correspond to Sec. 247, subpara. 2 of CA.

32 The two District Court decisions held the following: (i) the issuance was not made at an advantageous price (the court adopted the appraisal document prepared by an investment bank for NBS, which evaluated the issuance price with option pricing models) and (ii) the issuance was made in an unfair manner. On advantageous issuance and unfair issuance (see the review of legal framework prior to 2004 above, particularly note 12).

In the High Court, Livedoor, the appellee, omitted its motion on advantageous issuance and focused on the aspect of unfair issuance. This essay does not deal with the matter of advantageous issuance.

33 The District Court held that defensive measures can be allowed when a hostile takeover clearly deteriorates "enterprise value," whereas the High Court held that courts cannot and should not evaluate enterprise value. These rulings may suggest that the two courts focused on different rules. However, the author is inclined to believe that the "enterprise value" in the District Court decision and the interests of all shareholders (which is the ultimate standard in deciding on whether the defensive tactic is legal) in the High Court decision are almost the same or at least reconcilable.

34 It is possible that the judges who cited these scenarios in the ruling bore in mind apparently vicious cases of hostile takeovers witnessed in Japan (see note 14 above) or in the U.S. in the early 1980s.

35 There were other reasons for upholding this result: the decision of the NBS board was not based on information gathered from a negotiation with Livedoor's executives; the defensive measure the board adopted was preclusive, as it did not reveal the conditions by which the pill would be redeemed.

36 Kono (2006: 32) summarizes the general discussion on the pros and cons of the manner in which Japanese courts make rulings.

37 It is possible that these four scenarios are only examples and thus do not define a situation in which triggering a defensive measure is allowed as a general rule. At the same time, the four exceptions should and will be read narrowly so as to limit the abuse of defensive pills. The third scenario, which refers to a situation in which the acquiring person intends to exploit the target's assets as collateral of the acquirer's debt, does not necessarily imply that every leveraged buyout can be frustrated by the board's actions.

38 *Unocal Corp.* vs. *Mesa Petroleum*, 493 A.2d 946 (Del. Supr. 1985).
Kozuka (2006: 12, 17) proposed an interesting analysis of the traditional primary purpose test. Setting aside doctrinal analyses and focusing on economic results, both the court decisions—in 1990 and in 2005—ruled that while an incumbent management may solicit a white knight, the latter is required to contribute money equivalent to the price in the stock market. Consequently, the market for corporate control is functional in Japan. The doctrinal differences between the primary purpose test and the *Unocal* standard should probably be neither neglected nor emphasized.

39 See also Takahashi (2005: 236–9).

40 As in the NBS case, the Nireco case was addressed twice by the Tokyo District Court and once by the Tokyo High Court: *FSP Value Realization Master Fund Ltd.* vs. *Nireco*, 1186 Hanrei-Taimuzu 274, 1734 Shôji-Hômu 37 (Tokyo District Court, 1 June 2005); *FSP Value Realization Master Fund Ltd.* vs. *Nireco*, 1186 Hanrei-Taimuzu 265, 1735 Shôji-Hômu 44 (Tokyo District Court, 9 June 2005) (confirming the temporary injunction decided by other judges in the same instance); *Nireco* vs. *FSP Value Realization Master Fund Ltd*, 1900 Hanrei-Jihô 156, 1735 Shôji-Hômu 48 (Tokyo High Court, 15 June 2005) (denying the appeal).

41 See Note 10 of the Guidelines.

42 TSE had already issued a warning on 21 April 2005 that a defensive plan such as that of Nireco could cause damage to innocent shareholders and could confuse market participants, and was thus inappropriate; however, the TSE did not mention the name of Nireco. Nireco was listed on another exchange called JASDAQ, which followed suit on the same day.

43 *Yumeshin* vs. *Nihon Gijutsu Kaihatsu* [JEC], 1909 Hanrei Jihô 87 (Tokyo District Court, 29 July 2005).

44 When this case was disputed, it was practically impossible to sell or buy the new shares generated by the split during the offer period because of the clearance of share transactions. With the improvement in share transfer and the clearance system in December 2005, a stock split can no longer play a defensive role. Instead, recent rights plans devise a share warrant with a discriminatory exercise clause, as is shown above.

45 Since a stock split was not considered to come under the category of issuance of new shares as provided in Sec. 280-10, this section did not apply directly to the facts of the case. It is difficult to interpret the part of the decision that denied the analogous application of the section to the facts. It could be understood that a stock split would not be subject to injunctive relief in any case. However, it could also be interpreted that because the relevant facts in this case did not demonstrate that the stock split at issue was unfair, it was not enjoined.

The same issue exists with respect to the pro rata allocation of share warrants without consideration (Sec. 277 of CA) that is commonly used in structuring Japanese poison pills (see above). Sec. 247 of CA, which provides for injunctive relief, does not contemplate its application to a pro rata allocation according to Sec. 277. Recent decisions on a dispute between Steal Partners and Bull-Dog Sauce clearly stated that Sec. 247 is applied analogously to a pro rata allocation of share warrants when used as defensive tactics, and that the allocation of warrants at issue was not unfair and thus not enjoined. *Steel Partners Japan Strategic Fund SPV II L.L.C.* vs. *Bull-Dog Sauce Co. Ltd.*, 1805 Shôji-Hômu 43 (Tokyo District Court, 28 June 2007); *Steel Partners Japan Strategic Fund SPV II L.L.C.* vs. *Bull-Dog Sauce Co. Ltd.*, 1806 Shôji-Hômu 40 (Tokyo High Court, 9 July 2007); *Steel Partners Japan Strategic Fund SPV II L.L.C.* vs. *Bull-Dog Sauce Co. Ltd.*, 1273 Kinyû Shôji Hanrei 2, (Supreme Court, 7 August 2007).

46 Jacobs (2006a, 2006b) recommends that the Japanese people adopt a gradual approach in improving the legal framework for M&As.

47 In fact, legal fees for introducing defensive plans was rather expensive during 2005; however, supposedly, the cost has been constantly decreasing. As of 2005, for giant law firms, planning skills with regard to structuring pills were considered to be not only a source of profits but also a symbol that differentiated them. However, such skills spilled over to dozens of quasi-large firms. On the other hand, it appears that in terms of making profits, financial advisers have no particular preference between the U.S. and the EU systems.

48 The patterns of shareholding and the mechanisms of generating and allocating social welfare have been evolving in each country for nearly a century. See Vitols (2001).

49 See Hansmann and Kraakman (2001).

50 Milhaupt and West (2004 179 et seq.) present the view that a market for corporate control is not only a mechanism to police corporate managers but an effective channel to promote the organizational diversity among companies. According to them, corporate governance systems that promote organizational diversity are more likely to produce firms that are adaptable to new technologies, and an active market for corporate control promotes this diversity.

51 Kahan and Rock (2002) observe that the poison pills had successfully ensured maintaining a fine balance between institutional investors and corporate managers. Bainbridge (2002) advocates that the director-primacy model, which claims that corporate decision-making efficiency can be ensured only by preserving the board's decision-making authority, is superior to both managerialism and shareholder primacy in explaining Delaware corporate law.

52 It seems that Japan is going a different way in its use of poison pills from that of the U.S. See Osugi (2007), which discusses later cases and subsequent development of M&A practices in Japan.

Bibliography

Bainbridge, S.M. (2002) "The Board of Directors as a Nexus of Contracts," *Iowa Law Review*, 88: 1–34.

Bälz, M. (2006) "Liberalized Rules for the Restructuring of Japanese Companies: Mergers, Demergers, and Share Exchanges under the New Company Law," *Zeitschrift für Japanisches Recht* 21: 19–35.

Davies, P. and K. Hopt (2004) "Control Transactions," in R. Kraakman *et al.*, *The Anatomy of Corporate Law: A Comparative and Functional Approach*, Oxford: Oxford University Press: 157–191.

Gilson, R.J. (2004) "The Poison Pill in Japan: The Missing Infrastructure," *Columbia Business Law Review* 2004: 21–44.

Hansmann, H. and R. Kraakman (2001) "The End of History for Corporate Law," *Georgetown Law Journal* 89: 439–468.

Jacobs, J.B. (2006a, 2006b) "Implementing Japan's New Anti-takeover Defense Guidelines, Part I—Some Lessons from Delaware's Experience in Crafting 'Fair'

Takeover Rules—and Part II—The Role of Courts as Expositor and Monitor of the Rule of the Takeover Game," *University of Tokyo Journal of Law and Politics* 3: 83–101, and 3: 102–118.

Kahan, M. and E.B. Rock (2002) "How I Learned to Stop Worrying and Love the Pill: Adaptive Responses to Takeover Law," *University of Chicago Law Review*, 69: 871–915.

Kanda, H. (1998) "Comparative Corporate Governance Country Report: Japan," in K.J. Hopt *et al.* (eds.) (1998), *Comparative Corporate Governance*. Oxford: Oxford University Press: 921–942.

Kono, T. (2006) "Soto kara Nihon hô wa dou miete iruka [How Japanese Law Looks from Foreign Perspectives]," *Jurisuto* 1312: 30–36.

Kozuka, S. (2006) "Recent Developments in Takeover Law: Changes in Business Practices Meet Decade-Old Rule," *Zeitschrift für Japanisches Recht* 21: 5–18.

Milhaupt, C.J. and M.D. West (2004) *Economic Organizations and Corporate Governance in Japan*. Oxford: Oxford University Press.

Milhaupt, C.J. (2005) "In the Shadow of Delaware? The Rise of Hostile Takeovers in Japan," *Columbia Law Review* 105: 2171–2216.

Osugi, K. (2007) "What is Converging? Rules on Hostile Takeovers in Japan and the Convergence Debate," *Asian-Pacific Law & Policy Journal* 9: 143–162.

Takahashi, E. and T. Sakamoto (2005) "Japanese Corporate Law: Two Important Cases Concerning Takeovers in 2005," *Zeitschrift für Japanisches Recht* 21: 231–239.

Vitols, S. (2001) "The Origins of Bank-Based and Market-Based Financial Systems: Germany, Japan, and the United States," in W. Streeck and K. Yamamura (eds.), *The Origins of Nonliberal Capitalism: Germany and Japan in Comparison*. Ithaca: Cornell University Press: 171–199.

3   What shapes corporate law in Japan?

Hideki Kanda

Introduction

In the United States, whether Delaware corporate law is the result of the "race to the bottom" or the "race to the top" has been much debated. More recently, Professor Mark Roe has shed new light on this issue from a new perspective, and has reminded us of the importance of the race between state corporate law and federal law.[1] These debates have one thing in common: corporate law in the United States has been shaped and developed through competition among legislators. What about Japan? Japan does not have a federal system, and thus there is only one set of corporate law in Japan. This simply suggests that competition between states or between state and federal legislators does not exist in Japan. Does this mean that there are no competitors in Japanese corporate law? Surely, there are competitors outside Japan, and indeed, Japanese corporate law has been influenced by the corporate laws of other jurisdictions. More generally, the familiar debate on convergence or divergence of corporate laws around the world suggests that there is competition among corporate laws worldwide. Yet, what about competition within Japan?

This short essay submits an additional argument to the debate: there is competition in shaping corporate law within Japan, and that competition exists among enforcers. More specifically, regulation, in particular a set of rules commonly called securities law or regulation, is a competitor to what is commonly called corporate law.

The dual system of corporate law and securities regulation

In Japan, the Companies Act of 2005 (CA) applies to all joint-stock companies. The CA provides for private law rules about joint-stock companies. It is a consolidation of the statutes that existed in 2005 in respect of joint-stock companies. Until such consolidation, corporate law rules were primarily codified as part of the Commercial Code. The Commercial Code has a German origin, but as far as rules on business corporations are concerned, it transplanted many American rules after World War II.[2]

Today, the CA also reflects numerous amendments made to the Commercial Code over the years, and captures the results of historical developments in Japan. The CA today thus has its own, somewhat unique landscape.[3]

The Financial Instruments and Exchange Act of 1948 (FIEA) applies to large publicly held companies.[4] The name of the Act was changed to its present name by the amendments in 2006 (effective from 30 September 2007). Until then, it was called the Securities and Exchange Act (SEA). The SEA (now FIEA) was modeled on the U.S. Securities Act of 1933 and Securities Exchange Act of 1934, but again, it reflects the unique historical developments in Japan. The FIEA therefore has its own characteristics, and the substance of the rules in the Act is not identical to that in the U.S.

Sometimes the CA and the FIEA regulate the same matters. For instance, both Acts require public companies to prepare financial statements and have them audited by professional auditors. In usual practice, companies prepare those documents and have them audited just once so as to satisfy the requirements under both Acts.

The CA is a private law, and there is no administrative branch or agency of government which enforces the rules under the CA. As an exception, public registry offices are understood to enforce the rules applied in matters that must be registered, but this is not discussed in this essay. Of course, courts enforce the rules of the CA. In contrast, the FIEA has an administrative body of the government, the Financial Services Agency (FSA), and an enforcement body, the Securities and Exchange Surveillance Commission (SESC). Needless to say, the FIEA is also enforced by courts.

In the following sections, I look at three topics as examples. The first is private litigation. Here, the FIEA does not provide effective means of enforcement, and the CA is considered to be important. The second topic is accounting fraud, where both the CA and the FIEA provide similar (or perhaps overlapping) rules, and the FIEA rules are enforced by the FSA and the SESC. Here, competition in enforcement occurs. The third topic is hostile takeovers and defenses, where the rules of the two statutes do not overlap but are related. Here, the enforcement analysis is not simple because the coverage of the substantive rules by both statutes is different.

Private litigation

In Japan, neither the FIEA nor the CA recognizes the class action system. This means that if individual investors suffer losses through an illegal activity by a large publicly traded company or certain misconduct by directors of such a company, it is not realistic for them to sue the company or the directors for damages. Because the amount of the loss suffered by each investor is usually small, it is costly for each investor to bring a legal action against the company or its directors in order to recover such loss. This is true for a claim under the CA and under the FIEA. In contrast, if a company suffers a loss from misconduct or illegal activity of directors, a shareholder of such a company can sue the directors through a derivative action under the CA. It is not costly to bring a derivative action today, and such actions have been popular. To that extent, the CA is enforced in Japan.[5] This does not mean, however, that in practice shareholders routinely win on the merits of the case, because courts usually do not find a breach of duty by the defendant directors.[6] However, as is well known, courts have found a violation of laws and awarded large amounts of damages in some derivative suit cases.[7]

Comparing derivative actions with direct actions is unwarranted when one attempts to compare the level of enforcement between the CA and the FIEA. If the CA or the FIEA were to recognize a class action, it might be deployed without reducing the popularity of derivative actions. Thus, whether class actions should be recognized in Japan is an independent policy question from that of recognizing derivative actions. However, for the purposes of this essay, it must be noted that a derivative action or a similar mechanism is not recognized under the FIEA. Thus, one can say that the lack of derivative action or a similar mechanism under the FIEA makes the CA more important in the practice of private litigation involving public companies in Japan.

Before 1990, shareholder derivative actions were rare. Since 1990 they have become popular. Why this should be so has been thoroughly debated and examined.[8] A far more important question seems to be why Japan imported derivative actions but not class actions. It may be that the class action is a more general system and therefore more difficult to import. A political-economy reason may also be possible. In any event, it is noteworthy that in the field of private litigation, the CA seems to be more important than the FIEA.

Two further points must be noted. First, it is common in Japan for customers to sue brokers for damages when they suffer investment losses from trading securities. This phenomenon is not discussed in this essay. Second, very recently, a few damage actions against companies and their directors have been brought under the FIEA by investors who alleged that they suffered losses from accounting fraud or for other reported reasons. However, such actions do not seem to be popular, compared to derivative litigation under the CA.

Accounting fraud

Financial auditors are liable for damages both under the CA and the FIEA if they act negligently in regard to the financial statements and other accounting documents of the company.[9] The exact content of the rule is not identical between the CA and the FIEA, but the differences are not important for the purposes of this essay.[10] More importantly, the FIEA, in addition to damage liability, provides for administrative fines for violations of the mandatory disclosure rules (as well as the anti-fraud rules) under the

Act.[11] Both for disclosure and anti-fraud rules, the SESC is empowered to make necessary investigations, and the SESC reports the results of its investigations and makes recommendations to the FSA. The FSA then has the power to impose an administrative fine. This system of administrative fines was introduced by the amendments to the FIEA (then SEA) in 2004 and became effective in 2005. As of the end of June 2007, fines had been ordered in 23 cases (18 insider trading cases and 4 false disclosure cases).[12]

The FSA also has supervisory power over public accountants and auditors under the Certified Public Accountants Act (CPAA). It is empowered to make disciplinary orders and even to remove the license of an auditor/accountant whose misconduct is found to be serious.[13]

In the early 1970s, a company listed on the Tokyo Stock Exchange (TSE) failed, and a large accounting fraud was uncovered. The SEA was not triggered. Deficiencies in the CA (at that time the Commercial Code) were blamed, and it was amended in 1974. As a result of the amendments, large companies are required to have their financial statements audited by financial auditors before they are submitted to annual shareholder meetings. In 2004–2006, accounting frauds were discovered at a few companies listed on the TSE. The CA was not triggered, and the FSA played an active role. Administrative fines were imposed,[14] and disciplinary action against the auditors was ordered.[15] As a result, one large auditing firm was liquidated on 31 July 2007. This is somewhat similar to the Enron debacle in the United States. The FIEA also requires each reporting company to establish an internal control system so as to ensure proper financial reporting.[16] Importantly, the CA was not amended, and there was no driving force in that direction. The CA is thus less important today in this field. The FIEA is far more important.

The role of stock exchanges, in particular the Tokyo Stock Exchange, is also changing in Japan. The TSE traditionally did not make corporate governance or other conduct rules for its listed companies. However, in recent years, the TSE has changed its position, and begun to promulgate such rules.[17] The rationale is that the TSE is responsible for providing measures for investor protection and maintaining fair capital markets. Because the TSE is an institution licensed under the FIEA, this means that, while the TSE's rules are not the rules of the FIEA and are sometimes characterized as soft law, the TSE acts in the shadow of the FIEA, not of the CA. Indeed, certain activities by joint-stock companies are permitted under the CA, but they are prohibited or restricted under the TSE rules. For instance, listed companies are not allowed to issue non-voting shares (with the exception of certain preferred shares). The TSE also takes the position that certain activities are not desirable from the perspective of investor protection and maintaining fair capital markets. In a recent example, a listed company made a large-scale reverse stock split (ten to one) as a part of its management buyout program so as to eliminate small public shareholders, and the TSE issued a public warning that such a reverse stock split negatively affects the rights of the individual investors in the company. In short, for listed companies, the CA is less important today. The rules of the TSE are far more important.

One might ask, then, why the CA does not respond to governance issues or other questionable activities that the TSE considers important. One might say that the purpose of the CA does not include maintaining fair capital markets. One might also say that the CA basically provides for rules that are common to both large public and small-scale companies. For the purposes of this essay, however, it is important to note the enforcement aspect. That is, the TSE enforces its rules. Theoretically, the TSE enforces its rules as part of the listing contract with the listed firm, which means that ultimately the courts enforce the rules. Generally speaking, any private party is free to impose conditions on the counter party in respect of activities which would be otherwise permissible under the CA, and such contractual conditions are enforced by courts if they are valid and lawful. As a realistic matter, however, the TSE rules are wide ranging and uniform, and thus they serve as de facto corporate law rules for listed companies.

Hostile takeovers and defenses

Finally, let me take up hostile takeovers and defenses. This area is also a bit complicated in respect of the law's coverage. The FIEA regulates tender offer processes, while most of the defensive measures raise legal issues under the CA, not the FIEA. In this sense, the distinction between the FIEA and the CA roughly corresponds to that between the federal (and state) securities law and state corporate law in the U.S. It is interesting to note that the validity of some of the defenses was challenged before the courts, and in those cases the relevant issues were those under the CA, not the FIEA.[18] In fact, current tender offer regulation under the FIEA permits the target company to adopt a defense action even after the commencement of an official tender offer by a hostile bidder. Thus, as in Delaware, case law under the CA shapes the landscape, although the substance of the case law is not identical between Delaware and Japan.

In a recent well-known case, in May 2007, Steel Partners, a U.S. buyout fund, commenced a hostile tender offer for all outstanding shares of Bull-dog Sauce, a Worchester sauce producer and a listed company on the TSE. Bulldog Sauce did not have any "pre-bid" defense plan (see below). As a post-bid defense, the board of Bulldog Sauce intended to issue share warrants to all shareholders, including Steel Partners and its affiliates (collectively SP), with the condition that SP could not exercise the warrants. The warrants had a redemption feature, by which the warrant holders other than SP received common shares in exchange for the warrants, whereas SP received cash. Thus, the securities were structured as a scheme to dilute the voting rights of SP without causing economic loss to SP ("economic" does not include the value of voting right). The Bulldog board introduced the proposal at the annual shareholders' meeting on 24 June 2007, and the plan was approved by more than 80 percent of the shares. SP sued to enjoin the issuance of the warrants. The Tokyo District Court held on 28 June 2007 that the scheme was valid. The decision was affirmed by the Tokyo High Court on 9 July 2007 and then by the Supreme Court on 7 August 2007. The relevant issues were those under the CA, and not the FIEA.[19]

Also, a number of public firms in Japan have one of two types of "pre-bid" defensive measures. The one is a poison-pill scheme using a trust or similar structure,[20] and the other (more popular) plan is known as an advance warning defense.[21] As of 25 May 2007, 359 listed firms (out of an approximate total of 3,900 listed firms in Japan) have pre-bid defensive plans. For listed firms on the Section One of the Tokyo Stock Exchange, 283 out of total of 1,753 companies have adopted such plans. Among those 359 firms, 349 have adopted some form of advance warning plan, and 10 have a trust-type or similar warrant schemes.[22]

It is interesting to note that under the CA, defensive plans using a separate class of shares are possible. For instance, a firm may issue a special class of shares which does not have voting power for the part of the shares exceeding the 20 percent stake of all outstanding shares. In order to issue such shares, the CA requires that the rights and designations of such shares be specified in the firm's charter. A firm issuing common shares may convert them into such special class shares by a charter amendment, which requires two-thirds approval at the shareholders' meeting. However, in practice, no company has yet introduced such class shares. There is discussion in academia as to whether such shares are always lawful, and the Tokyo Stock Exchange takes the view that such shares are not appropriate for existing listed firms, as opposed to firms making initial public offerings (IPOs).[23]

A different type of share was once issued. In November 2004, a listed firm, an oil company, issued a "golden share" (a special class share), which gave the holder of the share a veto right over any proposal submitted to its shareholders' meetings. However, the share was issued to the government, and it was understood that the oil company should be permitted to issue such shares to the government from a public-policy standpoint.

From the perspective of this essay, the point is that the CA is important for critical issues in the area of hostile takeovers and defenses, and courts play an important role in applying the relevant rules under the CA. The Tokyo Stock Exchange also plays an important role in shaping the landscape in this area. This is because such issues are not directly regulated by the FIEA, and thus there is no room for enforcement by the FSA in this area.

Conclusion

This essay has shown that, in Japan, enforcement affects developments in corporate law, and in that sense, the Financial Instruments and Exchange

Act equipped with administrative enforcement is more important for companies to which the statute applies. With respect to the matters that are not covered by the Financial Instruments and Exchange Act, the Companies Act inevitably plays a role, and courts play an important role in creating case law in such areas. Whether this can be called competition may be controversial. However, the development of corporate law in Japan cannot be well understood without considering its enforcement aspects.

Notes

1 Roe (2003, 2005).
2 See for example West (2001a).
3 See for example Kanda (2004).
4 A company whose securities are listed on a stock exchange, traded "over the counter," or the number of whose registered shareholders is 500 or more is subject to the periodic reporting requirements of the FIEA. A company that makes a public offering is also subject to the same reporting requirements.
5 For the detailed developments of shareholder derivative actions, see Tomotaka Fujita, in this book.
6 See Fujita, above. See also West (2001b).
7 See Aronson (2003).
8 See West (2001b).
9 See, for example, Article 429(1) of the CA; Articles 21(1)(iii), 22(1) and 24-4 of the FIEA.
10 See, for example, the Tokyo District Court Judgment on 24 February 2005, 1931 Hanreijiho 152 (an investor unsuccessfully sued the auditing firm for damages).
11 Articles 172–175 of the FIEA.
12 See the SESC Annual Report 2005–2006; same 2006–2007.
13 A special organization called the Certified Public Accountants and Auditing Oversight Board (CPAAOB) was established in April 2004. It is responsible for oversight of accountants and auditors and makes necessary investigations. For FSA disciplinary actions, see, for example, FSA News Release, 24 May 2006 (removal of license); same, 7 July 2006 (disciplinary order for big four auditing firms); same, 30 November 2006 (removal of license).
14 See above, note 13.
15 See above, note 13.
16 Article 24-4-4 of the FIEA.
17 See generally the Tokyo Stock Exchange, Comprehensive Improvement Program for Listing System 2007 (24 April 2007).
18 See Kenichi Osugi in this volume.
19 See Osugi, above.
20 Under a typical trust-based scheme, the firm issues share warrants to a trust bank with designated shareholders as beneficiaries of the trust. When a hostile bid occurs, the pill is triggered and the trust bank transfers the warrants to the shareholders. The warrants have a discriminatory feature and the bidder has no right to exercise them, as the terms and conditions of the warrants usually provide that the warrants are not exercisable by those shareholders who own 20 percent or more of the firm's outstanding shares.
21 The advance warning plan varies from company to company but its typical style is as follows. The board, sometimes with approval of the shareholders' meeting, makes a public announcement that if a shareholder attempts to increase their stake to 20 percent or more of the firm's outstanding stock, before the

shareholder does so, that shareholder is required to disclose and explain, in accordance with the details specified in the announcement, their intent to hold such stake and what they would do for the firm. If the shareholder does not answer these questions or the target board considers the shareholder's explanation to be unsatisfactory, then a defensive measure will be triggered. Such defensive measure is typically to issue stock warrants to all shareholders, but those shareholder having 20 percent or more cannot exercise the warrants. Instead, the warrants of such shareholder can be redeemed at a fair price at the option of the company. Thus, typically, warrant issuance has the effect of "cashing out" the hostile bidder.

22 See the material submitted to the METI Corporate Value Study Group on 29 May 2007.

23 See Tokyo Stock Exchange, *Interim Report of Advisory Group on Improvements to TSE Listing System* (13 April 2007).

References

Aronson, Bruce E. (2003) "Reconsidering the Importance of Law in Japanese Corporate Governance: Evidence from the Daiwa Bank Shareholder Derivative Case," *Cornell International Law Journal* 36: 11–57.

Kanda, Hideki (2004) "Understanding Recent Trends Regarding Liabilities of Managers and Directors in Japanese Corporate Law," *Zeitschrift für Japanisches Recht* 17: 29–36.

Roe, Mark J. (2003) "Delaware's Competition," *Harvard Law Review* 117: 588–646.

—— (2005) "Delaware's Politics," *Harvard Law Review* 118: 2491–2543.

West, Mark D. (2001a) "The Puzzling Divergence of Corporate Law: Evidence and Explanations from Japan and the United States," *University of Pennsylvania Law Review* 150: 527–601.

West, Mark (2001b) "Why Shareholders Sue: The Evidence from Japan," *Journal of Legal Studies* 30: 351–382.

Part II
Korea

4 A tale of three companies

The emerging market for corporate control in Korea

*Hwa-Jin Kim**

Shakespeare could hardly have written a more convoluted tale of sibling rivalry, palace intrigue and thirst for power.[1]

Introduction

Contested mergers and acquisitions emerged in the business world of Korea in the mid-1990s and have since served as a popular topic for the media. The surprising takeover of Hannong Corporation by Dongbu Group in 1994 opened the gate for such transactions in Korea. This was followed by the abolition of the statutory protection of control as of 1 April 1997. Since the early 2000s, two or three hostile takeover attempts have taken place every year, even targeting member companies of the largest corporate groups such as Hyundai and SK. The largest company in Korea, Samsung Electronics, is also said to be vulnerable to takeover threat by foreign competitors or hedge funds. KT&G's fight against Carl Icahn and Steel Partners in early 2006 provoked public discussion about the market for corporate control and hedge fund activism in Korea.

This essay describes and analyzes the current status of corporate control in Korea by summarizing three recent cases, together with relevant laws and regulations: SK Corporation's (SK) fight against Sovereign Asset Management; the contest for control over the Hyundai Group (Hyundai); and KT&G's fight against Carl Icahn and his allies. Active policy discussions in respect of the market for corporate control and takeover defenses and the reshaping of large corporate groups are all ongoing and should lead to new legislation. This essay focuses in particular on the role of takeovers in the improvement of the corporate governance of Korean companies, as dramatically exemplified by the three cases.[2]

The setting

Corporate governance and takeovers

It is well known, through numerous reports and scholarly works, that many efforts to improve the corporate governance system of Korean companies have been undertaken since the 1997 Asian financial crisis (Kim 2002; Black *et al.* 2001; Kim 1999; Seo 2006; Black, Jang and Kim, 2006). The Korean Securities and Exchange Act (KSEA), which stipulates rules regarding the corporate governance of public companies, has gone through 16 revisions since 1997, and the Korean Banking Act has seen 11 revisions. The Korean Commercial Code has also been subject to four revisions and at the time of writing is being scrutinized again for another major amendment.[3] It is also noteworthy that various sectors have continuously engaged in endeavors to improve corporate accounting practice and capital market structure, as evidenced by the enactment of the Securities Class Action Act, *inter alia.*[4] Legislators are also working on integrating the seven individual acts covering the capital market and developing a new infrastructure for developing investment banks in the Korean capital markets.[5]

Contested mergers and acquisitions are no longer viewed unfavorably. In fact, as mentioned above, a number of corporate control contests and hostile takeover attempts have since taken place. Especially following the critical period in 1997, contested mergers and acquisitions have played a valuable function in improving corporate governance, and this has led the way to the amendment of many laws to facilitate and promote hostile takeovers.[6] As a result, advocates of takeover defensive tactics for the protection of incumbent management face objections. Additional restrictions are being imposed on member companies of large corporate groups instead, and the government is also considering implementing a number of regulations for the ownership structure of conglomerates, in an effort to make them subject to market discipline. Two of the most noted devices are investigation of the discrepancy between control rights and cash flow rights within the large conglomerates, and making the ownership structures known to the public.[7]

Now that the business environment in Korea is no longer so favorable to current owners/directors, they are urging new means of takeover defense such as the poison pill[8] and dual-class common shares.[9] At the same time, they are busy searching for other legitimate ways to protect their management control. Amid this state of alert, some yet to be legally proven tactics, such as the golden parachute, are quite popular. The court cases on takeover defenses are not informative, and the available cases are limited to the most commonly used methods, such as rights offerings[10] and selling treasury shares to friendly parties. In particular, sale of treasury shares has been the favorite tactic of Korean corporations in their attempt to protect their corporate control, but since 2006 a decision prohibiting the practice has thrown this tactic into doubt.[11]

Foreigners at the gate

Following the 1997 crisis, the growth of the Korean mergers and acquisitions (M&A) market has been remarkable, and the door to the Korean market is now much more accessible to foreign investors and businesses.[12] The proportion of foreign-owned shares in Korean companies has increased markedly. According to data from Bloomberg, foreigners owned on average 55.7 percent of the 10 largest corporations in Korea as of 22 June 2006.[13] As much as 83.4 percent of Kookmin Bank, the largest financial institution in Korea, is owned by foreigners, and 51.8 percent of Samsung Electronics, the largest company in Korea. Those foreign investors have also firmly expressed their interest in corporate governance and control. The Korea Financial Supervisory Service reported that 301 foreign investors owned more than 5 percent of public companies, based on the 5 percent reporting (Large Holding Report) as of the end of 2006, and 100 of them reported that they had obtained the stock in order to influence management.[14] The cases discussed below, as well as the example of Norwegian Golar LNG's attempt to take over Korea Line Corporation in 2004, have certainly left Korean corporations on alert for the possibility of losing their control in the boardroom to foreign investors. Even mammoths such as Samsung Electronics[15] and POSCO[16] are not exempt from the fear.

Recently, stressing the threat to corporate control imposed by foreign funds, Korean companies have been demanding that the government reform the existing systems; they want to have more secure means available to protect their corporate control, or to be free of the series of restrictions under the Korean Anti-Monopoly and Fair Trade Act (AFTA). Samsung Electronics, in particular, went so far as to submit a constitutional petition to the Constitutional Court of Korea in 2005, reasoning that the restrictions under the AFTA had rendered the entire Samsung conglomerate vulnerable to takeover attempts, and the instability of laws and regulations had made it nearly impossible to set out its long-term corporate strategies.[17] But the unveiling of serious problems in its corporate governance put Samsung under heavy pressure from the press before the petition could make its way to the justices. Samsung in the end pledged a large-scale corporate responsibility drive and made a huge donation to charity.

The attitude of the Korean government has been true to principles, at least until recently. In other words, the government and grassroots organizations, including PSPD (People's Solidarity for Participatory Democracy, one of the largest grassroots organizations in Korea, which has enjoyed increased power since the 1997 Asian financial crisis) (Kim and Kim 2001), seem to think that there is no logic in dampening the expectation that contested mergers and acquisitions function to improve corporate governance. Although foreign funds and investors involved in hostile takeover attempts are, in general, regarded with suspicion, they are finding advocates in the Korean market, some of whom even claim that there is no particular reason to bar foreign takeover attempts in key national industries. It is known that the United States, in the recent FTA negotiations, expressed its interest in abolishing the 49 percent limitation imposed on foreign ownership of the key-industry companies such as KEPCO and KT. Some members of the

Korean National Assembly are working on a bill modeled after the U.S. Exxon-Florio Act.[18]

SK

Background

The SK case, uniquely, provides empirical data and resources showing that, first, its problem-ridden corporate governance triggered a hostile takeover attempt, and then the takeover threat brought about major improvements in corporate governance. Furthermore, it raised fierce political and economic controversies because

1 the hostile takeover threat came from a foreign investment fund
2 energy was the core business of SK Group, and
3 SK Group's most important member company was the key tele-communications provider, SK Telecom, which was the 450th largest company based on its total market capitalization as of 31 March 2005.

At the center of SK Group is SK Corporation, which is controlled by SKC&C, which in turn is controlled by Chairman and CEO Chey Tae-won, the eldest son of the late head of SK Group, Chey Jong-Hyun. Under the control of SK Corporation lies a number of affiliate companies, including SK Telecom, SKC, SK Networks (former SK Global), and SK Shipping.[19]

The beginning of SK Group is traced back to half a century ago, when Chey Jong-Hyun's brother Chey Jong-kun founded Sun Kyoung Textiles, the mother company of SK Networks, in 1953. In 1967 came the birth of Sun Kyoung Synthetic Fiber, which later became SKC. Following the death of Chey Jong-kun in 1973, Chey Jong-Hyun succeeded his brother in 1978 and spurred the dramatic growth of SK Group in the 1980s and 1990s. Before his death in 1998, he entered into the mobile telecommunications industry and acquired the oil refining business Yukong, each of which is remembered as his greatest achievements. Following the death of Chey Jong-Hyun, SK Group was led by the group Chairman, Chey Tae-won, and SK Telecom CEO Son Kil-seung, known as the most successful professional manager in Korean business history, until 2003. While taking the office of CEO at SK Telecom, Son Kil-seung also served as the president of the Federation of Korean Industries (FKI). But in the wake of the "SK Saga," Son Kil-seung claimed to be responsible and resigned from both SK Telecom and FKI at the same time.

The development of "SK Saga" occurred during the 1997 Asian financial crisis. SK Securities incurred a huge loss from financial derivatives deals with JP Morgan prior to 1997, and this led to lawsuits in both Korea and the U.S. In an effort to bring about reconciliation between the two parties, SK Global involved its overseas subsidiary, but PSPD deemed this illegal and filed a complaint against the SK management with the Public Prosecutor's Office. Furthermore, fearing the loss of his corporate control due to the reinstatement of the legal limitation on total investment,[20] Chey Tae-won exchanged his Walker Hill stock for SK Corporation stock and unexpectedly became subject to judicial restraint with respect to the exchange. To make matters worse, SK Global was found to have committed a large-scale accounting fraud, and the stock prices of all the SK Group companies plummeted. When SK Corporation's stock price fell to 6,100 Korean won, Sovereign Asset Management suddenly emerged as the largest shareholder.[21]

When Sovereign entered the picture, the public viewed it as a mysterious entity and scorned it as an ill-intentioned speculator. But Sovereign claimed to be a serious corporate governance fund. It was believed that not only were Sovereign's actions in Korea unpredictable and lacking in consistency, but also the fund seemed to be without any fundamental strategies. Sovereign persistently assailed SK Group's corporate governance flaws and eventually demanded the removal of Chey Tae-won, doubting his leadership qualifications as the head of SK Group. Further, Sovereign attempted to gain control of the board of SK Corporation by nominating outside director candidates. Notwithstanding the suspicion that Sovereign intended to take over SK Corporation, Sovereign focused its public announcements on the issue of corporate governance alone and expressed no plan to engage in management and business. But the press cast doubt on Sovereign's true intentions. Its ambiguous moves in the process of ownership disclosure and reporting of foreign investment created confusion in the market and resulted in major changes in the 5% Large Holding Report. The change required that a very detailed description of investment objectives be made public.[22]

Struggle

Sovereign vied for control of SK at two annual shareholder meetings. At the March 2004 meeting, it tried to remove the clause on cumulative voting from the articles of incorporation of the company and to elect outside directors of its choice, but these attempts failed. With strong support from the National Pension Service and minority shareholders, the vote was in favor of the company by 51.5 percent to 39.5 percent.[23] Prior to the March 2004 shareholder meeting, SK had tried to increase the share of its allies by disposing of its treasury shares to friendly parties. Sovereign asked the court for a preliminary injunction, but the court's ruling was not favorable to the contender. The Seoul District Court ruled in its 23 December 2003 decision that the disposal of any treasury shares should not be prevented, provided that the shares were not originally acquired to perpetuate the existing management and the controlling shareholder(s).

Around October 2004, Sovereign demanded that SK hold an extraordinary meeting of the shareholders to amend SK's charter so as to disqualify anyone with a criminal conviction from being a director of the company, and to elect certain persons designated by Sovereign as outside directors of SK. SK refused Sovereign's request to hold the meeting, stating that the proposal to amend the SK charter was, in substance, identical to the proposal that had been rejected at the 2004 annual meeting, and that since the 2005 annual meeting was close at hand, there was no reason to urgently hold an extraordinary meeting to elect outside directors. In response, Sovereign filed a petition with the court seeking permission to hold an extraordinary meeting. The court rejected Sovereign's petition.[24] Sovereign then made a shareholder proposal to include the amendment of SK's charter and election of outside directors on the agenda of the 2005 annual meeting. SK and Sovereign carried out a proxy contest in relation to the issue.[25]

The March 2005 shareholder meeting began in a highly tense atmosphere; while Sovereign had demanded Chey Tae-won's removal from the board, the meeting agenda included renewal of Chey's term as director. But again, by a wide margin the result of the shareholder voting allowed the company to defend its corporate control and Chey Tae-won was re-elected to the board. The Seoul High Court convicted Chey Tae-won in June 2005 but he was saved from imprisonment and allowed to remain on probation. Sovereign, in July 2005, disposed of its entire stake in SK and gained about 1 trillion Korean won in profit, which is as an outstanding performance for a corporate governance fund. The fund thereafter invested in LG Group, again putting the market on alert, but sold its stock after six months and left the Korean market altogether.[26]

Viewpoint

Sovereign's withdrawal from the Korean market evoked wild speculation, but Professor Park Sang Yong of Yonsei University evaluated Sovereign's strategies from an academic perspective.[27] According to Park, unlike undervaluation due to the "Korea discount," which results from a multitude of factors, undervaluation that is triggered by a discount of subsidiary shares due to matters relating to poor corporate governance creates unique opportunities for arbitrage, and the SK case exemplifies the latter. The aggregate value of SK Corporation's listed stock fell below 40 percent of the value of its equity investment (20.85 percent) in SK Telecom at the outset of Sovereign's hostile takeover attempt. During the period subject to analysis, while the rate of increase of share price of other oil-refining corporations did not even reach the rate of increase of the composite stock price index, SK's rate far exceeded it. Such a phenomenon cannot be explained by anything other than a hostile takeover threat.

While under the threat of Sovereign's hostile takeover, SK Group assiduously worked on improving its corporate governance. There are several apparent reasons for this effort. First, it was not a surprise that it saw the need to fix its corporate governance, since it triggered public criticism and disgrace. Second, Chey Tae-won was in prison, awaiting trial. SK needed to make public that it was striving to improve its corporate governance system in order to render the situation favorable to the chairman. Third, Sovereign assailed the corporate governance of SK, which was lagging behind global standards.

SK Corporation's effort to restructure its board by appointing a majority of outside directors was not a token political move. SK Group even went so far as to reform the boards of its private member companies into outside-director dominated boards, which was not required by law. Regardless of the motive for such drastic change, the result was the creation of a well-functioning board and a reputation as the pacesetter for high-standard corporate boards in the Korean market. Professor Hasung Jang's widely quoted comment summarizes well the overall impact: "Sovereign achieved in one year what the Korean government could not in many years." SK Group also tried to transform itself into a loosely integrated entity within which the member companies shares its brand. While the current market was infested with problems caused by complicated relationships among the member companies of large conglomerates, SK's move was praised as a prudent strategy. Finally, in April 2007, SK Group announced its plan to transform itself to a holding company structure. The market applauded the move.

Hyundai

Background

Similarly, the Hyundai case reflects a corporate governance issue resulting in a hostile takeover attempt, but it is much more complicated than the SK case in terms of its historical background and the high level of politics involved. Both the bidder and the incumbent in the Hyundai case vied for support from the shareholders on a platform of improving corporate governance. This case demonstrates that corporate governance issues can lead to a hostile takeover attempt or disputes over corporate control.

The history of the Hyundai Group[28] is integral to the history of the Korean national economy. In 1947 the now-deceased founder and honorary chairman of Hyundai, Chung Ju-yung, founded Hyundai Engineering & Construction, which was the foundational entity of Hyundai and later became Hyundai Construction in 1950. Chung Ju-yung's professional career included holding the office of the president of FKI for 10 years; and once he even assembled a political party and ran for president of Korea. Founded in 1972, Hyundai Heavy Industries left a legend that it once obtained funds from Barclays Bank of England solely on the basis its plan for shipbuilding business and the pictures of the site. The extraordinary history of Hyundai reached its peak in the late 1990s. Honorary Chairman Chung Ju-yung herded 1,001 cows to North Korea in June 1998, which certainly created drama, and met with the ruler of North Korea, Kim Jong Il, the following October. The historic event resulted in the founding of Hyundai Asan in 1999, initiating business with North Korea.

The Hyundai Group, however, faced a crisis in 1999. With Hyundai Construction close to insolvency and the North Korean business getting out of hand, the Group had severe liquidity problems and was forced by its creditors to restructure its affiliated companies. As a result, Hyundai Group disposed of or separated 23 of its 49 affiliated companies and categorized the remaining 26 companies into the five key industries of heavy engineering, automobiles, electronics, construction, and finance. Each of the five categories was turned into a form of small group, which was reorganized as an independent business entity. Not included in the five key industries, Hyundai Department Store was given to the chairman's third-eldest son, Chung Mong-keun, Hyundai Development Company to his third-younger brother, Chung Se-young, and Kumgang Korea Chemical (KCC) to his fourth-younger brother, Chung Sang-young, for independent management.

In 2000 an event dubbed "The Feud of the Princes" occurred. The conflict was a power struggle over the succession of Hyundai corporate control among Chung Ju-yung's sons, Mong-hun, Mong-koo, and their respective aides. Following the conflict, Mong-hun was selected as the successor to take over Hyundai Group, Mong-koo would control Hyundai Motor and Mong-joon would control Hyundai Heavy Industries. After the death of Chung Ju-yung in March 2001, Hyundai continued its North Korean business with the Kim Dae-jung administration, thus honoring Chung Ju-yung's will. As Hynix Semiconductor and Hyundai Construction faced critical liquidity issues, Mong-hun gave up on the two companies and focused on running Hyundai Asan, the North Korean business. Mong-hun was investigated for accounting fraud in Hyundai Merchant Marine, which was connected to the allegation that he had passed money to North Korea illegally. He committed suicide in August 2003.

Contest

After Mong-hun's death, his widow, Hyun Jeong-eun, succeeded him and a foreign fund began to actively purchase the stock of Hyundai Elevator, the flagship of the Hyundai Group. Claiming to be salvaging Hyundai Group from foreigners, the brothers' uncle and the president of KCC, Chung Sang-yung, who disliked the officers associated with the late Mong-hun and was displeased with Hyun's taking over Hyundai Group, contended for a hostile takeover.[29] Amid the family conflict, Mong-koo and Mong-joon remained neutral. Hyundai Group tried to increase its capital through a large-scale public offering, but it was enjoined by the court. The court ruled that Hyundai's public offering infringed the pre-emptive right of the shareholders.[30] However, Hyundai Group's attempt to avert the hostile takeover attempt by KCC succeeded, because KCC was found to be in violation of the 5% Rule for material omission in reporting[31] following a fierce proxy fight.[32] No efforts were made at reconciliation.

During the course of the legal battle, Hyundai emphasized that the 5% Rule should not be understood just as an "early warning system."[33] The purpose of the Rule was, rather, to protect minority shareholders who did not have the necessary resources to collect information on other (large) shareholders' intent. Certain empirical studies done by U.S. scholars[34] were heavily cited in the brief of Hyundai's counsel. The court accepted the argument and severely sanctioned KCC's violation of the 5% Rule.[35] The ruling of the court was perceived as extraordinary by the Korean bar, partly because the Korea Financial Supervisory Service did not accept Hyundai's argument that the entire filing for over 5 percent made by KCC should be treated as invalid.[36]

Chung Sang-yung had mentioned during the dispute that he would stop doing business with North Korea once he took over Hyundai Group, but the new chairman, Mrs. Hyun, successfully defended her management control and visited North Korea with one of her daughters to meet Kim Jong Il.[37] Hyundai's business with North Korea continues to this date.

Before the crucial shareholders' meeting of 30 March 2004, KCC announced that it would withdraw from the contest if it would lose the proxy contest. Indeed, KCC sold its stock (of Hyundai Group) to Schindler Holding of Switzerland and withdrew from the scene in early 2006. In May 2006, Hyundai Heavy Industries unexpectedly took over the shares of Hyundai Merchant Marine[38] from Golar LNG and became Merchant Marine's largest shareholder. Hyundai Heavy claimed that its takeover of the shares was an act in support of existing management, but the Hyundai Group did not accept the claim. Hyundai Merchant Marine is the key corporation of Hyundai Group and owns a large portion of Hyundai Construction stock.[39] In fact, Hyundai Group was preparing a bid for Hyundai Construction. There was speculation that it was a strategic move for Mong-joon's succession to the Hyundai Group while Mong-koo of Hyundai Motor was in prison for a large corporate scandal. Once again, it became clear that Mong-hun and Mong-joon do not have a friendly relationship. As of this writing, the dispute is dormant, but it may become active again.[40]

Viewpoint

It is interesting to note that the incident that directly triggered KCC's attempt at a hostile takeover was a foreign fund's large-scale purchase of Hyundai stock. Hyundai Heavy also made a remark that was equally interesting, that the purchase of Merchant Marine stock was motivated by its concern over a potential hostile takeover by a foreign entity. Furthermore, the data and materials on the disputes over corporate control between Hyundai Group and KCC reveal that the main issues were not so much about creating synergies through mergers and acquisitions as about calling attention to the problems affecting the corporate governance system and promising to correct the flaws therein. After the successful takeover defense, Hyundai Group's leadership promised investors that it would focus further on "responsibility, transparency and ethics" in managing the member companies.[41]

It is also noteworthy that, whereas the growth of Hyundai Group in the preceding decades had taken place in the most patriarchal setting in Korea, management assailed KCC for basing its hostile takeover attempt on what Hyundai itself exemplified. That Hyundai Group tried to rely on citizens (and "netizens," or citizens active on the internet), employees and small investors as a means of protecting its corporate control also was quite uncharacteristic. Lastly, an extraordinary situation emerged in which a female, the current Hyundai chairman, was under attack. She elicited solid support from female executives in Korea.

KT&G and Carl Icahn

Background

KT&G[42] is an outgrowth of the Monopoly Bureau founded in 1952 and Korea Tobacco and Ginseng Corporation founded in 1989. In 1999, the Corporation spun off its red ginseng business division and was listed in the same year. Issuing global depository receipts (GDRs) and disposing of stock owned by the government in 2002, it was entirely privatized and renamed KT&G. As of 30 September 2005, Kiup Bank was the largest domestic shareholder, with 5.75 percent. KT&G listed its GDRs in the Luxembourg Stock Exchange and its management is run by professional managers and an independent board of directors.

KT&G implemented the cumulative voting system, a method that allows a group of shareholders to consolidate all its proxies behind one candidate for a board seat, increasing that candidate's chances of election.[43] Since 2004, KT&G has been selected every year by the Korea Corporate Governance Service as the company with the best corporate governance practice.[44] According to the sources from the Korea Exchange, the rate of return to shareholders of KT&G during the period between 2003 and 2005 was 96.09 percent, a record rate in Korea.

Carl Icahn's attack on KT&G in early 2006 caught Korea by surprise.[45] It was quite shocking to see KT&G fall prey to a hedge fund, which belittled its past glorious records of dispersed ownership and professional management, and its recognition for excellent corporate governance. The incident raised an alert as to the soundness of the Korean criteria for evaluating corporate governance. Actually, during the dispute many flaws in KT&G management and corporate governance were revealed.

Carl Icahn went about his usual way in the KT&G case,[46] and in his doing so, the Korean capital market was able to draw lessons on the strategies and techniques of international hedge funds. His key suggestions included, *inter alia*:

1   selling down non-core assets
2   spinning off and listing of Korean Ginseng Corporation

3 restructuring KT&G's vast real estate portfolio
4 increasing dividends so that the company's dividend yield would be in line with other world-class tobacco companies, and
5 buying back shares, through tender offer if necessary, and canceling shares to the extent legally permissible.[47]

On 23 February 2006, immediately after sending the "proposals for enhancing stakeholder value," the Icahn group proposed that KT&G acquire additional KT&G shares at 60,000 Korean won (at a 13 to 33 percent premium). The Icahn group was prepared to commit an aggregate of approximately two trillion Korean won (two billion US dollars) of its own equity capital towards the consummation of the transaction and was sure about the possibility of additional debt financing. The proposal was rejected by KT&G in a letter dated 28 February 2006.

Showdown

Despite winning a favorable outcome in the proxy contest[48] with support from Institutional Shareholder Services and Glass Lewis, due to a material blunder by one of his local counsel who failed to file a proper shareholder proposal, Icahn had to settle for appointing one outside director of his choice to the board at the March 2006 shareholders' meeting.

There were six directorships up for election at the meeting, consisting of two slots for outside directors and four slots for outside directors who would also serve on the audit committee. While the Icahn group's three candidates appeared on the agenda as candidates for election to the board, they would only be available to compete for the two non-audit committee directorships. By reserving four of the six directorships for directors who would also serve on the audit committee, KT&G had strategically ensured that all of its nominees would fill these positions, as candidates for such positions may only be selected by the board. The Icahn group claimed that such an approach unlawfully infringed its right to submit the shareholder proposals.[49]

However, on 14 March 2006, the Daejeon District Court rejected the petition by Carl Icahn and his allies, allowing their three nominees to vie for only two seats of KT&G's outside directorship. The Court overruled Icahn's claim, saying,

> We do not find that KT&G's separate voting system for regular and audit directors encroaches upon the minority shareholders' right to a choice of directors as Carl Icahn and his partners claim ... Both separate and collective voting for directors are consistent with the current Commercial Code and Securities Exchange Act. Which to choose between the two depends on the board as long as there is no special proposal from shareholders during a shareholder proposal period ...

The Carl Icahn consortium did not take issue with the voting method itself during the shareholder proposal period, although they argued that it was not in line with the law. All they wanted was to include three nominees they recommended as candidates for directors.[50]

The four audit-committee member positions on the 12-member board were assured to go to KT&G's candidates, but one of the two outside director positions was almost certain to go to an Icahn candidate because neither side would win the 66.7 percent support needed to take both seats. Carl Icahn and his partners succeeded in getting their candidate on the board through cumulative voting. The remaining three candidates for the two seats for which the Icahn candidates were eligible received far fewer votes. In August 2006 KT&G accepted practically all of the suggestions made by Icahn.[51] Carl Icahn, in December 2006, disposed of its entire stake in KT&G and gained about 100 billion Korean won in profit (44.22 percent net return).[52]

New issues

At the time of dispute, one commentator went as far as to say, "If Sovereign was a grade school kid, Icahn is a college student. Now a group of graduate students like KKR will flock to the Korean market. Are Korean companies ready to defend their corporate control?"[53] As peculiar as it may sound, the statement turned out to be quite convincing. The international mix of shareholders elicited participation by many international players during the KT&G and Icahn dispute. KT&G was advised by Goldman Sachs and Lehman Brothers, and Georgeson Shareholder Communications acted in the proxy solicitation at the shareholders' meeting.

KT&G triggered an explosion of debates on the merits of leaving Korean companies exposed to the possibility of hostile takeover attempts.[54] Many economists have asserted the disciplinary function of a hostile takeover attempt; a hostile takeover attempt puts a rein on directors, thereby serving as an effective external controlling mechanism. In light of the positive effect, some argue for no limitation on hostile takeover attempts. According to the liberal advocates, the need for securing takeover defensive tactics as demanded by companies lacks sound judgment. Numerous companies that belong to corporate groups are already free from any hostile takeover attempts because of cross and circular shareholdings and complicated ownership structures. Therefore, the government should focus more on untangling ownership structures of Korean corporations and allow hostile takeover attempts to function effectively. They further argue that KT&G could not avoid being the target of the hedge fund because its dispersed ownership was characteristic of Western corporations and because it did not belong to a conglomerate. The threat imposed on KT&G by the hedge fund in the end benefited the shareholders and other interested parties and increased the value of the company.

The KT&G case also opened a new era in the discussion of directors' obligations and liabilities in control contests and takeovers. In the course of the defense against Carl Icahn and his allies, KT&G considered selling treasury shares to friendly local banks. On 13 March 2006, Industrial Bank of Korea, KT&G's third-largest shareholder with a 5.96 percent stake, and Woori Bank asked KT&G to allow due diligence for a possible purchase of KT&G's 9.75 percent treasury shares. It was reported that Icahn and his allies would take legal actions against the board of directors of KT&G if they were to push ahead with such a sale. According to Icahn, a sale of treasury shares to the banks "would constitute a breach of the board's fiduciary duties to the shareholders."[55] It is not known whether such a warning did in fact influence the decision of the KT&G's board, but one of the most popular takeover defensive tactics in Korea was not used by KT&G against Carl Icahn.

The issue of directors' liabilities arose again when Korea Securities Depository (KSD) decided not to accept the KT&G foreign shareholders' votes electronically from local custodians from 9 March 2006.[56] The Icahn group demanded that KT&G take action to rectify the situation, and reminded that

> [E]ach member of the board of directors is responsible and liable as fiduciaries to protect the integrity of a fair election process. In that capacity, it is incumbent on the board of directors to use all available means to force the KSD to exercise its authority to continue the electronic voting process and not cut off any shareholder's voting rights. [We] intend to hold each director personally responsible for any failure to satisfy his duties to shareholders ... and will take any and all legally available means against those that are responsible for such actions."[57]

As the decision of KSD was regarded as not depriving the voting rights of foreigners, no legal action was taken by the Icahn group. However, its course of action clearly showed a different approach, namely holding the directors personally liable for possible misconduct, not legally challenging the corporate act itself.

Conclusion

The cases discussed above show that a company's corporate governance bears a close link to hostile takeover attempts. Problems rooted in the corporate governance of a company can ignite hostile takeover attempts. In the case of SK, a takeover attempt resulted in tangible improvements in corporate governance. The Hyundai case demonstrates that the takeover issues befell a traditional Korean family business as it was growing into a mega-corporation and going through generational changes. The developments had close links to a hostile takeover attempt from outside. Although no empirical evidence is provided by this case, it is possible to conclude that the M&A market is exerting a positive influence on corporate governance. The KT&G case attests that Korean companies are not exempt from the international current of hedge fund activism[58] and must promptly learn the survival and adaptation skills necessary in a market undergoing a paradigm shift in corporate governance.

The three cases were entangled in legal disputes. As a result, they all contributed to improving legal principles on mergers and acquisitions in the Korean market. The contribution is quite significant, since the relatively short history of the Korean market means a shortage of rich M&A resources. In particular, the SK and Hyundai cases called for developing various defensive tactics against takeover attempts, and battles over the legitimacy of the new tactics unfolded in the courts. All the major Korean law firms were mobilized in these cases and some U.S. law firms with long experience in the areas took part indirectly. Milbank Tweed Hadley & McCloy played a major role in the SK case. And yet, there are not enough resources to provide guidelines for directors in control contests and hostile takeovers,[59] because, in Korea, a dispute hardly ever develops around directors' liabilities, but rather around the legality and legitimacy of a certain defensive tactic. Putting more weight on director liabilities is necessary to advance the board system, and thus it needs to be addressed.

Another interesting point is that an occurrence of disputes in the Korean M&A market, arising from foreign ownership of stock and listing on foreign exchanges, almost always calls for the involvement of Western investment banks, law firms, and consulting firms. When they are involved, the Western institutions bring in a multitude of advanced financial techniques and takeover defensive tactics and thereby help to raise the competency of professionals and professional services companies of Korea. Given the impact of such professionals' roles and performance in developing an efficient M&A market and corporate governance (Coffee 2006; Choi and Fisch 2003), the importation of Western skills is commendable.

Finally, in view of the foregoing discussion, we may quite safely conclude that Henry Manne (Manne 1965)[60] was right after all. Further, he was right in an Asian civil law country under Confucian culture, such as Korea, some forty years after he presented the thesis that the market for corporate control functions as a disciplinary mechanism for corporate governance. The cases described in this article show, even empirically in the SK case, that the validity of his thesis may transcend national jurisdictions and cultural differences. The Korean case, in particular the SK case, also shows that the increasing exposure of control to the market could eliminate the "inefficient controlling shareholder system" (Gilson 2006: 1676–1677).[61]

Notes

* The author thanks N. Alice Kim for invaluable assistance. The author would also like to thank Professors Hideki Kanda, Curtis Milhaupt, Kon Sik Kim, and

other authors' workshop participants at the University of Tokyo Faculty of Law and faculty seminar participants at the Seoul National University College of Law for commenting on earlier drafts of this article. The author is grateful to the Seoul National University for the financial support of the Research Settlement Fund for the New Faculty Members. The author also benefited from the financial support of the Seoul National University Center for Rule of Law.

1 *Financial Times*, 5 May 2006, 28 (on Hyundai saga).
2 Korea may be qualified as one of the "inefficient controlling shareholder systems" under the taxonomy proposed by Gilson (2006). See, e.g., Bae *et al.* (2002).
3 See Korean Ministry of Justice Press Release, 4 October 2006.
4 Choi (2004) (discussing the impact of class actions and whether securities class actions would be beneficial in Korea). See also Chung (2004).
5 See Korean Ministry of Finance and Economy Press Release, 29 June 2006.
6 For the current situation in Japan, see Milhaupt (2005).
7 See, e.g., Korea Fair Trade Commission Press Release, 13 July 2005 (showing improvements). For the current developments in and discussions on the law of corporate groups in Korea, see Kim (2006b). For the reform in Italy, see Ferrarini, Giudici and Richter (2005).
8 David A. Katz and Laura A. McIntosh, Corporate Governance Update: Poison Pills – Maintain Flexibility in Takeover Defense (Wachtell, Lipton, Rosen & Katz Memorandum, January 26, 2006). Cf. Subramanian (2003).
9 The Korean Commercial Code, Article 369, Paragraph 1, adopts the one vote per share system. It is a mandatory rule and as such is understood to be a rule which a company cannot overturn by its articles of incorporation. However, restrictions on voting rights are stipulated not only under the Korean Commercial Code but in numerous other laws and regulations in Korea. A primary example is the requirement that a shareholder may exercise only up to 3 percent of the total number of issued and outstanding shares in the appointment of a statutory auditor. The Commercial Code, Article 409, Paragraph 2. It should be noted that the dual-class share system should not be perceived simply as a means to retain incumbents' control of management. The dual-class share system is relatively more transparent compared to cross-shareholdings or pyramid-type structures. See Lucian Bebchuk and Oliver Hart, "A Threat to Dual-Class Shares,'"*Financial Times*, 31 May 2002 (warning that if the dual-class share system were abolished in Europe, the relevant companies would attempt either to adopt cross-shareholding or to create a pyramid-type corporate structure to protect their managements' interests).
10 Under the Korean Commercial Code shareholders of the stock companies have pre-emptive rights. Commercial Code, Article 418, Paragraph 1. However, the Code provides that the board of directors has the authority to issue new shares to third parties and/or shareholders not in proportion to the current shareholding ratio under certain circumstances. Commercial Code, Article 418, Paragraph 2. Thus, the issuance of new shares can be an effective tool that incumbent management can use to fend off hostile bidders.
11 Seoul Western District Court, Decisions of 24 March 2006 and 29 June 2006, Case Nos. 2006-Kahap-393 and 2005-Gahap-8262, respectively (outlawing the disposition of treasury shares to the controlling shareholder). Cf. Seoul Central District Court, Decision of 23 December 2003, Case No. 2003-Kahap-4154 (allowing the sale of treasury shares to friendly financial institutions for the purpose of takeover defense).
12 See Kim (2001).
13 For cross-listing of Korean companies on foreign exchanges, see Kim (2003). As of December 2006, eight Korean companies have listed their ADRs on the New York Stock Exchange: www.nyse.com/international/nonuslisted/int_listed. html.

Thus far, no study has been made on the effect of the Sarbanes-Oxley Act of 2002 on cross-listed Korean firms. See generally, Litvak (2007).

14 Korea Financial Supervisory Service Press Release, 31 January 2007, 2.

15 Samsung Electronics, Study on the Restrictions on the Exercise of Voting Rights by Financial Affiliates (October 2004) (Korean) (on file with the author). In 2004, Samsung Electronics' expenditure in R&D amounted to 40.1 percent (3.5 trillion Korean won) of the total R&D expenditures made by Korean companies. That single company contributed 6 percent to GDP and 14.8 percent to exports, respectively, in the same year. The corporate governance of and control over Samsung Electronics has become a national agenda.

16 See 'POSCO Might Need to Steel Itself for Pressure by Activist Investors,' *Wall Street Journal*, 6 March 2006, C10.

17 A financial or insurance company belonging to a business conglomerate with at least two trillion Korean won in assets may not exercise the voting rights it holds in a domestic affiliate. Exceptionally, it may exercise the voting rights up to 30 percent in corporate control-related matters. AFTA, Article 11.

18 Cf. Schmidt (1993).

19 http://eng.skcorp.com.

20 The so-called limitation on total investment amount is one of the means employed by the AFTA to curb undue concentration of economic power in a few hands; the other such means being (chiefly) the prohibition of cross (or recipro-cal) equity investment, the prohibition of debt guarantees for an affiliate, and the limitation on voting rights of financial and insurance companies. While these latter prohibitions and limitations apply to companies belonging to any business group with at least two trillion Korean won in assets, the threshold for applying the limitation on total investment amount is five trillion Korean won in assets. A company belonging to a business group with at least five trillion Korean won, and thus subject to the limitation on total investment amount, may not acquire or hold stock of other domestic companies in excess of 25 percent of its net asset amount. See generally Jung and Chang (2006).

21 See Ok-Rial Song, "Legal Issues of the SK Case," *Business Finance Law* 3 (2004), 23 (Korean).

22 The new KSEA explicitly makes it obligatory to file a report of the "Purpose of Ownership" (that is, the purpose of influencing the management control of the issuer) in addition to the "Status of Shareholding" which is stipulated as a matter to report under the old KSEA. KSEA, Article 200-2, Paragraph 1. The New KSEA also states that persons who have reported the purpose of their ownership as "for the purpose of influencing the management control of the issuer" will be, from the time of the filing of the report until the expiration of the fifth day, prohibited from acquiring additional equity securities of the issuer or exercising the voting rights on the shares that the persons own (as filed in the report) (newly added). KSEA, Article 200-3, Paragraph 2. Any one of the following acts falls under the definition of "an act to influence the management control": (1) the appointment or removal or suspension of office of a director or auditor, (2) amendment of the articles of incorporation in relation to the company's corporate bodies such as the director and board of directors, (3) change in the company's capitalization, (4) influence regarding dividend policies, (5) merger (including short-form merger and small-scale merger) or division of the company, (6) stock swap or transfer of stock, (7) acquisition or transfer of all or a material part of the business, (8) the disposition or transfer of all or a material part of the assets, (9) lease of all or material part of the business, delegation of management, or entering into or amending or terminating a contract whereby the company will be sharing all the profit and loss of the business with another company, or entering into other contracts of a similar nature, (10) exercising de facto influence

on the company or its officers or minority shareholders' rights or delegating such influence for the purpose of dissolving the company. Presidential Decree to the KSEA, Article 86-7.

23 *Hankuk Kyongje*, 13 March 2004, 13.
24 Seoul Central District Court Decision, 15 December 2004, Case No. 2004-Bihap-347. However, the court viewed Sovereign's petition as not abusive.
25 Sovereign had a tough fight. SK demanded that Sovereign provide certificates of registered seal impression of the shareholders who issued proxy to Sovereign. Surprisingly, Sovereign complied with the company's demand. Therefore, the issue of the means and standards for confirming the veracity of a proxy did not arise at the shareholders' meeting of SK.
26 See *Maeil Kyungje*, 24 August 2005, A1.
27 Sang Yong Park, "The Political Economy of Corporate Governance: Hostile Takeovers and Labor's Participation in Management," *Korean Management Review* 34(2) (2005), 569 (Korean).
28 www.hyundaigroup.com.
29 See *Hankuk Kyongje*, 5 November 2003, 1. See also *Hankuk Kyongje*, 8 December 2003, A14 (Chung Sang-yung's half-page open position letter).
30 Suwon District Court Yeoju Branch, Decision of 12 December 2003, Case No. 2003-Kahap-369. See *Hankuk Kyongje*, 18 November 2003, 3.
31 See Korea Financial Supervisory Service Press Release, 11 February 2004; Suwon District Court Yeoju Branch, Decision of 23 March 2004, Case No. 2004-Kahap-51. Grounds for sanctions such as restraint on voting rights include not only defective reporting, but also false reporting and omission in reporting. More specifically, the KSEA has the following penal provisions: (i) a person who, in intentional violation of the obligation to file a Large Holding Report, did not report the status of shareholding, purpose of ownership and the details of the change, or has falsely reported or omitted to state material matters, will be restricted from voting the shares that are in violation of the reporting requirement, as mentioned above, among the portion that exceeds 5% of the issued and outstanding voting shares for a period of six months; and (ii) a person who has delayed the above reporting or corrective reporting by mistake shall be subject to the same restraint from the date of the acquisition (or change) until the date that the correction report is made. In both cases, for the respective periods of time, the Korea Financial Supervisory Commission may order disposition of the shares that are in violation of the law. KSEA, Article 200-3, Paragraph 1; Presidential Decree to the KSEA, Article 86-8. Also, the New KSEA adds a penal provision stipulating that a person who fails to file a Large Holding Report may be subjected to up to one year of imprisonment with labor or up to 5 million Korean won fine. KSEA, Article 210, No. 5-2. See Korea Financial Supervisory Service, *Understanding Korea's "5% Rule"* (December 2005).
32 At the shareholders' meeting held on 30 March, 2004, duplicative proxies representing about 300,000 shares (5.4 percent of issued and outstanding shares of the company) were presented and treated as invalid.
33 See generally Jennings *et al.* (1998); Carney (2000). For the British 3% Rule, see Davies and Gower (2003). For the rule in Germany, see Klaus Peter Berger, "'Acting in Concert' nach §30 Abs. 2 WpÜG," *Die Aktiengesellschaft* 49 (2004), 592.
34 See Gilson and Black (1995: 903) (citing a study that shows higher abnormal rate of return in the case of compliance of the 5% Rule).
35 Seoul Central District Court, Decision of 26 March 2004, Case No. 2004-Kahap-809. The petition for the preliminary injunction was filed by Hyundai Securities.
36 See *Hankuk Kyongje*, 30 March 2004, 3.
37 See *Maeil Kyongje*, 6 August 2005, A7.
38 www.hmm21.com/hmm/jsp/eng/index.jsp.

39 *Hankuk Kyongje*, 3 May 2006, A26.
40 See *Money Today*, 2 May 2006, 3; *JungAng Ilbo*, 1 May 2006, 3.
41 See *Hankuk Kyongje*, 2 April 2004, A15 (full-page advertisement).
42 www.ktng.com/eng/index.jsp.
43 This is the default rule under the Korean Commercial Code. See Korean Commercial Code, Article 382-2. See generally Gordon (1994).
44 www.cgs.or.kr/eng/biz/b_model.asp.
45 See "Icahn's Push in Korea Shows Rise of Raiders is Roiling New Markets," *Wall Street Journal*, 2 March 2006, A1.
46 See Ken Auletta, "The Raid: How Carl Icahn Came Up Short," *New Yorker*, 20 March 2006, 132–143.
47 Icahn group's letter to KT&G dated 23 February 2006 (on file with the author).
48 The KSEA (Article 199), its Enforcement Decree (Article 85), and the Regulation on Securities Issuance and Disclosure promulgated by the Korea Financial Supervisory Commission apply to a proxy contest in Korea. With certain exceptions, in order to solicit votes from other shareholders, the solicitor must send to shareholders a proxy statement complying with the relevant rules. KSEA's Enforcement Decree, Article 85, Paragraph 1. The solicitor who violates the rules may be subject to imprisonment of two years or less or a penalty of 10 million Korean won or less. KSEA, Article 209, No. 9. The first ever proxy contest in Korea took place in 2003. This was a proxy contest over a shareholders' meeting of Hanaro Telecom between LG supported by Carlyle Group on the one hand and Hanaro Telecom supported by Newbridge/AIG Consortium and Hanaro's labor union on the other. The latter won the fight. Hanaro's board of directors decided to receive foreign investment from Newbridge/AIG Consortium and, to achieve this purpose, approved several agenda items on the shareholders' meeting which LG opposed, including determination of the minimum price for the issuance of new shares and issuance of new shares.
49 See Icahn group's letter to KT&G dated 15 February 2006 (on file with the author). For comment, see Ok-Rial Song, "Takeover Defense Through Composition of the Audit Committee," *Business Finance and Law* 20 (2006), 93 (Korean).
50 Case No. 2006-Kahap-242. For discussions on shareholder proposals in the United States, see generally Bebchuk (2003); Lipton and Rosenblum (2003); Bebchuk (2005).
51 'KT&G Bows to Icahn Demand to Return Cash to Shareholders,' *Financial Times*, 10 August 2006, 1.
52 See *Maeil Kyungje*, 6 December 2006, A2.
53 See *Money Today*, 13 April 2006: www.moneytoday.co.kr/view/mtview.php?type=1&no=2006040914422600450.
54 See, e.g., Korea Corporate Governance Service, Report on the Experts' Discussions held on 23 February 2006 (Korean): www.cgs.or.kr/review/0605/report_05.asp.
55 "Icahn Threatens to Sue KT&G Board," *Financial Times*, 15 March 2006, 22.
56 This was a surprise to many local custodians who had expected that the deadline would be 10 March, which was four business days before KT&G's annual general meeting of shareholders to be held on 17 March 2006, which has been the normal practice with KSD and the local custodians.
57 Icahn group's letter to KT&G dated 12 March 2006 (on file with the author).
58 For discussions on hedge fund activism, see "How to Handle Hedge Fund Activism," deallawyers.com webcast, 9 May 2006; "The Alpha Effect: How Hedge Funds Are Reshaping Deals," *International Financial Law Review*, June 2006. Cf. Hu and Black (2006).
59 Kim (2006a).
60 See also Easterbrook and Fischel (1981). Cf. Lipton 1979, together with Gilson and Kraakman (2005).

61 Other strategies suggested by Professor Gilson are improving the legal system and improved access to global capital markets. See Gilson (2006): 1673–1678.

Bibliography

Bae, Kee-Hong *et al.* (2002) "Tunneling or Value Added? Evidence from Mergers by Korean Business Groups," *Journal of Finance* 57, 2695.

Bebchuk, Lucian A. (2005) "The Case for Increasing Shareholder Power," *Harvard Law Review* 118, 833.

—— "The Case for Shareholder Access to the Ballot," (2003) *Business Lawyer* 59, 43.

Black, Bernard S. *et al.* (2001) "Corporate Governance in Korea at the Millennium: Enhancing International Competitiveness," *Journal of Corporation Law* 26, 537.

Black, Bernard S., Hasung Jang and Woochan Kim, "Does Corporate Governance Predict Firms' Market Values? Evidence from Korea," (2006) *Journal of Law, Economics, and Organization* 22, 366.

Carney, William J. (2000) *Mergers and Acquisitions: Cases and Materials*, New York: Foundation Press.

Choi, Stephen (2004) "Evidence on Securities Class Actions," *Vanderbilt Law Review* 57, 1465.

Choi, Stephen and Jill Fisch (2003) "How to Fix Wall Street: A Voucher Financing Proposal for Securities Intermediaries," *Yale Law Journal* 113, 269.

Coffee, John (2006) *Gatekeepers: The Professions and Corporate Governance*, Oxford: Oxford University Press.

Chung, Dae Hwan (2004) "Introduction to South Korea's New Securities-Related Class Action," *Journal of Corporation Law* 30, 165.

Davies, Paul L. and L.C.B. Gower (2003) *Principles of Modern Company Law*, 7th edn., London: Sweet & Maxwell.

Easterbrook, Frank H. and Daniel R. Fischel (1981) "The Proper Role of a Target's Management in Responding to a Tender Offer," *Harvard Law Review* 94, 1161.

Ferrarini, Guido, Paolo Giudici and Mario Stella Richter (2005) "Company Law Reform in Italy: Real Progress?" *Rabels Zeitschrift für ausländisches und internationals Privatrecht* 69, 658.

Gilson, Ronald (2006) "Controlling Shareholders and Corporate Governance: Complicating the Comparative Taxonomy," *Harvard Law Review* 119, 1641.

Gilson, Ronald and Bernard Black (1995) *The Law and Finance of Corporate Acquisitions*, 2nd edn., New York: Foundation Press.

Gilson, Ronald and Reinier Kraakman (2005) "Takeovers in the Boardroom: Burke versus Schumpeter," *Business Lawyer* 60, 1419.

Gordon, Jeffrey N. (1994) "Institutions as Relational Investors: A New Look at Cumulative Voting," *Columbia Law Review* 94, 124.

Hu, Henry and Bernard Black (2006) "The New Vote Buying: Empty Voting and Hidden (Morphable) Ownership," *Southern California Law Review* 79, 811.

Jennings, Richard W. *et al.* (1998) *Securities Regulation*, 8th edn., New York: Foundation Press.

Jung, Youngjin and Seung Wha Chang (2006) "Korea's Competition Law and Policies in Perspective," *Northwestern Journal of International Law and Business* 26, 687.

Kim, Hwa-Jin (1999) "Living with the IMF: A New Approach to Corporate Governance and Regulation of Financial Institutions in Korea," *Berkeley Journal of International Law* 17, 61.

—— (2001) "Taking International Soft Law Seriously: Its Implications for Global Convergence in Corporate Governance," *Journal of Korean Law* 1, 1.

—— (2002) "Toward the 'Best Practice' Model in a Globalizing Market: Recent Developments in Korean Corporate Governance," *Journal of Corporate Law Studies* 2, 345.

—— (2003) "Cross-Listing of Korean Companies on Foreign Exchanges: Law and Policy," *Journal of Korean Law* 3, 1.

—— (2006a) "Directors' Duties and Liabilities in Corporate Control and Restructuring Transactions: Recent Developments in Korea," *Oxford University Comparative Law Forum* 7, 2.

—— (2006b) "Corporate Governance in Groups of Companies," *Korean Bar Association Journal* 362: 6.

Kim, Jooyoung and Joongi Kim (2001) "Shareholder Activism in Korea: A Review of How PSPD Has Used Legal Measures to Strengthen Korean Corporate Governance," *Journal of Korean Law* 1, 51.

Lipton, Martin (1979) "Takeover Bids in the Target's Boardroom," *Business Lawyer* 35, 101.

Lipton, Martin and Steven A. Rosenblum (2003) "Election Contests in the Company's Proxy: An Idea Whose Time Has Not Come," *Business Lawyer* 59, 67.

Litvak, Kate (2007) "Sarbanes-Oxley and the Cross-Listing Premium," *Michigan Law Review* 105, 1857.

Manne, Henry G. (1965) "Mergers and the Market for Corporate Control," *Journal of Political Economy* 73, 110.

Milhaupt, Curtis J. (2005) "In the Shadow of Delaware? The Rise of Hostile Takeovers in Japan," *Columbia Law Review* 105, 2171.

Schmidt, Patrick L. (1993) "The Exxon-Florio Statute: How It Affects Foreign Investors and Lenders in the United States," *International Lawyer* 27, 795.

Seo, Jeong (2006) "Who Will Control Frankenstein? The Korean Chaebol's Corporate Governance," *Cardozo Journal of International and Comparative Law* 14, 21.

Subramanian, Guhan (2003) "Bargaining in the Shadow of Takeover Defenses," *Yale Law Journal* 113, 621.

5 Improving corporate governance through litigation

Derivative suits and class actions in Korea

Ok-Rial Song

Introduction

Among many corporate monitoring tools, corporate litigation—class actions and derivative suits—have a distinctive feature: a relatively feasible *ex post* remedy for *serious* governance failure. Since they deprive managers of money, prestige, or even their jobs, these suits serve an important threatening or disciplinary function that can deter management from engaging in wrongdoing. Moreover, such deterrent effect may well be emphasized once the limited role of the current monitoring measures is taken into account. Recent research using U.S. data found that *ex ante* corporate governance devices may not be as efficient as expected. Outside or independent directors, for instance, have little effect on firm performance (Lin 1996: 921–939; Fisch 1997: 276–278; Millstein and MacAvoy 1998: 1310–1317; Bhagat and Black 1999: 940–950); executive compensation schemes not only fail to reduce agency costs, but may result from or magnify such costs (Bebchuk, Fried and Walker 2002; Levmore 2001); and institutional investors lack sufficient incentive to monitor. The market for corporate control, which commentators tend to prefer, seems to have disappeared even in the U.S. market (Bebchuk and Ferrell 1999; Bebchuk, Coates and Subramanian 2002). In this situation, corporate litigation may be the last resort for an efficient corporate governance system. This essay explores why and how to establish corporate litigation in Korea.

During the decade following the East Asian financial crisis, Korea struggled to establish a transparent and accountable corporate governance system. Since then, as widely noted, corporate law and securities regulation have experienced a rapid change primarily by adopting an Anglo-American-style legal framework for corporate governance issues. As a result, Korean corporate law and securities regulation are generally deemed to provide near-world-class investor protection (Kim 1999: 70–81; Song 2002: 220–226). To name a few changes, shareholder proposals, voting by mail, cumulative voting, stock options, and audit committees have been provided for in the statutes. Appointment of several independent directors was mandated for listed companies, and large firms should have more than 50 percent independent directors. Minimum shareholding requirements for exercising certain share-holders' rights were dramatically diminished. As far as the statutory level of regulation is concerned, therefore, it can be fairly said that the Korean legal framework is now not very different from that of the U.S. or other Western developed countries.

As we can see in recent corporate scandals involving several major business groups (*chaebols*), however, the actual practice of Korean *chaebols* seems to persist despite the recent statutory reforms. The shameful description of Korean corporate governance, and for the *chaebol* system in particular, that Professors Shleifer and Vishny made before the above institutional reforms still holds, to some extent.[1] Several observations may provide a clue as to why this is so. Outside directors, for instance, are likely to be chosen by managers or controlling shareholders. Stock options are simply regarded as a windfall, because the informational efficiency of the Korean stock market is not yet firmly established, and thus firm value is imperfectly reflected in stock price. Even the market for corporate control is not working in Korea.

Worst of all, class actions and derivative suits do not help, simply because almost no such suits have been filed. Fewer than ten derivative suits have been filed since the late 1990s, and a class action has never been filed since its statutory adoption in 2005. Moreover, most of the derivative lawsuits have been not initiated by shareholders or entrepreneurial lawyers, but rather by an NGO called People's Solidarity for Participatory Democracy (PSPD) (Lee 2002: 353–356). The chances are, however, that such derivative suits may be poorly attuned from the point of view of efficiency, because they are filed not for pecuniary reasons, but rather with a mission to cure the Korean corporate governance system. Due to lack of financial and human resources, the PSPD was only able to bring a few lawsuits against a limited number of large corporate groups such as Samsung or Hyundai. Thus, although the derivative lawsuits that the PSPD filed attracted much attention, little deterrent function was achieved. At least as of now, when managers and controlling shareholders violate their fiduciary duties or commit securities crimes, they are more likely to be criminally prosecuted (as we saw in the recent corporate scandals) than to be privately sued by investors.

Against this backdrop, this essay, using a comparative approach, examines why class actions and derivative suits have been rarely used in Korea despite the statutory similarities with the U.S. and Japan, and argues that, in order to activate such litigation, it is necessary to change the structure of the legal service market in Korea. The essay asserts that the emergence of a lawyer-driven litigation market quite similar to the U.S. model is more desirable in improving the Korean corporate governance system.

Before we argue that corporate litigation should be activated, however, there are several caveats to address. Contrary to conventional understanding, the empirical tests mainly based on the U.S. data show that class actions and derivative suits are very unlikely to result in an increase of shareholder value in terms of stock price gain (Fischel and Bradley 1986; Romano 1991). Even a recent study using Japanese derivative litigation data reports no significant shareholder gain associated with filing a derivative suit (Milhaupt and West 2004: 23–28). Assuming these results are accurate, why should we believe that it is a good idea to encourage investors to sue? My view on this question is that the social gain from litigation, which should be distinguished from the stock-price gain of specific shareholders of the defendant company, may already be incorporated in the stock price of each company in that jurisdiction, and thus bringing a lawsuit might not be associated with any abnormal returns. The social gain comes from the *ex ante* disciplinary or threatening nature of the suits, and thus the mere possibility of litigation, not the actual bringing of lawsuits, accounts for social gains. Therefore, the magnitude of such gain depends on the extent to which the shareholders—in a specific jurisdiction—are likely to bring lawsuits if managerial wrongdoing is revealed. Put differently, the actual filing of a suit is not an empirical event, or at best tells something other than the social benefit associated with the disciplinary effect of corporate litigation.

The other concern is collusive settlement between defendant managers and plaintiffs' attorneys, as witnessed in the U.S. class actions and derivative suits. As widely noted, such practice enables the U.S. plaintiffs' lawyers to file frivolous suits. The efficiency concern about collusive settlements and frivolous suits is that, if disputes are likely to end up in settlements which do not depend on the merits of the claims, deterrence may not be generated. Why, then, should we think that the concept of a "lawyer-driven" litigation system is still convincing in Korea? This essay suggests several possibilities. First, culture may differ from country to country, and thus such practices may be controlled by the invisible hand. Second, the law may explicitly establish several barriers to this practice. The PSLRA of 1995 in the U.S. may be the most notable example, and the Securities Class Action Act in Korea also stipulated the same provisions. Third, several procedural rules in civil lawsuits may prevent frivolous suits from being filed. Fourth, if the problem is serious, legislators or the judiciary may enact special rules designed to cut off the profits of plaintiffs' lawyers from settlements. Therefore, we do not have to be concerned about the "abuse" of corporate litigation at the outset. In fact, it should be emphasized that excessive attention to abusive practices may involve some risk of paralyzing the corporate litigation system itself. As we can see below, the Korean Securities Class Action Act is a precise example of this mistake.

Although this essay focuses on derivative suits and class actions, the role of corporate litigation in improving corporate governance should not be exaggerated. The negative feature of lawsuits—as an *ex post* liability measure—in comparison with the market for corporate control is that they are applied to the limited and manifest violation of fiduciary duties. In other words, shareholders are not able to sue managers who lack management skills but are nonetheless loyal, while the market for corporate control is capable of punishing inefficient managers. Therefore, relying on corporate litigation certainly helps to prevent managers from betraying shareholders, but it may fail to achieve economic efficiency. That is why corporate litigation should never be regarded as a substitute for other monitoring devices, such as market for corporate control.

This essay proceeds as follows. The first two parts describe the Korean derivative suit and class action mechanisms, respectively, from a comparative perspective. A comparison of derivative suits between the United States, Japan, and Korea shows that the statutory differences between the three countries are quite minimal and thus not sufficient to explain the differences in reality. In fact, it seems easier for shareholders in Korea to file a lawsuit than for shareholders in the United States. Similarly, a comparison of class actions between the United States and Korea reveals that the differences, if any, are negligible. Nevertheless, the overall shape of corporate litigation in the two systems is totally different. The third part addresses several questions, such as the sources of such ineffective corporate litigation, the assessment and plausible reform proposals of the current system, and several solutions for abusive practices.

Derivative suits

A derivative suit is a unique feature of U.S. law. German corporate law, from which the Korean and Japanese corporate law originated, did not have this feature—instead, shareholders were only able to require auditors to bring a lawsuit against directors. Thus, the Korean and Japanese derivative suit mechanism is a direct import from U.S. corporate law. It follows that the statutory framework of derivative suits in Korea, Japan, and the U.S. is seemingly identical, with minimal and negligible distinctions. The different practice of derivative suits in those countries, despite the legistative similarities, is therefore quite puzzling.

To illustrate, consider the Japanese case. Japan had witnessed almost no derivative actions since its adoption in 1950. Shareholders in Japan filed fewer than 20 derivative suits from 1950 to 1990 (West 1994: 1438). In 1993, Japan reduced the filing fee to about $80 (JPY8,200), and the change brought about an explosion in derivative litigation.[2] Relying on this fact, commentators tend to believe that reducing the litigation fee may have "caused" such an explosion, but it is not convincing (Milhaupt and West 2004: 10). Korea, for instance, has since the early 1990s fixed the filing fees at a nominal amount—about $50 (50,000 won) prior to the financial crisis, and currently about $240 (230,000 won).[3] Nevertheless, shareholders in Korea are very reluctant to bring a lawsuit. In fact, filing fees have never been a critical issue in Korea; the nominal increase in filing fees was not an attempt to block lawsuits, just a reflection of a general price increase. Setting aside the effect of the filing fees, what prevents Korean shareholders from bringing a lawsuit? What exactly is it that Japan and the U.S. have, but Korea does not have? This Part will be devoted to comparing the basic legal structures of derivative suits between Korea, Japan, and the U.S.

Who can bring a suit?

Traditionally, the minimum shareholding requirement imposed on a plaintiff has been regarded as the most significant barrier preventing shareholders from bringing a derivative suit (Kim and Kim 2003: 386). Prior to the financial crisis, the statutory threshold for bringing a suit was 5% of shares in the company. Compared to the U.S.[4] and Japan,[5] where a shareholder with only one share may bring a derivative suit, the 5% requirement was blamed for paralyzing the derivative suit mechanism. Considering the fact that even the controlling families in Korean *chaebols* directly own, on average, less than 10% of controlled firms, the threshold of 5% seemed to be too high. Immediately after the financial crisis in 1997–1998, therefore, the shareholding threshold for filing a derivative suit was dramatically reduced to 0.01% in the case of listed companies.[6] It is not clear that a threshold of 0.01% is still a significant hurdle for derivative lawsuits.

Another apparent barrier to bringing a suit is a holding period requirement, which is found in Japan but not in the U.S.[7] Like Japanese law, the Korean Securities and Exchange Act requires that a shareholder hold shares "continuously" for 6 months before bringing a suit.[8]

On the other hand, however, Korean corporate law, like Japanese law, does not have a "contemporaneous shareholder rule," which is universal in U.S. state corporate laws.[9] Under this rule, the plaintiff shareholder must have been a shareholder "at the time of the alleged wrongdoing." There are two rationales for the contemporaneous shareholder rule. One is a concern with individuals purchasing shares simply for the purpose of bringing a frivolous suit. The other is that, since the market price reflects the losses that the directors' wrongdoing might incur, granting recovery to individuals who buy stock after wrongdoing damaged the corporation allows them to obtain a windfall (Gevurtz 2002: 396–399). Since there is no such rule in Korea, individuals can bring a suit simply by purchasing a few shares[10]— after noticing managerial wrongdoing in a listed company, although no one has attempted to do this. Arguably, the purpose of the two rules is the same: They aim at preventing a frivolous suit, through different institutions—the holding period requirement in Korea and Japan, and the contemporaneous shareholder rule in the U.S.

How can board interrupt?

Under Delaware corporate law, a plaintiff shareholder, prior to bringing a suit, must make a demand on the corporation's board of directors to take action, "unless the demand would be futile" (Gevurtz 2000 401). In Korea, on the contrary, demand on the board is universal,[11] as the Revised Model Business Corporation Act (RMBCA) and the Amercan Law Institute's (ALI) Principles of Corporate Governance provided,[12] and a plaintiff shareholder must wait for 30 days before filing suit. Only if the demand and waiting 30 days for the board's response might cause the company "irreparable damage," may shareholders bring suit without demand.[13] Put another way, the so-called "demand required, demand excused" distinction in Delaware jurisprudence has not been adopted in Korea and Japan; even though the demand would be "futile," shareholders must make a demand unless irreparable harm to the corporation would be incurred. The result is that the directors have enough time to take defensive measures at corporate expense, and a lawsuit is delayed for at least 30 days in Korea. Japan has a very similar procedure, except that shareholders must wait for at least 60 days.[14]

On the other hand, most of the procedural complexities in relation to the demand issue in the U.S. derivative suit mechanism do not exist in Korea. In particular, the board is essentially incapable of barring the complaint from proceeding to court. The U.S. board has two major tools to interrupt shareholders and prevent them from proceeding: refusal to bring a suit and special litigation committees. First, the board may simply refuse to take action. Applying the business judgment rule to such refusal, courts have held that the litigation may go forward only if, for example, the plaintiff can prove directors' conflicts of interest or bad faith (Gevurtz 2000: 408). Such proof may be readily available, but in any event, a shareholder in Korea is able to proceed without showing directors' conflicts of interest or bad faith.[15] Second, U.S. corporate management can ward off derivative suits by appointing special litigation committees. Since the mid-1970s, such committees, almost without exception, have concluded that the derivative suit was not in the corporation's best interest (Gevurtz 2000: 412).[16] In Korea, however, such practice is not expected to emerge in the near future.

Taken together, U.S. shareholders must be concerned about the strategies that the board can employ to drop the suit, while in Korea and Japan the demand requirement is merely procedural. A shareholder has to wait for several days, but after doing this, the suit automatically proceeds. The only way for the Korean company's board to bar a derivative suit is to accept the demand and have the company itself file the suit. In these respects, a derivative suit is more easily brought in Korea (and Japan) than in the U.S.

Litigation costs

To bring a suit, a plaintiff shareholder incurs filing fees—currently about $240—and attorney's fees. Theory suggests that such costs may significantly deter a shareholder from suing directors. Since it is the injured company that receives the actual recovery, a plaintiff shareholder can obtain only a proportional—typically *de minimis*—benefit from a "corporate" recovery in a suit. Accordingly, the U.S. rule is that a shareholder "prevailing" in a derivative suit should be fully reimbursed by the company for the filing fees and attorney fees incurred. Economically, the full reimbursement of litigation costs by the corporation is equivalent to the imposition of litigation costs on all the shareholders, pro rata, and therefore the free-rider problem can be resolved. By the same reasoning, therefore, the reimbursement of filing fees and attorney fees is statutorily provided in Korea[17] as well as in Japan.[18]

Nevertheless, shareholders and attorneys in Korea still have to bear a significant risk in connection with filing a derivative suit. First, the reimbursement of litigation costs is awarded only if a plaintiff prevails. Should he or she fail, the company is not obliged to pay the cost incurred, even though the suit was brought in good faith. Combined with the cost-allocation rule mentioned below, such a possibility raises significantly the expected cost of bringing a suit. Second, the reimbursement is, in principle, limited to the "reasonable or appropriate amount," but the scope of reasonableness is not yet clear. The current level of legally justifiable litigation costs is provided by Supreme Court Rule,[19] and thus, if plaintiff attorneys are paid more than this Rule prescribes, they are unlikely to be fully reimbursed. Most notably, this Rule calculates litigation costs on the basis of the amount pursued in a suit,[20] and does not employ any special method—such as the "lodestar" method in the U.S. cases—for a derivative suit. Since a derivative suit is perceived as being quite time consuming as compared to an ordinary suit for the same amount of damages, the final amount of attorney fees permitted by this Rule may be lower than the fee calculated under the lodestar method. Thus, attorneys are subject to the risk of not being fully compensated.

A plaintiff shareholder in Korea bears another risk in relation to litigation costs. Korea follows the British rule: a losing plaintiff must pay the litigation costs—including attorney fees—reasonably incurred by the defendant.[21] As a result, uncertainty with regard to litigation costs in Korea may raise the expected costs of filing a derivative suit for two reasons: (1) if a plaintiff shareholder wins, he is not sure of being fully reimbursed; and (2) if, on the other hand, a shareholder loses, he faces the British rule and bears the litigation costs reasonably incurred by both parties.

On the other hand, mainly due to a concern about frivolous suits, roughly one-third of the U.S. states require that the plaintiff shareholder should post security to cover the expenses that the corporation may incur. New York enacted the first security for expenses statute in 1944,[22] though Delaware has not followed this route. Although Korean corporate law is not very concerned about the abusive practice of derivative suits, the security for expenses clause has been incorporated in the statute since its origin.[23] Thus, the court may, at the request of the defendant directors who proved that the suit was brought in bad faith, order the plaintiff to post an adequate amount of security for expenses. To be sure, a shareholder who brings a meritorious suit does not have to post security, but in actuality, the posting requirement depends primarily on the court's interpretation of the "bad faith" of a plaintiff.

Summary

Table 5.1 summarizes the basic legal framework of the derivative suit system set forth above.

As stated above, the basic structure of the litigation system looks quite similar in the U.S., Japan and Korea. This is not surprising, though, because Korea and Japan imported the U.S. model without substantial modifications. The only notable distinction between Korea and Japan is that Korean law requires a shareholder to possess more than 0.01% of the total shares. Compared to the U.S. system, on the other hand, a shareholder in Korea has several advantages: he does not have to be a contemporaneous shareholder, the possibility of the board blocking the suit is very limited, and the court may decide in favor of the plaintiff with regard to the security deposit. The only disadvantages for a shareholder of a Korean company are, again, the minimum holding requirement and the holding period of six months.

Thus, an immediate response would be, why are derivative suits not brought in Korea, while the U.S. and Japan have trouble with too many suits? Can the holding requirement and uncertainties in association with litigation costs cause that much trouble to a shareholder who intends to bring a derivative lawsuit? We will revisit this issue in the third part of this essay.

Securities class actions

What about class actions? The National Assembly of Korea passed a Securities Class Action Act that came into effect on 1 January 2005. Was it a good idea? Securities class actions have always been controversial, even in U.S. legal academia. The externalities from the omission or misrepresentation

Table 5.1 Comparison of statutes

	United States	Japan	Korea
Minimum shareholding	–	–	0.01%
Holding period	–	6 months (public)	6 months
Contemp. shareholder	Yes	–	–
Demand on board	Futility test	60 days' delay	30 days' delay
If board refuses	BJR applies	Can file suit	Can file suit
Litigation committee	Yes	–	–
Filing fees	$100 (fixed)	$80 (fixed)	$190 (fixed)
Attorney fees if prevail	Reimbursed	Reimbursed	Reimbursed
Cost allocation	American rule	American rule	British rule
Security for expenses	Yes	Yes (if bad faith)	Yes (if bad faith)

of material information are, in nature, purely pecuniary (Friedman 2000: 35), and thus allowing a buyer of a security to be compensated by the company may merely result in a windfall to the seller, and vice versa. A diversified investor could be worse off if a class action system were adopted. From an *ex post* point of view, indeed, the description given a decade ago by Professor Alexander still holds: "payments by the corporation to settle a class action amount to transferring money from one pocket to the other, with about half of it dropping on the floor for lawyers to pick up. Such transfers are not in the economic interests of continuing shareholders" (Alexander 1996: 1503).

Such a skeptical view—mainly stressed by the business circle—prevented the Korean government from adopting the class action system for several years after the financial crisis. Setting aside the theoretical issues, needless to say, the strongest arguments of the opponents included abusive practices, such as a frivolous suits or collusive settlement. If, the argument went, it is true that the U.S. has experienced such trouble with class actions and thus enacted the Private Securities Litigation Reform Act of 1995 (PSLRA) to change abusive practices, Korea's sudden jump into the class action system may not be desirable. Another group of opponents placed emphasis on differences in the legal and cultural environment between the two countries. In addition to the traditional "common law versus civil law" distinction, for instance, they argued that class actions are the unique feature of the U.S. legal system, which would inevitably fail to be in harmony with the Korean civil procedure law, under which it is strictly prohibited for any person to exercise or dispose of another's legal entitlements.

Arguably, the most critical issue was whether the newly introduced class actions would be able to have a disciplinary effect against corporate directors. While the proponents argued that the new system could enhance the transparency and accountability of corporate management,[24] the business sector exaggerated the malicious effect of a class action by arguing, for instance, that filing a suit is likely to destroy the company's reputation in the market and thus eventually lead it to go bankrupt. Many seminars, conferences, and even moot courts were held in preparation for the defense against class actions, and large companies were gradually equipped with expanded in-house legal counsel. Ultimately, however, both sides turned out to be wrong. As of now, no movement toward a class action has been detected; no class action has been filed, and no law firms or private attorneys voluntarily entered this business.

Limited applicability

Arguably, one of the most important features of the Securities Class Action Act is that it resulted from a social compromise. Since it was the first time a class action system had been enacted in an East Asian country, and since there were many concerns about the negative effects of the new legislation, the Act incorporates several provisions—mostly modeled after the PSLRA—to curtail abusive practices.

In this context, the Act provides that a class action may be brought in very limited circumstances,[25] such as

1   violation of duty of disclosure in the public offering[26]
2   negligence in periodic reporting by a registered company[27]
3   market manipulation or insider trading, and
4   fraudulent audits.

These restrictions are not found even in the PSLRA, and it is clear that the government wanted to implement the institution very carefully. In fact, the original bill went further, stating that a class action may be brought only against a company with assets of two trillion won—equivalent to roughly two billion U.S. dollars—or more,[28] but it was argued that such a restriction was too extraordinary, and in any event the size of assets fluctuates continuously. Moreover, securities fraud tends to be more prevalent among smaller public companies. Since it was very hard to find the policy justification for such an unusual restriction, this provision was disregarded. Instead, however, the Act did not apply to smaller listed companies until 1 January 2007,[29] except in cases of manipulation or insider trading.

Immediately after approval of the Act, debate about its applicability to accounting fraud became heated. Several scholars pointed out that it is statutorily feasible for a company which committed accounting fraud long ago, say, in 1980, to be held liable to the shareholders in 2006, because the effect of the fraud is likely to be reflected in the 2006 financial statements. For this reason, they argued, unless the company discloses the accounting fraud committed in the past and then "reverses" the accounting process, it may be held liable for accounting fraud in a class action. This argument does not make any sense, because the Act explicitly states that a class action may be brought for the action "that is committed after the Act comes into effect."[30] Nevertheless, the Act was amended in March 2005 to take account of such concerns, and now explicitly provides that accounting fraud committed in the past will not be subject to a class action if the company discloses the fraud and "reverses" the accounting process to correct it by 31 December 2006.[31] Ironically, however, few companies made use of this provision, and thus this amendment may end up enabling a shareholder to bring a class action if the company committed accounting fraud in the past, because this provision assumes that such lawsuits are perfectly legal—a silly drafting error.

Class members and opt-out provision

The Act considered three issues to determine a "class":

1   the basic structure of class formation is designed after the U.S. model, or Rule 23 of the Federal Rules of Civil Procedure
2   the inconsistency of the "class" concept with the principles of civil procedure law should be minimized by providing notice requirements more precisely, and again
3   several provisions to prevent the abusive lawsuits.

First of all, under Rule 23 of the Federal Rules of Civil Procedure, for a class action to be maintained, the class should satisfy several requirements provided in Rule 23(a) and Rule 23(b). These are also found in the Korean counterpart. For instance, the class members must be numerous;[32] the questions of law or fact should be common to class members;[33] the lead plaintiff should fairly and adequately protect the interest of the class;[34] and finally, a class action should be superior to other measures for protection of the interest of class members and efficient adjudication of the dispute.[35] Thus, it is no exaggeration to say that the basic structure of the Korean class action is modeled on the U.S. law.

Copying was easy, but the government had to coax the opponents into accepting the bill. Legal scholars, for instance, argued that it is in violation of the principles of civil procedure to extend *res judicata*, binding force of the judgment, to persons who did not take part in the lawsuit or did not acknowledge the filing of the suit.[36] To be sure, this is one of the core elements of class actions, but it is also true that such extension is inconsistent with the Korean adversarial system. Taking the criticism, the Act allows members to opt out of the class by filing a written declaration of exclusion with the court.[37] In order for class members to decide whether to remain or not, they must be notified of the filing of a class action, and thus the Act provides details about notifications.

The problem with the notification requirements is that they are likely to increase the cost associated with filing a suit, without substantial benefits. The notification should be made by ordinary mail to class members, and the court is obliged to make every effort to identify the addresses.[38] But this system does not make sense. The class action assumes the situation in which individual damages are so small that each victim has no incentive to sue. That is, even if the individual member is notified of the filing of an action, he still has no incentive to think about it. Moreover, opting out from the class—contrary to the legislative intent—does not mean that the member preserves his right to sue. Rather, because the member will not file an individual suit, there will be no recovery at all. Acknowledging this, no one will file a written declaration of exclusion. Why should the court incur large costs to notify individual investors? Arguably, lowering the cost incurred in notifying investors should be preferred to protecting the individual right to sue, and perhaps the notification by an announcement in the newspaper alone might be sufficient for that purpose.

Finally, minimum class size is stipulated to prevent abusive lawsuits. Rule 23 in the U.S. only requires that the class be "so numerous that joinder of all members is impracticable,"[39] but the Act requires that the class consist of 50 members or more and the class hold at least 0.01% of the total number of securities issued by the defendant company.[40] This provision reminds us of the minimum shareholding requirement in the case of a derivative suit.[41] Again, it seems obvious that the legislators were unreasonably obsessed with the abuse issue.

Lead plaintiff and lead counsel

The qualifications and restrictions on lead plaintiffs and lead counsels are the most controversial aspects of the Act. As widely noted, the PSLRA in the U.S. reformed securities class actions in various aspects, especially in relation to the lead plaintiff and lead counsel, primarily in order to prevent "professional plaintiffs" from filing frivolous suits, and to encourage institutional investors to actively participate in the class action.

In U.S. class actions, several provisions serve this purpose.

1 The lead plaintiff should file a sworn certification with the court that he did not purchase the securities only for the purpose of bringing a class action.[42]
2 A person may be a lead plaintiff in no more than five class actions in any three years.[43]
3 The court must determine who is most able to represent the interests of class members, and in such determination of the court, the person who has "the largest financial interest" in the suit should be presumed to be the most adequate plaintiff.[44]
4 If a lead counsel directly owns or otherwise has a beneficial interest in the securities that are the subject of the litigation, and therefore the conflict of interest is significant, the court may disqualify the attorney.[45]

Almost the same provisions are found in the Korean Securities Class Action Act,[46] with very slight modification and addition. Contrary to U.S. class actions, for instance, the number of class actions in any three years that will disqualify the lead plaintiff is reduced to three, and such restriction is applied to lead counsel as well. In particular, the restriction that prohibits the lead counsel from bringing more than three class actions during any three-year period has been blamed for impeding the development of experienced professional class-action law firms. Arguably, it is almost inconceivable for major law firms in Korea to bring a class action as a lead counsel against their client companies, and thus the only way for a class action to be brought is to encourage small law firms to specialize in this area. Perhaps the Act should have given more incentives to the smaller law firms.

The fundamental question is whether such kinds of strict restrictions were in fact necessary, given the different legal and social environments between the U.S. and Korea. These provisions were, of course, based on the opponents' perception that the introduction of a class action system might have a huge impact on the daily operation of the business community and that abusive lawsuits were also quite likely in Korea. Contrary to this expectation, however, no class action has yet been filed. Even several attorneys who work for NGOs say that they have no intention to engage in the class action business because of the restrictions involved. Perhaps the real effect of the Act is not to promote litigation, but to sound the death knell for them. We will return to this issue in the final part of this essay.

Litigation costs

Class actions in Korea are likely to impose a huge financial burden on lead plaintiffs or lead counsels. First of all, they have to incur filing fees. The Act does not provide for a flate rate; instead, the filing fees are, in principle, determined according to the amount of damages claimed as in ordinary lawsuits. The flat rate was not adopted, because a class action was perceived to be a suit in which investors are pursuing "their own" damages—just like ordinary lawsuits. Moreover, the cases are generally more complicated. Of course, considering the fact that the amount pursued in a class action is generally large, the Act allowed a 50 percent discount off the regular fees, and placed a cap of 50 million won—equivalent to 50,000 U.S. dollars.[47] In comparison with the flat rate of $240 in a derivative suit, however, this amount is still so large as to dicourage filing of a class action.

Another financial burden is expenses, which must be paid *in advance*. At the beginning stage of the discussion, the government tried to require the plaintiff to post security to cover the damages the company might suffer, just as provided in a derivative suit, and the original proposal of the Act contained such a provision. Faced with criticism from NGOs, however, the final bill did not adopt this requirement. Instead, the plaintiff must pay in advance the costs incurred in the court's notices to the public and appraisal process in the lawsuit.[48] In general, the costs incurred in a class action are borne by the attorney, and they are compensated by the contingent fee arrangement if the plaintiff prevails. Taken together, therefore, the initial investment which attorneys have to make to file a class action is not negligible.

Summary

As examined above, the PSLRA in the U.S. was imported word for word into the Korean Class Action Act. Given the ineffective derivative suit system as described previously, the emphasis in designing the new class action system should have been placed on structuring it to effectively discourage managers from engaging in wrongdoing. The Act as enacted, however, contains many so-called "anti-abuse" provisions that will effectively discourage investors from filing a suit. In terms of preventing frivolous suits, the Act went further than the PSLRA.

Discussion

Despite the statutory similarities or advantages in comparison with the U.S. and Japan, Korea has not witnessed any "explosion" of derivative suits. Although the filing fee has been a fixed amount of $50 to $240 since 1992,[49] no derivative suit was filed for 5 years after the fee was fixed. Also, as mentioned, no class action has been brought since the enactment of the Securities Class Action Act. The first question, therefore, is why is there is almost no corporate litigation in Korea?

Few derivative suits

The legal environment for fiduciary duty changed dramatically after the financial crisis, mainly through the active filing of lawsuits by the PSPD. In fact, the PSPD filed the first derivative suit in Korean history, in 1997, against the directors and officers of Korea First Bank. In that case, Korea First Bank made a decision to make a large loan to Han-Bo Steel, which went bankrupt in early 1997, and minority shareholders alleged that the directors and officers of the bank violated their duty of care (no investigation of the overall risk of Han-Bo Steel) and duty of loyalty (bribery from Han-Bo Steel). One year later, the Seoul District Court rendered a decision that the directors were liable,[50] and the Supreme Court endorsed the ruling.[51]

In 2001, another high-profile derivative suit was reviewed by the court: a lawsuit against Samsung Electronics again brought by the PSPD. It was filed in 1998, and the plaintiffs alleged that the controlling shareholder and directors of Samsung Electronics were liable for breach of duty of care in acquiring a company which eventually went bankrupt. The Soowon District Court also held that they were liable,[52] and, although the Supreme Court finally reversed it,[53] this case may be called a Korean version of *Van Gorkom*,[54] because it was argued in the District Court that, in making a takeover decision, the board members, like the Trans Union managers, were not well informed about the target company.[55]

In addition to these two high-profile cases, two or three more cases were resolved without drawing public attention, and several cases are pending at the district court level. Some recent derivative suits were brought by the Korean Deposit Insurance Company (KDIC), but still, the KDIC is not an ordinary investor, and at the same time such suits are very rare. Overall, derivative suits have been very rarely brought since the financial crisis.

Admittedly, the above two cases—First Korea Bank and Samsung Electronics—had a great impact on business law and practice, and the substance of fiduciary law in Korea now is quite different from what it was prior to these two cases. But two is a small number. Contrary to the complaints from the business sector, the number of derivative suits is too small for corporate management to be threatened. Most importantly, derivative suits were not initiated by investors or entrepreneurial lawyers, but rather by the

PSPD. Arguably, there would have been no derivative suits but for the PSPD. They filed suit not for pecuniary reasons, but rather with a mission to cure the Korean corporate governance system. Although the activities performed by the PSPD have been generally evaluated as more successful than initially expected, the organization lacks human and financial resources to monitor all the major companies in Korea. Thus, the PSPD adopted a strategy, which turned out to be quite smart, of bringing a small number of lawsuits against a limited number of large corporate groups such as Samsung, Hyundai, or LG. The controlling shareholders and managers of other corporate groups are still free of the threat of litigation.

Litigation costs and legal profession

Why are Korean practices different? One of the possibilites, perhaps the most notable one, is the litigation cost structure, and commentators tend simply to suggest that the reduction of these costs may encourage plaintiffs to file a suit. The deterrent effect of litigation costs was discussed above, but this cannot fully explain the different practices across the countries.

Derivative suits and class actions are different forms of remedies in terms of the legal structure, but from economic perspectives, they have much in common. Perhaps most notably, both are lawsuits in which the plaintiff has to incur his or her own costs to protect other investors' interests. Obviously, a shareholder lacks incentives to file a derivative suit even if he knows about managerial wrongdoing, because a shareholder bears the total litigation costs but is only able to obtain a fractional benefit of the increase in the firm's value. Since each shareholder has only a small proportion of shares, he is not willing to take part in the suit unless the costs are negligible. The incentive structure associated with filing a class action, in which a lead plaintiff brings a lawsuit on behalf of other class members, is the same. Even though the litigation costs are not too high, the shareholders still have to bear costs that may be higher than the fractional benefit from the suit, and thus have little incentive. What, then, is the convincing argument for the "explosion" of corporate litigation in the U.S. and Japan?

Cultural differences are often suggested, but this argument cannot stand on solid ground.[56] When there was no shareholder litigation in Japan, for instance, the belief that Japanese people have an "inherent" aversion to litigation was remarkably pervasive among scholars, but the observation turned out to be false. The "culture" argument does not explain the sharp increase in the number of derivative suits in Japan since 1993, because it is unreasonable to believe that there was a sudden change in Japanese culture. Moreover, once the globalization of the capital market is taken into account, this argument seems obviously flawed. Global investors in the Korean stock market have no reason to follow Korean corporate culture.

One mechanism the U.S. law has developed to cure the problem of lack of incentive is "professional lawyers." A derivative suit or a class action is typically brought by a plaintiff's attorney, who is a professional specialist in such lawsuits. The attorney, and not the nominal plaintiff, bears the litigation costs (Klein and Coffee 1996: 196). It might be argued that, therefore, no matter how significant the litigation costs, there will be attorneys who are willing to make an investment at each risk–return combination. To be sure, higher litigation costs may reduce the number of lawyers who engage in this business, but if, for example, market competition becomes more fierce, the effect of the litigation costs is likely to be offset by the pressure of market competition. In this case, therefore, the fundamental problem is not the litigation costs themselves, but the structure and competition in the legal service market. Changes in the legal service market take much longer, but this observation seems timely, since the legal service market in Korea is now undergoing revolutionary changes: the number of lawyers has been dramatically increased in recent years and the opening of the domestic legal service market to foreign law firms is imminent. In a more competitive market, a small number of lawyers are willing to organize corporate litigation within the constraints of the existing cost structure.

In Korea, however, such a theory is not a perfect fit. Suppose that all of the litigation costs examined above are negligible. Even in such a case, a plaintiff shareholder in a derivative suit or a lead plaintiff in a class action in Korea must bear two significant legal uncertainties associated with litigation costs, even if American-style professional attorneys emerge.

The one relates to a "retainer" practice. It is quite common in Korea that attorneys demand payment in the form of a "retainer" before the litigation begins. The retainer may be reimbursed by the defendant company if a plaintiff prevails in a derivative suit, and also the retainer paid in a class action may be credited if a class defeats the defendant. Assuming the plaintiff wins, it does not matter whether or not the payment is made in advance, but the plaintiff does not always win. The retainer is not refundable to a losing plaintiff. Thus, the retainer practice may be viewed as an insurance policy granted to the attorneys, by which the risk associated with the investment is transferred from the attorney to the plaintiff. Such risk allocation may aggravate the moral hazard problem of the attorneys. As a result, shareholders or investors are discouraged from filing a suit even though the attorneys are available, and the professional attorneys are also likely to engage in opportunistic behavior.

The other risk associated with filing a suit is the British rule, as stated above.[57] Korea follows the British rule in allocating litigation costs: a plaintiff losing the suit must pay the litigation costs—including attorneys' fees—reasonably incurred by the defendant. It should be kept in mind that the plaintiffs, not the plaintiffs' attorneys, are obliged to pay the costs. Thus, plaintiffs are not willing to file a suit unless there is an agreement— whether it is confidential or not—that the attorneys will bear the litigation costs in full, including the costs incurred by the defendant according to the court order, and such agreement is effectively enforced by the court, or at least by a reputation mechanism in the legal services market. Taken together, it is hard to perfectly eliminate the possibilities for shareholders to bear any costs.

In this context, recent research on derivative suits in Japan shows several interesting results. According to Professor Mark West, plaintiffs usually lose derivative suits in Japan.[58] Therefore, the risk of losing a retainer fee is quite significant in Japan (Japan does not follow the British rule with respect to attorneys' fees). Arguably, the expected costs on the plaintiff-shareholders' side may not exceed the expected value of a pro rata increase in the value of his shareholding. Why, then, do shareholders in Japan file derivative suits? Professor West reported several interesting changes in the Japanese legal services market. Most importantly, many attorneys reduced their retainers.[59] Small retainers and large contingent fees become standard legal practice. In addition, to avoid high risk, attorneys select their cases carefully and avoid investing in cases that the business judgment rule governs (West 2001: 370). To reduce the risk on the plaintiff-shareholders' side and thus induce them to file a suit, several attorneys made confidential agreements on fee-kickbacks, giving the plaintiff a part of the attorneys' fee received from the companies (West 2001: 371). Taken together, it can be concluded that the attorney-driven market for derivative suits has already emerged in Japan.

It should be noted that, in Japan, the possibilities for shareholders to bear litigation costs have been eliminated by private arrangements with plaintiffs' attorneys, not by statutory reform. If such arrangements are invalidated as unfair or deceptive practices, it would probably be the death knell of derivative suits even in Japan. The same "lawyer-driven" litigation will be witnessed in Korea when the legal services market is sufficiently competitive.

What about the British rule on allocating the litigation costs? One way to change this rule is to statutorily make an exception specifically for derivative suits and class actions. Since such suits aim mainly at deterrence, rather than at compensating victims for damages, it may be convincingly argued that the cost-allocation rule should treat them as such. This is not the only way, however. Given that the British rule is effectively enforced, another way to implement this arrangement is, again, by contract. Since entrepreneurial lawyers must solicit a few investors—who are concerned about the British rule and thus are reluctant to get involved—to file a suit, they are likely to make a confidential agreement that they will pay the defendant's attorneys' fees and other costs incurred if the suit fails. As long as such an agreement is continuously enforced by the court, the British rule will not prevent the lawyer-driven market from emerging.

Policy issues of "lawyer-driven" market

What is the cost of creating a lawyer-driven litigation system in Korea? Some scholars and politicians are concerned about the abuse of derivative suits and class actions, and argue that implementing such a system is never a good strategy for a small economy such as Korea. In other words, "regulation through litigation" is very costly in a small emerging market. In particular, the U.S. experience tells that litigation has almost nothing to do with regulating the agency costs of managers, and in fact, filing a suit may be regarded as yet another agency cost. These two results are closely connected. That is, since the litigation is very likely to end up in a settlement which does not depend on the merits of the suits (agency cost), they have no impact on improving the corporate governance system.

Collusive settlement

Many empirical and theoretical papers on derivative suits and class actions report on the collusive settlement practice between defendant managers and plaintiffs' attorneys.[60] The problem with this practice is not merely that the lawyers file frivolous suits to threaten innocent persons, but rather that the final settlement does not depend on the merits of the suit. If the managers are forced to settle, and thus the managers are sued regardless of their violation of fiduciary duty, then managers do not have any reason to expend extra costs to exercise care, for example.

In the corporate litigation setting, both parties—plaintiffs' attorneys and defendant managers—have strong incentives to settle. On the attorneys' side, early settlement may reduce the downside risks by eliminating the possibility of losing the suit—assuming that such risks are borne by the attorneys. Morevoer, if the attorneys are paid only on a contingent fee basis, without consideration of hourly fee, their incentive for early settlement will be much stronger. On the defendant managers' side, on the other hand, directors and officers who are named as defendants may expect indemnification by the company or compensation by D&O insurance. Since such indemnification or insurance is generally not available to the defendants if they are found liable by the court for a breach of their fiduciary duties, the defendant directors and officers prefer early settlement to obtaining a final judgment. Both the attorneys and managers, in fact, are agents of the investors, but they collusively agree to harm the principal (what might be called a "dual" agency cost).

Since the agency costs are generated on both sides, several solutions are also possible from both sides. Take the managerial incentive first. It may be suggested, for instance, that a mandatory cap be imposed on settlement amounts to prevent managers from paying too much. D&O insurance companies may be involved by not compensating the entire amount of the settlement. In any event, punishing managers in case of settlement is the intuition behind these proposals, but the regulation has an *ex ante* externality on the market for directors (Kraakman, Park and Shavell 1994: 1738). In other words, any effort to regulate managerial incentives to settle may raise the reservation price for managers to be willing to work for the company and, as a result, the expenses that the company incurs in order to attract talented managers must be raised. Since adjusting the liability of managers is closely related to the managerial incentive for a specific company, the agency cost problem generated on the managers' side is unlikely to be resolved.

On the other hand, however, the regulation of plaintiffs' attorneys' incentives is relatively feasible. It is worthwhile to note that one of the causes of the disappearance of the deterrent effect is that attorneys are allowed to retain the same monetary compensation when the disputes are settled as when they are litigated to a judgment. Thus, it may be proposed that the attorneys be deprived of their expected compensation package and thus be reimbursed only for costs that are actually incurred and proved, if the suit ends up in settlement. While the court should be generous in enforcing contractual contingent fee agreements if the suits are finally adjudicated, strict scrutiny of attorney fees should be made in case of settlement. Plaintiffs' attorneys will then select cases with a higher probability of winning.

Still, however, there remain several reasons for plaintiffs' attorneys to agree on settlement. Early settlement reduces uncertainties, and thus if the manager is willing to settle, the attorney does not have any reason to reject it. Is the concept, then, of a "lawyer-driven" litigation system still convincing for Korea? The anwer may be positive for several reasons. Perhaps the culture or implicit norms of the Korean legal profession, or even reputation mechanisms, may play a (limited) role. The Korean legal profession is still a small, closed society, and thus the reputation mechanism may work for some time.

Furthermore, there are at least two procedural rules to prevent attorneys from filing a frivolous suit. Most notably, the discovery process is absent from the Korean Civil Procedure Act. Plaintiffs' attorneys who do not know specifically about managerial wrongdoing or securities fraud can not attempt to file a suit for the purpose of obtaining its settlement value. Considering that the PSLRA in the U.S. introduced an automatic stay of the discovery process,[61] its absence may play a significant role in this context. Another procedural rule is the British rule, as stated above. From the above discussion, it was concluded that the effect of the British rule would be ultimately imposed on the plaintiffs' attorneys, through statutory reforms or private agreement. Therefore, the fee-shifting rule constrains the attorneys—not plaintiffs themselves—from bringing a frivolous suit.

Most importantly, however, the relevance of this debate on Korean corporate governance should not be exaggerated. In the long run, arguably, plaintiffs' attorneys may come to believe that filing a suit just for the settlement value is never profitable. The emphasis on abusive practices, however, may harm the system in the short run. The overheated debates on this issue caused several anti-abuse provisions to be inserted into the Securities Class Action Act in Korea, as described above, but the pure effect was not to prevent abusive lawsuits, but just to paralyze the class action system itself. In fact, the Act should not have followed the PSLRA. For the time being, Korean legislators should have thought about how to make it fully functioning, rather than worrying about the over-functioning of the system.

Social benefits?

Several studies have been undertaken to measure the social benefits of good corporate governance, in terms of abnormal stock price gains or increases in firm revenue or profit, but sometimes the empirical results turn out to be puzzling. For instance, outside or independent directors do not improve firm performance. Also, contrary to the conventional understanding, empirical tests show that class actions and derivative suits are very unlikely to result in an increase of shareholder value in terms of the stock-price gain (Fischel and Bradley 1986; Romano 1991). Even a study using the Japanese derivative litigation data reports no significant shareholder gain associated with filing a derivative suit (Milhaupt and West 2004: 23–28). Based on this research, commentators might hastily conclude that encouraging investors or attorneys to sue directors and officers is unlikely to increase the national wealth. If the empirial research is accurate, what are the social benefits of activating derivative suits and class actions?

This issue should be more deeply debated, but this essay makes two comments. First, it was already examined that, in fact, filing a suit itself may be regarded as another agency cost. If litigation is very likely to end up in settlement, it is unlikely to have an impact on improving corporate governance. Such agency costs are mixed with the social benefit, and thus the above research may be interpreted as failing to isolate the pure benefit of the litigation. As discussed above, litigation does not necessarily result in agency costs if collusive settlement practice is properly regulated.

Second, and more importantly, the empirical results concerning derivative suits and class actions should be distinguished from those about the firm-level corporate governance tools. Independent directors, for instance, may be adopted by an individual firm, and the investors may take into account the adoption itself and the quality of independent directors in pricing the firm. In this case, therefore, the finding of insignifinant stock-price gains associated with the election of independent directors implies that independent directors have nothing to do with firm performance. On the contrary, transforming the litigation system and legal profession to be more conducive to filing suit will have an impact on all companies in that jurisdiction, whether suits are actually brought or not. In other words, the social gain may already be incorporated in the stock price of each company, and thus bringing a lawsuit might not be associated with any abnormal returns. The social gain comes from the disciplinary or threatening nature of the suits, and thus the mere possibility, not the actual bringing, of lawsuits accounts for the gain. Therefore, the magnitude of such gain depends on the extent to which shareholders or investors—in a specific jurisdiction—are likely to bring law-suits if managerial wrongdoing is revealed. Put differently, the actual filing of a suit is not an event, or at best tells something other than the social benefit associated with the disciplinary effect of corporate litigation. In conclusion, the social benefits from bringing suit have not been yet been cleared rejected.

Conclusion

In the situation in which *ex ante* monitoring or incentive mechanisms such as independent directors, executive compensation, institutional share-holders, and the voting system are inherently or practically defective and in which the market for corporate control does not perform a disciplinary function on managers, derivative suits and class actions may be the last and most plausible candidate for institutional reform to improve corporate governance. Korea has tried to activate the derivative suit system, and it recently enacted the Securities Class Action Act. This essay has compared the statutory differences regarding corporate litigation between Korea, Japan, and the U.S., and argued for activating the system.

To be sure, there are several negative effects of filing a frivolous suit, and the Korean example—several anti-abuse provisions in the Securities Class Action in particular—may show how business people and politicians make use of these concerns to destroy such a disciplinary mechanism. The emphasis on abusive practices, however, may not be appropriate in present-day Korea, where the agency costs of controlling shareholders are not yet adequately regulated and the private benefits of control are still large. Managers should be more subject to the threat of being sued, and this heightened threat may create positive social results.

Notes

1 Shleifer and Vishny (1997: 742) described, "Korean chaebol sometimes sell their subsidiaries to the relatives of the chaebol founder at low prices.... In many countries today, the law protects investors better than it does in Russia, Korea, or Italy."
2 West (2001: 351–356) reports that 84 suits were pending in 1993, but there were 174 suits in total by the end of 1996, and 286 suits by the end of 1999, including 95 filed in 1999 alone.
3 Korean Civil Action Filing Fees Act § 2(1) (providing that if the litigated amount is more than 10 million won and less than 100 million won, the filing fee is "the litigated amount × 45 / 10,000 + 5,000 Won"); Supreme Court Regulation on Civil Action Filing Fees §§ 15(1), 18-2 (providing that, regardless of the amount of damages alleged, 50 million and 100 won is regarded as the litigated amount of derivative suits). The filing fees are thus calculated as 50,000,000 × 45/10,000 + 5,000, or roughly 230,000 won. Prior to the year of 2001, the same provisions of the Act and Regulation provided that the litigated amount of derivative suits were 10 million and 100 won, and the ratio to be multiplied to this amount was 5 /1,000. As a result, the filing fees prior to the crisis were 10,000,000 × 5 / 1,000, or roughly 50,000 won.

4 Rev. Model Bus. Corp. Act § 7.41 (no limitation).

5 Japanese old Commercial Code § 267(1) and (new) Company Law § 847(1), (2) (no limitation).

6 Korean Securities and Exchange Act § 191-13(1). In case of non-listed companies, the shareholding threshold was also reduced to 1%, which still seems high (Korean Commercial Code § 403(1)).

7 The holding period requirement was amended in the new Japanese Company Law. See Japanese old Commercial Code § 267(1) (six months) and (new) Company Law § 847(1), (2) (generally six months, but not required in case of non-public companies).

8 Korean Securities and Exchange Act § 191-13(1). In case of non-listed companies, instead of requiring higher shareholding ratio, there is no holding period requirement (Korean Commercial Code § 403(1)).

9 Del. Code Ann. tit. 8, § 327; Cal. Corp. Code § 800(b)(1); N.Y. Bus. Corp. Law § 626(b); Rev. Model Bus. Corp. Act § 7.41(a).

10 But the amount must be over 0.01% of total shares and the plaintiff must wait for 6 months after purchasing the shares.

11 Korean Commercial Code § 403(1).

12 Rev. Model Bus. Corp. Act § 7.42; American Law Institute, Principles of Corporate Governance § 7.03.

13 Korean Commercial Code § 403(4).

14 Japanese Company Law § 847(4).

15 Korean Commercial Code § 403(3).

16 For judicial review of the committee's recommendation to drop suits, see *Auerbach* vs. *Bennett*, 47 N.Y.2d 619 (1979) (minimal review); *Zapata Corp.* vs. *Maldonado*, 430 A.2d 779 (Del. 1981) (two-step test).

17 Korean Securities and Exchange Act § 191-13(6) (reimbursement of "full" litigation costs); Korean Commercial Code § 405(1) (reimbursement of "reasonable or appropriate" litigation costs).

18 Japanese Company Law § 852(1).

19 Korean Civil Procedure Act § 109(1).

20 Supreme Court Rule on the Calculation of Reasonable Litigation Costs § 3(1).

21 Korean Civil Procedure Act § 98. The British rule does not apply if the parties agree to settle. In case of settlement, the American rule—each party bears its own costs—applies (Korean Civil Procedure Act § 106).

22 N.Y. Bus. Corp. Law § 627.

23 Korean Commercial Code §§ 403(7), 176(3), (4).

24 Enhancing the transparency of corporate management was also mentioned as a purpose of the Act (Korean Securities Class Action Act § 1).

25 Korean Securities Class Action Act § 3(1).

26 Korean Securities Exchange Act § 14. This provision is a "catch-all" clause, and includes all the liabilities of §§ 11, 12(a), 12(b) of the Securities Act of 1933 in the U.S. except that the buyer of a security in the secondary market does not have standing as a plaintiff.

27 Korean Securities Exchange Act § 186-5. The periodic reporting like 10-K or 10-Q is mandatory for all listed companies in the Korean Stock Exchange market or KOSDAQ market. Article 186-5 is a Korean version of the Rule 10b-5, with limited applicability.

28 In June 2004, the number of the company with assets of two trillion won or more was only 66; 63 companies were listed in the Korean Stock Exchange and 3 companies in the KOSDAQ.

29 Korean Securities Class Action Act, Appendix § 3.

30 Korean Securities Class Action Act, Appendix § 2.

31 Korean Securities Class Action Act, Appendix § 4.

32 Fed. R. Civ. P. § 23(a)(1); Korean Securities Class Action Act § 12(1) 1. The minimum size of the class is also provided.

33 Fed. R. Civ. P. § 23(a)(2); Korean Securities Class Action Act § 12(1) 2.

34 Fed. R. Civ. P. § 23(a)(4); Korean Securities Class Action Act § 11(1).

35 Fed. R. Civ. P. § 23(b)(3); Korean Securities Class Action Act § 12(1) 3.

36 Korean Securities Class Action Act § 37.

37 Korean Securities Class Action Act § 28(1).

38 Supreme Court Rules on Securities Class Action § 15.

39 Fed. R. Civ. P. § 23(a)(1).

40 Korean Securities Class Action Act § 12(1) 1.

41 Korean Securities and Exchange Act § 191-13(1).

42 Securities Act of 1933 § 27(a)(2)(A); Securities Exchange Act of 1934 § 21D(a)(2)(A).

43 33 Act § 27(a)(3)(B)(vi); 34 Act § 21D(a)(3)(B)(vi).

44 33 Act § 27(a)(3)(B)(i), (iii); 34 Act § 21D(a)(3)(B)(i), (iii).

45 33 Act § 27(a)(9); 34 Act § 21D(a)(9).

46 (1) The member who wishes to be a lead plaintiff should file an application that says he or she did not purchase the securities only for the purpose of bringing a class action or at the request of the attorney (Korean Securities Class Action Act § 10(3), 9(2), hereinafter in this endnote "Act"). (2) A person who is involved as a lead plaintiff or lead counsel in *three* or more class actions for the most recent three years may not be a lead plaintiff or lead counsel (Act § 11(3)). (3) The lead plaintiff should be a person who is able to adequately represent the interests of class members, such as the person who has the largest financial interest in the suit (Act § 11(1). (4) If a lead counsel directly owns or otherwise has a beneficial interest in the securities that are the subject of the litigation, and therefore the court determines that the conflict of interest is significant, he or she may be disqualified (Act § 5(2)).

47 Korean Securities Class Action Act § 7(2).

48 Korean Securities Class Action Act § 16.

49 Korean Civil Action Filing Fees Act § 2(1).

50 Seoul District Court, 97 Ga-Hap 39907 (24 July 1998).

51 Supreme Court, 2000 Da 9086 (15 March 2002).

52 Soowon District Court, 98 Ga-Hap 22553 (27 December 2001).

53 Supreme Court, 2003 Da 69638 (28 October 2005).

54 Smith v. Van Gorkom, 488 A.2d 858 (Del. 1985).

55 For detailed description of the above two high-profile cases, see Kim and Kim (2003: 389–392).

56 West (1994: 1439–1441) says, "Ending the inquiry with a cultural explanation avoids the next logical query; namely, why does culture dictate nonlitigiousness, if it does at all? If this second-order question remains unanswered, a satisfactory response to the primary inquiry is impossible." Ramseyer (1987: 39–40) also argues, "Cultural values are fragile things.... Whether hostile takeovers will eventually become as common in Japan as in the United States, therefore, ultimately may depend on the extent to which Japanese firms find... that takeovers pay.... [M]ost writers have overestimated its uniformity and coherence and underestimated the extent to which individuals manipulate it strategically."

57 Supreme Court Rule on the Calculation of Reasonable Litigation Costs § 3(1).

58 West (2001: 357–358) reports that, from a database consisting of 73 derivative suits filed between 1993 and 1999, only 2 cases resulted in victory for plaintiffs and 4 cases are pending because of appeals by defendants.

59 West (2001: 368–369) describes that a retainer of $30,000 for the damages claimed of $1.5 billion; under the Fee Rules, the retainer would be over $30 million.

60 Coffee (1986: 698–700) mentions that the most interesting empirical observation is that "[shareholder litigation] results in very few litigated victories for plaintiffs."

Macey and Miller (1991: 45) also says "The attorney may also agree to an inappropriately low settlement on the merits in exchange for the defendant's implicit or explicit promise to allow the attorney to expend additional risk-free hours in order to build up a fee." Thomas and Hansen (1992: 428), citing Romano, says, " [S]hareholder litigation is a weak, if not ineffective, instrument of corporate governance."

61 33 Act § 27(b); 34 Act § 21D(b)(3)(B) (during the pendency of any motion to dismiss).

Bibliography

Alexander, J.C. (1996) "Rethinking Damages in Securities Class Actions," *Stanford Law Review* 48: 1487–1537.

Bebchuk L.A. and A. Ferrell (1999) "Federalism and Corporate Law: The Race to Protect Managers from Takeovers," *Columbia Law Review* 99: 1168–99.

Bebchuk, L.A., J.C. Coates, and G. Subramanian (2002) "The Powerful Antitakeover Force of Staggered Boards: Theory, Evidence, and Policy," *Stanford Law Review* 54: 887–951.

Bebchuk, L.A., J.M. Fried, and D.I. Walker (2002) "Managerial Power and Rend Extraction in the Design of Executive Compensation," *University of Chicago Law Review* 69: 751–846.

Bhagat, S. and B. Black (1999) "The Uncertain Relationship between Board Composition and Firm Performance," *Business Lawyer* 54: 921–63.

Coffee, J.C., Jr. (1986) "Understanding the Plaintiff's Attorney: The Implications of Economic Theory for Private Enforcement of Law Through Class and Derivative Actions," *Columbia Law Review* 86: 669–727

Fisch, J.E. (1997) "Corporate Governance: Taking Boards Seriously," *Cardozo Law Review* 19: 265–90.

Fischel D.R. and M. Bradley (1986) "The Role of Liability Rules and the Derivative Suit in Corporate Law: A Theoretical and Empirical Analysis," *Cornell Law Review* 71: 261–97.

Friedman, D.D. (2000) *Law's Order: What Economics Has to Do with Law and Why It Matters*, Princeton, NJ: Princeton University Press.

Gevurtz, F.A. (2000) *Corporation Law*, MN: West Group.

Kim, H. (1999) "Living with the IMF: A New Approach to Corporate Governance and Regulation of Financial Institutions in Korea," *Berkeley Journal of International Law* 17: 61–94.

Kim, K. and J. Kim (2003) "Revamping Fiduciary Duties in Korea: Does Law Matter to Corporate Governance" in C. Milhaupt (ed.) *Global Markets, Domestic Institutions: Corporate Law and Governance in a New Era of Cross-Border Deals*, New York: Columbia University Press.

Klein, W.A. and J.C., Jr. Coffee (1996) *Business Organization and Finance: Legal and Economic Principles*, New York: Foundation Press.

Kraakman, R., H. Park, and S. Shavell (1994) "When Are Shareholder Suits in Shareholder Interests?" *Georgetown Law Journal* 82: 1733–75.

Lee, B. (2002) "Don Quixote or Robin Hood? Minority Shareholder Rights and Corporate Governance in Korea," *Columbia Journal of Asian Law* 15: 345–71.

Levmore, S. (2001) "Puzzling Stock Options and Compensation Norms," *University of Pennsylvania Law Review* 149: 1901–40.

Lin, L. (1996) "The Effectiveness of Outside Directors as a Corporate Governance Mechanism: Theories and Evidence," *Northwestern University Law Review* 90: 898–976.

Macey, J.R. and G.P. Miller (1991) "The Plaintiffs' Attorney's Role in Class Action and Derivative Litigation: Economic Analysis and Recommendations for Reform," *University of Chicago Law Review* 58: 1–118.

Milhaupt, C.J. and West, M.D. (2004) *Economic Organizations and Corporate Governance in Japan*, New York: Oxford University Press.

Millstein, I.M. and P.W. MacAvoy (1998) "The Active Board of Directors and Performance of the Large Public Traded Corporation," *Columbia Law Review* 98: 1283–1321.

Ramseyer, J.M. (1987) "Takeovers in Japan: Opportunism, Ideology and Corporate Control," *UCLA Law Review* 35: 1–64.

Romano, R. (1991) "The Shareholder Suit: Litigation Without Foundation?" *Journal of Law, Economics and Organization* 7: 55–87.

Shleifer, A. and R.W. Vishny (1997) "A Survey of Corporate Governance," *Journal of Finance* 52: 737–83.

Song, O. (2002) "The Legacy of Controlling Minority Structure: A Kaleidoscope of Corporate Governance Reform in Korean Chaebol," *Law and Policy in International Business* 34: 183–245.

Thomas, R.S. and R.G. Hansen (1992) "Auctioning Class Action and Derivative Lawsuits: A Critical Analysis," *Northwestern University Law Review* 87: 423–57.

West, M.D. (1994) "The Pricing of Shareholder Derivative Actions in Japan and the United States," *Northwestern University Law Review* 88: 1436–1507 (1994).

—— (2001) "Why Shareholders Sue: The Evidence from Japan," *Journal of Legal Studies* 30: 351–82.

6 The role of judges in corporate governance

The Korean experience

*Kon-Sik Kim**

Introduction

In comparative corporate governance discourse, a debate is still under way among researchers in different parts of the world as to whether (and the extent to which) law matters in improving corporate governance.[1] It seems now generally agreed, however, that law in practice matters far more than law on the books.[2] What makes law in practice approach law on the books is enforcement. Although enforcement is now being discussed widely, the concept of enforcement seems to differ depending on the commentator. Although the focus has been traditionally placed on enforcement of law (hard law, to be precise), the term "enforcement" is now often broadly defined as a process of generating a desirable behavior on the part of market participants.

In this broad sense of the word, enforcement may depend on various elements of society. Not only formal elements such as government agencies, self-regulatory organizations (SROs), outside directors and private lawsuits but also informal elements such as market pressure, mass media and NGOs all affect corporate governance practice in one way or another. Although enforcement consists of various factors, law enforcement occupies a central, if not dominant, position. And in conventional law enforcement, judges play a crucial role, although their exact role differs depending on the country.[3]

As for Korea, law did not matter much in corporate governance prior to the financial crisis in 1997. Lawsuits filed in relation to corporate governance disputes were rare, if not totally absent. The judge's role on the corporate governance stage was insignificant. Since the crisis, however, the situation has changed dramatically. Corporate governance lawsuits are rapidly on the rise. The increase of such lawsuits may be attributable to various factors. First, the corporate statutes have been revised to make it easier to file a shareholder derivative suit. Second, shareholder activists, especially those affiliated with People's Solidarity for Participatory Democracy (PSPD), have been relying heavily on lawsuits in achieving their objectives.[4] PSPD has been taking a variety of legal measures, civil as well as criminal, against managers of *chaebol*, family-controlled conglomerates in Korea. Third, since the crisis, the share of foreign investors in the stock market has gone up tremendously. As of the end of 2006, they accounted for 37.3 percent (in terms of the market capitalization) of the shares listed in the prime section of the Korea Exchange.[5] In blue chip firms, however, their share is even higher: for example, 83 percent in Kookmin Bank (the largest commercial bank in Korea), 62 percent in POSCO and 49 percent in Samsung Electronics.[6] Foreign investors tend to be less patient than their domestic counterparts and some of them are less inhibited about filing lawsuits.

With the increase of lawsuits, the role of judges is becoming crucial in corporate governance practice in Korea. Their decisions may not only determine the outcome of a particular corporate governance dispute but also shape (or distort) the actual picture of corporate governance. Since 1997, the judiciary has been faced with various corporate governance disputes. Dealing with these disputes, judges show a somewhat "schizophrenic" attitude. They sometimes adopt a highly formalistic approach, sticking to the letter of a statutory provision, while in other cases they will liberally digress from the statutes to reach an outcome not explicitly supported by the statutes. The purpose of this essay is to examine the role of judges in Korea's corporate governance on the basis of these decisions, showing different attitudes in judicial decision making.

This essay proceeds as follows: it begins with a survey of the status of corporate governance lawsuits and a discussion of the factors causing the increase of such lawsuits and cover diverse types of such lawsuits. The next part introduces a sample of corporate governance lawsuits which appear contradictory in judicial reasoning. Then several perspectives are presented from which one may explain these apparently inconsistent decisions. The final part is a conclusion.

Rise of corporate governance lawsuits

Lawsuits related to shareholder resolutions

Under Korean law, shareholder lawsuits may arise in various contexts of corporate governance. For example, a shareholder may sue to vacate a shareholder resolution for violation of law or the articles of incorporation, or to nullify a merger or issuance of shares. Minority shareholders holding a certain number of shares may file a lawsuit to seek dismissal of a director for violation of law or illicit behavior (Art. 385 II) or a derivative suit against a director for damages (Art. 403).

Prior to the 1997 financial crisis, shareholder lawsuits were largely confined to those seeking to invalidate a shareholder resolution.[7] As such lawsuits have long been addressed by the Commercial Code (Arts. 376–381), lawyers are generally familiar with them. The prevalence of such lawsuits in Korea may be primarily due to the following two factors. First, unlike shareholder derivative suits, even a shareholder holding one share is qualified to file this kind of lawsuit. Second, the general shareholders' meeting (GSM), in smaller firms in particular, is often conducted in disregard of formal procedures under the corporate statutes. As long as there are no disputes among shareholders, no one pays much attention to this kind of technical flaw. Once a feud between business partners arises, these flaws may be picked up as a pretext for attack.

The lawsuit invalidating a shareholder resolution is indeed a powerful weapon against majority shareholders. This remedy, however, is not without limits. First, it may not address the real complaint of discontented shareholders. Such a lawsuit is often a product of a long, ruptured relationship, not just one-time misconduct. Invalidating a particular move by majority shareholders does not help restore the broken relationship. Second, more significantly, this remedy is of limited relevance in corporate governance disputes. The limitation derives from the limited power of the GSM as a corporate organ. Under Korean law, the jurisdiction of the GSM is broader than in the United States. For example, dividends are declared by the GSM, not the board of directors, under Korean law. Still, the power of the GSM is largely limited to fundamental changes such as mergers and amendments to the articles of incorporation. The division of power between the GSM and the board is not as strict as in the United States, as the power of the GSM may be liberally expanded by the articles of incorporation. It may not be a practical option, however, to further expand the power of the GSM, because it will then hinder timely and flexible corporate decision making. Thus, material business decisions are mostly made in the boardroom. From a corporate governance perspective, it is thus more important to restrain the behavior of the board and individual directors, than of the GSM.

Lawsuits aimed at the board and directors

Korea has a statutory framework designed for restraining abuse by directors. The corporate statutes recognize a Korean version of fiduciary duties, i.e., the "duty of care of a good manager" (Civil Code, Art. 681) and the duty of loyalty (Art. 382-3) introduced in 1998. Academics still dispute the conceptual relationship between the two duties. It is now well accepted, however, that the two duties can be interpreted as a functional equivalent of the fiduciary duties imposed on directors under the U.S. corporate law.[8]

The two statutory duties, however, failed to grow into an equivalent of their American counterpart. This is largely due to the inadequacy of shareholder derivative suits under Korean law. Although the shareholder's derivative suit was adopted in KCC in 1962, no derivative suits were recorded until 1997. The absence of derivative suits did not signify the absence of wrongs against shareholders. A primary cause of the absence of such suits was a 5 percent shareholding requirement imposed on a plaintiff shareholder. For a large listed firm, this shareholding requirement served as a virtually insurmountable hurdle.

Inadequacy of criminal sanctions

The absence of shareholder derivative suits does not necessarily mean that management abuse was completely beyond control. Tunneling activities by managers may constitute a breach of trust, a crime under the criminal code in Korea (Art. 355(2)). Managers of bankrupt firms in particular have often been indicted and convicted of breach of trust. Examples of criminal sanctions against top executives abound, including scandals involving SK, Hyundai, Doosan and Samsung. This approach of imposing criminal sanctions on corporate managers does have its merits, as it is familiar, powerful and flexible. It has its own shortcomings as well. First, prosecutors may be susceptible to public pressure. Although they no longer receive the cue from the Blue House, the office of the president, they are not entirely free from political considerations. Indeed, prosecutors have been exercising much discretion in indicting managers. In a recent case, for example, the CEO of a medium-sized company was indicted and then found guilty of breach of trust for acquiring private placements of bonds with warrants at a substantial discount.[9] In contrast, in a nearly identical case involving Samsung Group, a leading *chaebol* in Korea, prosecutors showed a different attitude. Samsung Everland, a non-listed real estate developer and a de facto holding company of Samsung Group, issued convertible bonds by private offering to Chairman Lee's son and daughters. This transaction was severely criticized as the young children of the chairman allegedly gained an enormous windfall profit in the process. In 2000, a group of law professors filed a charge against the top executives with the prosecutor's office, but the prosecutor's office refused to indict them. Then, in 2005, more than four years after the charge had been filed, the prosecutor's office changed its mind and indicted the two representative directors. The defendants were convicted by the trial court.[10]

Second, as breach of trust is subject to criminal punishment, the scope of misconduct covered by it should be limited to highly reprehensible behavior. Indeed, a breach of duty, a central element of the crime of breach of trust, is rather vague and amenable to a quite liberal interpretation.[11] In a recent Supreme Court decision, a CEO who engaged in a leveraged buyout transaction was convicted of breach of trust.[12]

Third, the level of criminal sanction imposed on managers who engage in wrongdoing is regarded as relatively low in Korea. This is well illustrated in a recent criminal case involving yet another *chaebol*. Several members of its controlling family were found to have long engaged in usurping tens of millions of dollars from firms under their control.[13] Under the criminal statutes, the defendants could be sentenced to anything from a minimum of 5 years to life.[14] Unlike other white-collar criminals in a similar situation, however, they were not even arrested, even though the facts were not disputed. They were all convicted, but got away with suspended sentences.[15] Finally, even if the wrongdoing controlling shareholder is sent to prison, he is normally released from prison after a few months and eventually resumes his position. The government will feel strong pressure from the business community and the media to place him back at the helm, by staying the sentence or granting amnesty.

Corporate governance reform after the crisis

From this analysis, we can see that criminal sanctions should not be allowed to take the front seat in corporate governance. Since the financial crisis, the government has made efforts to facilitate shareholder suits. Through a series of revisions, the shareholding requirement for a derivative suit has been substantially alleviated. For a large listed firm, the shareholding threshold has been reduced to as low as 0.01 percent of the shares (Securities Exchange Act Art. 191-13(1)). If the firm is really large, it may still not be easy to clear this hurdle. In such a case, the only realistic option is to form an alliance with a foreign institutional investor.

Attorney fees are known to be a critical element in shareholder lawsuits. Now, there is a possibility that plaintiffs' lawyers may be compensated for their services. Korea has finally enacted a provision entitling plaintiff shareholders to seek reasonable compensation from the company for their litigation costs (Art. 405; SEA, Art. 191-13(6)), which include attorney fees. It will be up to the court to determine the "reasonable" amount of attorney fees that the company should pay to the successful plaintiff. It is not entirely clear, however, whether Korean judges will be as generous as their U.S. counterparts in determining attorney fees. In Korea, it is still a foreign idea to provide an incentive to private individuals to file a lawsuit in the interest of others.

Rise of lawsuits against managers

Given the cumbersome shareholding requirement and the lack of incentive to sue, it is somewhat surprising to observe shareholders' derivative suits in Korea at all. So far, PSPD and a small number of public-minded lawyers have been behind these few lawsuits. These lawsuits have sent shockwaves throughout the Korean business community by holding managers liable for breaches of fiduciary duties. The first landmark decision was in the Korea First Bank (KFB) case.[16] The case was based on KFB's questionable loans to the Hanbo Group, which failed after making a string of overly optimistic investments. At the time of the loan decisions, Hanbo was regarded as "unqualified" under KFB's own internal loan standards. Moreover, KFB's top executives received bribes from the chairman of Hanbo. A group of shareholders organized by PSPD filed, for the first time in Korea, a shareholder derivative suit against directors for damages. Although the defendant directors argued that their decision was basically a business judgment, the district court rejected this argument by saying that "the directors made a mistake that cannot be passed over lightly and that exceeded their scope of discretion."[17]

The Korea First Bank Decision attracted much attention from the mass media, partly because the directors were held liable for as much as 40 billion won (roughly 40 million dollars), an exorbitant sum of money for salaried managers.[18] Less spectacular, but more influential, are the lawsuits filed by Korea Deposit Insurance Corporation (KDIC) against responsible managers of bankrupt financial institutions and debtor firms. Since the financial crisis, KDIC, like the U.S. Federal Deposit Insurance Corporation following the savings and loans crisis, has been suing those responsible managers. As of the end of 2005, KDIC filed civil liability actions against 9,144 executives of 489 financial institutions for more than 1.6 trillion won in total. Also, KDIC has demanded that financial institutions file lawsuits against 698 managers of 132 distressed firms.[19] The litigation activities of KDIC will not continue indefinitely, however. KDIC may exercise its broad litigation power only in exceptional circumstances where public funds are injected into a distressed financial institution (Deposit Protection Act, Art. 21-2).

Duty of care

In the KFB case, it was the duty of care that was violated. But the case involves a conflict-of-interest aspect, as defendant directors were found to have received a bribe from Chairman Chung of Hanbo. Indeed, cases where a director is held liable purely on the grounds of the duty of care are rare, as Korean courts recognize a version of the business judgment rule.[20] It is not clear, however, how far the business judgment rule reaches. As shown later, there are cases where related-party transactions are at issue. In theory, it may be treated as a duty of care case for those directors who are not "specially interested" in the transaction in question. Then the court could apply the business judgment rule to the directors' decision to approve the transaction. Holding the directors liable for damages, the court made no distinction between the two duties, nor did it discuss the business judgment rule. In one recent case, outside as well as inside directors were held liable for approving an unfair related-party transaction.[21]

The duty to monitor, a subset of the duty of care, is growing increasingly relevant, especially for outside directors.[22] Primarily under the influence of the Sarbanes Oxley Act, the concept of internal controls is now being discussed and has been adopted in the statutes. If strictly enforced, this concept may lead to an increase in cases regarding the duty of care. It is not clear, however, how the courts will react to this concept.

Duty of loyalty

In Korea's corporate governance practice, the duty of loyalty may be far more relevant. Except for a small number of former government-owned firms privatized during the last decade (e.g., KT, POSCO, KB and KT&G), even the largest firms in Korea generally have controlling shareholders. Although the cash-flow rights of controlling families have been on the decline – below 5 percent in some business groups – the controlling family enjoys effective control over all the group companies by means of complicated circular and pyramid shareholding schemes.[23] As Table 6.1 shows, there is a wide gap between the controlling shareholder's voting rights and cash-flow rights. In other words, the so-called voting power multiplier (VPM: voting rights over cash-flow rights) is high for controlling shareholders. According to Table 1, VPM for 14 business groups with more than 5 trillion won in assets is as high as 7.47.[24]

The dwindling cash-flow rights of the controlling family, coupled with the family's effective control over group firms, provides a strong incentive to engage in "tunneling" activities, to the detriment of minority shareholders. Related-party transactions among affiliated companies are rampant and not effectively regulated. An endless stream of scandals involving controlling families demonstrates the inefficacy of the corporate statutes in restraining abuse.

Korea's corporate statutes have many gaps in regulating conflict-of-interest transactions arising from the *chaebol* structure. For example, the statutes do not explicitly recognize the concept of controlling shareholders per se, nor do they cover corporate opportunities.[25] But the statutes are bound to be incomplete in this area, as there are so many different ways of tunneling.[26] It is up to the judges to fill these gaps by way of statutory interpretation. As discussed later, however, Korean judges do not seem to be enthusiastic about playing this crucial role.

Since the financial crisis, the statutes have been strengthened as regards related-party transactions. Related-party transactions encompass a wide variety of transactions, including sale of assets or issuance of securities to

Table 6.1 Cash flow and voting rights of the 14 largest business groups (2006)

	Cash flow	*Voting*	*Voting/ ownership*
Samsung	4.20	29.00	6.91
Hyundai Motors	6.28	38.51	6.13
SK	2.21	36.32	16.42
LG	5.58	38.08	6.83
Lotte	9.94	47.85	4.81
GS	18.58	51.98	2.80
Hanwha	4.02	50.39	12.53
Doosan	4.63	53.82	11.62
Kumho-Asiana	13.45	50.96	3.79
Dongbu	16.43	55.53	3.38
Hyundai	4.65	21.50	4.62
CJ	13.18	48.24	3.66
Daelim	12.33	43.32	3.51
Hite Beer	15.22	46.13	3.03
Average	6.36	37.65	7.47

affiliates of the controlling shareholders. What has come into the spotlight in recent years is the sale of shares of a non-listed firm. Under the revised statutes, these transactions are now subject to board approval and disclosure requirements. However, the board approval requirement has turned out not to be as effective as expected in filtering out suspect transactions.

Under the corporate statutes, a director "specially interested" in a transaction in question is not allowed to vote on a board resolution (Commercial Code, Arts. 391(3), 368(4)). The concept of "special interest", however, seems rather narrowly construed by commentators. For example, suppose Firm A is selling a major asset to Firm B, an affiliated firm under the control of the same controlling shareholder, C. The sales transaction is required to be approved by the boards of both firms (Securities Transaction Act, Art. 191-19(2); Fair Trade Act Art. 11-2). Although C is excluded from voting in Firm A's board meeting, other inside directors may, and do, vote unless they serve on Firm B's board at the same time. It is not difficult to predict how these insiders, mostly long-time subordinates of C, would vote on this matter. True, listed firms are now required to have outside directors—up to 50 percent of the board in large listed firms. However, since such transactions are normally presented as legitimate transactions on fair terms, passive outsiders would not dare ask awkward questions in the board meeting. It is thus no wonder that controversial related-party transactions, which later caused lawsuits, were formally approved by the board.[27]

As a matter of principle, shareholders may still sue directors for damages if they can prove loss to the firm incurred as a result of a particular transaction. In reality, however, it is difficult to obtain information to prove the unfairness of the transaction. Even if a shareholder has all the information, it still must meet the burdensome shareholding requirement. Once a derivative suit is filed, however, the court may make its own judgment as to the fairness of the transaction. In a few recent cases involving a sale of unlisted shares, the court has examined in detail the fairness of the price.

Lawsuits arising from control disputes

Prior to the financial crisis, the controlling family normally enjoyed almost absolute control even in the largest firms in Korea. Together with shareholdings of affiliate firms, the controlling family could normally secure more than 50 percent of the voting rights. Consequently, a hostile takeover attempt was quite rare. Things have changed somewhat since the crisis, however. As Table 6.1 above shows, the voting power of the controlling shareholders fell below 50 percent in many *chaebol*, and even below 30 percent in some *chaebol*. As the figures in Table 6.1 refer to the group average, the actual percentage for individual firms, large firms in particular, may be even lower.

A vacuum created by the dwindling holding of controlling shareholders has been filled by institutional investors, especially foreign investors. As mentioned earlier, foreign investors now occupy more than 37 percent of the Korea Exchange. As their investment concentrates on blue-chip firms, their share is now hovering over 50 percent in top firms such as Samsung Electronics and POSCO. As a result, the controlling family's control is no longer as secure as before.

An immediate consequence of this change is a small, but growing number of instances where the controlling shareholders are challenged by minority shareholders (see H.J. Kim in this volume). Legally, challenge against the controlling family may take the form of a formal tender offer. Formal tender offers, however, are rarely employed even in a hostile takeover context. Proxy contests are more common. Proxy contests have been initiated not only by foreign investors such as Tiger Fund, Sovereign, and Carl Icahn, but also by domestic investors. In connection with the proxy contest, interested parties often file various lawsuits, including lawsuits seeking preliminary injunction. Disgruntled shareholders may, for instance, attempt to gain access to the books and accounts of the firm, or to block the firm's issuance of equity securities to a white knight. On the other hand, management may seek to prevent the raiders from voting shares acquired in violation of the 5% Rule under the Securities Transaction Act, which requires an investor to report to the financial regulator when its shareholding in a listed company reaches 5 percent (Art. 200-2).

These new types of corporate governance lawsuits pose a challenge to judges, who are not well versed in the policy implications of control disputes. Korea does not have a developed set of statutory rules applicable to takeovers, except for tender offer provisions included in the Securities Transaction Act. Thus, judges are the ones expected to make rules in this area. Defensive measures available to management under the current corporate statutes are quite limited. Dual-class voting shares are not allowed.[28] More importantly, poison pills, a widely popular and powerful weapon against hostile takeovers in the U.S. and increasingly in Japan, are not available, largely due to strict statutory provisions on securities. Pyramidal and circular shareholding patterns commonly observed in almost every *chaebol* may be regarded as a functional substitute for poison pills. It is difficult to predict how long controlling families can afford to maintain these complicated ownership structures. With the increase of challenges against the controlling family, however, we will observe an increasing number of corporate governance lawsuits of various types.

Recent corporate governance lawsuits

As shown above, corporate governance lawsuits have become more common and diverse in the corporate governance scene of post-crisis Korea. Dealing with these lawsuits, judges seem to have adopted somewhat inconsistent attitudes, depending on the circumstances. In some cases, the court employs a rather formalistic approach, sticking to the letter of the statutes. In other cases, however, the court liberally exercises discretion in statutory interpretation to reach a preferred outcome not explicitly supported by the statutes. This kind of inconsistency in case law may be unavoidable to a certain extent, and is observed in other jurisdictions as well. It seems notable, however, that decisions issued during a relatively short period of time show such contrasting perspectives. This part will illustrate the contrast by presenting a selected group of leading court decisions.

Decisions adopting a formalistic approach

Civil law judges are still generally believed to be more formalistic in their mindset than their common law colleagues. It is not difficult to find in the corporate governance area decisions based on a formalistic reasoning. Here, only two will be discussed.[29]

Samsung Electronics CB case

A prime example showing the formalistic mindset of Korean judges in the corporate governance area is the famous Samsung Electronics Convertible Bond Case.[30] On 24 March 1997, Samsung Electronics, the flagship company of the Samsung group and by far the largest listed firm in Korea, issued by private offering convertible bonds (CBs) in the amount of 60 billion won: 15 billion won to Samsung Corporation, a member firm of the Samsung Group, and 45 billion won to the 29-year-old son of Chairman Lee of the Samsung group. The terms and conditions were as follows:

Due date: 24 March 2002
Conversion price: 50,000 won
Conversion period: from 25 September 1997 to 24 March 2002
Interest rate: 7 percent

On 29 September 1997, Lee Jr. exercised his conversion right and acquired about 900 thousand common shares, 0.9 percent of the total shares of Samsung Electronics. PSPD filed a lawsuit to invalidate the CB issuance, arguing, among other things, that the conversion price of 50,000 won was unduly low, given the fact that the share price at the time of issuance was 56,700 won and that the conversion price of CBs issued two months later was 123,635 won.[31] Although the Seoul High Court admitted that the conversion price was relatively low, it refused to invalidate the CBs, stating:[32]

This fact may justify a shareholder's claim for injunctive relief prior to the issuance of the CBs, a claim against directors for damages, or a claim against the purchasers of the CBs in question for additional payment. It by no means justifies, however, invalidation of the CBs already issued.

The formalistic attitude of the court is well illustrated in the following passage:

> The current Commercial Code does not require an advance notice or public announcement to the shareholders concerning the total amount of CBs, issue price, terms of conversion, conditions for the shares to be issued as a result of conversion, and conversion period at the time of issuance. It may be acknowledged that such a legal deficiency should be remedied. But even when the board of directors has deprived a shareholder of an opportunity to exercise his right to enjoin by secretly and promptly issuing CBs without making an advance public announcement of such matters, the issuance of the CBs should not be held illegal.

The Supreme Court upheld the lower court decision on basically the same grounds. The Supreme Court also stated that even the CBs suspected of being issued for purposes of prearranged inheritance, gift or control transfer cannot be invalidated without other grounds. Emphasizing the so-called "stability of the marketplace", the Supreme Court stated that issuance of CBs may be invalidated only on limited grounds such as material violation of law or material impact on shareholders' interests. Upon learning that the CBs were issued, PSPD sought a preliminary injunction enjoining the listing of the CBs on the stock exchange. The preliminary injunction was granted. The Supreme Court, however, did not place much value on the injunction, stating that it could not block a sale outside the exchange. The Supreme Court did not discuss whether Lee Jr. had sold the converted shares to a third party. On a similar note, stating that shareholders may recover damages instead by filing a shareholder derivative suit, the court did not go into whether or not the plaintiff shareholder can satisfy the shareholding requirement for a derivative suit.

Double derivative suit case

Another example showing the judiciary's formalistic approach to statutory interpretation is a recent decision by the Supreme Court denying the so-called double derivative suit. The facts of the case are summarized as follows: Y, the defendant, was the representative director of Company A, who was alleged to have misappropriated A's funds. X, the plaintiff, was a minority shareholder of Company B. Company B was the 80 percent shareholder of Company A. Although X was not formally a shareholder of Company A, he filed a derivative suit against Y. The most significant issue involved was whether or not a shareholder of the parent company has standing to file a derivative suit against directors of the subsidiary company. In other words, the issue was whether to recognize a double derivative suit, an issue of first impression in Korea. The Seoul High Court surprised the legal profession by holding in favor of X.

Criticism of the double derivative suit is twofold. The first criticism is based on a literal interpretation of the statutes. Under the statutes, a derivative suit may be brought by shareholders holding a certain percentage of shares

(Article 403 of the Commercial Code, Article 191-13 of the Securities Exchange Act). One may argue that shareholders of the parent are not counted as shareholders of the subsidiary. The second criticism is based on the practical consideration that shareholders of the parent have alternative remedies. According to this line of reasoning, the parent's shareholder may first demand that the parent's board of directors take action against the subsidiary's directors. If the board refuses to act, the shareholders can file a regular derivative action against the parent's directors for violating the duty of care to protect the parent's investment in the subsidiary.

The Seoul High Court, however, allowed a double derivative suit on the following practical grounds. First, it may be very difficult to appraise the indirect loss of the parent company caused by the act of the subsidiary's director. Second, if a double derivative suit is not permitted, managers controlling both the parent and the subsidiary may shield themselves from legal liability by having a director of the subsidiary commit an illicit act. Third, a double derivative suit would not only have a deterrent effect on the subsidiary's directors but also help the parent reduce its damages.

It is noteworthy that the court emphasized "the necessity of a double derivative suit" in interpreting "shareholders" under Article 403 of the Commercial Code as including "shareholder of a corporate shareholder." The Supreme Court, however, rejected this flexible interpretation of the High Court. Turning a blind eye to the effect of the decision, the Supreme Court simply stated that the double derivative suit is not allowed, as the shareholders under Art. 403 refer to those of the company involved, not its parent.

Although the case involved a relatively small firm, it was closely watched by big business and PSPD. Many firms in Korea now have subsidiaries. If a subsidiary enters into a dubious transaction with an affiliate, minority shareholders of the parent company have no effective remedy under the current law.[33] In relation to recent corporate scandals, PSPD is reported to have given up on the double derivative suit as it was not sure of the legality of such suits under the current law. The bill to revise the corporate statutes prepared by the Ministry of Justice first included a provision which explicitly allowed a shareholder of a parent company to file a derivative suit against the directors of its subsidiary (Art. 406-2). This provision was heavily criticized by the Federation of Korean Industries, a main trade association for *chaebol*. PSPD, on the other hand, was also critical of this provision, arguing for further relaxation of the requirements.[34] The Ministry of Justice eventually dropped the provision from its final draft.

Decisions adopting a liberal approach

Despite the popular perception that civil law judges are relatively passive in statutory interpretation, Korean judges sometimes digress from the letter of the statute to reach a conclusion they find appropriate. Two examples will be discussed here.

Samsung Electronics derivative suit

The first example again relates to Samsung Electronics. In 1998, PSPD filed a shareholder derivative suit against directors of Samsung Electronics, including Chairman Lee and the top executives. Although this case deals with many interesting issues, only an issue related to damages will be discussed here. In December 1994, Samsung Electronics sold to an affiliated company the shares of another affiliate it had acquired 8 months before. The sale price was 2,600 won per share, a 74 percent discount from the purchase price of 10,000 won per share. Samsung Electronics followed a widespread practice of retaining a reputable accounting firm to determine the value based on a valuation formula for unlisted stock under the Inheritance and Gift Tax Law. The formula is a combination of the net asset value and the profit value. The accounting firm came up with 2,361 won per share (50 percent × 4,723 won + 50 percent × 0 won). The accounting firm reached the final figure, 2,597 won, by adding a 10 percent control premium. But the Suwon District Court held that the tax law formula should not govern as the context is different, and that the fair value should have been calculated based on the net asset value only. The court independently calculated a net asset value of 5,733 won. Finding no factors justifying the low sale price as opposed to the net asset value, the court held that the directors had violated the duty of care and had to pay more than 62 billion won in damages. The Seoul High Court upheld the district court decision, but reduced the damages by as much as 80 percent based on various mitigating factors.[35] The High Court decision was upheld in 2005 by the Supreme Court. The Supreme Court based the reduction of damages on "the ideal of equitable allocation of losses." As mitigating factors considered in reducing the damages, the court enumerated not only factors related to the conduct causing the damages but also general factors such as the degree of the directors' past contributions to the firm.

This decision is particularly noteworthy because it appears inconsistent with Article 400 of the Commercial Code, which requires the consent of all the shareholders to reduce the liability of directors. Although Article 400 has been widely criticized as unduly restrictive, the courts have been reluctant to moderate its rigidity. In one recent case, the Supreme Court even held that the consent of shareholders holding 96 percent of the shares is not sufficient.[36] Prior to this decision, it had been generally believed that there was no other way to reduce the liability of directors. The judges could thus achieve by way of interpretation what even the 96 percent shareholders could not achieve. In the process, they showed how flexible and creative even civil law judges could be in reaching a favored conclusion which appears to contradict the explicit letter of the statutes.

Preliminary injunction related to the shareholders' meeting of SK

The court's creativity is also revealed in the second case, which derived from a well-publicized dispute between SK and Sovereign, a Dubai-based private fund run by two New Zealanders.[37] The controversy started when Sovereign bought in early 2003 about 15 percent of the shares of SK Corporation, a de facto holding company of the SK Group. At the time of the purchase the SK Group was in trouble, as Chairman Chey, the controlling shareholder of the SK Group, was indicted for accounting and share transfer scandals. In June 2003, the Seoul Central District Court sentenced Chairman Chey to three years' imprisonment for, among other things, a criminal breach of trust and accounting fraud.[38]

After the purchase, Sovereign began a campaign to oust Chairman Chey and enhance SK's transparency. In March 2004, it vigorously waged a failed proxy fight against the management. Sovereign nominated five candidates, all respectable Korean nationals. In an effort to boost the public image of SK, Chairman Chey presented his own slate of distinguished outsiders. At the general shareholders' meeting (GSM), Chairman Chey managed to defeat Sovereign by a narrow margin, filling all five slots of the board with his nominees. In connection with the GSM, Sovereign also submitted a proposal to include in the articles of incorporation a provision excluding from the board those sentenced to imprisonment, a provision obviously aimed at Chairman Chey. Although this proposal garnered slightly more than 50 percent of the votes, it was not passed because the Commercial Code requires a two-thirds majority for amendments to the articles of incorporation (Art. 434).

In October 2004, Sovereign requested that SK Corporation call an extraordinary GSM exclusively to deal with the same charter amendment issue.[39] When SK Corporation's board rejected Sovereign's request, Sovereign filed a petition for the court's approval of an extraordinary GSM. In December 2004, the Seoul District Court rejected Sovereign's petition.

Under the statutes, a shareholder holding at least 1.5 percent of the shares for the last six months is qualified to call a GSM with the court's approval (SEA Art. 191-13(5)). Commentators generally agree that the court must approve the request unless the minority shareholder's exercise of this right amounts to "an abuse of right." Holding that there was no abuse of right, the court still refused to approve Sovereign's petition. The court stated that in approving the shareholder's request, it should consider the necessity of an extraordinary GSM from a paternalistic perspective based on various factors such as the possibility of passing a resolution or impact on the national economy. The court mentioned many different factors. The court stated, for example, that "because continuous instability in management control might lead to the departure of investors and the decline in the investment value, given the nature of SK Corp's business, requiring long-term investment and business plan, a benefit from stabilizing management control at least until the GSM next year is not insignificant." The court also noted that in exercising shareholder rights, a corporate, as opposed to individual, shareholder is "more likely to sacrifice the interests of the corporation for its own firm's interest." The court even mentioned that "it is not impossible for SK Corp to voluntarily propose to make a similar change to the articles of incorporation at the annual GSM to be held in March 2005."

At the March 2005 GSM, Chairman Chey was re-elected to the board, receiving 55.3 percent of the votes. In May 2005, the Seoul High Court upheld the lower court's ruling denying Sovereign's petition. Unlike the lower court, the High Court chose to adopt a simpler reasoning, holding that Sovereign's request to call the GSM constituted an "abuse of right." An abuse of right is normally recognized in extreme situations. The High Court set forth the two requirements (subjective and objective) for the abuse. Subjectively, one must exercise his right solely to inflict harm on the opposite party without any benefit to himself. Objectively, the exercise of the right must be in violation of public policy. In actual reasoning, however, the High Court flatly ignored the subjective requirement, concentrating exclusively on whether or not the exercise of the right was in conflict with the original purpose or function served by the minority shareholder's right to call an extraordinary GSM.

Like the lower court, the High Court enumerated various factors to support its ruling. The court noted that such an amendment was not in the interest of the firm and the shareholders as it would exclude even a competent director who had been sentenced to imprisonment for a traffic accident. Outside directors with serious criminal records are not allowed to sit on the board under the Securities Transaction Act (Arts. 191-12(3)(iii), 54-5(4)(i)). From the court's perspective, as SK Corporation already had seven outside directors, it appeared unreasonable to impose a strict qualification requirement on the remaining three inside directors.

Not long after the decision, Sovereign sold its SK holdings, achieving a profit of almost one billion dollars. Sovereign has been widely depicted by the media as a prime example of a greedy foreign investor.

Conflicting decisions concerning the sale of treasury shares

The formalistic and liberal decisions discussed above relate to different corporate law issues. In one example, however, different judges took conflicting attitudes toward the same issue. The issue relates to the sale of treasury shares in the presence of takeover threats.

SK case

The first case again derives from SK Corporations's fight against Sovereign. As a defensive measure against Sovereign's challenge to Chairman Chey, SK Corporation came up with a plan to sell treasury shares carrying 10.4 percent of the votes to a group of friendly banks, which promised to vote the shares in favor of Chairman Chey at the March 2004 GSM. Sovereign sued to enjoin SK Corporation from selling the shares. Although the Commercial

Code provides for shareholders' pre-emptive rights for newly issued shares (Art. 418(1)), it is silent on the sale of treasury shares. Sovereign, however, argued that the company should not favor a particular group of outsiders to the exclusion of the existing shareholders in selling the shares. Rejecting Sovereign's argument, the Seoul District Court allowed the sale to go forward.[40] According to the court, an adverse impact of the proposed sale on Sovereign's position was not enough to block the sale. The court implied such a sale may be blocked in a situation where keeping management is not in the interest of general shareholders. In the absence of any evidence suggestive of such a situation, the court stated that "the decision by SK Corp's board, which was made to defend its management control against Sovereign's takeover attempt, should be held legal."

Daelim Trading case

In 2006, a different court adopted a contrary attitude on the same issue. The case involves Daelim Trading (Daelim), a listed firm largely owned by two factions of the same family. The facts can be summarized as follows. As of the end of 2004, Factions A and B controlled 34.11 percent, and 29.98 percent, respectively. The dispute arose in 2003 as a member of Faction B was ousted from management dominated by Faction A. In 2005, Faction A caused Daelim to sell a large block of treasury shares to Faction A, and issue new shares to the existing shareholders. At the end of these transactions, Faction A could control 47.49 percent of the vote while Faction B's share (including shares of its allies) amounted to 30.24 percent. When Faction A called the GSM for dividing the company, Faction B filed a petition for preliminary injunction, enjoining Faction A from voting the shares acquired from Daelim. Contrary to the Seoul Central District Court decision above, the Seoul Western District Court granted the preliminary injunction[41] and then held the sales transaction invalid.[42]

Until this decision, the SK ruling discussed above was the only decision on the sale of treasury shares. In 2006 there was a ruling on the issuance of shares. When there was a fight for control of Hyundai Elevator, a de facto holding company of Hyundai Group, Hyundai Elevator attempted to issue a large number of shares to the general public.[43] Its primary purpose was to dilute the share of KCC, the raider. At the request of KCC, the court enjoined Hyundai Elevator from conducting the offering.[44]

Although the Commercial Code explicitly provides for a lawsuit for invalidating issuance of shares (Art. 429), it is silent as to the invalidation of the sale of treasury shares. Central to the reasoning of the court is the fact that the sale of treasury shares is functionally similar to the issuance of shares. A leading corporate law expert criticizes this decision for exceeding the scope of interpretation.[45] The sale of treasury shares, his argument goes, is not different from the sale of company assets and so the company should be free to sell those treasury shares to a particular shareholder.

Understanding the decisions

As noted above, traditionally, civil law judges were believed to be less active than their common-law colleagues in their role of making rules. It is now widely agreed that the differences between continental courts and common-law courts are not as wide as is commonly thought.[46] The sample of decisions described above is certainly too small to warrant a definitive conclusion on this issue. The judges' attitudes revealed in the cases are somewhat confusing. In some decisions, judges were quite flexible in interpreting statutes to reach a conclusion they desired. Judges invoked general and flexible concepts such as "equity" or "good faith," and made an inquiry into the "purpose or function" of a legal provision. In other decisions, judges adopted a formalistic attitude, turning a blind eye to the practical consequences of their reasoning. How do we understand these conflicting attitudes of the judges? One may try three possible explanations: favorable, neutral, and cynical.

Favorable explanation

One may argue that judges' vacillation between formalism and liberalism in statutory interpretation represents their efforts to reach the right conclusion. In other words, as judges primarily care about results, they are ready to sacrifice consistency to achieve a just result in each case. Indeed, for the judiciary, this explanation may be most favorable, as it assumes the judges to be both capable and acting in good faith.

This kind of judicial attitude, however, is not acceptable. If the judge adopts a formalistic approach in a particular decision, it will be difficult to know the real reasons for the conclusion. An answer that the conclusion is mandated by the statutes does not alone suffice. As the judge is generally capable of finding a way to avoid the statutes, she should disclose the reason why she did not try to digress from the literal interpretation of the statutes.

Neutral explanation

One may try a more neutral explanation: the inconsistent decisions mentioned earlier may reflect different ways of thinking on the part of Korean judges. Like other parts of Korean society, the judiciary is also in transition. The mindset of judges varies depending on the individual. Some judges are more conservative in the sense that they place much weight on the letter of the statute. Other judges are more liberal in the sense that they emphasize potential consequences of a decision.

The conservative tendency of Korean judges may be attributable to their upbringing. Law school training in Korea still emphasizes deductive reasoning unrelated to sophisticated policy considerations. Their heavy caseload also makes judges reluctant to tread on unfamiliar territory, experimenting with novel concepts or theories. It may be far more tempting to a busy judge to stick to a formalistic approach.[47]

Cynical explanation

One may also explain these cases from a more cynical perspective. It may be interesting to examine these cases from the perspective of who won and who lost. Start with formalistic decisions. In the Samsung CB case, Samsung Electronics won, and PSPD lost. In the double derivative suit case, the decision was favorable to *chaebol* firms with numerous subsidiaries, and detrimental to shareholder activist lawyers. Turn to the liberalistic decisions. In the Samsung Electronics derivative suit case, the court's decision to reduce the amount of damages was beneficial to Samsung's top executives. The SK GSM decision was obviously favorable to SK Corporation, and detrimental to Sovereign, a foreign shareholder. In the SK Treasury Share ruling, the court, adopting a formalistic approach, refused to grant an injunctive remedy to a foreign fund challenging the controlling shareholder of a major *chaebol*. On the other hand, in the Daelim Trading case, which derived from a family feud among domestic shareholders, the court granted a remedy based on flexible reasoning emphasizing the practical effect of the decision.

By now, readers will hardly fail to notice a trend in this group of decisions. Regardless of the type of reasoning adopted, parties related to big business won, while activist shareholders and foreign investors lost. True, given the small size of the sample, one must not place too much weight on this rather cynical observation. One may point to other decisions which may contradict this observation. Indeed, shareholder activists have recorded a victory in a small number of lawsuits against *chaebol*, in which judges reached a result favoring minority shareholders based on a substantive analysis. The decisions discussed above may be more important, however, in terms of number and significance. They are by no means aberrations, but mainstream decisions carefully written by elite judges.

It is difficult to find a proper word for this kind of pro-*chaebol*, anti-shareholder activist, and anti-foreign investor attitude. Let's use the adjective "conservative" for the sake of simplicity. A cynical observer may try to explain the conservative tendency of Korean judges, elite judges in particular, as follows: First, elite judges may be close to business executives working for *chaebol* and lawyers representing these *chaebol* clients. They may be tied to each other by common educational, professional, and social backgrounds. Second, and of more significance may be the career pattern of Korean judges. Most judges, including even former judges of the Supreme Court, practice after retiring from the bench, often affiliating with top law firms representing *chaebol* firms. One may presume that retired judges known for an anti-*chaebol* record may have a hard time landing a position with a major law firm, let alone finding *chaebol* clients. In a sense, judges, like other players of Korean society, may not be immune to *chaebol* interests.

What exacerbates this pro-*chaebol* mindset is a growing antipathy towards foreign investors, and towards the activism of foreign funds, to be more precise. Recently, the local media, business dailies in particular, have been attacking foreign funds on various grounds, such as seeking short-term profits and threatening management control.[48] It is now becoming increasingly awkward even for an academic to take sides with foreign investors in public. It may be difficult to expect the judiciary to ignore this pressure in making a decision.

Evaluation

It is not clear which of the three explanations is most persuasive. All three may have at least some truth. Regardless of the explanation, one may feel rather uncomfortable after reading the decisions discussed above. It must be emphasized, however, that the picture of case law in the corporate governance area may change in the future in accordance with Korea's changing corporate governance environment.

Concluding remarks

The more discretion courts are allowed, the more likely it becomes that courts will abuse that discretion. One obvious solution to this kind of abuse may be enacting more detailed statutory rules. The solution may not be technically feasible, however. As there are numerous ways in which a conflict of interest develops between managers and shareholders, a flexible and general concept, such as fiduciary duty, is essential for addressing such conflicts. For conflict-of-interest transactions, it may be better, if not inevitable, to leave law "incomplete".[49]

In Korea, relying on judges may not be as bad as in other countries. First, the judiciary is relatively clean, compared with other sectors of Korean society. True, a corruption scandal involving judges is exposed from time to time, and the general public's perception of judges is not necessarily favorable. It may be safely said, however, that a judge would not change her ruling in return for an outright bribe.[50] Second, most judges are quite capable.[51] In terms of integrity and competence, it may be difficult to find those who are better qualified than judges. This does not mean, however, that judges are perfect. Although they would not accept a cash bribe from the parties, they may be prone to a more subtle form of pressure. It is still a widespread practice in Korea that parties select counsel based on the strength of social ties between the presiding judge and counsel. Also, career judges with no business experience may often lack sophistication in business matters. This may not be a serious defect, however, in the long run. Fast learners, judges will quickly achieve a level of expertise as they are exposed to more cases.

It may not be realistic to expect Korean judges to become as flexible as their common-law colleagues in a short period of time. So even in the presence of fiduciary duties in the corporate statutes, it may make sense to put more concrete provisions into the statutes. The provision on de facto directors (KCC Art. 401-2) is a prime example. Along this line of reasoning, the draft of the new Commercial Code includes a provision on double derivative suits (Art. 406-2) and expands the scope of self-dealing transactions under Art. 398.

Admittedly, the role of judges in restraining management behavior in seeking private benefits of control is still limited. It may be particularly relevant in Korea to activate market pressure on owner-managers. Market pressure may turn out to be more effective because it tends to restrain even undesirable behavior not formally constituting a violation of fiduciary duty. So far, pressure from the market for corporate control has been minimal, if not totally absent, in Korea. If cross or pyramidal share ownership schemes crumble, threats of hostile takeovers will loom large. At that point, Korea may need to consider introducing a Korean version of the poison pill. In such an event, the role of judges will become even more crucial. It is not clear whether Korean judges are well prepared to take up such a delicate role. Indeed, as the new draft Commercial Code gives management more freedom on finance matters such as dividends and types of securities, judges are expected to play a more active role in minimizing management abuses. It will be fascinating to observe how the role of Korean judges evolves in the coming years.

Notes

* I express my gratitude to Hideki Kanda, Joo-Young Kim and Curtis Milhaupt for valuable comments.
1 For a short description of this discourse, see, e.g., Kim and Kim (2003: 373).
2 Regarding the relationship between corporate governance and enforcement, see, e.g., Berglöf and Claessens (2004).
3 On the role of judiciary in corporate law, see, e.g., Coffee (1989).
4 For a survey of the role of NGOs in corporate governance in Asia, see Milhaupt (2004).
5 Financial Supervisory Service (2007)
6 http://stock.naver.com/sise/sise_foreign_hold.nhn (accessed 16 January 2006).
7 The situation is similar in other civil law countries as well. For Italy, see Enriques (2002); for Germany, see Pistor and Xu (2003).
8 This paragraph is partly based on Kim and Kim (2003: 373, 381)
9 Supreme Court, Judgment No. 2001 Do 3191 (28 September 2001).
10 Seoul Central District Court, Judgment No. 2003 Kohap 1300 (4 October 2005).
11 Punishing managerial misconduct with the crime of breach of trust is heavily criticized by commentators. Lee (2006a).
12 Supreme Court, Judgment No. 2004 Do 7027 (9 November 2006).
13 The whole scheme was disclosed to the public by a disgruntled family member who had been ousted from the chairman's office.
14 Act relating to the Heightened Punishment for Certain Economic Crimes, Art. 3 (1)(i); Criminal Code, Art. 355.
15 This incident has led to yet another controversy. A few days after this decision, the chief justice of the Supreme Court severely criticized the overly lenient attitude

of judges at a dinner with senior judges. He was reported to have said, "If a thief steals one hundred million Won, you will surely send him to prison for a few years at least. If a person who stole from his company tens of billion Won is set free with a suspended sentence, how would the general public react?" www.e-goodnews.co.kr/sub_read.html?uid=43965&section=section3 (accessed 16 January 2007).

16 For details of this famous decision, see Kim and Kim (2003: 389–391).

17 Seoul District Court, Judgment No. 97 Kahap 39907 (24 July 1998).

18 The amount was later reduced to one billion won on appeal.

19 Korea Deposit Insurance Corporation, (2006: 81–83).

20 Regarding the business judgment rule in Korea, see, e.g., Kim and Yi (2004).

21 Seoul Southern District Court Judgment No. 2003 Kahap 1176 (17 August, 2006).

22 The director's duty to monitor is now well recognized by the court. Supreme Court, Judgment No. 84 Daka 1954 (25 June 1985); Supreme Court, Judgment No. 2002 Da 60467, 60474 (10 December 2004).

23 In 2006, the Fair Trade Commission's attempt to revise the Anti-monopoly and Fair Trade Act to regulate practices of circular share ownership ended in failure due to all-out opposition by the big business.

24 Fair Trade Commission (2006).

25 The proposed government bill to amend the Commercial Code attempts to include a provision on corporate opportunities.

26 Pistor and Xu (2003).

27 For a recent decision holding outside as well as inside directors liable for an unfair related party transaction, see, Seoul Southern District Court, Judgment No. 2003 Kahap 1176 (17 August 2006).

28 Non-voting preferred shares may be issued up to a certain limit.

29 Other examples of corporate governance decisions adopting a formalistic reasoning include Seoul Central District Court, Judgment No. 2006 Kahap 3203 (2 November 2006) (rejecting a preliminary injunction for gaining access to the shareholder register by a corporate governance fund); Daejon District Court, Judgment No. 2006 Kahap 242 (14 March 2006) (rejecting a preliminary injunction sought by foreign funds).

30 For a translation of the lower court decision, see Journal of Korean Law 1 (2001): 157. Disputes regarding related-party transactions involving Samsung Electronics are discussed in Jang and Kim (2002).

31 Although this case involved other interesting legal issues, only the conversion price issue will be discussed here.

32 Seoul High Court, Judgment No. 98 Na 4608 (23 June 2000).

33 They may file a criminal complaint against the managers involved.

34 The provision does not cover directors of a subsidiary's subsidiary. Moreover, a firm is counted as a subsidiary under the Commercial Code only when the parent holds more than 50 percent (Art. 342-2 (1)).

35 Seoul High Court, Judgment No. 2002 Na 6595 (20 November 2003).

36 Supreme Court, Judgment No. 2003 Da 69638 (28 October 2005).

37 The whole saga is narrated and discussed in chapter 6 of Milhaupt and Pistor (2008).

38 Seoul Central District Court, Judgment No. 2003 Kohap 237, 311 (13 June 2003).

39 This time, Sovereign attempted to exclude from the board those who were indicted.

40 Seoul District Court, Judgment No. 2003 Kahap 4154 (23 December 2003).

41 Seoul Western District Court, Judgment No. 2006 Kahap 393 (24 March 2006).

42 Seoul Western District Court, Judgment No. 2005 Kahap 8262 (29 June 2006).

43 Under the articles of incorporation, the shareholders do not have the pre-emptive right if shares are issued by public offering.
44 Suwon District Court (Yeoju Branch), Judgment No. 2003 Kahap 369 (12 December 2003).
45 Lee (2006b).
46 Pistor et al. (2002): "civil law courts have at times played a much more proactive role in shaping the contents of legal rules than the general principle that 'judges interpret, but do not make the law' may suggest."
47 Likewise, judges in the U.S. are believed to rely on heuristics (simplistic rule-like tests) to simplify their decision-making process. Sale (2002).
48 Foreign investors suffering from image or even legal problems are numerous, including Sovereign, Tiger Fund, Hermes, Lone Star, Newbridge Capital and Carl Icahn.
49 Pistor and Xu (2003).
50 Enriques (2002).
51 Each year, usually only around the top 10–20% of graduates from the Judicial Research and Training Institute are invited to join the bench.

Bibliography

Berglöf, E. and S. Claessens (2004) "Enforcement and Corporate Governance," World Bank Policy Research Working Paper No. 3409. Available at http://ssrn.com/abstract=625286.

Coffee, J. C., Jr. (1989) "The Mandatory/Enabling Balance in Corporate Law: An Essay on the Judicial Role," *Columbia Law Review* 89: 1618.

Enriques, L. (2002) "Do Corporate Law Judges Matter? Some Evidence from Milan," *European Business Organization Law Review* 3: 765.

Fair Trade Commission (2006) *Ownership Structure of Large Business Groups*, 11 (in Korean).

Financial Supervisory Service (2007) *Report on the Securities Transactions by Foreign Investors for December 2006*, 2 (in Korean).

Jang, Hasung and Joongi Kim (2002) "Nascent Stages of Corporate Governance in an Emerging Market: Regulatory Change, Shareholder Activism and Samsung Electronics," *Corporate Governance: An International Review* 10: 94.

Kim, Hwa-Jin and Tehyok Daniel Yi (2004) "Directors' Liabilities and the Business Judgment Rule in Korea" (April 15,). Available at http://ssrn.com/abstract=530442.

Kim, Kon Sik and Joongi Kim (2003) "Revamping Fiduciary Duties in Korea: Does Law Matter in Corporate Governance?," in Curtis Milhaupt (ed.), *Global Markets, Local Institutions*, New York: Columbia University Press.

Korea Deposit Insurance Corporation (2006) *Annual Report.*

Lee, Chul-Song (2006a) "Officers' Criminal Responsibility for the Issuance of Convertible Bonds at an Unfair Price," *Human Rights and Justice*, 359: 96 (in Korean).

—— (2006b) "Validity of the Unfair Sale of Treasury Shares," *Korean Journal of Securities Law* 7 (in Korean).

Milhaupt, C. J. (2004) "Nonprofit Organization as Investor Protection: Economic Theory, and Evidence from East Asia," *Yale Journal of International Law* 29: 169.

Milhaupt, C. J. and K. Pistor (2008) *Law and Capitalism: What Corporate Crises Reveal about Legal Systems and Economic Development around the World*, Chicago: University of Chicago Press.

Pistor, K. and Chenggang Xu (2003) "Fiduciary Duty in Transitional Civil Law Jurisdiction: Lessons from the Incomplete Law Theory," in Curtis Milhaupt (ed.), *Global Markets, Local Institutions*, New York: Columbia University Press.

Pistor, K., Y. Keinan, J. Kleinheisterkamp, and M.D. West (2002) "The Evolution of Corporate Law: A Cross-Country Comparison," *University of Pennsylvania Journal of International Economic Law* 23: 791.

Sale, H. (2002) "Judging Heuristics," *U.C. Davis Law Review* 35: 903.

Part III

Greater China (The Mainland and Taiwan)

7 Protecting minority shareholders in China

A task for both legislation and enforcement

Xin Tang

Introduction

Features of China's financial system (especially strict capital controls) helped to insulate the country from the 1997 Asian financial crisis (Fernald and Babson 1999: 12; Zhang 2006: 3), which was largely blamed on poor corporate governance. For China, the concept of corporate governance had appeared just a few years before the crisis (Wu 1993: 189–196, 268–271; Zhang 1994: 79; Qian 1995), and the first Company Law was passed in the same period.[1] However, from theory to practice, corporate governance has developed significantly since 1994. At the end of 2006, for the listed companies which are the key figures of corporate governance and the subject of this essay, the Share Structure Reform (*Guquan Fenzhi Gaige*)—a program to convert non-tradable shares held by the state into free-floating shares tradable on the national securities exchanges—is nearly finished, which means corporate governance of those listed companies will undergo even greater transitions.

Protecting minority shareholders from opportunistic expropriation of management or controlling shareholders is always a critical principle of corporate governance, but protection of minority shareholders was not the chief concern of the Company Law of 1994. The reason for this was not only that the Berle and Means image of the firm with separation of ownership and control, which dominated in Britain and the United States, did not fit the reality of China's prevailing principal owner type (state ownership). It was also that the enactment of the Company Law first aimed at setting down the political objective of transforming state-owned enterprises (SOEs) into stock companies (corporatization, or *Gufenzhi Gaizao*), establishing a legislative authority for this transformation, and preventing possible losses of state-owned assets in the transformation.[2] Thus the Company Law, which is considered to be a basic statute for the common business enterprises, was (at least partially) drafted as a law for converting SOEs into stock companies.[3] With this background, the rights of shareholders other than the state itself were either not available, not made clear, or not clearly associated with remedies (Howson 1997: 147–149).

In the years since the birth of the Company Law, the demand for investor protection has increased significantly in Mainland China for the following reasons:

1 the number of individual shareholders exploded due to the rapid expansion of the securities market;
2 scholars, some top officials of the China Securities Regulatory Commission (CSRC) and the media prompted awareness of the rights of investors after corporate scandals and market turbulence;
3 the importance of developing the stock market to lessen the oppressive pressure on banking finance was recognized by the government;
4 a majority of SOEs have been successfully converted into stock companies, so that providing guidance and privileges for such conversion was no longer the chief concern of the legislation.

All these elements have led to increased awareness of investor protection and corporate law enforcement as significant policy issues.

In October 2005, the most important laws concerning corporate governance of listed companies in China were extensively revised to introduce measures to further the protection of minority shareholders' interests.[4] Devices with the function of compensation and deterrence have been established under the laws, as well as administrative regulations and stock exchange rules to address chronic illnesses of corporate governance, especially looting of listed companies by their controlling shareholders. Although research has suggested that improvement of legal provisions would contribute to the performance of companies and the welfare of the shareholders, as we shall see, the new measures in the laws still fall short of fulfilling the demand for shareholder protection.

The next part of this essay introduces the protection of minority shareholders provided by the new laws and the formal enforcement measures in China. Plagued by enforcement problems, these public and private mechanisms fail to offer sufficient protection to investors. The part that follows discusses the possible alternative solutions to domestic enforcement regimes, including a "self-enforcing" corporate law model, cross-listings on foreign stock exchanges, and the possibility of nonprofit organizations acting as corporate law enforcement agents. Although none of the alternatives is a panacea for treatment of the governance problems, they do provide a range of partial answers to the underproduction of corporate law enforcement in China. After this, the penultimate part provides some thoughts on securities-related class action remedies, which are currently absent from the law but might be another means of achieving efficient corporate governance. The essay ends with a brief conclusion.

Revision of laws and the formal enforcement institutions

Since it was believed that poor protection for minority shareholders in China has hindered the improvement of corporate governance as well as development of the capital market, drastic modifications were made to China's 12-year-old Company Law. Lawmakers clearly announced that one of the major objectives of the reform was to strengthen the protection of minority shareholders and to improve corporate governance in China. Further, they hoped the revised Company Law would "normalize corporate governance of the listed companies, discipline those companies and their related personnel, and promote the stable and healthy development of the capital market" (Cao 2005). Revisions to the Securities Law were passed the same day to "improve the regulation of listed companies and raise those companies' performance" (Zhou 2005). At the end of 2005, a Revision Bill (*Xiuzhengan*) of the Criminal Law was also passed to combat "crimes that bring severe damages to the interests of listed companies and their public investors" (An 2005).

The new laws have been widely applauded in China (e.g. Liu 2005a; Zhao 2005; Fan and Wang 2006: 83–85; Zhou 2006: 16–21; Liu 2005b; Guo 2006; Tong 2006). The revisions (although only on paper) will raise China's scores in the "shareholder protection" index developed by La Porta and colleagues (La Porta *et al.* 1998: 1126–1134).[5] They will probably also increase the welfare of minority shareholders of listed companies (Shen *et al.* 2004; Shen *et al.* 2005).

In this part, I shall give a brief introduction to the protective provisions, especially for the minority shareholders under the Company Law, analyze the missing concepts in the statute, then discuss the formal enforcement institutions which are being relied upon to bring the provisions on paper into reality.

New protective provisions under the Company Law

Under the new Company Law, the controlling shareholders are specifically required not to abuse their shareholders' rights (§§ 20.1, 20.2). Unfair related-party transactions are strictly prohibited (§ 21). As responsibilities and powers of the board of statutory auditors (*Jianshihui*) have been expanded, the new Company Law also makes it more convenient to convene a board meeting (§§ 118.2, 119). Independent directors are required for the board of directors of listed companies (§ 123).[6] In addition to a pre-existing duty of loyalty, a duty of care is now established for board members and senior officers, although "bright line rules" are only set for the former (§§ 148, 149). A company's shareholders are given the right to bring actions in court against the company's directors and officers, in which they can seek damages on behalf of the corporation for violations of the directors' and officers' duties to the corporation (§ 152). Cumulative voting is recommended (although not required) for the election of members of the board of directors (§§ 106). A majority of outside shareholders may even petition the court to dissolve a company if it has met with such difficulty in its business operations that the continued existence of the company will cause serious losses to the interests of the shareholders, and such situation cannot be rectified by any other means (§ 183). Coupled with other protective measures already provided in the old Law, such as the "one share, one vote" principle (§ 106.1 of the old Law, § 104.1 of the new Law), a supermajority vote required for fundamental changes to a company (§ 106.2 of the old Law, § 104.2 of the new Law),[7] the Company Law (if only on paper) will provide some protection to minority shareholders.

Apart from the statutes, some mandatory rules of the CSRC and Listing Rules of the securities exchanges also contribute to the progress of corporate governance of listed companies in China. For example, the new Guide to Articles of Association of Listed Companies (*Shangshi Gongsi Zhangcheng Zhiyin*, GAALC)[8] limits the number of inside directors to no more than 50 percent of all the directors,[9] requires the accounting firm serving as the independent auditor of the company to be appointed at the shareholders' meeting instead of by the board of directors alone,[10] requires the companies to provide a means for shareholders to vote by mail or internet rather than only in person,[11] and entitles the independent directors to propose convening an interim shareholders' meeting.[12] The newest Rule for Shareholders' Meetings of Listed Companies (*Shangshi Gongsi Gudongdahui Guize*, (RSMLC))[13] requires that the company provide shareholders with all of the information they need to make an informed decision on the issues for which they are asked to vote,[14] orders a mechanism for providing reasonable assurance that the votes will be counted honestly, and provides for an independent tabulation team that should consist of attorneys, representatives of shareholders, and statutory auditors (*Jianshi*).[15] To convene a shareholders' meeting when the board of directors fails to provide the shareholders' list, the board of auditors or qualified shareholder(s) may apply to the Securities Registration and Settlement Company (*Zhengquan Dengji Jiesuan Jigou*) for the list.[16] The new Listing Rules of the two national securities exchanges also stipulate detailed rules of voting procedure and disclosure requirements covering all kinds of related party transactions.[17]

Missing concepts

Some authors have argued that because transition economies have a high proportion of companies that are controlled by a single shareholder or a small group of shareholders, and are also often characterized by relatively weak non-legal constraints (e.g., efficient capital and product markets) on the powers of managers and controlling shareholders to act at the expense of minority shareholders, these economies should have stronger rules to protect minority shareholders than those found in developed market economies (Kiseliov, *et al.* 1999: 204). Although great progress has been achieved, especially from the revisions of the Company Law, the provisions in the new laws may still not be good enough to yield thorough protection for minority shareholders in China.

In the statutes

The revisions to China's laws only provide limited protections to minority shareholders. For instance, mandatory cumulative voting for members of the board of directors is not the law. Even if listed companies opt for cumulative voting, there are no rules on minimum board size or provisions on staggering of board terms. The minimum percentage of shares that entitles a shareholder to make proposals at a shareholders' meeting, or to call for an extraordinary shareholders' meeting (3 percent and 10 percent, respectively), is set too high, and the Company Law fails to provide a procedure for shareholders to obtain a list of other shareholders in order to solicit support for their proposals, or to provide a means for shareholders to receive all of the information they need to make an informed decision on the issues for which they are asked to vote.[18] With regard to voting, there may be advantages in specifying the minimum vote required to approve fundamental changes to the company as a majority or supermajority of all voting shares, rather than a majority or supermajority of the votes of shareholders who participate in the voting, but even after the latest revisions of the Company Law, a quorum is not needed to validate a shareholders' meeting in China.[19]

The minimum percentage and period of shareholding that entitles a shareholder to bring a derivative law suit against the directors or controlling person is also set too high (the plaintiff must have individually or collectively held more than 1 percent of the shares of the company for more than 180 consecutive days, § 152.1 of the new Company Law). Redemption and appraisal rights of dissenting shareholders (§§ 75, 143.1(4)) are limited to very few situations—mergers or corporate divestures.[20] In addition to the right to authorize the number of shares that may be issued, shareholders may need additional protection during the issuance of new shares to prevent such shares from being issued at an unfairly low price to selected buyers, and to prevent the use of such issuances to reduce the influence of particular shareholders. However, under current law there are no prohibitions against a company issuing or acquiring its own shares at a price lower than market value. The law does not provide for mandatory pre-emptive rights as protection against underpriced stock issues, "targeted" sales of new shares to other parties, or general attempts to dilute the vote of existing shareholders.

Once control of a listed company has been acquired by a shareholder, the old Securities Law[21] provided for a system of "takeout" rights. Under this system, when an investor acquired 30 percent of the outstanding shares of a listed company, the investor was required to offer to buy all remaining shares at a fair price. This gave the remaining shareholders an opportunity to decide whether to remain as shareholders in the controlled company. The system of takeout rights has been adopted by several countries in Europe and is consistent with the rules envisaged in the EU directive.[22] However, the new Securities Law abandons the requirement that the shareholder who achieves control must extend a takeover bid to all the remaining shares (§ 88 of the new Securities Law, compared with § 81 of the old Law); the new Listed Company Takeover Rule even cancels the requirement of a fair offer price,[23] which cripples the protection to the minority shareholders. Rules to restrict freeze-out transactions are also absent from the statutes.

In the judicial explanations

The official explanation of the Company Law, without which courts will be impeded from hearing related cases, is still to be promulgated by the Supreme People's Court of the PRC (SPC).[24] Whether or not the derivative suit mechanism can provide some redress to damaged listed companies and their minority shareholders may depend on rules in this forthcoming Judicial Explanation (*Si Fa Jie Shi*). The critical points to be clarified by the Judicial Explanation are as follows:

1 The litigation fee: if the fee is set as a percentage of requested damages, as in other private litigation, the amount of fees will have a chilling effect on filing suits.
2 Recovery of expenses: as plaintiffs would not be able or willing to shoulder the burden of the litigation fee, they should have a right of recovery of such expenses from the corporation.
3 Security deposit: whether the court will require the plaintiff shareholders in every suit to provide an "appropriate" security deposit in consideration of possible losses the defendant may incur is critical.[25]
4 Liability of individuals: the deterrent effect of derivative litigations can be fulfilled only if the defendant directors and officers will be ordered to bear out-of-pocket liabilities (rather than being covered by insurance or company reimbursement).

Some other Company Law articles which provide shareholders with a private right of action may face similar problems.[26]

Control of tunneling to protect minority shareholders

Using "tunneling" as an example, let us consider whether the revisions of company law, securities law, and even the criminal law will be helpful in reducing looting of listed firms by their controlling shareholders.[27] In China, the principal forms of looting are failure by the controlling shareholders to pay for their capital contributions; direct or contingent loans to controlling shareholders; disadvantageous (to the listed company) transactions with the controlling shareholder; and even naked takings (Ho, 2003).

Private right of action

Many private liability provisions have been added to the Company Law, including:

§ 20.1 (prohibition against abuse of shareholders' rights)

§ 20.2 (shareholder's liability for compensation to the company and other shareholders for abusing rights)

§ 21.2 (shareholder's liability for compensation to the company for abusing "affiliation relationship"[28])

§ 152.3 (shareholder's right to bring a derivative suit against "a third party" who infringes upon the interests of the company),[29] and

§ 22.2 (shareholders' right to challenge the resolutions of a shareholders' meeting or a board meeting).

The new Securities Law provides further remedies to the public shareholders of a listed company, such as § 69 (a controlling person who knowingly directs a false statement to be made shall bear joint and several liability with the issuer).

Protections for the minority shareholders on the books do not seem bad, but legal enforcement remains a problem. First, the court system is not active in hearing corporate and securities cases. Listed companies and their officers still have a certain political backing, and Chinese courts are neither experienced nor politically powerful and are hence reluctant to take cases involving complicated reasoning and powerful defendants. The local courts have been reluctant and very inefficient in hearing securities-related claims, even though the SPC allowed them to take a limited category of those claims. According to a prominent securities lawyer, Yixin Song, since the first legal action filed in 1996, about 10,000 investors have initiated securities-related suits, but only about 1,000 have achieved some kind of compensation through settlements or judgments. In fact, the number of plaintiffs is probably fewer than 10 percent of all those who have been damaged and have standing to sue, while the damages claimed may be less than 5 percent of the total losses arising from the illegalities (Shentu and Chang 2006).[30] Second, class actions are not permitted in China. Although transplantation of the institution has been supported by many commentators,[31] class actions still appear to be infeasible for the foreseeable future. Third, without key institutions such as contingency fees and award of attorneys' fees, the "private attorney general" role of private litigation in the enforcement of law appears difficult to realize (*cf.* Coffee, 1983).[32]

Administrative liabilities under the Company Law and the Securities Law

The CSRC resolved to address the tunneling problem (especially misappropriation of listed companies' assets) in the Chinese market during

2006. That is, controlling shareholders would be made accountable for assets or profits transferred illegally from listed companies. Nevertheless, the agency has been hampered in several ways in meeting this goal. First, the Company Law does not provide the CSRC with any specific power to curb tunneling illegalities, while the new Securities Law only orders all listed companies to disclose their de facto controlling persons.[33] Further, as the supervisor of the controlling shareholders of listed companies,[34] the CSRC's principal legal weapon to combat looting is to declare concealment of the underlying transaction to be a "material omission" in the statutory reports of the listed companies, subjecting the issuer and its executives to modest sanctions.[35] The CSRC may declare the responsible persons unfit to engage in any securities-related business or be elected to the board of listed companies (*Shi Chang Jin Ru*), but it has not used this sanction very often.[36] Second, as a government agency with responsibility for both the enforcement of rules regarding disclosure and merit-based review of the investment quality of issuers, the CSRC has limited resources to enforce the law (Clarke 2003). Moreover, the agency still lacks sufficient administrative authority to discipline the high-level state-owned shareholders behind some listed companies. The ambitious anti-misappropriation plan is not likely to be achieved by the CSRC alone.

Disciplinary actions of the self-regulatory bodies

China's two national stock exchanges are joining the war against tunneling, but it is even more doubtful that they are equipped to achieve any breakthrough. The exchanges may administer private reprimands or public censures, which are not likely to be effective against unscrupulous offenders. For more serious measures they may delist a company or suspend its listing. However, even if the exchanges are willing to act, this sanction is more painful to the innocent shareholders than to the guilty controllers who hold "non-tradable shares" that are not listed on the exchanges. The exchanges may declare the offender to be unfit to serve on the board of directors or board of supervisors, and they may also advise the company to dismiss its secretary of the board of directors,[37] but the exchanges have seldom deployed those sanctions in recent years.

Criminal liability

Revisions to China's Criminal Law, passed in 2006, make the directors, managers, and even controlling shareholder(s), or de facto controlling person(s) of a listed company, subject to criminal liability if they knowingly make the company engage in actions causing substantial loss to the corporation.[38] While the revision still needs to be explained by the SPC, one critical issue remains: If the profits siphoned off or assets transferred out of the listed company were used to prop up troubled firms in the same state-controlled group (e.g. to pay salaries for workers in those firms), "criminal culpability," which is indispensable under the criminal law for an action to constitute a crime, may be very difficult to prove. Nevertheless, as the number of listed companies controlled by private capital is increasing year by year in China,[39] and looting by controlling shareholders has also happened in these companies, well-defined criminal liabilities should have some power to deter those illegalities.[40] Furthermore, corporate governance of Chinese listed companies is not just characterized as controlled by a dominant state-owned shareholder (*yigu duda*), but also as under "insider control" (*neibu ren kongzhi*) and "absent owner" (*suoyouzhe quewei*). While effective control rights are assigned to management, which generally has a very small, or even nonexistent ownership stake (Wei, 2000), assets of state-controlled listed companies may be converted through various subterfuges into the personal property of management (Clarke 2006: 147). Thus the games played by the government, management, and outside investors become more complex than those addressed in the traditional corporate finance models (Su, 2000; Li and Zhang, 2005; Zhao, Lowe and Pi, 2005). Criminal penalties have a role to play in curbing illegal self-interested actions of management as well.

Alternative solutions to domestic enforcement regimes

If China's formal corporate law enforcement regime remains problematic, it is useful to explore possible alternatives to improve corporate governance.

A self-enforcing model of corporate law

Professors Black and Kraakman (1996) argue that, in emerging economies, the best legal strategy for protecting outside investors in large companies while simultaneously preserving managers' discretion to invest is a self-enforcing model of corporate law. The self-enforcing model structures corporate decision-making processes to allow large outside shareholders to protect themselves from insider opportunism, with minimal resort to legal authority, including the courts. The model may be a feasible choice for emerging markets to protect minority shareholders, and China's legislators have been designing some of the Company Law provisions based (at least partly) on that model. For example, a rule requiring both shareholder and board-level approval for self-interested transactions is now in the law. Making loans to other enterprises or providing guarantees to individuals is permitted, when consent of the shareholders' general meeting or the board of directors has been obtained in accordance with the articles of association of the company. With the consent of the shareholders' general meeting, a company may even provide a guarantee to its controlling shareholder or de facto controlling person, and directors and officers may operate for themselves or others any business similar to that of the company for which they work.[41] Under the old Company Law, those acts were strictly forbidden.[42]

As the regulator of China's securities market, the CSRC has also been exploring ways to construct a self-enforcing corporate governance model for listed companies. In 1997, 2000, and 2001, the agency promulgated a series of important rules to strengthen the role of the shareholders' meeting and to introduce the independent director system.[43] Pursuant to another rule of the CSRC,[44] implementation of or application for the following matters can only be made upon the approval of the general meeting of a listed company (attended by holders of both the tradable shares and non-tradable shares), and the approval by more than half of the voting rights represented by the tradable shares' public holders:

1   issuing new shares publicly, issuing convertible bonds, and placing shares with existing shareholders
2   material asset restructurings, for which the total consideration for the assets has a premium of at least 20 percent of the audited net book value of such assets
3   repayment of debt owed to the company by a shareholder using the shares of the company
4   the overseas listing of a subsidiary of material importance to the company
5   relevant matters in the development of the company which have a material impact on minority shareholders.

When voting on the above matters, a company is required to provide its shareholders with a "network voting platform," so the shareholders may vote through the internet.[45] The rule on shareholder approval actually considers the "public shares" held by minority shareholders to be a different class of shares from those held by the controlling shareholders or de facto controllers of the company (often SOEs or even the local governments themselves).

The CSRC does not limit its corporate governance rules to the internal decision-making processes of listed companies. It also attempts to enlist assistance from the financial intermediaries who are deemed to be the "watchdogs" of the market. To cure false representations in the annual report and financial statements of listed companies, the CSRC requires issuers applying to make public share offerings or convertible corporate bonds issuances to appoint a qualified securities company as a "sponsor" (*Baojianren*). As the chief underwriter of the public offering, the sponsor must comply with the principles of honesty, trustworthiness and due diligence in conducting its review of the issuer's application. The sponsor must also supervise the operation and reports of the issuer even after its shares have been listed for one or two years (depending on various conditions).[46] The sponsor bears joint and several liability, with the issuer or the listed company, for losses suffered by the investors for false representations or material omissions in those documents or reports, unless they can prove that they are not at fault.[47] Misrepresentations or omissions in the sponsoring documents themselves subject the sponsor and responsible staff to fines and other administrative penalties.[48]

In the newest Takeover Rule, the CSRC establishes the key role of financial consultants (*Caiwu Guwen*) in maintaining order in takeover activities. Except for a few particular circumstances,[49] the rule obligates the acquirer of a target company to retain a financial consultant who will issue an expert opinion on whether the acquirer has fulfilled its obligations under the rule. The board of directors of a target company facing a tender offer, or the independent directors of a company facing a management buyout offer, must also retain financial consultants to help them confirm whether the offer is fair.[50] Moreover, the rule contains a special chapter defining the financial consultant's duties and responsibilities in the takeover of listed companies.[51] Some of these duties include due diligence and follow-up tracking during the takeover transaction, as well as continuous supervision after the takeover transaction. As with the aforementioned sponsors, financial consultants are qualified, supervised, and disciplined principally by the CSRC. As "watchdogs" in takeover transactions, they are responsible to the market regulator, not to the courts.

It remains to be seen whether the self-enforcing corporate law provisions or the market watchdogs will play a major role in overcoming China's enforcement problem. But as Black and Kraakman pointed out, even the self-enforcing model cannot respond completely to the need for legal provisions addressing liabilities and their formal enforcement.[52] The key point is, since company laws and securities regulations are inherently "incomplete," ambiguous provisions or gaps in the self-enforcing law will have to be explained or filled in by a regulator or court. Moreover, plagued by collective action problems, the general meeting of shareholders may be too weak to provide real protection to its members. Finally, the supporters of a self-enforcing model may overrate the effectiveness of "self-enforcing" laws in an emerging market with very weak judicial enforcement, imperfect market constraints, and faint reputation bonding.

The role of cross-listings

Professor Coffee predicts that when the large firms around the world opt into higher regulatory and disclosure standards, "bonding" themselves to governance standards more exacting than those of their home countries, the U.S. securities laws will accommodate functional convergence—through both migration and harmonization—raising governance and disclosure standards. According to Coffee, good enforcement can be attained when firms in weak enforcement regimes bond themselves to "good" corporate law in a regime imposing high disclosure requirements and subjecting listed firms to a stringent regulatory and private enforcement mechanism (Coffee 2002: 1757).

China's Securities Law of 1999 imitates the U.S. disclosure principle and numerous substantive provisions (evidence of formal convergence). As its U.S. counterpart (Coffee 1999: 690–691), China's Securities Law presently seems capable of regulating controlling shareholders to some extent through the following rules:

1 Articles 86 and 87 of the new Securities Law require any investor who has obtained a 5 percent shareholding in a listed company to disclose that fact within three days. The report must include the name and address of the investor, description and quantity of the shares held by it, and the date on which the shareholding or change in shareholding reaches the threshold. The takeover rule of the CSRC requires much fuller disclosure, including (among others) the identity of the investor and the persons who agree to act in concert with respect to attaining more than 5 percent of shares, purpose of the acquisition, and disclosure of transactions of the listed companies' shares in the six-month period preceding the acquisition.[53] As a result, the provisions, just like section 13(d) of the U.S. Securities Exchange Act, deny the possible new controllers of the company the veil of anonymity by requiring a transparent ownership structure.

2 Insider trading rules restrict (with criminal penalties) the controlling shareholders' ability to purchase or sell shares based on material, non-public information.[54]

3 The takeover rule assures, through both disclosure and substantive rules (particularly regarding timing, withdrawal, and proration rights), all shareholders of a listed company an equal opportunity to participate in any tender offer for their shares.[55]

4 The continuous disclosure system generally requires issuer's timely disclosure of the controlling shareholder's material developments relating to its shareholding.[56]

5 A controlling shareholder is subject to civil and administrative liabilities for disclosure of fraudulent information, misleading representations, or material omissions by the controlled company which cause investors to suffer losses in securities transactions.[57]

6 Rules provide the remaining shareholders a "sell-out right," that is, the right to sell their shares to the acquirer of a listed company at a fair price when the company is delisted following the completion of an acquisition. This rule allows shareholders a chance to escape possible oppression by the new controller.[58]

Nevertheless, plagued by the enforcement problem, those provisions may remain on paper, instead of being applied in fact. Therefore, some of the best firms seeking any variety of goals—to show a credible and binding commitment by the issuer and its controller not to exploit minority investors, to raise more equity capital, to increase share value, or to achieve worldwide recognition—

may decide to list on a developed stock exchange and thereby opt into foreign governance standards. This kind of immigration to the foreign market may help ease the enforcement problem in China.

Until now, some locally well-known companies have been listed in U.S., U.K., Hong Kong, or Singapore markets. Some companies and their officers and directors have been hit with class action lawsuits filed in the United States (e.g., Chinalife, Chinadotcom, NetEase). The chairman of a company listed on the Hong Kong exchange (Skyworth Digital Holdings Ltd.) was even sentenced to jail for misappropriating funds and conspiring to defraud in connection with the granting of share options. But it remains to be seen whether corporate governance in Mainland China can achieve convergence to global standards mainly by encouraging local companies to list in the U.S. or other developed markets. As of this writing, not many companies have been permitted to list their shares on developed markets. At the end of June 2007, there were only 60 Chinese companies listed on the London Stock Exchange, and even fewer listed on NYSE and NASDAQ (Zhu 2007).[59] The influence of those companies' governance on their locally listed counterparts may be limited. Also, as there have been very limited channels for domestic citizens to invest in foreign markets and the national exchanges in China have not been fully opened to foreign capital, real competition among national and foreign stock exchanges has not yet begun. Thus, exchange harmonization will be slow. Finally, cross-border supervision of cross-listed companies requires more efficient cooperation among regulators, and even courts of different jurisdictions, without which there will be a failure of enforcement.[60]

Cross-listing may help to improve corporate governance in some companies, but as Bernard Black pointed out, even if those firms have "escaped" their weak home-country institutions through foreign listings, such escape is only partial without the help of local enforcement and other institutions.[61]

The role of the nonprofit organizations

Professor Milhaupt maintains that nonprofit organizations (NPOs) have emerged as perhaps the most important corporate law enforcement agents in Korea, Japan, and Taiwan, and their action may be another partial solution to the problem of weak investor protection and corporate law enforcement (Milhaupt 2004).

As is widely known, China does not have a tradition of active NPOs, but a similar organization of securities lawyers has recently emerged.

After the CSRC published its administrative penalties against Kelon (a listed company which submitted false accounting reports) and Deloitte (an international accounting firm which gave an unreserved opinion on the financial report of Kelon), 60 lawyers from 45 law firms around the country formed a "Justice claiming team for the compensation from Kelon and Deloitte's false statement" (*Kelong, Deqing Xujiachenshu Minshi Peichang An*

Quanguo Lushi Weiquantuan). The Justice Claiming Team consists of lawyers who have been participating in securities-related civil compensation
lawsuits in the country. Boasting rich practical experience, the team released
its Movement Statement through high-profile media, claiming that the lawyers' group was a loose and open-ended organization that would accept any
qualified Kelon shareholders' actionable claims. Most importantly, the
group announced that if there were any similar misrepresentation cases in
the future, all the members of the team would automatically form a new
Justice Claiming Team (Shentu and Chang 2006). According to Yixin Song,
one of the conveners of the Justice Claiming Team, the team is the biggest
lawyers' group focused on a single case in China's history, with three tasks:

1 organizing the member lawyers to discuss difficult law issues in the
   Kelon and Deloitte cases, coordinating the lawyers and law firms
   involved in the case, and exploring ways to improve securities-related
   civil suits and the private compensation law system;
2 coordinating with the CSRC, the SPC, and related lower courts, accepting
   their guidance, providing professional comments and advice; and
3 providing practical legal education to investors and persuading them "to
   believe in the strength of the law, and believe in the strength of themselves"(Yue and He 2006).

The Justice Claiming Team is not likely to be registered with the local government as an NPO; rather, it is now a forum for securities lawyers to
exchange experience and information gathered from the cases they have
represented.[62] But that difference does not seem so important. Unlike in
Japan or Korea, there appears to be less public antipathy in China toward
allowing lawyers to play a greater role (even if basically for profits) in the
resolution of economic problems, at least before the emergence of real corporate and securities law-related NPOs in the country. In such an environment, the high-profile group of activist lawyers could still be a partial (if
transitory) response to the public goods problem of corporate law enforcement. In the future, the role of the NPOs may also be played by a govern-
ment-sponsored "Securities Investor Protection Fund Limited Liability
Company" (SIPFLLC) in charge of the financing, management, and use of
the Securities Investor Protection Fund.[63] The attitude of the court system
will be the most important determinant of the role of NPOs in the corporate governance of China's companies (See Yu 2006).

Class actions

China's Civil Procedure Law and Securities Law do not provide for a U.S.-
style class action suit. The Judicial Explanations relating to civil liability for
misrepresentation in the securities market made it clear that plaintiffs in
securities litigation can adopt "representative suits with a fixed number of

litigants" (*Renshu Queding De Daibiaoren Susong*, § 54, the Civil Procedural Law),[64] but not "class actions".[65] For multiparty litigations (*Quntixing Susong*), in 2006 government agencies and the Lawyers' Association announced strict control over plaintiffs' lawyers.[66]

At the same time, since fraud has been so common in the securities market, and investor protection is far from sufficient, the regulators, stock exchanges, business lawyers, and public media have increasingly voiced their support for the establishment of a securities-related class action system (Cheng and Wu 2005, Xia 2005, Wang 2005).

Whether a securities-related class action system should be established in China may be examined by balancing the pros and cons. The answer to the question also depends on how the system, the securities regulation framework, and the overall legal infrastructure are set.

Overview of conflicting arguments

Since the adoption of the Civil Procedure Law in the early 1990s, scholars have noted the differences between "representative suits without a fixed number of litigants" (*Renshu Buqueding De Daibianren Susong*) under China's Civil Procedure Law and U.S.-style class actions. Many scholars argued that the "representative suits without a fixed number of litigants" had better support in the theory of civil procedure law and might be better suited to meeting the demands of local conditions. In the intervening years, however, more scholars have become inclined to endorse a class action system.

Advantages of a class action system

The primary benefit of allowing securities-related class action lawsuits is the expansion of the effect of the judgment, meaning the ruling of the court will bind those who have not actually opted into the lawsuit, thereby providing an efficient means of giving relief to a much larger class. Thus, a class action helps to overcome the collective action problem among dispersed individual plaintiffs. Without the system, the damages claimed by a single plaintiff may be minimal and the cost of litigation prohibitive, thus precluding any incentive for plaintiffs to litigate individually. Finally, a class action system will effectively deter fraud and irregularities when limited administrative penalties cannot achieve the same result.

Problems of a class action system

There are, on the other hand, many problems entailed in a class action system. First, class actions permit some plaintiffs to appoint themselves as the representative of the entire plaintiff class, which conflicts with the prevailing legal theory. Second, if China does not have the political, social, and judicial infrastructure to accommodate a class action system, the courts may decline to hear class actions even if they are introduced into law. Third, class action litigation is not the only means of providing relief to a group of individuals. Government regulators, local governments, and local or industrial self-regulatory organizations may be in a better position to solve social problems. Fourth, it is almost impossible for the class members to supervise the actions of their representatives and lawyers. Fifth, instead of realizing social justice, class actions may be abused by corporate attorneys who only focus on their potential profitability. Sixth, the influx of numerous class actions could create a huge burden on the potential defendants (especially securities issuers and financial intermediaries) and the courts. Finally, it cannot be overlooked that the U.S. has experienced problems with class actions; to date no other major jurisdiction has widely used the institution.

The need for a class action system

In view of a variety of factors, introducing a class action mechanism for securities suits is both necessary and possible. China's securities market is nascent. Cultural, legal, and market constraints are too weak to provide practical protection to inexperienced individual shareholders, who constitute the main body of investors. A robust enforcement mechanism such as the class action institution is needed to address gaps in the supply of investor protection and corporate law enforcement which cannot be filled by other means. Moreover, government officials and commentators agree that some brazen misconduct in the securities market should be punished to achieve deterrence. Securities-related class actions are highly technical and professional, which makes it possible to insulate them from politically sensitive public-policy issues. After more than 10 years' construction, a set of comparatively detailed securities statutes and rules has been established, making it much easier than before to discover and confirm illegalities. The adoption and revision of the Securities Law and related Judicial Explanations have provided private rights of action to sue wrongdoers. Through the handling of these cases, some intermediate and superior courts have gained first-hand experience in hearing misrepresentation cases. More and more research on the U.S. class action system has been introduced into China, making it easier to draw lessons from the U.S. experience. A team of institutional investors has been born to provide potential candidates for lead plaintiffs. The rapidly expanding group of business lawyers and law firms has been able to provide qualified legal services to litigants. After the revision of the Securities Law, the CSRC is even better equipped to detect and punish illegalities, signaling to the plaintiff's bar that attractive cases are available. The agency will also be very helpful in providing expert opinions as *Amicus curiae*.

According to experience in U.S. and Korean markets,[67] devising an efficient class action regime for China involves balancing three separate problems:

1 the problem of blocking frivolous suits while allowing meritorious suits
2 the agency problem between plaintiffs' attorneys and the plaintiff class, and
3 the lack of incentives of plaintiffs' attorneys to focus on smaller companies (Choi 2004: 1510).

While implementation is of concern, the reform should first focus on misrepresentation cases, with which some courts have become familiar. The SPC ought to permit experimental practices of "representative suits without a fixed number of litigants" (§ 55, the Civil Procedural Law), and then establish a class action system.

Infrastructure for a class action system

Plaintiff lawyers

In large Chinese cities, an active, professional corporate and securities bar is forming, although most business lawyers still focus on work other than litigation. However, familiarity with corporate and securities law grants them particular advantages in becoming trial lawyers and developing expertise in pursuit of a securities class action. Today, China has only a few large law firms with over one hundred attorneys. Thus, diversifying the risk that any given class action may not result in a positive return for the firm may be problematic. Nevertheless, diversification may still occur across firms, as several plaintiffs' firms may jointly share in the co-representation of different classes in several different lawsuits.

Institutional investors

The presence of institutional investors who are able to take an active role in class actions is one of the keys to success of the system. A group of institutional investors (including securities investment funds, insurance companies, Social Insurance Funds, securities companies, Qualified Foreign Institutional Investors (QFIIs), and Foreign Strategic Investors) have appeared in China. However, some of the institutional investors—especially the Securities Investment Funds—are widely criticized as being inclined to make speculative and risky investments instead of maintaining stable shareholdings (e. g., Li 2002: 72–3). They appear unconcerned with listed companies' governance and share few interests in common with individual investors. They have even been involved in market manipulation and other scandals (Ping and Li 2000; Xu 2005: 79). Another main type of institutional investor, the local Social Insurance Funds, have been reported to have severe governance problems for themselves (Hu *et al.* 2006). It is thus doubtful whether these institutional investors can actually be counted on to act as lead plaintiffs. In the future, responsible institutional investors have to be raised.

Judges and courts

Specialized judges and courts have better ability to handle class actions. They may develop expertise in distinguishing between frivolous and meritorious claims, and may be able to sanction frivolous suits. Specialized judges may also apply doctrines (such as reliance and causation, or measures of damages) more consistently, contributing to the predictability of judicial outcomes, and increasing the probability of settlement. To some extent, China should employ a number of specialized sub-courts (*Shen-panting*) in the Peoples' courts. For example, the intellectual property sub-courts with specialized judges in major cities have successfully earned a reputation as comparatively efficient and professional. Employing similarly specialized courts with expert judges for corporate and securities cases may provide significant benefits for a shareholder class action system.

Concluding remarks

China's corporate governance has undergone more than ten years' development. As awareness of investor protection created a significant policy issue, the most important statutes related to corporate governance have been revised to meet the increasing demand for protection. Research has suggested that improvement of formal legal provisions would contribute to the performance of companies and the welfare of shareholders. However, when plagued by enforcement problems, some good law provisions on paper would fall short of fulfilling the demand for better governance. The alternative solutions to public and private enforcement regimes include a "self-enforcing" corporate law model, cross-listings on foreign stock exchanges, and the possibility for nonprofit organizations to act as corporate law-enforcement agents. They will help to partially ease the chronic illnesses of the securities market, but there is no complete substitute for institutions at the heart of a good national investor-protection system and corporate governance, especially formal enforcement mechanisms. Among other mechanisms, a securities-related class action system may be a good institutional choice for China in the future.

Notes

1 Company Law of the People's Republic of China (adopted by the 5th Session of the Standing Committee of the 8th National People's Congress on 29 December 1993, and effective 1 July 1994), hereinafter "Company Law of 1994" or the "old Company Law".
2 See §§ 81, 80.1, 24.1, the Company Law of 1994.
3 For example, as stated in the Company Law of 1994: The Law was promulgated "with the aim to establish a modern enterprise system . . . " (§ 1); The state assets held by a company belong to the state (instead of to the company itself) (§ 4.3); When a SOE is to be converted into a company, the conversion of management style shall be conducted in accordance with laws and administrative regulations (§ 7); Where a SOE is converted into a stock company, the state assets are strictly

prohibited to be under-valued in exchange for shares, sold at prices below the prevailing market price, or allocated to any person without consideration (§ 81); The establishment of a stock company (the only type of company which has access to equity financing market) shall have the approval of the ministries authorized by the State Council or the relevant provincial government (§ 77).

4 Company Law of the People's Republic of China (revised by the 18th Session of the Standing Committee of the 10th National People's Congress on 27 October 2005, and effective 1 January 2006) hereinafter "Company Law of 2006" or the "new Company Law"; Securities Law of the People's Republic of China (revised by the 18th Session of the Standing Committee of the 10th National People's Congress on 27 October 2005, and effective 1 January 2006), hereinafter "Securities Law of 2006" or the "new Securities Law".

5 Just as Allen, Qian and Qian (Allen *et al.* 2005: 57–116), we give China a score on shareholder rights law following the LLSV law and finance methodology. For old company law provisions applying to listed companies China was assigned an antidirector rights score of 3 (out of 6). After the revision, the score is now up to 4. The old score put China's shareholder rights score below the English-origin average (4) but above both the German-origin average (2.33) and French-origin average (2.33), which would make China rank right at the average of all LLSV countries (developed and developing) for shareholder rights if China had been in the LLSV list of countries. With the new score, China is now doing as well as the average of English-origin jurisdictions, and would be in the upper part of the LLSV country list.

6 Principles of Corporate Governance for Chinese Listed Companies (*Zhongguo Shangshi Gongsi Zhili Zhunze*) issued by the CSRC in 2002 required companies to "establish an independent director system in accordance with relevant rules." According to an even earlier Guidance Opinion on the Establishment of an Independent Director System in Listed Companies (*Guanyu Zai Shangshi Gongsi Jianli Duli Dongshi Zhidu De Zhidao Yijian*), listed companies were required to have at least two independent directors by 30 June 2002, and such directors were to constitute at least one-third of the board by 30 June 2003. "Independent directors" does not find its place in the law until the revisions of the Company Law in 2005.

7 Such fundamental changes include, e.g., amendments of the article of association, increasing or decreasing the charter capital, merger, division (or separation) or liquidation of the company.

8 Revised and entered into effect since 16 March 2006.

9 GAALC § 96.3, "insider directors" means those directors who also serve as executive officers or the representatives of employees of the company.

10 GAALC § 159. The Company Law (§ 170.1) entitles the company's articles of association to determine if the board should also have the power to hire or dismiss the auditor of the company.

11 GAALC § 44.2.

12 GAALC § 46.1. If the board declines the independent directors' proposal to convene such a shareholders' meeting, it has to publicize the reasons, see GAALC § 46.2.

13 Revised and entered into effect on 16 March 2006.

14 RSMLC § 16.

15 RSMLC § 37.

16 RSMLC § 11.

17 Shanghai Securities Exchange Listing Rule and Shenzhen Securities Exchange Listing Rule (revised and entered into effect on 19 May 2006), Chapter 10 "Related-party Transactions".

18 Similar requirements are provided for in the CSRC rules, as mentioned before. But the requirements in the rules are set too narrowly, and sometimes the provisions

are so important (e.g., rights to information) that they should be included in the law itself.

19 "The lack of any mention of a quorum requirement (with respect to share-holders' meetings) ... does not evidence any consciousness on the part of the Company Law drafters of the rights of minority shareholders." Howson (1997: 146–147).

20 There should have been a number of other instances where appraisal and redemption rights can be made available: (1) for a charter amendment that limits shareholder rights; (2) for a reorganization; and (3) for a major transaction. A judge or an independent appraiser is also needed to determine the value of the redeemed shares.

21 Securities Law of the People's Republic of China (adopted by the 6th Session of the Standing Committee of the 9th National People's Congress on 29 December 1998, and effective 1 July 1999), hereinafter "Securities Law of 1999" or the "old Securities Law".

22 Principle 10 and Rule 9, The City Code on Takeover and Mergers (UK); Article 35, The Securities Acquisitions and Takeovers Act (Germany); Article 5, Directive 2004/25/EC of the European Parliament and of the Council of 21 April 2004 on Takeovers.

23 § 35, Measures for Administration of Takeover of Listed Companies (*Shangshigongsi Shougou Guanli Banfa*, revised and published on 31 July 2006).

24 The first Judicial Explanation of the new Company Law was published on 28 April 2006, which only address the coordination of the new and old Company Laws.

25 High shareholding thresholds for the exercise of important shareholder rights and the significant economic risks of filing suit have historically been major obstacles to shareholder activism in other East Asia jurisdictions. See Milhaupt (2004: 169).

26 E.g., § 22.2 (Shareholders' right to challenge the resolution of a shareholders' meeting or a board meeting); § 183 (In very limited situations, shareholders may petition the court to dissolve the company).

27 The term "tunneling" is used as in Johnson *et al.* (2000) to refer to the transfer of assets or profits out of a company to its controlling shareholders.

28 "Affiliation relationship" refers to the relationship between the controlling shareholder, de facto controlling person, director, supervisor, or senior officer of a company and the enterprise under their direct or indirect control and any other relationship that may lead to the transfer of any interest of the enterprise. However, the enterprises in which the state holds a controlling interest do not have an affiliation relationship between them simply because the state holds a controlling interest in them. See § 217(4) of the Company Law.

29 Although not stated clearly, "a third party" can be understood to refer especially to the controlling shareholder and/or de facto controlling person of the company.

30 In our statistics to the middle of 2006, since the SPC permitted the shareholders to sue the listed companies and their executives for misrepresentations in the prospectus and other statements (SPC 2003), about 120 companies (and related executives, controllers, and accountants) have met the strictly formulated criteria to fall into the small group of possible defendants. Among them only 17 companies have been sued, and even fewer have been held responsible for or have agreed through settlements to pay the losses of the plaintiff investors. Source: News reports on the financial newspapers, such as *China Securities* (*Zhongguo Zhengquan Bao*), *Shanghai Securities* (*Shanghai Zhengquan Bao*), *Securities Times* (*Zhengquan Shibao*).

31 Supporters of securities-related class actions include the Chairman of CSRC, CEO of Shenzhen Securities Exchange and many commentators. See section on "Class actions" in this essay.

32 E.g., under the Lawyer Service Fee Regulatory Rule (*Lushi Fuwu Shoufei Guanli Banfa*, April 2006) promulgated by the State Development and Reform Commission and the Justice Ministry, a contingent fee is not permitted in multiparty litigations.

33 §§ 54, 66, 67.2(8), the Securities Law of 2006. Under the Company Law, the term "de facto controlling person" means any person who is not a shareholder of a company but has de facto control of the acts of the company by means of investment relationship, agreements, or any other arrangements.

34 § 71.1, the new Securities Law. Under the new Company Law, the term "controlling shareholder" means a shareholder whose capital contribution accounts for more than 50 percent of the total capital of a limited liability company, or a shareholder whose shareholdings account for more than 50 percent of the total equity of a company limited by shares, or a shareholder whose capital contribution or shareholdings account for less than 50 percent but who holds the voting rights on the strength of its capital contribution or shareholdings that are enough to have an important influence on resolutions of the board meeting or the shareholders' general meeting. See § 217(2), the Company Law of 2006.

35 § 193, the new Securities Law.

36 Since 1997 when the CSRC provided itself with the power of *Shi Chang Jin Ru*, it has used the power in about 30 securities law cases. See CSRC (2006).

37 E.g., §§ 17.3, 3.2.4 of Listing Rules of Shanghai Stock Exchange and Shenzhen Stock Exchange (2006).

38 The harmful actions include: (1) providing funds, commodities, services, or other assets to other units or persons without consideration; (2) providing or accepting funds, commodities, services, or other assets under manifestly unfair conditions; (3) providing funds, commodities, services, or other assets to manifestly insolvent units or persons; (4) providing collateral for the debts of manifestly insolvent units or persons, or providing collateral for the debts of any units or persons without justified reasons; (5) disclaiming a property right or bearing a debt for others without justified reasons; (6) damaging the listed company in other ways. See § 169-1, the Criminal Law of PRC (revised on 29 June 2006).

39 As of the end of 2004, listed companies with a collectively owned enterprise, privately owned enterprise, foreign enterprise or limited liability company as the largest shareholder amounted to 390, about 28.32% of all listed companies. The other 987 companies (71.68% of all listed companies) were still controlled by the goverment or by SOEs. As of the end of 2003, the corresponding figures were 347 (26.96%) for non-state-controlled companies and 940 (73.04%) for state-controlled companies respectively. See CSRC (2004 and 2005).

40 In March 2006 alone, at least three controlling persons of several listed companies were facing criminal charges for looting those companies. They are Qiu Baozhong, chairman of the board of directors of ST Long Chang (600772, SH), de facto controlling person of both Fujian Sannong (000732, SZ) and Zhejiang Haina (000925, SZ); Zhang Liangbin, chairman of the board of directors of Zhaohua Jituan (000688, SZ); Zhong Xiaojian, chairman of the board of directors of Shuma Wangluo (000578, SZ). In August 2006, the chairman of board of ST Sanlong (000732.SZ) was also arrested. As reported, since the "tunneling" problems were revealed in the listed companies controlled by the privately owned enterprises, about 15 company chairmen or CEOs have been under investigation, detained or arrested. See He (2006).

41 §§ 16, 149, Company Law (2006) of PRC.

42 See §§ 60.1, 60.3, 61.1 and 123.2, Company Law (1994) of PRC.

43 See especially the Guidelines for the Articles of Association of Listed Companies (*Shangshi Gongsi Zhangcheng Zhiyin*), issued on 16 December 1997, revised on 16 March 2006; Regulatory Opinions for General Meetings of Listed Companies

(*Shangshi Gongsi Gudongdahui Guifan Yijian*), issued on 18 May 2000, revised on 16 March 2006; and Guidance Opinion on the Establishment of an Independent Director System in Listed Companies (*Guanyu Zai Shangshi Gongsi Jianli Duli Dongshi Zhidu de Zhidao Yijian*), issued on 16 August 2001.

44 The Certain Rules Regarding Strengthening the Protection of Interests of Public Shareholders (*Guanyu Jiaqiang Shehui Gongzhonggu Gudong Quanyi Baohu de Ruogan Guiding*), issued by CSRC on 7 December 2004.

45 § 1.1, Certain Rules Regarding Strengthening the Protection of Interests of Public Shareholders.

46 §§ 11.1, 11.2, the new Securities Law; §§ 4, 29, 30 (among others), Provisional Measures of Sponsorship System for Issuing and Listing of Securities (*Zhenquan Faxing Shangshi Baojian Zhidu Zanxing Banfa*) (28 December 2003).

47 § 69, the new Securities Law.

48 § 192, the new Securities Law; §§ 60, 65, Provisional Measures of Sponsorship System for Issuing and Listing of Securities.

49 Such as in the administrative allocation of state-owned stocks, in the transfer of stocks that does not result in the change of the de facto controller, and the obtaining of stocks by inheritance.

50 §§ 9, 17, 28, 32, 51, Measures for Administration of Takeover of Listed Companies.

51 §§ 65–71, Measures for Administration of Takeover of Listed Companies.

52 "We can only reduce, not wholly avoid, the need for official enforcement" (Black and Kraakman 1996: 1918). Also see Black 2001: 790–791 (Effective regulators, prosecutors, and courts are the most important institutions that control information asymmetry, which is critical for developing strong public stock markets).

53 § 16, Measures for Administration of Takeover of Listed Companies.

54 Shareholders who hold 5 percent or more of the shares of the company, the de facto controlling person of the company and its directors, supervisors and officers are deemed to be "insiders"; it is illegal for them to buy or sell securities of the company or divulge such information or procure others to buy or sell such securities before related insider information is made public. See §§ 73–76, 202 of the new Securities Law, § 180 of the Criminal Law.

55 Especially §§ 37, 42, 43.1, Measures for Administration of Takeover of Listed Companies.

56 § 67 of the new Securities Law.

57 §§ 69, 193.3 of the new Securities Law.

58 § 97.1 of the new Securities Law, § 44, Measures for Administration of Takeover of Listed Companies.

59 As a comparison, at the end of 1996, there were 416 foreign listings on NASDAQ, 305 on the New York Stock Exchange, and 63 on the American Stock Exchange, for a total of 784, and this number continued to grow rapidly. See Licht 1998: 566.

60 E.g., presently there are more and more finance scandals revealed in the Mainland China companies listed in Hong Kong, but the local regulators and courts of Hong Kong have felt impotent in the inquiries and legal enforcement against those companies' illegalities, since the companies' assets, business, and even the illegal facts are all in the Mainland instead of Hong Kong, the key personnel may choose to stay in the Mainland or have been detained there, and thus will not be reached by Hong Kong's law enforcers. See Wang (2006).

61 "A company's reputation is strongly affected by the reputations of other firms in the same country. And reputation unsupported by local enforcement and other institutions isn't nearly as valuable as the same reputation buttressed by those institutions." See Black (2001: 784).

62 "We don't need or plan to register the Justice Claiming Team as a corporation or association" Yixin Song 2006.

63 As to § 134 of the new Securities Law, a securities investors' protection fund (SIPF) has been established by the state government. The fund comprises funds contributed by the securities companies and other funds raised. According to § 7 of the Measures for the Management of Securities Investor Protection Funds (*Zhengquan Touzizhe Baohu Jijin Guanli Banfa*) (issued by the CSRC, Ministry of Finance and Peoples' Bank of China on 30 June 2006), the funds of the SIPF are only used to compensate securities investors as customers of a securities company when it goes into bankruptcy, is closed, or taken over by the government. The SIPFLLC was registered on 30 August 2006.

64 § 14, Supreme People's Court "Several provisions on the adjudication of civil suits for damages arising out of false representations in the securities markets" (*Zuigao Renmin Fayuan Guanyu Shenli Zhengquan Shichang Yin Xujia Chenshu Yinfa De Minshi Peichang Anjian De Ruogan Guiding*), issued on 9 January 2003, hereinafter "2003 SPC False Representation Provisions."

65 "Class action is not applicable to securities related actions," see § 4, Circular of the Supreme People's Court Concerning Issues Relating to Acceptance of Civil Tort Suits Filed Due to False Representation on the Securities Market (*Zuigao Renmin Fayuan Guanyu Shouli Zhengquan Shichang Yin Xujia Chenshu Yinfa De Minshi Qinquan Jiufen Anjian Youguan Wenti De Tongzhi*), issued on 15 January 2002, hereinafter "2002 SPC False Representation Circular."

66 Under the Lawyer Service Fee Regulatory Measures (*Lushi Fuwu Shoufei Guanli Banfa*, issued in April 2006) promulgated by the State Development and Reform Commission and the Justice Ministry, a contingent fee is not permitted in multiparty litigations. Under the Guideline to Multiparty Litigations (*Zhonghua Quanguo Lushi Xiehui Guanyu Lushi Banli Quntixing Anjian Zhidao Yijian*, issued in March 2006) promulgated by the National Lawyer Association, those litigations are subject to "supervision" of the Association.

67 Several theoretical issues (especially frivolous litigation and the relationship between the professional plaintiffs' attorneys and the plaintiff class of investors) exist in contemplating the value of private securities class actions in the United States. The U.S. enacted the Private Securities Litigation Reform Act of 1995 to address these issues. Modeled after the U.S. securities regime, Korea has adopted a securities-related class action law that took effect in January 2005. See Chung (2004: 165) and Song in this volume.

Bibliography

Allen, Franklin, Jun Qian, and Meijun Qian (2005) "Law, Finance, and Economic Growth in China," *Journal of Financial Economics*, 77: 57–116.

An, Jian (Deputy Director of the Legal System Working Commission of the Standing Committee of the National People's Congress) (2005) "*Guanyu 'Zhonghua Renmin Gongheguo Xingfa Xiuzhengan (Liu) (Caoan)' De Shuoming* [An Introduction to the Revisions of Criminal Law of the People's Republic of China (VI) (Draft)]", reported to the Standing Committee of the National People's Congress of the People's Republic of China, 24 December 2005. Available at www.npc.gov. cn/was40/detail?record=1&channelid=20179&searchword=%20(%20FSRQ%3E% 3D%272005%2F12%2F1%27+AND+FSRQ%3C%3D%272005%2F12%2F31%27+ AND+BIAOTI%3D%D0%CC%B7%A8%D0%DE%D5%FD%B0%B8++%29+and +%28+IDS%3D%27350751'%20 (accessed 15 August 2006).

Black, Bernard and Reinier Kraakman (1996) "A Self-enforcing Model of Corporate Law," *Harvard Law Review* 109: 1911–1981.

Black, Bernard S. (2001) "The Legal and Institutional Preconditions for Strong Securities Markets," *UCLA Law Review* 48: 781–849.

Cao, Kangtai (Director of the Legal Affairs Office of the State Council) (2005) *"Guanyu 'Zhonghua Renmin Gongheguo Gongsifa (Xiuding Caoan)' De Shuoming* [An Introduction to the "Company Law of the People's Republic of China (Draft Revisions)]", reported to the Standing Committee of the National People's Congress of the People's Republic of China, 25 February 2005. Available at www.npc. gov.cn/was40/detail?record=1&channelid=20179&searchword=%20(%20BIAOTI %3D%B9%AB%CB%BE%B7%A8++%29+and+%28+IDS%3D%27343120'%20 (accessed 15 August 2006).

Cheng, Yong and Zhanyu Wu (2005) "Shang Fuling (Chairman of the CSRC): the 'Eleven Five Plan' Will Promote 5 Basic Institutions [Shangfuling: 'Shiyi Wu' Litui Wuxiang Jichuxing Zhidu Sheji]", on *Shanghai Securities*, 3 November 2005.

Choi, Stephen J. (2004) "The Evidence of Securities Class Actions," *Vanderbilt Law Review* 57: 1465–525.

Chung, Dae Hwan (2004) "Introduction to South Korea's New Securities-related Class Action," *Journal of Corporation Law* 30: 165–80.

Clarke, D.C. (2003) "Corporate Governance in China: An Overview," *China Economic Review* 14: 494–507.

—— (2006) "The Independent Director in Chinese Corporate Governance," *Delaware Journal of Corporate Law* 31: 125–228.

Coffee, John C., Jr. (1983) "Rescuing the Private Attorney General: Why the Model of the Lawyer as Bounty Hunter is not Working," *Maryland Law Review* 42: 215–88

—— (1999) "The Future as History: The Prospects for Global Convergence in Corporate Governance and Its Implications," *Northwest University Law Review* 93: 641–707.

—— (2002) "Racing Towards the Top? The Impact of Cross-Listings and Stock Market Competition on International Corporate Governance," *Columbia Law Review* 102: 1757–1831.

CSRC (eds.) (2004) *China Securities and Futures Statistical Yearbook 2004* [*Zhong-Guo Zhengquan Qihuo Tongji Nianjian, 2004*], Beijing: China Finance (*Zhongguo Jinrong Chubanshe*).

—— (2005) *China Securities and Futures Statistical Yearbook 2005* [*ZhongGuo Zhengquan Qihuo Tongji Nianjian, 2005*], Beijing: China Finance (*Zhongguo Jinrong Chubanshe*).

CSRC (2006) File. Online. Available at www.csrc.gov.cn/cn/jsp/index.jsp?path=ROOT > CN > %D6%A4%BC%E0%BB%E1%B9%AB%B8%E6 (accessed 1 September 2006).

Fan, Jian and Jianwen Wang (2006) *Corporation Law* [*Gongsifa*], Beijing: The Law Press (*Falu Chubanshe*).

Fernald, John G. and Oliver D. Babson (1999) "Why Has China Survived the Asian Crisis So Well? What Risks Remain?" FRB International Finance Discussion Paper No. 633. Available at SSRN: http://ssrn.com/abstract=154629.

Guo, Feng (2006) "The New Securities Law: A Balance Between State Intervention and Deregulation [Xin Zhengquanfa: Guojia Ganyu Yu Fangsong Guanzhi Zhi Pingheng]", 21st Century Economic Report (*21 Shiji Jingji Baodao*), 9 January 2006.

He, Jun (2006) "Presently 29.4 Billion Yuan Have Been Misappropriated From 123 Listed Companies [Muqian Liangshi Haiyou 123 Jia Shangshigongsi Bei Zhanyong Zijin 294.05 Yiyuan]," in *Shanghai Securities* (1 September 2006).

Howson, Nicholas C. (1997) "China's Company Law: One Step Forward, Two Steps Back? A Modest Complaint," *Columbia Journal of Asian Law* 11: 127–73.

Ho, Betty M. (2003) "The 'Dominant Shareholder Problem' of Chinese Listed Problems: diagnosis should precede prescription [Zhongguo Shangshi Gongsi 'Yigu Duda' De Wenti: Shangwei Zhenduan, Ruhe Xiayao]," in Wang Baoshu *et al.* (eds.), *Protection of Interests of the Investors [Touzizhe Liyi Baohu]*, Beijing: Social Science (*Shehui Kexue Chubanshe*), 101–124.

Hu, Runfeng *et al.* (2006) "Shanghai Scandal Exposes Social Security Risks [Shanghai Shebao: Weixian De Touzi]," *Caijing Magzine*, 2006 (17).

Johnson, Simon *et al.* (2000) "Tunneling," *American Economic Review* 90: 22–27.

Kiseliov, Alexander Ivanovich *et al.* (1999) "General Principle of Company Law for Transition Economies," *Journal of Corporation Law*, 24: 196–293.

La Porta, Raphael, Florencio Lopez-de-Silanes, Andrei Shleifer, and Robert W. Vishny (1998) "Law and Finance," *Journal of Political Economy* 106(6): 1113–1155.

Licht, Amir N. (1998) "Regulatory Arbitrage for Real: International Securities Regulation in A World Interacting Securities Markets," *Virginia Journal of International Law* 38: 563–638.

Li, Weian and Guoping Zhang (2005) "Research on the Top Management Governance Evaluation Index and Empirical Study on Relationship between the Index and Governance Performance: Based on Corporate Governance Evaluation of Publicly listed Companies in China [Jingliceng Zhili Pingjia Zhishu Yu Xiangguan Jixiao De Shizheng Yanjiu: Jiyu Zhongguo Shangshi Gongsi Zhili Pingjia De Yanjiu]," *Economics Review* [*Jingji Yanjiu*] 2005(11): 87–98.

Li, Xiangqian (2002) "Research on Institutional Investors, Corporate Governance and Stability of the Capital Market [Jigou Touzizhe, Gongsi Zhili Yu Zibenshichang Wending]," *Nankai Economic Review* 2002 (2): 69–73.

Liu, Junhai (2005a) "The Institution Innovations of the New Company Law [Xin Gongsifa De Zhidu Chuangxin]." Available at http://finance.sina.com.cn/g/20051101/09502083807.shtml (accessed 25 March 2007).

—— (2005b) "A Securities Law with Institutional Innovations [Yibu Zhidu Chuangxin De Zhequanfa]," *China Securities* [*Zhongguo Zhengquan Bao*], 17 November 2005.

Milhaupt, Curtis J. (2004) "Nonprofit Organizations as Investor Protection: Economic Theory and Evidence From East Asia," *Yale Journal of International Law* 29: 169–207.

Ping, Hu and Jing Li (2000) "The Inside Story of Securities Investment Funds: An Analysis of the Report of Investment Funds' Actions [Jijin Heimu: Guanyu Jijin Xingwei De Yanjiu Baogao Jiexi],"*Caijing Magazine* 2000 (2).

Qian, Yingyi (1995) "The Corporate Governance Structure and Financing Reform in China [Zhongguo De Gongsi Zhili Gaige He Rongzi Gaige]," in Aoki (ed.), *Corporate Governance in Transitional Economies: Insider Control and the Role of Banks* [*Zhuangui Jingji Zhong De Gongsi Zhili Jiegou: Neiburen Kongzhi He Yinhang De Zuoyong*], Beijing: China Economy (*Zhaoguo Jinji Chubanshe*), 115–150.

Shen,Yifeng, Nianhang Xu, and Yi Yang (2004) "Test on the Law Protection of Minority Investors in Different Stages [Wuoguo Zhongxiao Touzizhe Falu Baohu Lishi Shijian De Shizheng Jianyan]," *Economic review* 2004 (9): 90–100.

Shen,Yifeng, Ming Xiao, and Juanjuan Huang (2005) "Investor Protection and Corporation Cost of Equity [Zhongxiao Touzizhe falu Baohu Yu Gongsi Quanyi Ziben Chengben]," *Economic review* [*Jingji Yanjiu*] 2005 (6): 115–124.

Shentu, Qinnan and Qing Chang (2006) "Justice Claiming Team for the compensation from Kelong and Deloitte's False Statement: Establishment of Investor Protection Association Becomes Imperative [Kelong An Lushi Weiquantuan: Jinkuai Sheli Touzizhe Baohu Xiehui]," in *China Securities [Zhongguo Zhengquanbao]*, 24 July 2006.

Song, Yixin (2006) "The Underground Stories of the Justice Claiming Team for the Compensation From Kelon and Deloitte [Kelong, Deqing Weiquantuan De Muhou Gushi]," in *China Securities*, 14 September 2006.

SPC (2003) "Several provisions on the adjudication of civil suits for damages arising out of false representations in securities markets [Guanyu Shenli Zhengquan Shichang Yin Xujia Chenshu Yinfa De Minshi Peichang Anjian De Ruogan Guiding]," issued 9 January 2003.

Su, Dongwei (2000) "Corporate Finance and State Enterprise Reform in China," 20 November. Available at SSRN: http://ssrn.com/abstract=250802 or DOI: 10.2139/ssrn.250802

Tong, Daochi (2006) "The Revision of the Criminal Law and Deterring Power of Regulation [Xingfa Xiuding Yu Jianguan Weisheli]," Shanghai Securities [*Shanghai Zhenquanbao*], 13 January 2006.

Wang, Lu (2005) "Appeal for Class Action Arises From Zhengbaiwen Case [Zhengbaiwen An Yinfa Jituansusong Huyu]," on *Shanghai Securities*, 6 December 2005.

Wang, Yuexin (2006) "The Haiyu Event Tortures Cross-boarder Supervision [Haiyu Shijian Kaowen Kuajing Jianguan Nanti]," on *Shanghai Securities*, 2 August 2006.

Wei, Gang (2000) "Incentives for Top-Management and Performance of Listed Companies [Gaoji Guanliceng Jili Yu Shangshi Gongsi Jixiao]," *Economics Review [Jingji Yanjiu]*, 2000 (3), 32–39.

Wu, Jinglian (1993) *Reform of Large and Middle-sized Enterprises: Founding of a Modernized Enterprise Institution [Dazhongxing Qiyegaige: Jianli Xiandaihua Qiye Zhidu]*, Tianjin: Tianjin Peoples' (*Tianjin Renmin Chubanshe*).

Xia, Lihua (2005) "Shenzhen Securities Exchange Advices Judicial Explanations to be Drafted to Support Securities-related Litigation [Shenjiaosuo Jianyi Chutai Sifajieshi Zhichi Zhengquan Susong]," in *China Securities*, 29 December 2005.

Xu, Longbing (2005) "Institutional Investors: Trading Behavior on China Stock Markets through Multi-Securities Accounts [Zhongguo Gushi Jigoutouzizhe Duo Zhanghu Jiaoyi Xingwei Yanjiu]," *Economic Review*, 2005 (2).

Yue, Jinfei & He, Jun (2006) "The Members of the Justice Claiming Team has Amounted to 60; the Lawyers Come from 45 Law Firms around the Country [Weiquantuan Chengyuan Yida 60 Ming, Fenshu 45 Jia Lushishiwusuo)]," in *Shanghai Securities*, 24 July 2006.

Yu, Haitao (2006) "The Guangzhou Intermediate Court Still Does Not Accept the Case; the Deloitte Case Meets a Deadlock [Guangzhou Zhongyuan Zanting Lian, Deqingan Shenxian Jiangju]," in *21 Century Economic Report [21 Shiji Jinji Baodao]*, 16 August 2006.

Zhang, Weiying (1994) "The Evolvement and Newest Development of Western Enterprise Theories [Xifang Qiye Lilun De Yanjin Yu Zuixin Fazhan]," *Economics Review*, Vol. 11, 1994: 70–81.

Zhang, Zhichao (2006) "Capital Controls in China: Recent Developments and Reform Prospects". Available at SSRN: http://ssrn.com/abstract=883647.

Zhao, Chao, Julian Lowe, and Lili Pi (2005) "Shareholder's Structure and CEO Turnover in Chinese Listed Companies [Zhongguo Shangshi Gongsi Guquan Jiegou Yu Zongjingli Biangeng]," *Reform [Gaige]*, 2005 (1): 93–100.

Zhao, Xudong (2005) "A Lecture of the Company Law [Gongsifa Jiangzuo]," Available at www.lawyoo.com/bbs/dispbbs.asp?boardid=21&id=165 (accessed 25 March 2007).

Zhou, Yousu (2006) *New Survey on Corporation Law* [*Xin Gongsifa Lun*], Beijing: The Law Press (*Falu Chubanshe*).

Zhou, Zhengqing (Deputy Director of the Finance and Economics Commission of the NPC) (2005) "Guanyu 'Zhonghua Renmin Gongheguo Zhengquanfa (Xiuding Caoan)'De Shuoming" [An Introduction to the Securities Law of the People's Republic of China (Draft Revisions)]," reported to the Standing Committee of the National People's Congress of the People's Republic of China, 24 April 2005. Available at www.npc.gov.cn/was40/detail?record=1&channelid=20179&searchword=%20 (%20FSRQ%3E%3D%272005%2F3%2F1%27+AND+FSRQ%3C%3D%272005% 2F5%2F30%27+AND+BIAOTI%3D%D6%A4%C8%AF%B7%A8++%29+and+% 28+IDS%3D%27343116'%20 (accessed 15 August 2006).

Zhu, Zhouliang (2007) "2007, China's Enterprises Will Launch a New High Tide in Overseas Listing [Zhongguo Qiye Haiwai Shangshi Jiang Xian Xingaofeng]," in *Shanghai Securities*, 11 June.

8 The role of non-legal institutions in Chinese corporate governance

Donald C. Clarke

Introduction

Chinese corporate governance has recently become a popular subject of academic research. Scholars of economics and business have tried to test the relationships between performance and corporate governance, each measured in various ways. Legal scholars have looked both at the substantive norms and, to a lesser extent, at the institutions—for example, the court system and the China Securities Regulatory Commission—for enforcing those norms.

Little attention has yet been paid, however, to the institutions outside the state regulatory structure that make up the environment in which corporate governance norms, both formal and informal, are expected to function.[1] This chapter focuses on these non-state institutions and the degree to which they can support the realization of corporate governance norms.

Although this chapter purports to be about non-state institutions, to speak of non-state institutions in China courts inaccuracy. The Chinese political system does not fundamentally accept the existence of an independent civil society; in principle, the state permits the existence of *no* organization not subject to government direction. Any institution of any influence is going to be subject to at least some degree of state direction. Moreover, I include within the category of "non-state institutions" certain mechanisms and structures (for example, independent directors) that ultimately depend in some sense on the state legal system for their effectiveness. Even though a clear line cannot, therefore, be drawn between state and non-state institutions of corporate governance, I believe that it is still useful to attempt to single out the latter for special examination, if for no other reason than that so far so much attention has been concentrated on the former.

There is also a more important reason: non-state institutions can contribute to more effective corporate governance if allowed to do so. China's corporate governance regime relies heavily on the announcement of rules by government authorities and relatively little on institutions for making those rules meaningful. Lawmakers seem to expect that regulated parties will read the legal texts and voluntarily obey; if they do not, their lack of "legal consciousness" (*falü yishi*) is generally blamed, not the lack of institutions (state or non-state) that would require them to obey, whether they had the requisite legal consciousness or not.

At the same time, the corporate governance regime does not look to non-state institutions for the making and enforcement of rules and standards. One reason for this is simply political: as noted above, China's current political system does not accept the existence of institutions that are both powerful and independent of the state. Furthermore, both Imperial China and China under the planned economy have left their legacy in official culture: state officials find it hard to believe that the unplanned workings of the market might produce a better set of rules or procedures than they could come up with themselves.

Yet in relying on the state legal and administrative system to make and enforce norms, the state has in a sense chosen to play its weakest card. For all its progress over the quarter century, the post-Mao Chinese legal system remains an institution of only modest importance in the polity. It may be that institutions outside the state legal system could do much more than they now do.

Non-state institutions of corporate governance in China

This chapter will generally (but not exclusively) focus on a narrow conception of corporate governance. It centers on issues of agency cost and has a normative goal: preventing those who control corporate assets from exploiting those (in particular, equity holders) who supply them (Jensen and Meckling 1976).

This limited conception of corporate governance contains two types of agency problem: vertical (the exploitation of shareholders as a whole by management) and horizontal (the exploitation of minority shareholders by controlling shareholders). In each case, the exploiter extracts rents or private benefits, but can do so in different ways, and the means of mitigating such exploitation are different (Roe 2004). In addition, mitigating one kind of agency cost may mean exacerbating another. Dispersed shareholding, for example, can lead to high vertical agency costs, because collective action problems make it difficult for shareholders to monitor management. But one solution—concentrated shareholdings—may result in higher horizontal agency costs (Roe 2004).

In the United States, the main agency cost problem is vertical; in the rest of the world, however, and especially in transition economies, it is horizontal (La Porta *et al.* 1998; Denis and McConnell 2003). This chapter will show that China seems to be no exception to this pattern. What makes China exceptional is the identity of the controlling shareholder that is doing the exploiting: in most cases, it either is or is closely connected with a governmental entity. For this reason, some mechanisms for dealing with controlling-shareholder problems that work outside of China may not work within it because the controlling shareholder is too powerful.

This is just a specific example of a more general proposition: that rules and norms of corporate governance cannot be understood in the abstract. They function—or fail to function—within a particular institutional environment, and understanding and critiquing the rules requires understanding that environment.

Chinese commentators often complain, for example, that the rules of the Company Law are too broadly worded and not readily put into practice. Certainly this is sometimes true: how, for example, should one understand "relatively small in scale" in Article 52 of the new Company Law? But sometimes the expectations of the critics seem unrealistic. No rule formulated *ex ante* can spell everything out; the key is to have an alternative system available to supplement legislative gaps. Often the detailed standards that commentators cite with approval come not from the *ex ante* legislation of other jurisdictions but from case law.[2]

Commentators also complain that even when the Company Law's rules are clear, regulated parties do not obey them, and that the structures provided by the law, such as the board of supervisors, remain decoratively on the shelf but do not function as intended. Although they tend to blame the actors for failing to live up to the law's expectations, the real fault arguably lies in the law's inattention to enforcement mechanisms, in particular those that can be activated by parties hurt by non-compliance.

This chapter does not examine enforcement mechanisms (such as they are) that exist as formal state institutions. Instead, it looks at some particular examples of non-state (or semi-state) institutions in order to show both their abstract potential for playing a role in corporate governance and the specific possibility of their doing so in China.

Markets in general

There are several institutions that align the interests of managers and shareholders (Roe 2004). Among these are markets of various kinds—product markets, capital markets, and labor markets—because to the extent that a corporate governance scheme does not rely on public or private enforcement of legal obligations or simply the good conscience of parties to the corporate enterprise, it relies on markets to pressure parties to do the right thing. Those markets impose a certain discipline on management, but the constraints are not tight. It may take some time for selection pressures to affect firms operating sub-optimally.[3]

At the beginning of economic reform in China, markets did discipline managers, because very little economic activity of importance took place on a market basis. Over time, the importance of product and other markets has increased. Nevertheless, a number of companies remain in protected markets; this gives their management considerable slack.

The role of stock markets and external debt in corporate finance and corporate governance

Two markets of potential importance for Chinese corporate governance are those for external debt and for equity financing.

Historical background

Before the reform era, there was no financial market in the sense of firms seeking financing by offering competitive terms, or suppliers of funds offering financing in the same way. The traditional state-owned enterprise (TSOE) received all its funding from government bureaux of various kinds. There were banks that performed an intermediation function by collecting the funds of individual depositors, to be sure, but they passed these funds on to firms according to government direction, acting essentially as cashiers (Lardy 1998).

If the firm received money directly from a state body, the funds would be characterized as a grant; if the money came from a bank, it would be called a loan. But even if the funds came with the label of "loan," firms operated under a soft budget constraint and were under no particular pressure to repay. While firms still competed for money, they did so on a bureaucratic, not a market basis.

This system began to undergo reform in the 1980s. The People's Bank of China (PBOC) was carved out from the Ministry of Finance and set up as a central bank in 1984, with conventional banking to be handled by four specialized state-owned banks (the "Big Four") (Lardy 1998; U.S. Commercial Service 2007).

The 1990s saw the emergence of rivals to the Big Four state-owned banks and an effort to move toward more market-based lending. The so-called "policy banks" were created to handle non-market-based lending, and the government authorized the creation of domestic joint-stock banks owned by local governments together with other institutional and occasionally private investors. While these banks may be more profit oriented than the Big Four, they are still subject to significant political influence in their functioning and have not been able to escape the obligation to make "policy loans" (Green 2003a: 22). If local political leaders think a favored enterprise should get a loan, it generally gets it.

In part as a result of these political considerations, bank lending grew faster than the economy during much of the 1990s, and the non-performing loan (NPL) holdings of the banks grew concomitantly. By the late 1990s, the system was insolvent (Green 2003a: 22).

Although the stock markets had been in existence since 1990, it was in 1996 that national leaders, looking for an alternative to bank lending, turned to them as a way of providing a new source of financing for the troubled state sector. This marked the beginning of unequivocal state support for stock markets. It also solidified some key features of the Chinese stock markets: first, that their primary role has been not to allocate capital to the most efficient enterprises, but to raise money for restructuring SOEs (Zhang 2004: 2044), and second, that the state has been both regulator and cheerleader, with the specific mission of keeping stock prices up in order to support the financing of SOEs.

The stock market since the mid-2000s

Given the support China's stock markets have received from the state, it is not surprising that much writing on them assumes that they are critical to the Chinese economy. At least until very recently, this assumption has been questionable.

As of the end of 2005, China's two stock markets listed 1,381 companies, with a circulating share[4] capitalization of 1.06 trillion *yuan* (approximately \$132 billion) (CSRC website, 1 September 2007), or 6 percent of gross domestic product in that year. At that amount, China ranked around twentieth in the world in terms of absolute market capitalization. Looking at market capitalization as a percentage of GDP, the United States showed 150 percent in 2002, while Hong Kong showed 300 percent in 2005. Other transition economies such as the Czech Republic and Russia each show about 25 percent. In short, the stock market is not large by any measure.

Why, then, were there at the same time widespread claims that China's market capitalization was about US\$500 billion (e.g., Bai *et al.* 2003; AFP 2006; Securities Industry Association 2003), ranking China ahead of Hong Kong and behind only Japan in Asia? The answer is that such claims unrealistically valued non-circulating shares as if they were circulating shares. All the available empirical evidence shows that non-circulating shares—historically as much as two-thirds of capital stock—sell at a large discount to circulating shares, sometimes by as much as 90 percent (Chen and Xiong 2002; Chen *et al.* 2000).[5] An economically realistic valuation would therefore be much lower.

Beginning in the spring of 2006, the market capitalization of Chinese listed companies, however measured, rose dramatically. In the 14 months from the end of March 2006 to the end of May 2007, the market capitalization with all shares valued (unrealistically) equally rose from 3.54 trillion *yuan* (US\$468 billion) to 17.8 trillion *yuan* (US\$2.36 trillion). The market capitalization of circulating shares rose from 1.23 trillion *yuan* (US\$164 billion) to 5.94 trillion *yuan* (US\$786 billion) in the same period (CSRC website, 1 September 2007). This certainly makes Chinese stock markets more important than previously. At the same time, however, the current market surge may be a bubble.[6] By some measures, Chinese market capitalization exceeded Japan's as of late August 2007 (Dyer 2007a), a result that seems hard to justify.[7]

In terms of funds raised for investment, the stock markets do not loom large. In 2002, for example, the stock market provided only about 5 percent of external corporate financing: US\$8.9 billion compared with US\$217.7 billion from bank loans (Green 2003b; Green 2003a: 29; Allen, Qian, and Qian 2002: 17–19). More recently, statistics for the first quarter of 2006 show that bank loans constituted an overwhelming 91.3 percent of external financing for non-financial institutions[8] in China, compared with a paltry 0.5 percent share for equities (PBOC 2006: 13). On the whole, then, "[b]oth the scale and relative importance (compared with other channels of financing) of China's external markets are not significant." (Allen, Qian, and Qian 2005: 73.)

There are many reasons for the tiny amount of investment funded through equity issues. One is, of course, simply the youth of China's stock markets—they have been around only since the early 1990s. But there is more to it than that. More important is that equity financing has been repressed through state regulation.

First, initial public offerings were subject to a state-administered quota until 2000, and even now must be approved by the China Securities Regulatory Commission (CSRC), which continues to exercise control over the number and type of listings (Pistor and Xu 2004; Green 2003a: 160–4). Because the key role of the stock market is to raise funds for restructured SOEs (Green 2003a: 22), it is necessary to restrict the supply of equity securities in order to keep prices high. And prices have been high: in September 2002, for example, the average price/earnings (PE) ratio of Chinese listed companies was 40 to 50, and one in seven companies had a PE ratio of over 100 (Walter and Howie 2003: 136).[9]

Second, a significant portion of the stock of listed companies—approximately two-thirds—has been kept off the markets in non-circulating form. Even when SOEs listed, therefore, their state shareholders were forbidden by state policy from listing more than about one-third of their shares. This policy stemmed from a fear of privatization.

Third, regulations on share issues have a strong paternalistic flavor and attempt to make investment in securities as safe as possible. Prior to the 2005 revisions to the Company Law and the Securities Law, companies wishing to make a public issue of stock had to show profits for the preceding three years.[10] Such a rule favors established, stable companies such as large SOEs—precisely the companies that probably already have reasonably good access to bank loans. It automatically rules out young companies or companies whose business plan calls for initial losses funded by equity, to be set off by later profits. In other words, equity financing in the stock market has in principle been conceived as a supplement to debt financing, not as an alternative source of financing for companies that are, for one reason or another, unsuited to debt financing.

This bias has consequences not only for the economy—new firms whose main asset is the opportunity for growth will find it especially hard to get off the ground (La Porta *et al.* 2000: 19)—but for corporate governance as well. To the extent that the equity markets remain dominated by firms with a large state ownership stake, the rules and practices governing the relationships among minority shareholders, controlling shareholders, directors, supervisors, and management will have to take account of the special character of the controlling shareholder—a state institution. Moreover, what happens on the circulating share market will have a smaller disciplining effect upon management when the proportion of shares on that market is so small.

What about investors? China is often said to have 60 to 70 million stock market investors (see, e.g., Beijing Modern Business News 2005). This is, however, a wholly fanciful number based, among other things, on the premise that each stock account equals a separate investor, a transparently false assumption—investors typically hold an account at each of China's two stock exchanges—that was debunked years ago in both Chinese (e.g., Tianjin Daily 2001) and English sources. In 2003, Walter and Howie (2003: 48), on the basis of a variety of data, put the number of actual holders of shares at five to ten million, and estimated the number of active traders to be from 500,000 to two million.

The 2007 stock market boom did bring many new investors into the market,[11] but still far fewer than is commonly assumed. As noted above, many investors hold duplicate accounts—one in Shanghai and one in Shenzhen—and some control many more than two. And remarkably, fully two-thirds of existing stock accounts *hold no stock at all*—possibly being held in reserve for market manipulation (Kroeber 2007).

Moreover, the picture of the average investor as a naive retiree staking his retirement savings is false. Only 17 percent are over 55, and they tend to play the market as a pastime, like bingo.[12] Institutional investors, not fickle individuals, play the dominant role in market movements (Hong Kong Stock Exchange 2004).

Understanding who the investors are and how they behave has critical implications for corporate governance. First, it helps us understand whether equity markets can in fact serve a disciplining function. Do they respond to failures of corporate governance? Second, it helps us to assess the necessity and urgency of measures to help the small investor who, in the popular image of the stock market, is getting roughed up by the big boys. If small investors gave up hope and left, would it matter?

Current research presents a mixed picture. Knowledgeable commentators agree that institutional investors, not fickle individuals, play a large role in market movements. And the trading strategy they adopt is largely speculative: the average holding period in China is about one to two months, compared with 18 months in the United States (Xu and Wang 1999).[13] In addition, China's stock markets have a high degree of synchronicity: one study found that 80 percent of the stocks listed on the two exchanges moved in the same direction in a given week (Morck *et al.* 2000; see also Durnev *et al.* 2004 and Fox *et al.* 2003). This degree of synchronicity is the second highest among stock markets in 40 countries; it suggests that stock prices move in response to information about the market in general, not about specific firms (Chang and Wong 2003: 25). In other words, Chinese investors rationally worry more about the latest twists and turns in government policy or other market-level rumors than about corporate results.

Although the above picture is the dominant one, it may not be entirely accurate. Studies have found, among other things, that investors pay a premium for better-governed companies (Bai *et al.* 2003: 22) and that they react to accounting numbers (Chen *et al.* 1999)—a seemingly banal result, but one that is inconsistent with the thesis that investors don't care about fundamentals.

Inconsistent as some of these findings are, it is nevertheless possible to draw a few tentative conclusions from existing research. First, the picture of the Chinese stock market as solely speculative is probably overstated. Investors are more concerned with fundamentals and governance than observers give them credit for. Thus, good governance will ultimately be rewarded.

Second, while a great deal of speculation does take place on the market, it is driven by institutional investors, not individuals. Therefore, current government policy—which blames individuals for speculation and attempts to curb it by encouraging institutional investors who will, it is assumed, take a longer-term perspective—is unlikely to be successful.

Third, policymakers in the field of corporate governance should not worry so much about the small investor.[14] He is not a major source of funds, and in any case can be no more than a price taker. Contrary to government fears, a market downswing will not bring 100 million angry citizens into the street protesting the loss of their life savings. It would, of course, create massive discontent among a small elite of the wealthy and powerful, which may be an equally good explanation of government fear of a falling market. But it is not the same thing.

Banks

Capital structure can be a source of oversight: a corporation with dispersed ownership and low leverage is one in which the managers have a great deal of slack. Conversely, high debt levels can mean close monitoring by creditors. While creditors monitor in their own interests, and not those of the shareholders, their interests are sufficiently congruent most of the time to be beneficial to shareholders.

In many economies, banks play a critical role in corporate governance (Gray 1997). Unlike small shareholders, they are both able and willing to monitor the financial health of their debtors. Moreover, academic research suggests that investment financed with bank debt tends to be more efficient than investment financed with retained earnings, probably because the former must be justified to a possibly skeptical third party, whereas management's use of retained earnings is subject to no oversight (Jensen 1986).

Banks may also be sufficiently dubious of a prospective borrower's financial health to refuse to lend at all, thus hastening the departure of a poorly run or otherwise inefficient company from the economy. And they may themselves be major shareholders, as in Germany or Japan,[15] although not in the United States (Roe 1994).

Chinese banks, however, have historically been incapable of playing this monitoring role. This is because they lacked both the ability to monitor and the incentive to do so.

As discussed above, the traditional role of banks was that of cashiers for the state. Even after the reforms of the 1980s, lending decisions were based on political criteria and the perceived needs of SOE borrowers, not on the prospect of the loan being repaid from the proceeds of whatever project it was used to fund (Su 2000).

Bankers thus did not have the tools to understand whether a loan was being put to good use or not; that was not a question with which they were intended to concern themselves, and the accounting system at the time would not have provided an answer.[16] They were simply to supply the money when ordered to do so. Nor did they need to worry about defaults; profit was simply not the objective and played no significant part in the evaluation of bank executives.

The result of all this is that banks have lacked what might be called a culture of monitoring (Chow and Fung 1998; Tian and Lau 2001). The very lack of a monitoring culture in banks has shaped corporate law significantly, as the state has tried to do through corporate law what the banks seem incapable of doing for themselves: protecting their interests as creditors.[17] In other words, far from enlisting the help of active banks in monitoring corporations, China's corporate law sees them as passive victims that need protection.

Recent scholarship suggests that the value of bank monitoring in Germany and Japan is much less than was supposed during the 1980s, when German and Japanese corporate governance models were in vogue.[18] If German and Japanese banks find it hard to monitor effectively, it is unrealistic to expect Chinese banks to manage. And because banks are still often required to lend for political reasons, the result is that corporate management has been subject to the discipline neither of the credit market when seeking a loan nor of lender monitoring after obtaining it.

Asset management companies

A possible substitute for banks as monitors has been the four asset management companies (AMCs), one corresponding to each of the Big Four banks, created in 1999 as part of a plan to recapitalize the state banking sector. The AMCs, organized as wholly state-owned non-bank financial institutions in corporate form owned (it appears) by the Ministry of Finance (MOF), were capitalized at 10 billion *yuan* each by the MOF. They then purchased, at face value, some 1.4 trillion *yuan* in non-performing loans from their corresponding banks, paying with ten-year bonds that they issued with a soft guarantee from the MOF. The intent was that the AMCs would then use their position as creditors (or as owners via debt-for-equity swaps) to force restructuring on the debtor enterprises.[19] The AMC could then sell its interest in the now valuable enterprise to an outside investor.

Unfortunately, some—not all—of the same problems that prevented banks from being effective monitors have also stymied the AMCs, most notably the political clout of the debtor enterprises and their government owners (Studwell 2002: 259–260; Tenev and Zhang 2002: 63–64). An account of the efforts of one of them, Huarong, is worth quoting in full:

> Monkey King Group (MKG), an industrial conglomerate from Yichang city in Hubei province, is one of the country's 512 key SOEs and one of the big SOEs to benefit from the debt-for-equity swap scheme put in place by the central government. In August 2000, China Huarong Asset Management Company bought 622 million RMB in MKG debt from The Industrial and Commercial Bank of China (ICBC). Since then, Huarong, the main creditor of the group, has been unable to press MKG into a drastic restructuring plan. On the contrary, with the approval of Yichang city officials, in December 2000, MKG started a huge asset stripping manoeuvre that has shrunk group assets from 2.42 billion RMB to 371 million RMB, according to Huarong. MKG then petitioned for bankruptcy to escape a restructuring plan coming from its main creditor Huarong, without informing the board of directors of its listed company. Last March, Huarong publicly questioned the fairness of the liquidation committee appointed by Yichang court, as it was composed only of representatives of local government agencies.
>
> (OECD 2002: 180, citing Miller 2001)

Board of directors and board of supervisors

A key institution of corporate governance is an internal oversight body such as a board of directors and, in China, a board of supervisors. These function, ideally, as a committee of the shareholders, and represent an attempt to overcome the costliness of monitoring by individual shareholders. Needless to say, there are many obstacles to the effective functioning of the board in this way—management typically has a great deal of control over the election process, and thus can generally seat its preferred candidates when shareholding is widely dispersed (Bebchuk 2007).

Independent directors

Chinese corporate governance has high expectations for independent directors. In 2001, the CSRC issued a "Guidance Opinion" (*zhidao yijian*) calling for listed companies to have a one-third independent board by mid-2003, and virtually all have complied at least in form.[20]

Despite the attention devoted to independent directors, it is unlikely that they can play their hoped-for role. An important reason is that the Chinese independent director system does not provide for a good way of policing independence to ensure that it is genuine. The CSRC must vet candidates, it is true, but as a practical matter the CSRC cannot possibly know both before election and on a continuing basis whether directors meet the criteria, both in name and in fact, for independence.

Consider, by way of contrast, the American system of *disinterested* directors. In making their votes highly desirable as a way of insulating conflict-of-interest transactions from substantive scrutiny, corporate law gives them a role that requires, in case of dispute, examination of the degree to which they actually were disinterested in the transaction in question. Chinese corporate law—in this sense like the New York Stock Exchange rules on independent directors, among others—simply requires that directors meet some criterion of independence, but fails to provide a meaningful policing mechanism.[21]

The votes of independent directors in Chinese corporate law have no special significance. The CSRC has indeed attempted to legislate in this area by stating, in its Several Provisions on Strengthening the Rights and Interests of Public Shareholders (CSRC 2004), that several matters must be approved by a majority of independent directors. Yet what will happen if they are not? The CSRC's authority to legislate such substantive corporate governance rules is uncertain. It cannot nullify a material transaction between a firm and an affiliate that was undertaken without the desired independent director approval, nor can it make rules giving shareholders grounds to sue for the same event.

In short, if independent directors are an institutional solution to vertical agency problems, China has gone only half way: it has provided the form of the institution, but has not provided the accompanying institutions that would give it life and significance.

Board of supervisors

Another potential institutional solution to the agency problem is the board of supervisors (*jianshi hui*).[22] Chinese commentators often compare China's two-tier governance model to Germany's, where the law mandates a dual-board system for large publicly held corporations, but the similarities in fact are few. In Germany, each corporation has an elected supervisory board (*Aufsichtsrat*), which appoints a managing board (*Vorstand*) composed of senior managers. The supervisory board's job is to oversee the management of the company (Law on Stock Corporations § 111(1)), and its major powers are the power to appoint and dismiss members of the managing board and the power to represent the company in its dealings with members of the management board (Oppenhoff and Verhoeven 2003: § 24.03). The law explicitly allocates managerial power to the managing board (Law on Stock Corporations § 76(1)).

While German law gives real power to the supervisory board, the Company Law of China expects that the board of supervisors will perform a supervisory role essentially by simply saying that it will, without actually giving the board any significant powers or providing structurally for its independence from those it supervises. Like the board of directors, the board of supervisors is elected by shareholders.[23] There is no reason to expect that the interests that dominate director voting will fail to dominate supervisor voting. Moreover, in enterprises dominated by state ownership, supervisors are enterprise employees and are subordinate to the enterprise chief. Not surprisingly, they bend to his wishes (Jiang 2001; Gao 2002: 9; Wang and Feng 2002: 120).

As a result of these problems, the board of supervisors appears to play no important role in corporate governance in China. Indeed, the impetus behind the independent director drive has been the hope that they will play the monitoring role that the board of supervisors has been unable to play.

The large shareholder as monitor: the state

Large shareholders can often be reasonably effective in monitoring corporate managers; if they do not abuse their control rights, their efforts benefit small shareholders as well. In China, the dominant shareholder in listed companies is often a state body. Commentators often point to this absence of an ultimate human principal with rights to residual earnings at the top of the chain of agents as the reason for ineffective monitoring. But many non-profit organizations operate successfully without such an ultimate principal. On the other hand, it is clear that in fact the state often *is* ineffective; it is not collective action problems that prevent effective shareholder monitoring, since there is a large and possibly sole shareholder, but rather organizational problems internal to that shareholder. The result is the phenomenon of the "absent owner" (*suoyouzhe quewei*). What are these problems?

First, the state often simply does not want to encourage the profit-maximizing behavior that minority shareholders value. But even when it does, it suffers significant disabilities as a monitor.

It may, for example, have inconsistent and incommensurable goals, such as full urban employment, efficient operations, and a bar on foreign ownership or control for reasons of national security. But even if the state as principal had mutually consistent and easily measurable goals, its agents—the monitors of the enterprise managers—might not monitor well for those goals. First, the monitoring individuals may well be locally employed and salaried, while the formal ownership of the shares is lodged in a higher level of government. A monitor responsible to local government will not object to corporate policies such as high employment that are beneficial to local government at the expense of the central state shareholder. Second, a monitor working in a government agency may be less able to distinguish good from bad corporate policy than a monitor in a business-oriented institutional shareholder.[24] Third, an individual monitoring on behalf of the state is much less likely to have someone at some point above him in the chain of command making a strong demand for good corporate performance in companies held by the state.

Finally, the devolution of managerial authority has occurred in tandem with economic reform measures that have legalized new forms of trade and new privately controlled entities to which stripped assets can, by means of controlled transactions, be transferred. The complexity of property relations and ownership forms has outstripped the state's capacity to monitor, which remains designed for the simple structures of an earlier day, when private ownership of significant property was not allowed, and transfers between enterprises were physical and not financial (Ding 2000).

Shareholder coalescence devices

Corporate governance is enhanced by institutions that allow for the coalescence of shareholders and thus potentially overcome the monitoring problems of the small shareholder (Roe 2004: 10). Such institutions include proxy fights and takeovers: while it may not pay a small shareholder to figure out how the company could be run better, it may pay an outsider to do so if he can buy up the shares and reap the benefit. This set of institutions has its own costs, of course: if concentrated shareholding were free, we would never see dispersed shareholding.

So far, at least, there is no hostile takeover activity to speak of in China. When listed companies were takeover targets, this was typically so that the acquirer could obtain a "backdoor" listing and thus have access to the stock market without having to gain approval itself. In addition, recall that typically only one-third of listed company stock is actually available as circulating stock, with the rest held as state or legal-person shares by a small number of shareholders. If they are contented with management, they will not sell to a hostile bidder. If they are not contented with management, they have the power to change it. In short, in the great majority of listed companies, a particular management team would not be in place if it were not performing to the satisfaction of the holders of a majority of shares.

Even if more shares were available on the market, one study found a negative correlation between performance and the proportion of shares traded on the market (Chen 2001: 68–69). This suggests that management does not perceive a large number of circulating shares as a threat to its tenure.

Management compensation arrangements

A common method of tying management incentives to shareholder interests is through compensation arrangements, such as those that tie salary to stock price performance. Among those in China who recognize that the separation of ownership from control is an unavoidable problem, a frequently mooted solution is simply to make managers more like owners by giving them an equity stake in the firm. For example, Yang and Zhang (2000: 18) suggest letting large stockholders take on management roles and letting some managers be large stockholders. The first part of this solution is unexceptionable if understood to mean that corporate governance policy should not fear the role that can be played by large shareholders with an interest to protect.

The second prong of their solution is more problematic. If directors and other senior officers are not rich enough to own significant amounts of stock, should stock in such large amounts as to be significant be simply given to them? It might provide directors with more incentives, but would also involve a shockingly immense transfer of wealth to them.

Even a tiny percentage ownership stake in a listed company is a huge amount, given the amounts of money involved. A commonly suggested target for management ownership is 1 percent. If we value listed companies conservatively—at only the value of circulating shares—the total comes to about US$731 billion, or about US$495 million for each of the 1,477 listed companies.[25] To give management 1 percent means handing over on average about US$4.95 million. Surely a reduction in agency costs can be purchased more cheaply.

Moreover, such a small stake cannot be expected to have an appreciable effect on management incentives. A manager holding a 1 percent interest who expropriates US$100 from shareholders will still net US$99. Yang and Zhang (2000) themselves note that a CEO with a 25 percent interest in the company still has a large incentive to engage in expropriating transactions. Yet giving CEOs a big enough stake to make a real difference—say, 50 percent—is not just unrealistic and unjust, but also unnecessary. Other institutions manage to procure reasonable performance from their agents for less than this, and there is no reason why Chinese corporations cannot manage to do so as well.

Gatekeepers (1): lawyers and accountants

Persons and institutions involved in information distribution and gate-keeping—including lawyers, accountants, securities analysts, underwriters, and the financial press—play an important role in corporate governance in many jurisdictions. The theory is that because they are repeat players whose income depends on reputation, the gains from maintaining that reputation will outweigh the gains from defecting and cooperating in fraud and mismanagement. Corporate insiders, it is thought, have the opposite set of incentives (Gilson and Kraakman 1984: 595–607).[26]

To perform their function, all of these must of course be appropriately motivated. If lawyers and accountants bear no responsibility for their opinions, one cannot expect them to press their corporate clients to correct a state of affairs that damages shareholders. Similarly, one cannot expect much from the financial press if the rewards for providing accurate information are less than the rewards for not doing so.

Neither the legal nor the accounting professions in China are yet well equipped to play an effective gatekeeper role. The Securities and Exchange Commission has been able to farm out much of its supervisory burden to both professions in the United States because they are capable of handling the task. By contrast, China's lawyers are few in number and, like its accountants, not trained to handle complex financial matters.[27] The law schools do not teach such topics, and the modern legal profession has not yet accumulated enough experience to enable juniors to learn from seniors on the job.

The position of the accounting profession is even worse.[28] China suffers from an acute shortage of qualified accountants (Jopson 2006). A 2001 study of 32 randomly selected audit reports found "gravely inaccurate errors" in 23 of them (Hu 2002a). So bad did things become that then-Premier Zhu Rongji called for foreign auditing firms to conduct supplemental audits of all listed firms in China (Hu 2002b; McGregor 2002). And the securities industry seems almost beyond redemption: a CSRC investigation revealed that in the notorious market manipulation scheme of Lü Liang, 125 securities firms actively assisted him (Walter and Howie 2003: 156–157).

As suggested above, lawyers and accountants cannot be expected to play a gatekeeping role if they bear little or no penalty for failing to do so. The system in China imposes few such penalties. While law firms and accounting firms may occasionally be sanctioned by the CSRC, I know of no lawsuits by misled investors against either. And firms seeking listings continue to use the same group of law and accounting firms without suffering any apparent penalty in the market (Irvin 2005).

Gatekeepers (2): the financial press

A critical part of a healthy corporate governance system is information that is both demanded by and accessible to investors and other participants in the corporate enterprise. And a key institution in both creating or assembling information and making it accessible is an independent and competitive press (Black 2001: 798–799).

The story of China's financial press in terms of these desiderata is a mixed one. On the one hand, the last several years have seen a mushrooming of newspaper, journals, and websites purveying information about economic and financial issues. In addition to the most well-known journal, *Caijing* ("Finance and Economy"), these media include *21st Century Economic Report* (*21 Shiji Jingji Baodao*), *China Securities News* (*Zhongguo Zhengquan Bao*), *Economic Daily* (*Jingji Ribao*), *Securities Times* (*Zhengquan Shibao*), and *New Fortune* (*Xin Caifu*). There is no doubt that these media compete with each other, and *Caijing* in particular has produced some solid journalism with several exposés.[29]

On the other hand, these media all owe their existence to some kind of formal or informal government affiliation; one cannot simply decide to start a newspaper in China. Beyond the possible inhibiting influence of ownership ties, it must further be remembered that the state insists in principle on control over all information.[30] This control is a cornerstone of the Communist Party's system of political control and is unlikely to disappear before the Party itself.

In the early days of China's financial press, it was regulated quite strictly by the CSRC—in the interests not of accuracy but of stability (Hu 2003: 64). Following an exposé by *Caijing* of a scandal involving massive market manipulation by investment funds (Ping and Li 2000), however, the CSRC under Zhou Xiaochuan began to appreciate the positive role that could be played by the financial press and loosened the reins. This led to *Caijing*'s most famous scoop, the exposure of fraudulent dealings at Guangxia Corporation of Yinchuan (also known as Yinguangxia).

At present, however, *Caijing*'s successes are more exceptional than typical, and financial reporting remains hobbled in significant ways. Objective reporting is hampered by corruption: favorable press coverage can often be obtained, and unfavorable coverage suppressed, for a price (Liebman 2005: 39–40). Many financial reporters lack training in the field, resulting in superficial coverage. Journals that publish unwelcome stories may find themselves sued for libel (Liebman 2006: 69).

The picture is not completely bleak—in a recent libel case based on unfavorable press coverage, the court found that journalists should be immune from suit if their reporting is backed by a source that is reasonable and credible and not based simply on rumors.[31] Nevertheless, the overwhelming fact is continuing political restraints on what may or may not be published, a fact that is known and to some degree accepted by all, or at least most, within the industry.

Conclusion

This chapter has examined the non-state institutional environment for Chinese corporate governance. Several institutional approaches to corporate governance are possible, chief among them an ownership approach, a shareholder rights approach, and a market monitoring approach. A given jurisdiction will typically display a mix.

The institutions of ownership can play a monitoring function when there is concentrated ownership, and it pays the dominant shareholder to expend resources in monitoring because it will reap all or most of the benefit. This kind of monitoring need rely neither on minority shareholder rights nor on market signals in order to discipline management; the owner is already in charge and does not need the help of courts, and it can receive from its own analysis the signals that would otherwise be transmitted by the market.

The ownership approach does not, however, come free. Holders of large blocks of shares are less able to enjoy the benefits of a diversified risk-reducing portfolio. Companies too large for any single owner to control cannot use this governance method. And to the extent that the owner undertakes its own analysis instead of relying on market signals, it must expend resources instead of free riding on the activity of others.

Finally, while concentrated ownership can mitigate one set of agency costs—vertical, between managers and shareholders as a body—it can exacerbate another set—horizontal, between dominant shareholders and minority shareholders. As the former decrease, the latter may increase. Which effect will outweigh the other cannot be known a priori.

The shareholder rights approach attempts to solve the problems of minority shareholders who cannot avail themselves of ownership rights—not only do they not have the rights of owners, but they also do not have the same incentives as owners. If minority shareholders can enlist the aid of the legal system at an acceptable cost, however (including the cost of informing themselves), they can protect their interests and both correct and deter management misbehavior.

Like the ownership approach, however, this approach has its characteristic costs. The more power minority shareholders have to protect their legitimate rights, the more power they have to pursue illegitimate claims as well for their nuisance value. A corporation whose shareholders enjoy the fullest complement of rights is a paralyzed corporation. People rationally choose to hold a security that does not grant all the rights they might like for themselves because they know that other investors are similarly constrained. The key, therefore, is to strike the right balance.

Where that balance should be struck, however, will differ across jurisdictions, because the availability of substitutes will differ. If there is a good substitute for minority shareholder rights, then there is little reason to pay the cost of an extensive panoply of rights because the marginal benefit thereby purchased will be small.

This consideration leads to the third approach to corporate governance: the market monitoring approach. As discussed above, a firm operates in a number of markets that impose objective constraints on its management. At the most obvious level, the stock market and not management has the final word on the appropriate value of a company's stock. When markets are functioning well, monitoring is much simpler. If stockholders wish to judge whether the CEO's salary is excessive, they can look at salaries in comparable companies.

Needless to say, knowing that a CEO is paid too much is not the same as being able to do something about it, so the existence of a managerial labor market is not a complete corporate governance solution. But if the stock market shares this knowledge, then the stock price is discounted accordingly, and those who buy after this knowledge is incorporated into the stock price are not harmed by it. Thus, the small investor can free-ride off the valuation efforts of market professionals, and to the extent that the stock market effectively disciplines managers (and dominant shareholders if management does their bidding), the small investor needs no special protections.

Where does China fit into all this? For all the attention it receives, the shareholder rights approach—indeed, any approach that relies upon formal legal institutions—cannot be expected to form the mainstay of an effective corporate governance regime. The courts have neither the power nor the inclination to play a major role, and government agencies such as the CSRC do not have the resources to serve as a substitute.[32]

Nor does the ownership approach hold out much hope. At present, dominant shareholders seem either to abuse their control or to fail to exercise it entirely. There are two possible ways in which these problems could be remedied. The state could improve its internal management system so that it became a more effective monitor in the companies it dominated. Such a reform is imaginable, but fails to address the issue of abuse of control. The control of abuses rests ultimately, like the shareholder rights approach, on legal institutions—and as argued above, legal institutions are a weak reed on which to rely.

Unfortunately, the best available substitute approach, that of market monitoring, is disfavored by the state. The Chinese state prefers direct regulation by government agencies first, and indirect regulation by private litigation in the state's courts next. Regulation by the uncontrolled institutions of the market comes a distant third, and indeed it is hard to find such institutions in China. The stock markets are creatures of the state and exist only upon its sufferance; securities firms are established and owned by various governmental bodies; banks are either directly owned or else highly controlled by governmental bodies; the financial press is subject to significant state influence, both through ownership channels and through the state's pervasive regulation of the media.

In a state with limited administrative resources, it would make sense to rely as far as possible on the contributions of non-state actors. But Chinese corporate governance institutions are tilted toward the legal because the government generally suspects the institutions of the market and civil society in general. It wants rules, not incentive structures. There is an excessive emphasis on getting the rules right, and an inadequate attention to institutions that could be flexible in creating and enforcing rules as the situation warranted.

The Asian financial crisis of 1997–1998 gave governments of the region good reason to be concerned with corporate governance issues. Weak corporate governance, insofar as it saps the confidence of investors in their ability to forestall managerial expropriation, can exacerbate such crises (Johnson *et al.* 2000).[33] When times are good, insiders refrain from excessive expropriation of outsiders because they desire future financing and care about their reputation. As future prospects deteriorate, however, an endgame situation appears, and insiders step up their expropriation. This is perceived, and perhaps even foreseen, by investors, who attempt to liquidate their positions as soon as possible (calling loans that can be called in the case of banks and selling stock in the case of equity investors). This pushes the firm nearer to collapse and the stock price further down. As the lack of sound corporate governance is a national problem, there are no attractive alternative investments domestically, so the withdrawn capital flees, exacerbating the collapse of the currency as it goes.

That corporate governance is a matter of public as well as private concern, however, does not mean that the only or best solution to corporate governance problems is a public one initiated by the state. An important part of any solution to China's corporate governance problems, given its current set of administrative and legal institution, lies not in the state's actively beefing up those institutions, but simply in its relaxing its hostility to civil society institutions and understanding that corporate governance is too important a matter to be left solely to the state.

Notes

1 A partial exception is Liebman and Milhaupt (2007)—partial because the authors examine sanctions imposed by China's stock exchanges, which are quasi-governmental bodies.
2 See, for example, Xu and Li (2001), who cite with approval tests developed in U.S. law such as "interest or expectancy," "line of business," and "fairness."
3 See, for example, Elster (1986), who questions the applicability of the biological analogy to economic activity on the grounds that the economic environment changes rapidly relative to the speed with which inefficient firms are eliminated from competition, and that therefore at any given time we are likely to observe efficient and inefficient firms coexisting.
4 Listed company shares in China were traditionally classified as circulating or non-circulating. Circulating shares, as the name suggests, are available for trading on the public markets. Until very recently, however, they typically represented only one-quarter to one-third of the total share capital of listed companies. The rest was in the form of non-circulating shares that, with minor exceptions, could be held only by state entities (state shares) or other corporate entities (legal person shares). Such shares are highly illiquid. For a fuller account of share types, see Walter and Howie (2003: 71–87). At present, reforms are underway to gradually convert all non-circulating shares to circulating shares. Many shares have been reclassified as "circulating" shares, although some are still subject to lock-ups and may not yet be freely sold. At the time of this writing (September 2007), the website of the China Securities Regulatory Commission (CSRC) shows the market capitalization of circulating shares to be just one-third the value of total market capitalization (valuing all shares as circulating shares), showing that it defines as non-circulating about two-thirds of the outstanding shares of listed companies.
5 Chen and Xiong (2002) found that the non-tradable state-owned shares and legal-person shares in China on average had a 70–80 percent illiquidity discount when they were traded on informal markets. Walter and Howie (2003: 186) also present data for sales of legal-person shares in three companies, showing discounts of between 76 and 83 percent. For more extended discussions of how to value listed companies, see Green (2003b) and Walter and Howie (2003: 188–189).

6 I write this, of course, at the risk of looking very foolish by the time this chapter appears in print, since by then we will know whether it was a bubble or not.

7 In the words of Fraser Howie, a long-time observer of the Chinese market quoted in the story, "All reality has been suspended in China." (Dyer 2007a.)

8 Non-financial institutions include households, enterprises, and government agencies.

9 Although the authors do not specify, they are probably referring to the mean PE ratio. A better number, because not skewed by extremes, would be the median PE ratio; it might be lower.

10 Company Law (1993), art. 137. The 1993 version of the Company Law was amended in 2005, effective as of 2006 (Company Law 2005). Article 137 of the 1993 Company Law was removed in the 2005 revisions to the Company Law and the Securities Law (Securities Law 2005). Article 13 of that law required the ability to earn profits continuously and a healthy financial state, but did not specify the three-year rule.

11 For example, in the 18 months from mid-2004 to the end of 2006, the number of stock accounts rose from 71.5 million to 78.5 million. In the next six months, the number shot up to 107 million (CSRC website, 1 September 2007). On a single day—28 May 2007—investors opened 385,000 new accounts (Dyer 2007b). As noted in the text above, however, this is not the same as saying that 385,000 new investors came into the market.

12 For a full analysis of the investor community, see Green (2003b: ch. 4) and Walter and Howie (2003: ch. 7).

13 A subsequent study finds a turnover velocity of 509 percent in 2000 (Chang and Wong 2003); see also Hu (2002c).

14 This is the advice for developing and transition economies generally of Berglöf and von Thadden (1999).

15 For a discussion of various views on the "main bank" system, see Milhaupt (2001).

16 The Chinese accounting system in the pre-reform era was typical for a planned economy: it was about matching sources to uses to monitor the spending of funds as the funder intended. It was not about matching revenues to expenditures to ensure that investments were profitable. See generally Huang and Ma (2001: 25–28).

17 Of course, every mature legal system provides a range of protection for corporate creditors; in the United States, such protection is accomplished largely through state law restrictions on corporate distributions and state and federal rules on fraudulent transfers. In China, however, *corporate law* protection is viewed as necessary to save creditors from their own misguided lending decisions.

18 On the softness of German and Japanese bank monitoring, see Shleifer and Vishny (1997: 773) and the sources cited in La Porta *et al.* (2000: 17–18).

19 For a fuller description, see Asian Development Bank (2003: 58–60) and OECD (2002: 179–181).

20 For a full treatment of independent directors in China, see Clarke (2006), on which much of this discussion is based.

21 I discuss the differences among independent, outside, and disinterested directors in Clarke (2007a).

22 I treat the board of supervisors at greater length in Clarke (2006: 173–175).

23 The Company Law provides that up to one-third of the supervisors shall be elected by the employees of the company (Company Law 1993: art. 124; Company Law 2005: art. 118), but such elections are dominated by management and the supervisors so elected cannot provide an independent check.

24 For a fuller discussion, see Qi *et al.* (2000: 594–595); see also Mar and Young (2001: 282), who state that "although Chinese SOEs [(state-owned enterprises)]

have concentrated ownership (i.e., the state) the potential positive effect of such an arrangement is absent because of the dispersal of state representation. ... In short, many SOEs are simply monitored inadequately or ineffectively."

25 The data are as of 30 June 2007 (CSRC website, 1 September 2007).

26 But see Coffee (2002), who argues that reputation is not as effective a policing mechanism as is commonly assumed.

27 On the capabilities of the Chinese legal profession, see generally Lubman (1999: 157) and Peerenboom (2002: 343–393). On the accounting profession, see Tenev and Zhang (2002: 120–123).

28 See generally Irvin (2005), to which much of the discussion and the citations in this subsection are owed.

29 On *Caijing* and its editor, Hu Shuli, see Chandler (2001).

30 For an overview of Party and government controls over the media, see Liebman (2005: 41–65).

31 The case in question pitted the Guangzhou Huaqiao Real Estate Development Company against the journal *China Reform*. Excerpts from the text of the judgment as well as commentary by prominent attorney Pu Zhiqiang, who appeared for the defendants, can be found at www.epochtimes.com/gb/4/10/18/n694419.htm.

32 There is not space here to make this argument in detail; I do so in another unpublished paper (Clarke 2007b). Nicholas Howson's chapter in this volume lists several interesting cases bearing on the issue of court enforcement of shareholder rights, but in only three (perhaps four—one case report is unclear) of those cases can courts be said to have found a breach of duty to shareholders.

33 According to Johnson and his colleagues, governance variables such as investor protection indices and the quality of law enforcement are powerful predictors of the extent of market declines during the Asian financial crises, and explain the decline better than the macroeconomic variables that have been the usual focus of the policy debate.

Bibliography

AFP [Agence France-Presse] (2006) "China to Complete State-Share Reforms This Year," China Daily, internet edn, 24 April.

Allen, Franklin, Jun Qian, and Meijun Qian (2002) "Law, finance, and economic growth in China," Wharton Financial Institutions Center working papers series, No. 02–44 (23 December 2002). Online at http://fic.wharton.upenn.edu/fic/papers/02/0244.pdf.

—— (2005) "Law, finance, and economic growth in China," *Journal of Financial Economics* 77: 57–116.

Asian Development Bank (2003) "Asian Development Bank, private sector assessment: People's Republic of China."

Bai, Chong-En *et al.* (2003) "Corporate governance and market valuation in China," William Davidson Institute, working paper No. 564. Online at http://ssrn.com/abstract=393440.

Bebchuk, Lucien (2007) "The myth of the shareholder franchise," *Virginia Law Review* 93: 675–732.

Beijing Modern Business News (2005) "7000 wan gumin qunian meihu junping kuisun 2045 yuan [70 million stock investors lost 2045 yuan per person on average last year]," *Beijing Xiandai Shangbao* [*Beijing Modern Business News*] (5 January).

Berglöf, Erik and Ernst-Ludwig von Thadden (1999) "The changing corporate governance paradigm: implications for transition and developing countries," unpublished manuscript (June).

Black, Bernard S. (2001) "The legal and institutional preconditions of strong securities markets," *UCLA Law Review* 48: 781–855.

Chandler, Clay (2001) "China moves: business magazine thrives by crossing the party line," *Washington Post*, E01 (22 March).

Chang, Eric C. and Sonia M.L. Wong (2003) "Political control and performance in China's listed firms 25" (March). Available at http://www.hiebs.hku.hk/working_papers.asp?ID=89.

Chen, Charles J.P., Shimin Chen and Xijia Su (1999) "Is accounting information value relevant in the emerging Chinese stock market?" Available at http://ssrn.com/abstract=167353.

Chen, Jian (2001) "Ownership structure as corporate governance mechanism: evidence from Chinese listed companies," *Economics of Planning* 34: 53–72.

Chen, Zhiwu and Peng Xiong (2002) "The Illiquidity Discount in China," International Center for Financial Research, Yale University.

Chen, Zhiwu, Peng Xiong and Lin Yang (2000) "Faren gu paimai shizheng yanjiu [Empirical research into auctions of legal person shares]." On file with author.

Chow, Clement Kong Wing and Michael Ka Yiu Fung (1998) "Ownership structure, lending bias, and liquidity constraints: evidence from Shanghai's manufacturing sector," *Journal of Comparative Economics* 26: 301–316.

Clarke, Donald C. (2006) "The independent director in Chinese corporate governance," *Delaware Journal of Corporate Law* 31: 125–228.

—— (2007a) "Three Concepts of the Independent Director," *Delaware Journal of Corporate Law* 32: 73–211.

—— (2007b) "Corporate governance in China: dilemmas of reform and the institutional environment" (unpublished working paper, 2007).

Coffee, John C., Jr. (2002) "Understanding Enron: it's about the gatekeepers, stupid," *The Business Lawyer* 57: 1403–20.

Company Law (1993) "Zhonghua renmin gongheguo gongsi fa [Company Law of the People's Republic of China]" (effective 1 July 1994).

Company Law (2005) "Zhonghua renmin gongheguo gongsi fa [Company law of the People's Republic of China]" (as amended 27 October 2005, effective 1 January 2006).

CSRC [China Securities Regulatory Commission] (2004) "Guanyu fabu 'guanyu jiaqiang shehui gongzhong gu gudong quanyi de ruogan guiding' de tongzhi [Notice on the Issuance of the 'Several provisions on on strengthening the rights and interests of public shareholders']", *Zheng Jian Fa* (2004) No. 18 (7 December).

CSRC [China Securities Regulatory Commission] website. Available at http://www.csrc.gov.cn (accessed various times).

Denis, Diane K. and John J. McConnell (2003) "International corporate governance," *Journal of Financial and Quantitative Analysis* 38: 1–36.

Ding, X.L. (2000) "The illicit asset stripping of Chinese state firms," *China Journal* 43: 1–28.

Durnev, Art, Kan Li, Randall Morck and Bernard Yin Yeung (2004) "Capital markets and capital allocation: implications for economies in transition," *Economics of Transition*, 12(4): 593–634 (December).

Dyer, Geoff (2007a) "Chinese stock market bigger than Japan's," *Financial Times* (29 August).

—— (2007b) "Share trading accounts in China hit 100M," *Financial Times* (29 May).

Elster, Jon (ed.) (1986) *Rational Choice*, New York: New York University Press.

Fox, Merritt, Artyom Durnev, Randall Morck, and Bernard Yeung (2003) "Law, share price accuracy, and economic performance: the new evidence," *Michigan Law Review*, 102: 331–386.

Gao, Yong (2002) "Duli dongshi zhidu yu shangshi gongsi zhili [The Independent Director System and Corporate Governance in Listed Companies]", *Jingji Tizhi Gaige [Economic System Reform]* 1: 8–12.

Gilson, Ronald J. and Reinier H. Kraakman (1984) "The mechanisms of market efficiency," *Virginia Law Review* 70(4): 545–644.

Gray, Cheryl (1997) "Creditors' crucial role in corporate governance," *Finance and Development* 34: 29–32.

Green, Stephen (2003a) "China's stockmarket: eight myths and some reasons to be optimistic," The China Project, Royal Institute of International Affairs and Cambridge University (February).

—— (2003b) "Better than a casino: some good news from the frontline of China's capital market reforms," Royal Institute of International Affairs, Asia Programme, working paper No. 6.

Hong Kong Stock Exchange (2004) "Institutional investors in mainland China" (January). Available at http://www.hkex.com.hk/research/rpapers/IIMC.pdf.

Hu, Bei (2002a) "Mainland companies are reeling from a year of financial scandals during which the audacity of corporate wrongdoers has put their Western counterparts to shame," *South China Morning Post*, 1 (26 March).

—— (2002b) "Tough audit rules eased after outcry from interest groups," *South China Morning Post*, B3 (2 March).

—— (2002c) "Exposure to stocks unhealthy; trading mostly speculative," *South China Morning Post*, B4 (16 April).

Hu, Shuli (2003) "Let there be more light," *China Economic Quarterly* 7: 64–66.

Huang, Allen and Ronald Ma (2001) *Accounting in China in Transition: 1949–2000*, World Scientific Publishing Company Incorporated.

Irvin, Brent (2005) "The ecology of corporate governance in China," unpublished manuscript.

Jensen, Michael and Curtis J. Meckling (1976) "Theory of the firm: managerial behavior, agency costs, and ownership structure," *Journal of Financial Economics* 3: 305–360.

Jensen, Michael C. (1986) "Agency cost of free cash flow, corporate finance and takeovers," *American Economic Review* 76: 323–329.

Jiang, Qiangui (2001) "Gongsi zhili yu guoyu qiye gaige [Corporate governance and state-owned enterprise reform]," *Zhongguo Zhengquan Bao [China Securities News]* internet edn. (12 June).

Johnson, Simon *et al.* (2000) "Corporate governance in the Asian financial crisis," *Journal of Financial Economics* 58: 141–186.

Jopson, Barney (2006) "Beijing in overseas accountancy deal," *Financial Times*, internet edn. (25 July).

Kroeber, Arthur (2007) "China stock frenzy," *Financial Times* (2 July).

La Porta, Rafael *et al.* (1998) "Corporate ownership around the world," Harvard Institute of Economics, research paper No. 1840 (August 1998). Online at http://ssrn.com/abstract=103130.

—— (2000), "Investor protection and corporate governance," *Journal of Financial Economics* 58: 3–27.

Lardy, Nicholas R. (1998) *China's Unfinished Economics Revolution*, Washington, DC: Brookings Institution Press.

Law on Stock Corporations (Germany). *Aktiengesselschaften [Law on Stock Corporations]* (as amended 28 October 1994).

Liebman, Bejamin (2005) "Watchdog or demagogue? The media in the Chinese legal system," *Columbia Law Review* 105: 1–157.

—— (2006) "Innovation through intimidation: an empirical account of defamation litigation in China," *Havard International Law Journal* 47: 33–177.

Liebman, Benjamin L. and Curtis J. Milhaupt (2007) "Reputational sanctions in China's securities market," Columbia Law and Economics working paper. Available at http://ssrn.com/abstract=999698.

Lubman, Stanley (1999) *Bird in a Cage: Legal Reform in China After Mao*, Palo Alto: Stanford University Press.

McGregor, Richard (2002) "Creative Chinese accounting creates work for Andersen," *Financial Times*, 20 (28 January).

Milhaupt, Curtis J. (2001) "On the (fleeting) existence of the main bank system and other Japanese economic institutions," Columbia Law School, Center for Law and Economic Studies, working paper No. 194 (9 November 2001). Online at http://papers.ssrn.com/abstract=290283.

Miller, Matthew (2001) "Real monkey business," *South China Morning Post*, Business Post, 14 (29 March).

Morck, Randall *et al.* (2000) "The information content of stock markets: why do emerging markets have synchronous stock price movement?" *Journal of Financial Economics* 58: 215–260.

OECD [Organization for Economic Cooperation and Development] (2002) *China in The World Economy: The Domestic Policy Challenges*, OECD: Paris.

Oppenhoff, Walter and Thomas O. Verhoeven (2003) "Stock corporations," in Bernd Rüster (ed.), *Business Transactions in Germany*, Matthew Bender.

Peerenboom, Randall (2002) *China's Long March Toward Rule of Law*, Cambridge: Cambridge University Press.

[PBOC] People's Bank of China (2006) "Zhongguo huobi zhengce zhixing baogao er ling ling liu nian diyi jidu 2006 [Report on the implementation of China's monetary policy, first quarter 2006]" (31 May).

Ping, Hu and Jing Li (2000) "Jijin heimu [The inside story on investment funds]," *Caijing [Finance and Economics]*, 31 (5 October). Available at http://www.caijing.com.cn/ele/31.shtml.

Pistor, Katharina and Chenggang Xu (2004) "Governing stock markets in transition economies: lessons from China," Columbia Law and Economics Working Paper No. 262 (November 2004). Online at http://ssrn.com/abstract=628065.

Qi, Daqing *et al.* (2000) "Shareholding structure and corporate performance of partially privatized firms: evidence from listed Chinese companies," *Pacific-Basin Financial Journal* 8: 587–610.

Roe, Mark J. (1994) *Strong Managers, Weak Owners: The Political Roots of American Corporate Finance*, Princeton, NJ: Princeton University Press.

—— (2004) "The institutions of corporate governance," Harvard University, John M. Olin Center for Law, Economics, and Business Discussion Paper No. 488 (August 2004). Online at http://ssrn.com/abstract=612362.

Securities Industry Association (2003) "Written statement of the securities industry association," in *United States-China Economic Relations and China's Role in the*

Global Economy: Hearings Before the House Commission on Ways and Means, 108th Congress. Available at http://www.sia.com/testimony/2003/siatestimony10-03.html.

Securities Law (2005) "Zhonghua renmin gongheguo zhengquan fa [Securities law of the People's Republic of China]" (as amended 27 October 2005, effective 1 January 2006).

Shleifer, Andrei and Robert Vishny (1997) "A survey of corporate governance," *Journal of Finance* 52: 737–783.

Tenev, Stoyan and Chunlin Zhang (2002) *Corporate Governance and Enterprise Reform in China: Building the Institutions of Modern Markets,* Washington, DC: World Bank and International Finance Corporation.

Studwell, Joe (2002) *The China Dream: The Quest for the Last Untapped Market on Earth,* London: Profile Books.

Su, Dongwei (2000) "Corporate finance and state enterprise reform in China" (18 November). Online at http://ssrn.com/abstract=250802.

Tian, Jenny J. and Chung-Ming Lau (2001) "Board composition, leadership structure and performance in Chinese shareholding companies," *Asia Pacific Journal of Management* 18: 245–263.

Tianjin Daily (2001) "Woguo zhen gumin buguo yiqian wan [True shareholders in China not more than ten million]," *Tianjin Ribao [Tianjin Daily]*, 3 (13 December).

U.S. Commercial Service [Department of Commerce] (2007) "Banking—U.S. Commercial Service China." Available at http://www.buyusa.gov/china/en/bank.html (accessed 1 September 2007).

Walter, Carl E. and Fraser J.T. Howie (2003) *Privatizing China: The Stock Markets and Their Role in Corporate Reform,* Indianapolis: John Wiley & Sons.

Wang, Changbo and Hualan Feng (2002) "Lun duli dongshi zhidu yu jianshihui zhidu xiang jiehe de jian guan moshi [On the monitoring model combining the independent director system and the system of the board of supervisors]," *Shengchanli Yanjiu [Research in Productive Forces]* 1: 119–121.

Xu, Xiaonian and Yan Wang (1999) "Ownership structure and corporate governance in Chinese stock companies," *China Economic Review* 10: 75–98.

Xu, Yongqian and Yulong Li (2001) "Gongsi zhili yu gudong baohu [Corporate governance and the protection of shareholders]," paper for 21st Century Commercial Law Forum, Qinghua University (18 November 2001).

Yang, Shuming and Zhang, Ping (2000) "Chongsu gongsi faren zhili jichu xin linian: suoyou yu jingying fenli de tongyi [A new concept for recreating the basis of corporate governance: the unity of the separation of ownership and management]," *Xiandai Faxue [Modern Legal Studies]* 5: 18–21.

Young, Michael N. and Pamela Mar (2001) "Corporate governance in transition economies: a case study of two Chinese airlines," *Journal of World Business* 36: 280–302.

Zhang, Yelin (2004) "The roles of corporatization and stock market listing in reforming China's state industry," *World Development* 32: 2031–2047.

9 The doctrine that dared not speak its name

Anglo-American fiduciary duties in China's 2005 company law and case law intimations of prior convergence

Nicholas Calcina Howson[*]

Introduction

On 27 October 2005, the Standing Committee of the legislature of the People's Republic of China (PRC or China) adopted an amended corporate law statute, changing China's 1994 Company Law[1] almost beyond recognition. The new 2005 Company Law[2] represents a radical shift in the PRC's understanding and implementation of the "modern enterprise system" for China, and a serious challenge for China's untested and politically weak judicial institutions.

Among a large number of important changes in the Company Law of 2005,[3] perhaps the most intriguing is the inclusion of a new Article 148,[4] which for the first time[5] in China's corporate law, directly addresses directors' and officers' fiduciary duties, and in a distinctly Anglo-American way:

> *Article 148.* Directors, supervisory board members and high-level management personnel should abide by laws, administrative regulations and the company articles of association, *and have a duty of loyalty* (*zhongshi yiwu*) *and duty of care* (*qinmian yiwu*) *to the Company.*[6]

A new Article 149 immediately following new Article 148 fleshes out, in statutory form, the specifics of a duty of loyalty concept.

These developments in China present a puzzle of sorts for corporate law convergence and transplant theorists. Many observers would initially understand the injection of fiduciary duties concepts into the 2005 Company Law as an expression of symbolic *formal* convergence and wholesale transplant from an alien legal system—even in the face of indigenous doctrinal objections and well-identified institutional obstacles. Yet, initial research as to how lower-level Chinese courts have actually handled case disputes in the pre-2005 period—presented for the first time in this chapter—shows that the same PRC courts (and China's securities markets regulator) anticipated 2005's major legal change *as early as the mid-1990s*, a full decade before these important doctrines were formally written into

Chinese law. Thus, what many observers have assumed is mere formal convergence or an explicitly rendered transplant may be revealed as something quite different—a *post facto* confirmation of doctrines and methods already applied *spontaneously* by Chinese judges hearing actual cases. This remarkable development path may in turn provide us with new insights as to how corporate law develops in a transitional economy (set in a largely unreconstructed political-legal system), and the ways in which judicial institutions can and must rise to the challenges offered by economic and legal change.

This chapter proceeds as follows: The first section summarizes the process through which corporate fiduciary duties have become a living part of China's reform-era corporate law—formally and pre-formally—and speculates on the true dynamic at work. The following section sets out the formal state of corporate fiduciary duties under China's post-1 January 2006 corporate law. The next two sections then look back to detail the special challenges which should have stymied the introduction of corporate fiduciary duties into the Chinese legal system; and review the basic theoretical literature on corporate law convergence, and the contrasting normative cases for convergence, or divergence, in the Chinese context. The section that follows then addresses the seeming "formal" convergence of China's corporate fiduciary duties law with developed world (and specifically Anglo-American) forms, much in line with the theory summarized in the preceding section. Then, the penultimate section—through the review of actual case reports—addresses the application of corporate fiduciary duties by Chinese judicial actors even *before 2005* to describe a kind of "pre-formal" functional convergence. The final section concludes, and speculates how the processes described in this chapter also inform us about the winning effect of business association law on the general establishment of "rule of law" (and functioning courts) in the PRC, as well as the factors which in practice shape company law convergence or divergence.

Legal development of corporate fiduciary duties

As this chapter will show, China's firm organization and governance has seen a *formal* convergence with the Western shareholder-oriented model, as described in the PRC's national corporate statutes of 1994 and 2005, and abundant China Securities Regulatory Commission (CSRC) regulation commencing in the early 1990s. Notwithstanding that formal or rhetorical convergence, it remains broadly acknowledged that path-dependant factors specific to the Chinese political, economic, and cultural circumstance—both "structure-driven" and "rules-driven" (Bebchuk and Roe 1999)—have inhibited convergence in fact, or what one scholar has called *functional* convergence (Gilson 2001).

The Chinese grappling with the Anglo-American and common law mechanisms summed up by the term "corporate fiduciary duties" demonstrates this. As described in this chapter, the fiduciary duties concept was imported into modern Chinese corporate law in the early 1990s specifically and exclusively to serve the assumed minimum requirements of the international public capital markets for PRC-domiciled issuers accessing foreign (including Hong Kong) capital markets. This importation was first effected via a 1993 letter of comfort provided by China's (then) leading reform commission to the Hong Kong Exchange, glossing China's (then) sole national enactment authorizing the formation of joint stock companies, and then by rules supplementing the 1994 Company Law applicable only to PRC-domiciled firms seeking "overseas" listings. In a parallel development, between the mid-1990s and late 2005 the CSRC worked diligently and often alone to push the formal concept of corporate fiduciary duties into every corner of China's corporate law and regulation (some of that being securities regulation, but applied to corporate governance at listed PRC companies). Yet even this formal invocation of corporate fiduciary duties was problematic and openly resisted, given the prior investment by Chinese academic law specialists (often also serving as legislative drafters) in a different, albeit foreign, doctrinal tradition—the "civil" law system, as construed in what is over-broadly seen even in China as "Asia" (primarily Japan and Taiwan)—and the acknowledged deficiencies of the Chinese judicial system.

Few of the Chinese agents of this transplant or importation in the past decade had any real hopes for substantive implementation, or expectation of claims seeking enforcement, of the fiduciary duties doctrine by government regulators, judges, or shareholder investors. This was due in large part to a realistic and cold-eyed appraisal of the quality, political independence, and competence of China's People's Courts. Thus, the fiduciary duties project as conceived up until late 2005 was almost entirely symbolic—meant to signal "modernity" and perhaps establish greater coherence in China's company law, or indeed to communicate assurances to uneasy public market investors, domestic and foreign.

The same might be said for the sudden appearance after 2005 of Article 148—and specifically Anglo-American fiduciary duties—at least insofar as doctrinal innovation is concerned. Again in 2005 China's law drafters (and now, in a reversal, the Chinese academics supporting them) conspired to signal "modernity" and symbolic assurances regarding the standard whereby corporate fiduciaries may be held accountable *ex post*. Thus, in the still largely symbolic or political sphere, the stubborn application of the (Asian-style) "civil" law-family norms was discarded almost absolutely, and replaced with an explicit and formal recognition of corporate fiduciary standards derived from the Anglo-American and common law traditions. More importantly, this new import (or if not an import, this new declaration of doctrinal affiliation) was embedded in a completely new procedural context, and a vastly expanded role for *ex post* judicial actors—allowing: shareholders' direct action against directors, officers, and supervisory board members; a cause of action based in breach of duties of care and loyalty; a derivative suit mechanism; implicit fiduciary duties for controlling share-holders; and a new basis for piercing of the corporate veil via the courts. Accordingly, while cynics might easily dismiss Article 148 as more empty symbolism—or a continued appeal to Chinese and foreign shareholders anxious to protect firm assets from irresponsible or criminal insiders—the procedural aspects of the 2005 Company Law point to a doctrinal innovation actually meant to be used in real lawsuits by aggrieved shareholders and creditors.

The formal developments summarized here are not at odds with convergence theory as it is applied to corporate law and corporate governance development, whether: initial strong convergence (efficiency-based) ideas; Professor Coffee's softer version (tied to the specific effects of cross-border securities listings or the desire to bring off such listings); or the hankering for common law mechanisms (to build better and more useful securities markets) posited in the work of Professors La Porta, Lopez-de-Silvanes, Schliefer, and Vishny. Stated in summary terms, one might look at the formal adoption of Anglo-American fiduciary duties in China over the past decade as the necessary and expected effect of the following factors: early adoption of the *form* of the shareholder-oriented corporate entity for China as the most efficient and productive organizational model; the explicit and implicit demands of foreign and domestic investors (and securities market regulators); and the desire to employ common-law mechanisms to bring about the most vibrant and allocation-efficient capital markets possible (again, to fuel growth). Each of these motivating forces might be seen to have been opposed—first in form, and increasingly in function—by an abundance of path-dependant factors, including deeply rooted phenomena such as ideological commitment to state ownership and socialist orthodoxy, SOE/Ministry system (*xitong*) loyalty, power already ceded to incumbent management/insiders, traditional (but renascent) Chinese family or village capitalism, poor understanding of rule of law (however defined), and little concept of independent, or even technically sophisticated, civil courts.

The foregoing is all true at the "macro" level, or the level of formal changes and aspirations memorialized in national statutes such as the 2005 Company Law. However, the case opinions analyzed in the Appendix to this chapter reflect a rather different picture at the micro, and effectively pre-formal, levels. In those cases, we see Chinese judges wrestling with corporate fiduciary duties concepts even before they were the official doctrines of the land—in fact, in the complete absence of any fiduciary duties notion in China's corporate law! (This is particularly noteworthy in China's developing legal culture, which continues to require a (positive law) "legal basis" (or *falu yiju*) for application of legal principles.) Moreover, in these cases we are permitted to see judges acting in this manner without reference to foreign law ideas, or even the strong hints that the dogged CSRC attempted to smuggle into the corporate governance scheme for listed companies via insistent use of the characters "*chengxin zeren* and *yiwu*" (Howson 2005). This, then, is the exact opposite of the progress identified by Professors Kanda and Milhaupt with respect to transplant of "duty of loyalty" into Japan's corporate law. In that example, Japan formally instituted a duty of loyalty provision as early as the 1950s, which was only taken notice of and employed several decades later: "for almost forty years after it was transplanted, the duty of loyalty was never separately applied by the Japanese courts, and played little role in Japanese corporate law and governance" (Kanda and Milhaupt 2003: 888). Conversely, China has seen the bold invocation—and application—of fiduciary duties concepts by its poorly regarded judges long before formal inclusion of the doctrine in China's amended company statute (and without reference to what the reformist and very "modern" securities regulator was trying to inject into the mix).

This in turn leads to interesting speculation on how corporate governance reform and convergence really occur in a transitional society such as the PRC. In the Chinese example, we can be sure that Chinese courts before 2005 were not overly influenced—or influenced at all—by the many factors usually invoked for the assumption of a well-developed alien doctrine like common law-style fiduciary duties: outside-in pressures (foreign norms foisted on an underdeveloped system); top-down impositions (whether from a reformist CSRC, foreign transplants pushed by influential academics, or strong directives from the bureaucratically supreme Supreme People's Court in Beijing); as part of a deliberate project to revivify China's domestic markets; or to suit the regulatory imperatives of foreign (transnational) securities regulators. All of these factors can and are invoked as reasons contributing to the *formal* convergence identified in this chapter, capped by the explicit rendering of "duty of care" and "duty of loyalty" (and remedies to match) in China's late 2005 company statute. What, then, accounts for the invocation and use (or lament for the absence of) traditional Anglo-American-style corporate fiduciary duties by the Chinese courts even before the promulgation of the 2005 Company Law of the PRC?

The cases presented here indicate at least one strong reason: the lack of any substitute for corporate fiduciary duties once (formal) *corporatization* had been become official (legal) policy and is truly launched—even if that *corporatization* does not amount to full privatization. With China's *corporatization* program, and the rise of the corporate form in a landscape previously dominated by state-owned enterprises (SOEs), collectives and individual proprietors, a new species of property rights holder—the shareholding investor—required functioning mechanisms to (1) monitor and hold accountable, and (2) check the power and opportunistic behavior of the directors and officers appointed under the new corporate scheme to manage a common pool of assets (and in the Chinese context, state or legal-person majority owners managing such allegedly shared assets directly and without interference from the intervening corporate form).[7] Until 2005, there was no clear statutory basis for that type of accountability or check; nor in China's transitional circumstance were there other norms or established business or ethical practices (much less a tradition of altruism in non-"system" (*xitong*) or non-kinship business association) to serve this function. Finally, no public authority (i.e., the state)—at any level—was competent or independent enough to ensure good governance, for a combination of well-rehearsed reasons: ranging from resource and competency constraints (even for the justice-loving and relatively uncorrupt securities regulator, the CSRC) to the deep conflicts for the state resulting from continued public ownership and control of only nominally *corporatized* assets.[8] China's courts—the fruit of the PRC's two-decades-long program of "legal construction"—stood as the last, best hope for investors brave enough to part with value and place it under the trust of an independent (corporate) legal person.[9]

This is not to say that the Chinese court system does not suffer the same costs and limitations as the other possible instruments of protection posited above, and thus would not itself fall prey to difficulties arising from incomplete substantive law, competence constraints, or domination by superior political and economic actors. Yet, when dealing with actors not tied directly into national or local power structures, and as demonstrated here, Chinese courts have proven perfectly willing and technically able to invoke and enforce, on their own and without statutory authorization[10]—and with respect to individual cases having no precedent-like effect—basic corporate fiduciary duty norms. Here, even China's much maligned People's Courts may be seen striving to act in a fashion similar to common law judicial institutions, and put parties *ex post* into a relationship they would have assumed *ex ante*, but for the intervening actions of negligent or opportunistic actors.

Corporate fiduciary duties in Chinese law today

As noted at the start of this chapter, in October 2005 China introduced Anglo-American-style corporate fiduciary duties into the nation's corporate law. In addition, and as in the 1994 Company Law (but in a different article), the 2005 Company Law sets forth in accompanying Article 149 a number of bright-line prohibitions, violation of which would constitute breach of loyalty-type obligations.[11] However, the 2005 statutory formulation passes up the opportunity—even with a newly minted "duty of care"— to articulate a specific *standard* for the duty of care prong,[12] or any instruction to regulators or judges who might be employed as a "business judgment rule" for newly authorized duty of care inquiries.[13] The 2005 statute also provides for what is equivalent in effect to fiduciary duties-type responsibility for controlling *shareholders* in Chinese companies of all sizes, albeit only implicitly and in a subclause buried in another new provision much noted because of its separate introduction of a "veil-piercing" actionable by third-party creditors (as opposed to shareholders in the firm).[14]

As one Chinese commentator has stated so aptly—and specifically with respect to Articles 148 and 149 of the Law—"without remedies, there are no rights" (Zhao 2005: 264). Thus, the new 2005 Company Law also provides for a vastly different world on the remedies side, including:

1 a substantive prohibition against (and thus a cause of action for) directors, supervisory board members and high-level management personnel acting in breach of the newly specified duty of loyalty[15]
2 the disgorging by directors, supervisory board members and high-level management personnel of gains procured as a result of loyalty breaches[16]
3 damages for losses suffered by the *company* (and thus to be sought by shareholders using the new derivative action) arising from breach of "law" (designed to include the new duty of loyalty and duty of care under Article 148), the company articles of association (which will also contain substantive, if *contractual*, fiduciary duty commands)[17] or administrative regulations by directors, supervisory board members and high-level management personnel
4 a new derivative suit mechanism allowing shareholders to use the injured company as a plaintiff in seeking damages from directors and high-level management personnel, or even sue directly "on behalf of" the company,[18] and
5 a very broad private right of action bestowed upon shareholders to sue for breaches by directors and high-level management personnel *which directly injure the interests of the shareholders* (thus potentially obviating the need for derivative suits), as follows:

> *Article 153.* When directors and high level management personnel breach law, administrative regulation or the stipulations of the company articles of association, thereby *harming the interests of the shareholders, shareholders* may bring an action in the People's Courts.[19]

In one very significant spasm of amendments, then, China's legislators provided both the *substantive* basis for Anglo-American-style fiduciary duties, and the *procedural* basis for *ex post* enforcement of those doctrines through and by China's courts in response to company (derivative) suits or direct shareholder litigation.[20]

There is no mystery as to why corporate fiduciary duties were affirmatively invoked in China's 2005 Company Law or, said another way, what set of problems Chinese corporate law drafters were trying to address via this radical adjustment. Immediately upon commencement of China's *corporatization* program in the late 1980s and early 1990s, and through formal declaration of the "modern enterprise system" in 1993, China's significant corporate governance problems became readily apparent. These difficulties resulted from many factors, but in very large measure from the problematic capital structure of most post-*corporatization* Chinese firms, listed and unlisted—

where controlling shareholders representing state or local governments held 70–80 percent of the issued equity of any firm.[21] (This result was deemed politically and ideologically necessary at the time: even though Chinese SOEs and medium and small-sized factories and enterprises were being *corporatized*, they were not being *privatized*, or so conservative political leaders or incumbent cadre managers were assured.) This capital structure led to one of two problems, either (1) directly self-interested or opportunistic behavior by a tyrannical controlling shareholder or the "system" (*xitong*)[22] represented by such shareholder(s) (usually the former line ministry or state administrative bureau controlling the assets now placed under the corporate form) with respect to the subsidiary corporate form, or (2) the absence of any real "principal" (interested shareholders) to monitor duly appointed "agents" (directors and officers) ceded management power over Chinese firms, resulting in all manner of opportunistic or self-interested behavior by those insiders (Tenev, Zhang and Brefort 2002; Clarke 2003: 494 (in particular with respect to the often-overlooked "absent principal problem")). Even before the formal invocation of fiduciary duties in 2005, Chinese policymakers and regulators had in the decade prior addressed the problem and conceived solutions from both angles—principal and agent. First, China has taken steps to create real principals, or sell down the interest of the state (allegedly representing "all of the people") and increase the presence of real shareholders in Chinese firms. This has been accomplished by the 2004–2005 program to sell down the state's illiquid interest in *corporatized* (and listed) firms,[23] or—in sensitive industries such as commercial banking where state control is still deemed necessary—create a real "principal" to actively represent the dominant shareholder.[24] Second, so as to reform the effective monitoring of, and constraints acting on, "agents" at PRC firms, legal policymakers have progressively recrafted the relationship between owners and agents in Chinese firms by amendment of the Company Law to include corporate fiduciary duties and provide for *ex post* evaluation of these legal standards—the subject of this chapter.

The difficulty with corporate fiduciary duties in China

New Article 148, and Anglo-American-style, *judicially enforced*, fiduciary duties inserted into the 2005 Company Law, proved a stunning surprise on at least three counts. First, while the PRC has since the early 1990s clearly tilted towards the shareholder-oriented model of corporate law and governance, it was at the same time forced to design and implement an *ex post*-applied/standards-unfriendly, self-enforcing model of corporate governance. Second, the fiduciary duties mechanism is itself a notoriously complex instrument of corporate governance in definition, application, and enforcement, regardless of the nationality or state of development of the jurisdiction implementing it. Third, in the PRC the very question of fiduciary duties, and specifically the perceived Anglo-American model, had been hotly debated for more than a decade, and generally portrayed as something unsuitable or alien to China's allegedly "Asian" and "civil law" tradition(s) of law and governance.

Shareholder-oriented but necessarily self-enforcing corporate law

Chinese corporate law, as it developed since the late 1980s and particularly in the 1990s, appeared to combine most aspects of a "self-enforcing" corporate law for developing or emerging capitalist economies (Black and Kraakman 1996). The factors determining this design were clear: As Black and Kraakman note in their seminal writing on self-enforcing corporate law in emerging markets generally, and which is wholly applicable to China at its present stage of development, "[a] company law that depends on fast and reliable judicial decisions is simply out of the question" (Black and Kraakman 1996: 1914). As China's *corporatization* program gathered pace, foreign observers, Chinese reformers and legislative drafters were cognizant of significant deficiencies in China's developing legal (judicial) institutions (Clarke 1996; Peerenboom 2002; Xin 2003; and Liu 2006). Thus, the Chinese corporate law system—at least in form—had many features of the "self-enforcing" model, including enforcement of norms by a combination of voting rules and transactional rights granted to direct participants in Chinese corporations, reliance on procedural protections and even prohibitions with respect to disfavored transactions, and the attempt to set out bright-line rules, all as substitutes for judicial or administrative actor-articulated standards applied *ex post*.

Corporate fiduciary duties, at least in the Anglo-American tradition, are of course an aspect of the ultimate *non*-self-enforcing mechanism in corporate law, requiring strangers to the business association (judges) to apply standards *ex post* to complex factual situations, presumably to put the various participants into a relationship they might have bargained for *ex ante* if various transaction costs had not been prohibitive. (Stated in the alternative—and if transaction costs are deemed to include opportunism and informational asymmetries—those participants are permitted to recover a position that justice and fairness dictates.) The range of actors who may be expected to undertake this "gap-filling" mechanism in corporate law—such as judges (or a regulator with sufficient authority and technical competence)—is exceedingly narrow, and those same actors can only function if the supporting political-legal culture is sophisticated enough, institutions are technically competent enough, and those actors have the requisite political standing and power to enforce the application of such standards *ex post*.[25]

Fiduciary duties in particular

Among the broader menu of corporate governance mechanisms, the fiduciary duties concept is a special and difficult case for several reasons. First, fiduciary duties are closely identified with, and rooted in, the peculiar judicial and political institutions of long-standing common law systems, with politically powerful (or powerful enough) judges boldly applying (or threatening to apply) murky judicial standards to fact-specific situations, and often against nominally far more powerful economic and political actors. Second, the application of fiduciary duties requires extraordinary flexibility and complex fact analysis, and thus a demanding level of technical competence among the judicial corps (or state regulator) wielding the doctrine. Third, corporate fiduciary duties as an aspect of corporate governance may only become truly relevant when the underlying capital structure of firms shows widely dispersed and passive shareholders who delegate management and direction of the firm to a board of directors and officers. Stated otherwise, there may be no recognition of a need for strong fiduciary duties concepts when firms are dominated by a single or group controlling shareholder (a family, a financial institution, or—as in the PRC—some aspect of national or local government). (Ironically, the converse may also be true: widely dispersed shareholding structures may only come into being when there are assurances of a strong fiduciary duties doctrine and prospect of implementation of the same.) In sum, factors supporting the resilience and utility of the fiduciary duties mechanism in the Anglo-American corporate law tradition are the same qualities which make it so difficult to communicate and apply in different legal-political systems (Pistor and Xu 2003: 77–106), not to mention the radically distinct context presented by modern China.

Against China's alleged "Asian" and "civil law" traditions

Third, the inclusion of Article 148 in the new PRC Company Law, and the explicit mechanisms for judicial enforcement of the fiduciary duties standards contained therein, represent China's rejection of what—at least rhetorically—was the accepted doctrinal tradition allegedly shaping China's corporate and commercial law: the Japanese and Taiwanese "civil law" traditions.[26] Both Japan and Taiwan originally structured their relatively weak notion of directors' duties on a Roman law concept—translated through the *Bürgerliches Gesetzbuch* ("*BGB*")—of "mandate" (*mandatum* in Latin). The Roman law concept (translated in both Chinese and Japanese characters as "*weiren*" (委任)) as used in Japanese statutes such as the Japanese Commercial Code, and now Chinese academic writing,[27] comprehends a consensual contract—written or unwritten—in which one person (the mandator) requests another (the mandatary) to perform a service, without compensation, and the mandator promising to indemnify the mandatary against any loss. Under Roman law, the arrangement was necessarily gratuitous, as the mandatary was not supposed to act out of personal gain but instead based on a kind of moral duty—as a "friend" of the mandator. Consistent with that moral charge, and balancing the indemnification obligation, is a standard of care—or the requirement that the mandatary use something like reasonable care in performing under the mandate (Story 1874: Section 4).

This term of art—translated into Japanese (using *kanji* or Han Chinese characters)—is explicitly identified in the Japanese Commercial Code as the basis for a director's duties to the company. Japan's Commercial Code at Section 254-1(3) holds:

> The relationship between a company and its directors, shall be [understood] in accordance with the provisions regarding mandate (*weiren*).[28]

"Mandate" in turn is elaborated at Article 644 of the Japanese Civil Code to hold that the mandatary (in this case, the director) shall have a duty of "due care as a good manager" towards the mandator (in this case, the company).[29] Similarly, the Taiwanese Company Law long contained the following article describing the same legal relationship between a company and its directors:

> *Article 192*. The relationship between a company and its directors, unless otherwise stipulated in this law, shall be [understood] in accordance with the civil code stipulations for mandate (*weiren*).[30]

Moreover, Taiwan's Civil Code describes the same standard of care under "mandate" as does the Japanese Civil Code (set forth above).

As Lawrence Liu, a Taiwan law practitioner and professor, sometime government official, and now senior official in a large-scale investment operation, summed up correctly about Taiwan (and tangentially Japan) to 2001:

> Fiduciary duty, however, has not become an important corporate law principle in Taiwan until recently. Taiwan is not unique in this regard. By following the Japanese Commercial Code model for its Company Law, Taiwan suffered the same problems as Japan ... The same unfamiliarity with fiduciary concepts exists in Germany and the transition economies that transplanted German law. As a cultural matter, the duty of loyalty seems to be downplayed in the Asian civil law jurisdictions as a result of the prevalence of family control and ownership concentration. ... By contrast, the duty of "due care as a good manager" is a core concept in the contract of "mandate" under the civil law system, which governs the legal relationship between directors (and supervisors) and the companies they serve. By virtue of this duty, directors are held to a professional negligence standard for their performance.
>
> (Liu 2003: 405–6)

Yet both Japan and Taiwan subsequently built on the allegedly inherited German civil law system. Japan—under strong American influence in the post-World War II period—rather famously altered the mandate provision by directly importing a seemingly separate "duty of loyalty" into the Japanese Commercial Code at Section 254-3 (Kanda and Milhaupt 2003).[31] In a slightly different manner, Taiwan amended its Company Law in 2001 so as to (1) emphasize an Anglo-American notion of duty of loyalty, and (2) import from the Taiwanese Civil Code and make explicit in the Taiwan Company Law the "mandate"-inspired duty of care (i.e., duty of due care as a good manager) as follows:

> *Article 23.* The responsible persons of a company should loyally (*zhongshi*) implement their duties and do their utmost to take the duty of care (*zhuyi yiwu*)[32] of a good manager (*shanliang guanli ren*); if these duties are contravened so that the company suffers harm, then [such responsible persons] shall be liable for compensation of such harm.

The similar journeys of Japanese and Taiwan norms with respect to directors' fiduciary duties are important because they had such a strong influence on the PRC's grappling with the same set of doctrinal problems under its much newer "modern enterprise system." These developments in Japan and Taiwan also allow us to understand how significant Article 148 of China's 2005 Company Law is as a rather more radical departure from the allegedly shared "Asian" and "civil law" traditions.[33]

In the early and mid-1990s, just as China's *corporatization* program (and modern enterprise system) was gathering pace, there was very pronounced hostility among China's academic and law-drafting circles to any idea of introducing specifically Anglo-American-style corporate fiduciary duties doctrine into Chinese law. In most cases, this hostility was based not upon concerns about the competence or independence of China's judiciary, but upon a perceived lack of fit with what was too glibly identified as China's civilian legal tradition. A strong example of this hostility is the published writing of Professor Wang Baoshu, then of the influential Chinese Academy of Social Sciences Legal Research Institute, and long a key personality in the creation of China's corporate law. In late 1993, and just before the coming into effect of the 1994 Company Law, Professor Wang Baoshu preemptively rebutted the temptation to see traditional Anglo-American doctrine as the source of the legal relationship between directors and the companies they serve (or the shareholders):

After describing why the use of agency concepts is inappropriate to the Chinese legal system, Professor Wang critiqued the trust or fiduciary strain:

> For China's legislators and corporate law scholars, we must conform to our own national situation [*guoqing*], and introduce doctrine that is consistent with China's legal tradition.
>
> First, it is not easy to introduce the agency concept because there is such a great difference between China's agency system and the real situation vis à vis the relationship between directors and companies ...

Second, it is not easy to introduce the trust [fiduciary] concept. Although the Standing Committee of the National People's Congress [China's legislature] is presently applying itself to trust legislation, we have no idea about the scope that the trust law will cover.

More importantly, the trust [fiduciary] system originally comes from the Anglo-American legal system, which is very strange [*mosheng*] for China—a nation used to a very long tradition of the civil law system. If we use this concept [trust (fiduciary)] to explain the relationship between a director and the company, people will find it difficult to become accustomed to or accept in their hearts. Conversely, if we introduce the mandate [*weiren*] relationship to explain the relationship between a company and its directors, it pretty well conforms to the customs and traditions of the Chinese people. Worthy of attention is the fact that wherever we seek to evidence that the director's position is determined by the mandate [*weiren*] theory, there must be corresponding stipulations in the corporate law. With this in view, we should change the vague [*mohu*] statement of the relationship between companies and directors in the CLS Standard Opinion.[34] First, we should add further stipulations to the General Principles of Civil Law regarding mandate; ... second, we should clearly stipulate in the [forthcoming] Company Law that the relationship between the company and directors is determined by the stipulations on mandate [*weiren*].

(Wang 1994:5).

Many other prominent corporate law academics in the PRC took a similar line through the 1990s, if in a more considered way (Liu 1998: 216–9).[35] (It should be noted that some academic writers in the PRC took a more liberal line from even the early 1990s, hopefully counseling the wholesale adoption of Anglo-American fiduciary duties, notwithstanding doctrinal obstacles or the admitted deficiencies of the judiciary.) Given this rhetoric, and the general agreement about China's "Asian" and "civil law" heritage, any prediction that China would incorporate common law-type renderings of duty of care and duty of loyalty into the October 2005 revision of the 1994 Company Law might have seemed absurd—yet that is just what the PRC did in late 2005, with the result being new Article 148 of the 2005 Company Law.

The large change seen in China's company law at the end of 2005 with respect to corporate fiduciary duties is in fact far more significant than similar changes noted in the Japanese and Taiwanese corporate law systems in 1950 and 2001 respectively. Both Japan and Taiwan maintained the "mandate" rhetorical (and doctrinal) framework to describe the relationship between directors and the companies they serve—as stipulated in their respective civil or commercial codes—coupled with rather formal and initially unelaborated adjustments (both Japan and Taiwan adding a "duty of loyalty," and Taiwan additionally rooting the standard for duty of care in the mandate obligation). Yet the PRC has now veered abruptly towards a very different doctrinal tradition. China still does not have *any* mention whatsoever of "mandate" (as *weiren*) in its unified Contract Law,[36] in what passes for its civil code (the General Principles of the Civil Law),[37] or in *any* law, regulation, or model form, and has now imported at least the Chinese characters (phraseology) closely tied to the Anglo-American fiduciary duties tradition. Moreover, the 2005 Company Law, by providing such strong private rights of action for the injured company (and a derivative suit mechanism) and shareholders directly, makes clear that the duties are meant to be enforced by, and subject to a jurisprudence construed under, functioning judicial institutions.

In sum, Article 148 of the 2005 Company Law represents a definitive refutation of China's acknowledged need for self-enforcing corporate law (and not, incidentally, a challenge to China's unready judicial system),[38] an optimistic embrace of the complex and difficult fiduciary duty mechanism, and a very pronounced turning away from what is so often characterized in the Chinese-language discourse as an "Asian" and "civil law" system.

Theoretical frameworks: convergence or expressions of specific transplant?

The surprising advent of Article 148 of China's 2005 Company Law, and its accompanying remedies machinery, may be examined via long-standing theoretical debates about corporate governance development and reform—across the world, between "the West" and East Asia, and across notionally different legal systems.

The debate regarding global corporate governance—between convergence, on one hand, and path dependency or failure to converge, on the other—is now well rehearsed in the literature addressing corporate governance reform. The strongest theoretical articulation of necessary and seemingly unstoppable convergence holds that economic forces, and especially movement towards the most economically efficient form across an increasingly *globalized* world, have led to agreement (explicit or implicit) on the desirability of the Anglo-American shareholder-oriented model of firm organization and governance: both in terms of optimal capital structure (widely dispersed shareholdings, separation of ownership and management) and resulting corporate governance rules (Hansmann and Kraakman 2003: 439).[39] A different, but intuitively more appealing, characterization of a slightly weaker convergence holds that convergence pertains most strongly among the world's largest public or listed companies, as shaped by the apparently uniform expectations of the global capital markets and the way in which national or transnational *securities regulation* (and not the more domestically oriented corporate law) as applied to transborder issuances determines corporate structures, firm governance, and corporate governance rules (Coffee 1999).[40] Professor Gilson has developed perhaps the most nuanced vision of convergence, by identifying *functional* convergence (sometimes effected via mere *contractual* convergence) in national situations where the factors determining path dependency discussed below (politics, ideology, culture, etc.) restrict the possibilities for *formal* convergence (Gilson 2001).

A subsidiary, but related, line of inquiry addresses the phenomena of specific legal "transplants" across national legal systems, usually from more "mature" legal systems to "less developed" systems (Kanda and Milhaupt 2003; Milhaupt 2005)[41]—such transplants representing a specific vehicle for the broader corporate governance and corporate law convergence either identified or aspired to. And yet the literature on specific transplants is justifiably more cautious in its claims regarding the success (beyond mere "formal" adoption) of such transplants, given a myriad of historical, political, cultural, legal system, and institutional differences. The communication of corporate fiduciary duties is one of the most representative problem cases in this regard, and for reasons usually laid at the door of different (often labeled "underdeveloped") legal cultures or institutional infrastructures (Black and Kraakman 1996; Stout 2003; Pistor and Xu 2003).

At the base of much of this body of work and speculation are the dual notions that (1) the "Western" (i.e., Anglo-American, rather than continental European) capitalist system (often twinned with the common law tradition (La Porta *et al.* 1999)) is somehow superior to other developed and developing world systems, and (2) in an increasingly *globalized* world, economic forces reach over and through allegedly antiquated ideas of nation states, historical and political traditions, or domestic institutions. In fact, a substrain in the convergence-path dependency debate focuses on, and values, neatly identified "legal origins." Here the team writing as La Porta, Lopez-de-Silanes, Schliefer, and Vishny (LLSV) has tried to demonstrate that the *type* of legal system matters: countries with a common-law legal system tend to have more developed (and dynamic, and ultimately allocation-efficient) capital markets than countries situated in the civil law tradition. The LLSV authors provide two major rationales supporting this insight: First, common law systems are deemed to be more protective of property rights generally, and specifically the interests of minority shareholders participating in corporate entities. This insight is based in the idea that common law judges are able to apply extremely flexible fiduciary duty principles in regulating *ex post* (or making costly *ex ante*) the behavior of potentially opportunistic, oppressive, or fraudulent actors in the corporate scheme—whether directors, officers, or controlling shareholders. The civil system is deemed to be more rigid in application, and thus less successful at true and perceived protection of disempowered shareholders. These contrasting realities, as much as contrasting perceptions, are said to encourage small shareholders to be more willing to part with their investment capital towards firms governed under a common law system (applying common law doctrines). Second among the rationales is the idea that civil law systems in some sense "over-regulate" commercial activity, as least as compared to common law systems. Over-regulation is considered a negative where there is a true market economy, because it can actually, or is perceived to, discourage private ordering or over-determine privately desired or negotiated outcomes.

The contrary position in the corporate governance debate sees not convergence between corporate law and governance regimes, but divergence. Non-convergence scholars offer various theoretical bases for why divergence or persistent non-convergence occurs (Bebchuk and Roe 1999),[42]and in one case (Japan) what approaches empirical proof for the proposition (West 2001). The key insight of the non-convergence theorists is that historical development and political/ideological forces unique to the still-relevant national unit, labeled "path-dependant" factors, can result in specific capital structures and effectively insulate corporate law and governance from the impact of global competitive forces (or efficiency goals)—i.e., those forces which the convergence theorists see as driving convergence to the Anglo-American shareholder-oriented model.

The Chinese case—corporate fiduciary duties in Chinese law from 1992 to the present

The Chinese case, and in particular the use of the corporate form beginning in earnest in the early 1990s, shows an interesting example of what may be the very opposite of Professor Gilson's notion of functional but not formal convergence: at least *formal* convergence between Chinese institutions and (at that time) "foreign" legal and governance forms (and towards the Anglo-American shareholder-oriented form), yet with *functional* convergence stymied by path dependency.

Since 1992, China's central government and the various departments leading the drafting of China's company law (and securities statutes and regulations) accepted—with a couple of pronounced and rather awkward exceptions—the form of the "standard shareholder-oriented model" of firm organization and corporate governance. Some outside observers may even have looked at modern China's more than decade-long experience with company law and perceived in it vindication of full convergence and even "the end of history for corporate law" (Hansmann and Kraakman 2001). A review of the 1994 Company Law and a close analysis of some of the ameliorations wrought in the successor 2005 Company Law—and in particular their respective sections on companies limited by shares—reveal the desired (minimum) commonalities:

1 full legal personality for the firm, including well-defined authority to bind the firm to contracts (and bond those agreements with assets that are the property of *the* firm, not property of the *owners of the firm*)[43]
2 limited liability for shareholders[44]
3 shared ownership in the firm by investors
4 formal separation between ownership and management, with management being delegated by the owners (shareholders) to a board of directors, and then to a management group supervised by the directors, and
5 transferable share interests.[45]

At the same time, the 1994 Company Law, and to a far lesser extent the 2005 Company Law, evidence continuing loyalty to other, apparently discarded models, including the "manager-oriented" and "state-oriented" models (conflated into one) or the "labor-oriented" model. For instance, a separate and radically inconsistent chapter was inserted into the 1994 Company Law (and maintained in the 2005 Company Law)[46] to address so-called "wholly state-owned companies" (*guoyou duzi gongsi*)—state administrative-department "invested and established" legal-person entities, which have *no* shareholders' meeting, but which do have boards of directors which delegate management powers to an executive group.[47] In addition, a fealty to the European (specifically German) style of "labor-oriented" corporate entities was and is symbolized with the "supervisory board" requirement for almost all companies.[48] Notwithstanding these important exceptions, the statutes and associated rhetoric clearly favor the "standard model" (as has the law in application insofar as organization forms are concerned).[49]

The reasons for this generalized and *formal* convergence, and the introduction of the shareholder-oriented corporate form in the 1994 Company Law, are now fairly clear. They were occasioned by two overriding policy requirements: (1) the desire to increase productivity at mostly bankrupt SOEs (by formally separating management and ownership to magically bring about increased monitoring and accountability, and change internal firm governance and incentives, and the way in which firms and firm managers interacted with an increasingly *marketized* external economy) and (2) corporate finance requirements, or the use of newly *corporatized* entities and just-established domestic stock markets to attract (assuredly passive) retail and institutional, domestic and foreign, investment for the same SOEs. Those strong policy goals, and the larger economic reform program, required that China move away from the SOE system and allow the existence of shareholding companies as the key player in the "modern enterprise system" and the associated capital markets. It quickly became apparent, however, that China's adoption of the corporate form was merely that—adoption of a form—with very little underlying *functional* convergence in respect of implemented corporate governance. The reasons for this apparent dysfunction are described above and may be laid at the door of the reform program's allowance of mere *corporatization* rather than privatization—i.e., the maintenance of capital structures which left as much as 70 percent of the equity in firms securely in the hands of state- (or local government)-backed holding companies.

Convergence over the corporate *form*, at least initially, was a relatively costless exercise for China. Not so the introduction, or convergence over, some of the implied mechanisms of the corporate form and associated governance mechanisms—such as the doctrine encapsulated under the term "fiduciary duties." Here we may ask whether the factors used to explain convergence over the shareholder-oriented form itself can also be used to explain introduction into Chinese law of the specific mechanisms summarized by the terms "duty of care" and "duty of loyalty". One intuitive under-standing supporting perceived convergence in corporate governance gen-erally and with respect to fiduciary duties specifically—and long a theme of Professor Coffee's work—is the force of demands by *foreign* investors and regulators who participate in the international capital markets. The idea here is that before global capital exercises its abundant choice in deciding where to deploy investment, it requires certain common and acceptable forms, rights, and protections—ranging across corporate law, securities reg-ulation, governance norms, disclosure, and remedies, etc.[50]

The initial introduction of corporate fiduciary duties into post-1949 Chi-nese corporate law does seem to support intimations of the unique power of the global capital markets to dictate corporate governance norms: the very idea of corporate fiduciary duties was first raised, and then entirely *trans-planted* lock, stock, and barrel from Hong Kong jurisprudence of June 1993, specifically to support the listing of PRC-domiciled *corporatized* SOEs on the Hong Kong Stock Exchange. In this singular case, the PRC Com-mission on the Restructuring of the Economic System (CRES)—the now defunct PRC department in charge of the *corporatization* scheme through the early 1990s—declared to the Hong Kong Securities and Future Com-mission that a form of Chinese characters[51] in the 1992 CLS Standard Opinion (the pre-1994 Company Law's legal basis for corporate establish-ments) had the same doctrinal content under PRC law as "fiduciary duties" under Hong Kong law. The focus of this neat trick was one article of the CLS Standard Opinion which contained the following pithy embryos of duty of care and duty of loyalty:

> Directors and managers shall assume a duty of good faith (*chengxin*) and diligence (*qinmian*) to the company ... [and]
> ... shall not be permitted to engage in any activities which compete with or harm the interests of their own company.[52]

In 1992 the CLS Standard Opinion was the sole corporate organizing sta-tute of the PRC at the time of the initial public securities issuances by PRC-domiciled issuers to Hong Kong. Accordingly, the Hong Kong securities regulatory authorities demanded, and the CRES delivered to those Hong Kong authorities, a strange and wonderful letter, dated 10 June 1993, which assured those Hong Kong regulators and the broader world:

> the duty of good faith (*chengxin zeren*) recited in Article 62[53] of the Standard Opinion has the same type of meaning (*juyou leiside hanyi*) as *fiduciary duty*[54] under Hong Kong law.[55]

In one rather swift and compelling action then, a national-level Chinese governmental actor (the same actor, incidentally, which had conceived of and promulgated the CLS Standard Opinion)—and in the absence of any other authoritative body such as the State Council of the PRC, the National People's Congress, or the judiciary—had sought to transplant, wholesale and by incorporation, the entire Hong Kong (and thus English) jurisprudence on "fiduciary duty" into Chinese corporate law.[56] This presumably provided some formal comfort to Hong Kong regulators and potential Hong Kong and international purchasers upon China's first foray into the international capital markets. Surely there are few examples in the short history of corporate governance convergence of (1) a more complete transplant from an alien (developed world) legal system, and (2) the apparent call of the international capital markets behind such an ambitious move!

This bold absorption of an entire body of (Anglo, more than American) corporate fiduciary duties jurisprudence was immediately abandoned with promulgation of the 1994 Company Law, and sudden absence in the 1994 company statute of the CLS Standard Opinion language glossed by the June 1993 CRES Letter to Hong Kong Exchange. (Although the language was recovered via special rules of August 1994 applicable to the establishment, organization, and internal governance of PRC-domiciled issuers listing stock directly overseas (including Hong Kong) (Howson 1997).) Notwithstanding that slip, the CSRC, for one, continued throughout the 1990s to build a notion of corporate fiduciary duties (and the procedural mechanisms necessary to enforce it) in listed company-specific regulation (and mandatory corporate constitutions) (Howson 2005). It is not difficult to discern the several reasons why the CSRC in particular sought to impose (or re-impose for those who mourned the passing of the CLS Standard Opinion and the wonderful CRES Letter to Hong Kong Exchange) this doctrine on China's developing corporate law in the decade ending in late 2005: Many of the leading lights of the CSRC had received training in law, accounting, and finance overseas, particularly in common law financial centers such as the United States, Canada, Australia, the United Kingdom and—closer to home—pre-Handover Hong Kong. Acquainted with the very significant role played by corporate fiduciary duties in those jurisdictions, such personnel quite naturally sought to import the same mechanism into China' new corporate governance scheme. Related to this desire was a motivating force of much greater vintage (in China's case, stretching back to the late 1800s)—the desire to establish institutions that are "modern" (how modern could China's company law be without a bedrock principle such as fiduciary duty?). Third, and supporting the implications of the LLSV writing described above, many of the most active reformers recognized that (at least the appearance of) corporate fiduciary duties applied in the common law fashion would be a key component in the creation of trust for China's domestic capital markets, desperately needed to reorient the capital allocation system in transitional China and finance China's hoped-for growth. Without this doctrine and the assurance that fiduciaries/agents of the firm could be monitored and ultimately constrained in some fashion (or punished when engaging in breach of their fiduciary duties), CSRC drafters feared that investors would not part with their savings and place funds at risk. Thus, the constant invocation of fiduciary duties (through the heavily weighted use of the term of art *chengxin zeren/yiwu*) by the CSRC (Howson 2005) was designed as an essential aid to the growth of China's capital markets.[57] Fourth, foreign capital expectations and the demands of foreign regulators—intensely relevant when China-domiciled issuers began direct overseas (and Hong Kong) listings in the early 1990s—played a part in requiring some explicit recognition of fiduciary duties in Chinese law. Fifth, some of the CSRC reformers may have thought that, even beyond the above-described essentially symbolic uses, fiduciary duties doctrine might actually be used or enforced, as an admittedly weak mechanism to counter opportunistic behavior identified at all of China's public companies. (In fact, some CSRC officials maintained a rather subversive, if very long-term, agenda regarding corporate fiduciary duties—believing that introduction of the substantive doctrine into Chinese law would *eventually* provide for enforcement demands, and a new understanding and use of the legal order and judicial institutions).

The fact remains however that the early invocation of corporate fiduciary duties in Chinese law in 1992–93, and the CSRC's coded efforts to keep it alive from 1994 to 2005, had far more to do with symbolic or political motivations (in large part responding to the assumed demands of foreign capital), and little to do with autonomous investors or judicial actors in China forcing the most economically efficient, wealth-creating, or suitable corporate governance mechanism. In this way, and from the point of view of the CSRC and China's 1994 Company Law drafters, the introduction of corporate fiduciary duties after 1993 by the CSRC—albeit indirectly—was of a piece with the mostly symbolic motivations identified in China's convergence with the shareholder-oriented form.

The above being true, observers of this development are nonetheless presented with a puzzle: Even after the introduction of new Article 148 in the 2005 Company Law, few would expect Chinese *judicial institutions* to commence grappling with corporate fiduciary duties concepts, much less entertaining the possibility of convergence with foreign, shareholder-oriented, corporate forms. Unlike (many foreign-trained) officials at the CSRC, it could not be anticipated that the behavior of the Chinese court bureaucracy would be determined or influenced in any way by foreign-educated lawyers, barely understood expressions of "modernity" in statutory law, the demands of foreign stock purchasers and securities regulators, or the desire to create real capital markets (and better capital allocation) in China.

And yet, initial research shows something quite unexpected not only about what Chinese judicial actors *will* do, but what they have *already* done: for the oft-dismissed Chinese courts did recognize the existence of fiduciary duties doctrines, beginning in the 1990s, and even sought to apply them far outside the rarified world of international, or listed, companies—all in the absence of specific statutory authorization in China's governing company law and long before the explicit convergence and transplant-heavy insertion of Article 148 in October 2005.

Functional application of fiduciary duties in Chinese courts *before* formal convergence and transplant

In the future, it is certain that a number of sources and institutions—other than judicial opinions and law courts—will be critical in the construction and application of the fiduciary duties concept in Chinese law.[58] Notwithstanding that multiplicity of authorities, it is undeniable that the People's Courts at all levels (as judicial bodies) and the CSRC (as the securities regulator enforcing corporate governance at listed companies) will handle actual cases involving corporate fiduciary duties claims, and become deeply involved in the business of explaining and applying these complex standards.[59] Moreover, individual courts (and the CSRC) will look to case decisions from courts around the country, increasingly available in formal and informal reports of actual cases,[60] even in the absence of any mandate or systemic norm conferring persuasive power on such other opinions. This was certainly the view of Intermediate, Higher, and Supreme Court judges/ justices interviewed by me in July 2007.

Many observers can justifiably doubt that the weak and inexpert Chinese courts will be able to apply these concepts at all. Yet, as the Appendix shows in more detail, basic corporate fiduciary duties standards have *already* been applied by Chinese judges—and long before their formal sanction in Chinese law as of October 2005. A review of pre-October 2005 Chinese decisions gives us a much truer insight about actual—almost *pre-emptive*—convergence over fiduciary duties in China even before the widely hailed codification (and formally signaled transplant) of those principles in late 2005 and provision of a "legal basis" (*falu yiju*) for such doctrines in Chinese law or even CSRC-driven regulation.[61]

It is important to note at the outset that the several Chinese cases described in the Appendix are not "major" cases or necessarily "authoritative" judicial rulings, as we might see rulings by the U.S. Supreme Court or the Delaware Chancery Court (or the Delaware Supreme Court on appeal from the Chancery Court) in the United States or some other jurisdiction's highest and most authoritative court.[62] That is because such cases do not exist in China at the present time, and because real judicial decisions (as opposed to bureaucratic "explanations")—even if they somehow become known nationally—have little persuasive force across the system as it exists today. Yet, these few opinions are critically important in the quest to understand when corporate fiduciary duties have come to China, and how they will be applied in future, even as the legal and judicial order is transformed. For these reflect evidence of real Chinese panels deciding real facts, and applying a key corporate law doctrine in a unique (and sometimes completely unprincipled) way.

What do these case reports demonstrate?

First, even before Article 148 of the 2005 Company Law declared the existence of a "duty of care," the CSRC was enforcing a fiduciary duty of care standard against the directors of China-domiciled public companies,[63] just as the People's Courts were grappling with the same idea in the non-public company context.[64] The first unique case related in the Appendix allowed the CSRC to articulate what such a duty might comprehend, at least at the margins (i.e., where there is "gross negligence" and thus no possibility of business judgment-style protection). Perhaps most important, the CSRC (and its lawyers and the lawyers representing a defendant director) divined both the duty, and a standard under the duty, *without* any reference whatsoever to Chinese corporate law or general civil statute, public company regulation, or the norms of the outside world (whether the Anglo-American tradition, or the assumed "Asian" and civil law tradition). Instead, it asserted that directors, even self-proclaimed "independent" or (nonexistent in law) "societal" (*shehui*) directors, simply have a duty of care with respect to their management of the company. In the second duty of care case, we see the clear rejection by a Chinese court of one muddied aspect of China's hybrid corporate law regime—the agency powers and responsibilities of the Chinese enterprise legal person's "legal representative" (*fading daibiaoren*) (or "representative director" from the civil law system)—in favor of a relatively coherent appreciation of the duties of *all* directors, acting as decision makers participating in a central decision-making body that is the corporate board.[65] In the same case, Chinese judges hold that directors need not be overly involved in the actual operations of the company (which is left to the appointed management corps), while they are at the same time given significant latitude to support and direct corporate actions that are undertaken in good faith and with less than complete information.[66] While flawed in certain ways, this opinion gives observers the taste of a Chinese-style business-judgment rule—again, without any basis whatsoever in Chinese law, regulation, or legal tradition. Lastly, this case, along with the third duty of care opinion analyzed in the Appendix, highlights why, indeed, a broad "duty of care" was so urgently needed after promulgation of the 1994 Company Law and the large-scale *corporatization* that followed in its wake: As described above, the 1994 statute provided sanctions only for directors and officers who acted in violation of affirmative laws, regulations, or the stipulated articles of association of the company.[67] In effect, directors and officers could not be monitored or held accountable for breaches of a more generalized duty of care that did not rise to contravention of positive law or quasi-contractual stipulation (a limited scope which might be perfectly acceptable under a purely civil law system). These two opinions show careful Chinese judges severely limited in their ability to enforce fiduciary standards against directors and officers precisely because there was no duty of care or substitute available in China's governing corporate law statute.

The pre-2005 duty of loyalty cases described in the Appendix are remarkable. They show how Chinese judges—again *before* a specific "duty of loyalty" was declared in the 2005 Company Law—divine and apply such a principle, and in a way which separates it from fiduciary obligations explicit or implicit in employment or management contracts, or set forth in corporate articles of association, or the two deficient (at least in this regard) Chinese characters appearing in the 1994 Company Law.[68] Here Chinese courts can again be seen aggressively going *beyond* what is allowed in the 1994 Company Law—whether the thin reed that is the adverbial phrase (in Chinese) meaning "loyally" (*zhongshi*), or the bright-line prohibitions against self-dealing in the predecessor to Article 149—and proceeding to a full-throated jurisprudence which condemns certain actions by corporate officers[69] under what the courts announce (on their own) is breach of a broad "duty of loyalty."[70] Even more impressive, Chinese courts at the very lowest level create an *ad hoc* derivative action to allow enforcement of a loyalty standard against misbehaving directors and managers by plaintiff shareholders acting "on behalf of the company."[71]

Under both prongs of the traditional fiduciary duties inquiry, then, we see courts and the securities regulator anticipating subsequent substantive and procedural legal change—change which we might have been tempted to understand later as "convergence," transplant from alien legal systems, or resulting from interactions with external norms or the demands of international capital markets. The formal convergence or explicitly rendered transplant is thus revealed as a *post facto* confirmation of doctrines and methods *already* applied seemingly spontaneously, or arising from new legal-economic institutions such as the corporate form itself.

Conclusion

The process for China described in this chapter may in the end tell us more about the winning effect of corporate and business association law on the general establishment of "rule of law" (and functioning courts), than the factors which shape company law and corporate convergence or divergence. At the very least, the journey of fiduciary duties in China to date demonstrates how the assumption of a legal and economic form (like the company) carries with it basic doctrinal implications, implications which must take root even in soil as politically, economically, organizationally, and doctrinally unfriendly as that of reform-era China. It would be overly deterministic to conclude that *corporatization* and the conferring of property rights in the firm automatically lead to rights-consciousness, and pressure on under-developed or weak judicial institutions to act in the flexible common law (or equitable) tradition. Overly deterministic, but perhaps not completely absurd, as we are reminded by one Chinese scholar's "Trojan Horse"— conjuring hopes for the application of corporate fiduciary duties and its effect on the legal system:

Actually, in respect of company law implementation, we believe that the case law system of binding precedents is superior to the statutory system. Perhaps, as some of us hope, the combination of these two approaches [common law precedent and civilian instruction by the Supreme People's Court via "explanation"] will work best.

(Luo 2006)

These attitudes in turn augur well for the future of Anglo-American-style fiduciary duties in China, and the application of the doctrine outside of the merely symbolic context. At the present time, the fiduciary duties standard—at long last authorized in statute—both challenges and supports the systemic legal institutional reforms underway in the PRC. In the future, as those reforms take hold and China's judicial institutions become more competent and even more independent in the commercial sphere, the same institutions will have more confidence in applying fiduciary duties doctrine to serve the private ordering goals, and expectations of fairness, held by cooperating investors in Chinese firms.

Notes

* I wish to express my thanks to the participants of: the Author's Workshop—A Decade After Crisis: Transforming Corporate Governance in East Asia—held in Tokyo, Japan, 30 September–1 October 2006; the 2006 International Symposium of the Tsinghua University Commercial Law Research Center's "21st Century Commercial Law Forum," held in Beijing, China, 14–15 October 2006; and the Yale Law School China Law Center's Chinese Legal Reform Workshop on 3 November 2006 for their insightful comments on alternative versions of this chapter. I also wish to thank Ms. Cao Yue (Cornell Law School L.L.M.) and Mr. Wang Qifei (Michigan Law School J.D.) for their research assistance. Unless otherwise noted, all references to Chinese company law, regulation, forms, and normative documents are from CLC 2006, an authoritative PRC State Council company law and regulation compendium published in late 2006, and all English language renderings of the same material are by the author.

1 *Zhonghua Renmin Gongheguo Gongsifa* (The Company Law of the People's Republic of China), passed by the 5th Session of the Standing Committee of the 8th National Peoples Congress on 29 December 1993 (Share System Collection 1994: 21) (with the very minor 25 December 1999 amendments, hereinafter the "1994 Company Law").

2 *Zhonghua Renmin Gongheguo Gongsifa* (The Company Law of the People's Republic of China), passed by the 18th Session of the Standing Committee of the 10th National Peoples Congress on 27 October 2005 (CLC 2006: 1-1) (hereinafter "2005 Company Law").

3 The changes between the 1994 Company Law and the 2005 Company Law are significant: The 1994 law was in many ways an orthodox business regulation-type statute, with a number of unique aspects tied to China's transitional economy. Thus, it expressed very significant attention to state ownership and Communist Party participation in the corporate form, and was replete with mandatory rules governing the corporate entity's external powers and internal (shareholder, director, and officer) governance, with very little role for courts or any kind of administrative agency applying standards *ex post*. The 2005 statute has been

washed clean of most provisions relating to state (or Communist Party) involvement in enterprises, and is now characterized by (1) a host of enabling rules (permitting participants to contract into a wide variety of arrangements) and (2) a new and significant role for the Chinese People's Courts to apply judicial standards (like the fiduciary duties that are the subject of this article) *ex post*.

4 New Article 148 should be compared to the system created by Articles 123 and 57–63 of the 1994 Company Law. For "companies limited by shares" (or *gufen youxian zeren gongsi*, as distinguished from "limited liability companies" (*youxia nzeren gongsi*)) old Article 123(1) reads: "The directors and the managers should abide by the company's articles of association, loyally perform their tasks and protect the interests of the company; they may not use their position or functions and powers in the company to seek personal gain." Article 123(2) of the 1994 Company Law then, by cross reference, made Articles 57–63 of the 1994 Company Law (governing limited liability companies) applicable to companies limited by shares; that cross-reference in turn folded in the provisions of Article 59, different only from Article 123(1) in that Article 59 includes supervisory board members in the ambit of the stipulated duty. Thus, the most important clauses in the 1994 Company Law related to corporate fiduciary duties were: Articles 59 (directors, supervisory board members, and officers to act in conformity with law, regulation, and articles of association, and a prohibition against self-dealing), 61 (self-dealing and related party contracts, and disgorgement of profits to company) and 63 (compensation for damages resulting from violation of law, etc. (tracking Article 118 for companies limited by shares)). All of the substantive areas caught by Articles 57–63 and 123 of the 1994 Compnay Law are now addressed in new Chapter VI of the 2005 Company Law.

5 There is some residual debate among Chinese scholars as to whether Article 148 of the 2005 Company Law (and corporate fiduciary duties doctrine) is substantively new, or just a confirming expression of what everyone "hoped" or "assumed" could be read into the 1994 Company Law. (This is distinct from the separate debate concerning whether the notion of Anglo-American style fiduciary duties was advocated by mainstream PRC scholars through the 1990s.) I agree with the views of Professors Zhao Xudong ("China's original [1994] Company Law had some basic stipulations regarding the duties of directors, supervisory board members and senior management personnel, and only a relatively generalized rule on duty of loyalty; but it did not clearly stipulate duty of care (or the duty [of care] of a good manager") and Luo Peixin ("The duty of care requires directors and managers to perform with the same diligence as a prudent person, under similar circumstances, with respect to the management of his own affairs. In China, Article 118 of the [1994] Company Law provided that directors should be liable for damages, if their performance constituted breach of law or the articles of incorporation. However, such duties emphasizing non-violation were not consistent with duty of care, because duty of care emphasizes due diligence and intelligence applied in the service of the corporation"). See Zhao 2004: 82, and Luo 2006: 56. See also Howson 2005.

6 2005 Company Law, Article 148(1) (emphasis added). The duties apply with respect to both "limited liability companies" and "companies limited by shares." (PRC corporate law permits two basic corporate forms, both of which allow for limited liability for shareholders: companies limited by shares (*gufen youxian zeren gongsi*) and limited liability companies (*youxian zeren gongsi*). The former is similar to what in American parlance is called a joint stock company, with an unlimited number of shareholders, strict separation of ownership and management, and more readily transferable share interests; the latter is more like a close corporation or LLC, with fewer investors, less liquid investment interests, and the possibility of less formal separation between the investors and the managers.)

7 Creditors could not be assured to have the same interest, given the fact that most of the state-owned or state-dominated commercial banks have continued to lend on non-commercial (or non-credit) bases, are politically conflicted regarding defaulting borrowers, and had no useful corporate bankruptcy law to wield in enforcing their rights. (This last aspect has been remedied with passage of the PRC Bankruptcy Law in 2006.)

8 This conflicted identity for majority or controlling shareholders of Chinese firms also, of course, severely limits the ability of such block shareholders to monitor *themselves* or the insiders who they appoint to represent them.

9 "Independent" in the sense of its legal identity, and ownership of corporate assets; but hardly independent from its controlling (often state or government) shareholders. Ironically, many investments were, and are, made in the PRC alongside state or government co-investors in the hope of assured profits, even if the result is often assured opportunism and/or failed management by controlling shareholders or the insiders who act on their behalf.

10 In fact, often in excess of what is only narrowly permitted in statute (see the duty of loyalty opinions, Appendix).

11 See for example 2005 Company Law, Article 149(1) (misappropriation of company funds), (2) (use of company funds to create personal deposit accounts or accounts in the names of other parties), (3) (lending company funds or causing the company to post guarantees for other parties), (4) (transactions or contracts with the company), (5) (corporate opportunity or competing businesses, without shareholder approval) etc., and 1994 Company Law, Articles 60 to 62. For similar provisions from the 1994 Company Law and other regulations and mandatory forms, see Howson 2005.

12 Some of these standards may be found in mandatory articles of association promulgated for listed companies (both offshore listing and domestic listing), and principles of corporate governance described by regulators, at least for listed companies. In the run-up to final promulgation of the 2005 Company Law, a scholar's draft-proposed amendment was issued which contained a standard—the standard of "care of a good manager" under the Roman Law "mandate" doctrine—for the duty of care prong. This idea did not survive the promulgation of the 2005 Company Law (Company Law Scholar's Draft 2004: Article 145).

13 Other than a provision identical in both the 1994 and 2005 Laws which asserts potential director liability for directors' resolutions, but then exempts directors from liability where they can demonstrate a vote *against* a resolution which contravenes law, regulation or the articles of association. See Howson 2005, and 1994 Company Law, Article 118 and 2005 Company Law, Article 113 (with the only difference being that under the 2005 Company Law directors may now have liability for resolutions which contravene "shareholders' resolutions" as well as those which contravene "laws, regulations and the articles of association").

14 2005 Company Law, Article 20 ("Shareholders who oppressively use their shareholders' powers and cause losses for the company or the other shareholders shall be responsible for compensation according to law").

15 2005 Company Law, Article 149(8). (This prohibition gives rise to a cause of action for breach of the same, something missing entirely from the 1994 Company Law).

16 2005 Company Law, Article 149, final clause.

17 2005 Company Law, Article 150.

18 2005 Company Law, Article 152 (in cases of breach of Article 150 (the catch-all prescribing damages for breach of law, administrative regulation or the articles of association), allowing shareholders to petition the supervisory board (or if there is no supervisory board, then direct to the People's Court) to bring suit against the implicated directors and high-level management personnel, and in case of a failure to pursue the case, then a direct action by shareholders "on behalf of" the company.)

19 2005 Company Law, Article 153 (emphasis added). (The 1994 Company Law bestowed upon shareholders a private right of action to sue in the People's Courts only for an injunction and only based upon an "illegal" board or share-holders' resolution. See 1994 Company Law, Article 111. This deficiency was ameliorated slightly in respect of a private right of action for false or misleading disclosure in the securities markets pursuant to special Supreme People's Court regulations released in 2002 and 2003. See *Zuigao Renmin Fayuan Guanyu Shouli Zhengquan Shichang Yin Xujia Chenshu Yinfa de Minshi Qinfan Jiufen Anjian Youguan Wenti de Tongshi* (Supreme People's Court Notice on Issues Related to the Acceptance of Civil Infringement of Rights Cases Arising from False Dis-closure Involving Securities), 15 January 2002 and the subsequent *Zuigao Renmin Fayuan Guanyu Shenli Zhengquan Shichang Yin Xujia Chenshu Yinfade Minshi Peichang Anjian de Ruogan Guiding* (Several Rules of the Supreme People's Court on Civil Compensation Cases Arising from False Disclosure Involving the Secu-rities Market), 26 December 2002 (CSRC 2005: 1102 and 1111).

20 The 2005 Company Law gives unprecedented authority to China's judicial organs in *ex post* veil-piercing and annulment of "illegal" shareholders' meeting or board resolutions. See for example 2005 Company Law, Articles 20 (veil-piercing and prohibition against oppression by [controlling] shareholders) and 22 (annulment of resolutions).

21 This may be perceived in a snapshot of the capital structure of the Shanghai Stock Exchange's listed companies as late as the end of 2004. Of all the compa-nies listed on the Shanghai Stock Exchange for the year ending 31, 2004, fully 65.805% of the capitalization of such firms was made up of illiquid (non-trad-able) shares, with 52.806% consisting of outright state-owned shares (*guojia guoyou gufen* or in shorthand *guoyougu*) and 4.625% of the remaining more than 13% owned by Chinese "legal persons" (most often corporate identities of the state or state holders). These illiquid, often directly state-held, shareholdings are not at all widely dispersed: As of June 2004, China had 1,324 listed companies (on the Shanghai and Shenzhen Exchanges). Of those, a single shareholder has more than 50% of the issued shares of 486 companies, and one shareholder has between 20% and 50% of 724 companies (thus for 91.4% of China's listed firms, one shareholder owns between 20% and approximately 70% of the equity). The single largest (state) holder of state-owned shares (*guoyougu*) controls more than 50% of the shares at 419 companies, and the single largest (state) shareholder controls between 20% and 50% of the shares at 450 companies (thus for 65.6% of China's listed firms, the single largest state shareholder controls between 20% and approximately 70% of the equity) (Shanghai Stock Exchange 2004).

22 For a marvelous description of the *xitong*, formal and informal, see Lieberthal 1995: 194–208.

23 This is the so-called *guquan fenzhi* ("capital structure reallocation") program: first announced on 29 April 2005 via the CSRC's *Guanyu Shangshi Gongsi Guquan Fenzhi Gaige Shidian Youguan Wenti de Tongzhi* (Notice Regarding Relevant Questions Concerning the Listed Companies' Capital Structure Re-allocation Reform Experiment), then confirmed in the CSRC, PBOC, Ministry of Finance and Ministry of Commerce's jointly promulgated *Guanyu Shangshi Gongsi Fenzhi Gaige de Zhidao Yijian* (Guiding Opinion Regarding the Listed Companies' Capital Structure Re-allocation Reform) of August 2005, and finally reduced to regulation in the CSRC's *Shangshi Gongsi Guquan Fenzhi Guanli Banfa* (Mea-sures for Administration of the Listed Companies' Capital Structure Re-alloca-tion) of 4 September 2005 (CSRC 2005).

24 Such as *Huijin*, a kind of domestic PRC joint venture established by the PRC Ministry of Finance and the PRC State Administration of Foreign Exchange to funnel recapitalizing foreign exchange funds directly to three of China's "Big

Four" banks in exchange for half of "the state's" 60% plus equity in such banks. See the Hong Kong offering prospectuses for China Construction Bank and Industrial and Commercial Bank of China (China Construction Bank 2005; Industrial and Commercial Bank of China 2006). The lightly staffed *Huijin* proved an aggressive and very effective monitor of management assigned to the three PRC commercial banks involved, far more effective than the collective-action challenged public investors in the same banks. In 2007 it was announced that *Huijin* would be absorbed into China's new foreign investment vehicle patterned after Singapore's Temasek.

25 Here we are well advised to make a traditional distinction between duty of loyalty and duty of care, at least insofar as enforcement is concerned: most courts will be more hesitant in finding and punishing breaches of duty of care, given the difficulties in evaluating breach and the likely negative effects on risk-taking managers (the latter concern expressed through the business-judgment rule). Therefore, in evaluating the reality of China's 2005 reform, it is appropriate to focus more intently on the introduction of duty of care, as contrasted with the duty of loyalty.

26 While Japan conjured a great deal of animosity towards itself in China during the Anti-Japanese War and World War II, and Taiwan is still formally a "renegade Province" occupied by forces hostile to the PRC, both areas and their legal systems continue to exert a very strong attractive influence on Chinese law academics and lawmakers alike. There are many reasons for this phenomenon: the historical inheritance from late Qing Imperial China which looked to Japan's Meiji Restoration as a model for modernization and strengthening, the Chinese Nationalist government's incorporation of *BGB*-inspired Japanese and German legal norms in the 1920s and 1930s, the generalized perception in China that these areas share a "civil law"-type legal system (*dalu faxi*) predating even introduction of the *BGB* into Japan at the end of the nineteenth century, the fact that Japan and Taiwan are understood as "Asian" polities and political and legal units which must share some of the same assumptions as Chinese society (i.e., the common (China-sourced) Confucian heritage), the domination of firms by a single shareholder or controlling shareholder block (with cross-holdings in other firms), and Japan and then Taiwan's successful participation in the global capitalist economy stretching back to the end of World War II.

27 The translation path here is dizzying: if written Chinese characters were exported to Japan in the first millennium (to express in writing a language (Japanese) from an entirely unrelated language group), the combination of Han characters *weiren* used by the Japanese since 1900 to express a Roman-age Latin term has now traveled "back" to China in the 1990s to signify the same concept!

28 Japanese Commercial Code, Article 254-1(3).

29 Japanese Civil Code, Article 644.

30 Taiwan Company Law, Article 192.

31 "... directors owe to the company the duty to perform their functions faithfully, in compliance with laws, the company's charter provisions, and resolutions of shareholders' meetings." Japanese Commercial Code, Section 254-3 (originally written in as Article 254-2 but renumbered because of 1981 amendments). This is not an explicit enunciation of a "duty of loyalty," but the identical use of the adverb "faithfully" or "loyally" in the PRC's 1994 Company Law to carry duty of loyalty. There was much academic discussion over 20 years as to whether the added language in Section 254-2 actually constitutes a duty of "due care as a good manager" derived from the "mandate" doctrine. A 1970 Japanese Supreme Court Decision held that Section 254-3 merely makes more specific and restates the duty of care cross-referenced from the Japanese Civil Code, and does *not* constitute a separate or higher duty for corporate directors (Kanda and Milhaupt 2003).

32 A direct and unambiguous rendering in Chinese characters of "duty of care;" compare with the PRC's inability in 2005 to take the same very bold approach, abandoning *"zhuyi yiwu"*—which was suggested as the title for the duty of care provision in a 2004 scholar's draft (Company Law Scholar's Draft 2004: Article 145) but not in the legislature's July 2004 working draft (Company Law Draft Amendment 2004: Articles 20 and 67)—for *"qinmian yiwu."*

33 It is ironic that PRC scholars and law drafters took no formal notice of the "more English than the English" pre-handover system in Hong Kong, where there was a thriving common law system ripe for transplanting, not to mention learned judges, barristers, and solicitors, a highly developed commercial and corporate culture, and vibrant capital markets. It is doubly interesting because China had taken so much from the Hong Kong system in the 1990s, communicated into the PRC by the many Hong Kong investors and professionals who began to turn toward the PRC in the mid-1990s as the 1997 handover and return of sovereignty over the Colony became a *fait accompli.* As will be related below, the CSRC (and its predecessor reformist department the Commission for the Restructuring of the Economic System (CRES)) *did* in one notable case pay close attention to the Hong Kong corporate and securities law system, seeking to absorb more than a century of Hong Kong (and thus UK) corporate fiduciary duties jurisprudence into China's then only national corporate law.

34 Here Professor Wang Baoshu is referring to the Opinion on Standards for Companies Limited by Shares, China's first post-Liberation regulation (not statute) regarding modern corporations, or CRES, *Gufen Youxianzeren Gongsi Guifan Yijian* (Opinions on Standards for Companies Limited by Shares), 15 May 1992 (Share System Collection 1994: 1) (hereinafter, "CLS Standard Opinion").

35 Suggesting little difference between Anglo-American substantive standards for duty of care and "mandate" doctrine duty of due care as a good manager, and so advocating continued fealty to the "mandate" theory, but with explicit invocation of the Anglo-American style doctrine in China's company law and description of "mandate" in the PRC Contract Law (then being drafted in a unified form) and the General Principles of the Civil Law, and addition of a specific "duty of loyalty" prong, like Japan, to complement the duty of due care as a good manager standard.

36 See *Zhonghua Renmin Gongheguo Hetongfa* (Contract Law of the PRC), effective 1 October 1999, at CLC 2006: 8-1 (Chapter 21 (*Weituo* or "Entrustment" Contracts.)

37 See *Zhonghua Renmin Gongheguo Minfa Tongze* (General Principles of the Civil Law of the PRC), effective 1 January 1987, at CLC 2006: 1–111 (hereinafter "General Principles of the Civil Law"), Chapter IV, Section 2 (Agency). Even the proposed Civil Code of the PRC, assembled under the direction of Professor Wang Liming and published in 2004, contains no provision whatsoever on "mandate" (*weiren*) but only on "agency" (*daili*) (Articles 201–233) and "entrustment contracts" (*weituo hetong*) (Chapter 28). See Professor Wang Liming's draft Code and commentary at Wang 2004.

38 This is recognized by most perceptive PRC scholars. See for example Luo 2006 (Professor Luo of course identifies the 2005 Company Law's revolutionary introduction of judicially enforced fiduciary duties (Article 148), piercing of the corporate veil (Article 20), and appraisal rights (Article 75). Interestingly, he also sees a judicial role in articulating standards and enforcement of corporate social responsibility obligations (Article 5) and even the "conditions" for Communist Party involvement in the leadership structure of firms (Article 19)!)

39 "There is no longer any serious competitor to the view that corporate law should principally strive to increase long-term shareholder value. This emergent consensus has already profoundly affected corporate governance practices throughout the world. It is only a matter of time before its influence is felt in the reform of corporate law as well."

40 Although Professor Coffee ascribes the impetus behind the identified convergence to the individual firms seeking capital, not—as in the Chinese case—a reformist group inside the Chinese securities regulator with a strong political and regulatory agenda of their own.

41 The latter regarding adaptation of *Unocal* test in Japanese takeover guidelines used to evaluate defensive tactics.

42 Including well-articulated notions of structure-driven path dependency (capital structures) and rules-driven path dependency (substantive rules, procedural rules, judicial practices, institutional and procedural infrastructures, and enforcement capabilities). It must be noted that this theory really focuses on developed-economy corporate entities and governance.

43 This concept was contradicted in the 1994 PRC Company Law with the provision (Article 4) asserting that state-owned assets owned by a company belong to the state (effectively looking through the intervening corporate form to privilege one shareholder with direct ownership of a portion of a company's assets). See 1994 Company Law, Article 4(2). This inappropriate and theoretically troubling clause was deleted from the 2005 Company Law.

44 This aspect was also badly drafted in the 1994 Company Law, so that shareholders in PRC companies limited by shares might have enjoyed not limited liability, but *proportional* liability. See 1994 Company Law, Article 3(3) ("... shareholders shall be liable to the company only to the extent of the shares they hold (*yi qi suochi gufen wei xian*)"). Again, this problem was remedied with the amended 2005 Company Law, so that limited liability for shareholders vis à vis companies limited by shares is now determined by subscribed-for shares (and implicitly the subscription amount only). As noted above, the 2005 Company Law also introduces a "veil-piercing" mechanism which will deprive certain shareholders in PRC companies of the protection of limited liability.

45 This too is a work in process in the Chinese context; a multitude of restrictions work on the proposed transfer of share capital in China, listed or not, in most cases depending upon who or what owns and is seeking to transfer the shares. Increased liberalization on this score is being effected through selling down the state (and state-backed legal persons') interests in listed and unlisted companies, and the slow collapse of distinct foreign exchange and RMB yuan capital markets bounded by capital account foreign exchange controls.

46 1994 Company Law, Part II, Chapter 3, Articles 64–72 and 2005 Company Law, Part II, Chapter 4, Articles 65–71. (Part II of the 1994 and 2005 Company Laws addresses limited liability companies (closed corporations), and thus wholly state-owned companies may be seen as a subspecies of limited liability company, although the former are so distinct from either limited liability companies or companies limited by shares that such an understanding seems misleading.)

47 There seems little doubt that the referenced section was inserted into the 1994 Company Law (and the 2005 Company Law) as a sop to certain political and economic actors in China who saw *corporatization* as the prelude to real privatization. The wholly state-owned company form permitted under the 1994 Company Law, actually unnecessary with the continuing effectiveness of the *Zhonghua Renmin Gongheguo Quanmin Suoyouzhiqiye Fa* (Law of the People's Republic of China on Industrial Enterprises Owned by All the People) (SOE Law) as a legal basis for SOEs, provided critical assurance that the new form might accommodate old and comfortable habits.

48 1994 Company Law, Part III, Chapter 4, Articles 124–128 and 2005 Company Law, Part III, Chapter 4, Articles 118–120. The supervisory board, in implementation, has proven a bit of an embarrassment to China's corporate law drafters and observers, as many participants in the PRC corporate form have had significant difficulty in understanding exactly what the institution is to do! With

the 2005 Company Law amendment, this problem has been resolved in a very minor way, by making the supervisory board the first port of call in the event of a derivative suit demand.

49 For instance, with respect to China's confusion over the use and function of the supervisory board, instituted in Chinese corporate law because of the common assumption that China somehow inherits German and "civil law" forms.

50 This might be an easy explanation for China's entire *corporatization* scheme (and the accompanying corporate governance template) established in the mid-1990s, if China had not first implemented *corporatization* and a form of corporate governance as a successful strategy to soak up *domestic* investment, or did not already have in place the full menu of foreign direct investment (FDI) vehicles which did an adequate job of attracting asset/project-specific *private* foreign investment.

51 The same characters now used to indicate the "duty of care" in Article 148 of the 2005 Company Law (*qinmian*).

52 CLS Standard Opinion, Article 63. The CLS Standard Opinion also contains an intimation of duties for company limited by shares "promoters" (*faqiren*) in the pre-incorporation period, stating "The promoters of a company shall bear the following responsibilities: ... (4) where during the course of establishment, because a mistake (*guoshi*) on the part of the promoters leads the company [*sic*] to incur losses, [they] shall bear joint liability for compensation." CLS Standard Opinion, Article 21.

53 A minor issue is presented by the fact that Article 62 of the Standard Opinion does not actually contain the exact characters "*chengxin zeren*", but instead the clause "*chengxin he qinmian de yiwu*" ("duty of good faith and diligence").

54 The Chinese language original of the words "*chengxin zeren*"—translated here as "duty of good faith"—is followed in the Chinese text by the *English language* form of words: "(fiduciary duty)". There was meant to be no ambiguity regarding the meaning of the glossed Chinese characters in English, or under Hong Kong/English jurisprudence.

55 See *Guojia Tigaiwei Guanyu "Gufenyouxiangongsi Guifan Yijian" he "Guanyu Dao Xianggang Shangshi de Gongsi Zhixing 'Gufenyouxiangongsi Guifan Yijian' de Buchong Guiding" zhi Xianggang Liansuo de Han* (CRES Letter to the Hong Kong Stock Exchange Regarding The Opinion on Standards for Companies Limited by Shares and The Addendum Regarding Implementation of The Standard Opinion For Companies Listing in Hong Kong), 10 June 1993, *Tigai Hansheng*, No. 74, 1993 (hereinafter, "CRES Letter to Hong Kong Exchange"), Item 6 (Share System Collection 1994: 252). The CRES Letter to Hong Kong Exchange continues, "... this duty includes (but is not limited to) each principle to be undertaken by directors and senior management as set forth in the Mandatory Articles of Association for Hong Kong Listing Companies." (This statement makes the subsequent 1994 Mandatory Articles for Overseas Listing Companies, successor to the prior *Dao Xianggang Shangshi Gongsi Zhangcheng Bibei Tiaokuan* (Mandatory Articles of Association for Hong Kong Listing Companies), 10 June 1993 (Share System Collection 1994: 25), important as a guide for fiduciary duties concepts (Howson 2005).

56 This nimble act was repeated, only with more elaboration, with the promulgation of the 1994 Mandatory Articles for Overseas Listing Companies and the importation of what may be a tort standard "reasonably careful" director or officer. These Mandatory Articles remain compulsory for PRC-domiciled issuers offering shares on overseas markets (including Hong Kong).

57 China's policymakers and regulators may have been right to hold this view. In the period after promulgation of the new Company Law and Securities Law in late 2005, and substantial completion of the "capital structure reallocation"

(*guquan fenzhi*) program—and after five flat years where the Shanghai Exchange A Share Index hovering around the 1100 mark—after 1 May 2006 the Shanghai Index began a bull run.

58 Those other, non-judicial, sources include the following: First, pre-eminent in the formal hierarchy of authoritative sources determining the construction of fiduciary duties standards in China will be the forthcoming Supreme People's Court "Explanation" (or likely several "Explanations") (sometimes called "Opinions") on the 2005 Company Law. (The Supreme People's Court has already issued one quasi-Explanation on the 2005 Company Law, addressing technical questions regarding how courts are to handle corporate law-based claims which straddle the 1994 and 2005 statutes. See *Zuigao Renmin Fayuan Guanyu Shiyong "Zhonghua Renmin Gongheguo Gongsifa" Ruogan Wenti de Guiding* (Regulations of the Supreme People's Court on Several Issues Concerning the Application of the "Company Law of the PRC"), *fashi* [2006] No. 3, 27 March 2006—promulgated and made effective 9 May 2006.) That (those) Explanation(s), when issued, will be influential and in some cases decisive as Chinese courts at all levels rely upon the pronouncement of their own highest bureaucratic authority. It is said in Beijing that the Supreme People's Court will likely issue a first Explanation on certain procedural aspects of the new Law (for instance, the newly authorized derivative action), and only follow at some time in the future with an Explanation describing the doctrine supporting application of fiduciary duties. Equally important will be Supreme People's Court interpretations concerning specific (sometimes "model") cases and enforcement actions, and special non-enforcement letters/interpretations handed down by the same court. Second, the CSRC's Listed Companies' Corporate Governance Principles—while not law or binding regulation—will continue as an important basis for the standards applicable to corporate fiduciaries, at least with respect to *listed* companies. See CSRC, *Shangshi Gongsi Zhili Zhuze* (Corporate Governance Principles for Listed Companies), 7 January 2002, CLC 2006: 4–8 (hereinafter, "Corporate Governance Principles for Listed Companies"). Third, the Guidance Principles for Independent Directors (soon to be reconstituted as CSRC-promulgated "regulations" (*tiaoli*) with binding legal effect) contain (and the forthcoming "regulations" will contain) a good deal of material on the standard of conduct of *independent* directors—which for basic duties of care and loyalty should be indistinguishable for executive and other non-independent directors. (The exception under the Chinese scheme seeming to be that such independent directors have to "tilt" in the direction of protecting the interests of "minority shareholders" rather than all the shareholders.) With the massive sell-down of state-held illiquid shares in listed companies effected between 2004–2006, there may be reason to readjust the command for such PRC independent directors in the direction of protection of the interests of the entire shareholders' meeting, or the company. See CSRC, *Guanyu Zai Shangshi Gongsi Jianli Duli Dongshi Zhidu de Zhidao Yijian* (Guidance Opinion Regarding the Establishment of an Independent Director System at Listed Companies), 16 August 2001, CLC 2006: 4–22 ("Guidance Opinion for Independent Directors") and Howson 2005. Fourth, the CSRC has promulgated mandatory articles of associations for PRC-domiciled domestic listing- and overseas listing-companies, which contain their own *contractually* binding and presumably enforceable standards (and even remedies) for corporate fiduciary duties. See the 1994 Mandatory Articles for Overseas Listing Companies, and CSRC, *Shangshi Gongsi Zhangcheng Zhiyin (2006 nian Xiuding)* (2006 Amended Guidance Articles of Association for Listed Companies), available at www.csrc. gov.cn/cn/jsp/detail.jsp?infoid=1142933582100&type=CMS.STD&path, replacing a 1997 form (CSRC, *Shangshi Gongsi Zhangcheng Zhiyin* (Guidance Articles of Association for Listed Companies), 16 December 1997, CLC 2006: 4–26 (1997

Guidance Articles of Association for Listed Companies) and Howson 2005 (regarding the 1997 version)). Fifth, and as many Chinese scholars note, a good deal of the "law" describing the specifics of fiduciary duties in China will no doubt be declared via specific *ad hoc* regulation—primarily by the CSRC as the now accepted regulator of publicly listed companies. Sixth, and again with particular meaning in the Chinese context, the views of Chinese corporate law scholars will continue to have great significance, especially with the advent of a corporate law which is the product of so much direct input from a group of Beijing-based scholars.

59 This occurred with respect to access to the courts on private claims against false and misleading disclosure in the PRC securities markets, even in the *absence* of any legal basis under Chinese law and affirmative *rejection* (at least initially) of such private suits by terrified Chinese courts. (The 2005 Company Law of course provides an explicit legal basis for People's Court hearing corporate fiduciary duties claims, by the company, or as triggered by the shareholders suing derivatavely.) See the good discussion of this phenomenon, and the subsequent institution of a legal basis, by two PRC Supreme People's Court justices (Xi and Jia 2003: 33). The legal basis (issued as Court "rules") the Supreme People's Court was subsequently forced to promulgate to allow these suits (after temporarily banning them) is contained in: *Zuigao Renmin Fayuan Guanyu Shouli Zhengquan Shichang Yin Xujia Chenshu Yinfa de Minshi Qinfan Jiufen Anjian Youguan Wenti de Tongzhi* (Notice on Issues Related to the Acceptance of Civil Infringement of Rights Cases Arising from False Disclosure Involving Securities), 15 January 2002 (CLC 2006: 5–29) (lifting the ban) and *Zuigao Renmin Fayuan Guanyu Shenli Zhengquan Shichang Yin Xujia Chenshu Yinfade Minshi Peichang Anjian de Ruogan Guiding* (Several Rules on Civil Compensation Cases Arising from False Disclosure Involving the Securities Market), 9 January 2003 (CLC 2006: 5–25) (providing the legal basis for acceptance of such cases by the courts). In fact, this may be part of the design animating the inclusion of the Article in the 2005 Company Law.

60 See, for instance, the Beijing University collection being assembled at: www.lawyee.net.

61 China's developing legal system does not yet produce easily accessible summaries or court opinions on any matter, much less something as difficult or complex as the duties of directors, supervisory board members, or managers in the corporate setting as construed *ex post* by judicial actors. This is especially true with respect to what might be construed as *duty of care* cases. For example, one case collection and commentary published in late 2005 by the Beijing No. 1 Municipal Intermediate People's Court describes six cases under the chapter headed "Responsibilities and Duties of Directors and Officers" and yet all of the situations described pertain to prohibited loyalty breaches or undertaking of competitive activities (Beijing No. 1 Municipal Intermediate People's Court 2005: 359–425). The CSRC is regulator of China's listed companies records and announces the large volume of fines or declarations of what it calls "breaches of fiduciary duties" by corporate directors and officers. These, however, relate almost uniformly to false, misleading, or less than timely disclosure by insiders at China's listed companies, or breach of the CSRC's own administrative, bright-line, regulation of self-dealing or conflicted transactions. To find, and analyze, such cases in modern China, analysts are forced to look to rare case reports by PRC courts, summary reports written up in Chinese-language teaching materials, and even informal media reports.

62 As are available in similar Japan-concerned studies (Milhaupt 2005).

63 As exemplified in the Lu Jiahao ("Flower Vase director") case, Appendix.

64 See Ye Jianmin case, Appendix.

65 See Ye Jianmin case, Appendix.
66 As is seen in the Ye Jianmin, Appendix, the court in its opinion veers towards automatic exculpation of any single director insofar as a collective board decision has been made.
67 See Ye Jianmin and Beijing University Campus Company cases, Appendix.
68 See Huayuan Pensioners case, Appendix.
69 Even where such directors or officers are not the defendants! See the Shidu Trademark case, Appendix.
70 See the Beijing Self-dealing, Shidu Trademark and Beijing Hua'er cases, Appendix.
71 See the Beijing Self-dealing case, Appendix, and the lower court's permitting one shareholder to sue firm directors and officers "on behalf of the company".

Appendix: pre-2005 Chinese Opinions Invoking Fiduciary Duties

Duty of Care—"Flower Vase"[1] Director Case (CSRC, Beijing Intermediate People's Court, 2001–2)—Director's Gross Negligence

On 27 September 2001, the CSRC brought an enforcement action[2] against twelve individuals, including the 71-year-old English language Professor Lu Jiahao. Lu and the others individuals had been directors of a company idiomatically known as "Zhengbaiwen" (a name as notorious in China as "Enron" is in the U.S.).[3] The CSRC fined the chairman and vice-chairman of the board of directors of Zhengbaiwen RMB 300,000 yuan and RMB 200,000 yuan respectively, and each of the other ten directors (of which unfortunate Professor Lu was one) RMB 100,000 yuan (US$12,000). The alleged defect in the directors' action arose from the board's unanimous recommendation that shareholders vote in favor of a proposed reorganization of Zhengbaiwen (and repurchase of their shares), which was on its face profoundly detrimental to the shareholders' interest (and later found to be fraudulent). Professor Lu objected to the application of the CSRC fine to him, and for a number of interesting and somewhat picturesque reasons.[4] Upon announcement of the the CSRC penalty, Professor Lu made application for administrative rehearing (*xingzheng fuyi*) before the same administrative body pursuing the enforcement action—the CSRC—seeking exemption from the CSRC fine. On 8 April 2002, the CSRC denied Lu's petition for rehearing of the administrative fine, and responded to Lu's objections as follows:

> Lu Jiahao is a director, he is responsible for the approval of directors' resolutions which relate to the truth and completeness of the listed company's application materials and annual reports submitted. [He may not] seek to avoid the fine by using rationales like the fact that he holds the position of an "independent" director, or because he does not work at the company or participate in everyday business management, or because he does not receive any compensation or subsidies [from the company].

Seeing the CSRC would not relent, plucky Professor Lu then took the almost unprecedented step of suing the CSRC in the Beijing No. 1 Intermediate People's Court, even naming the Minister-level Chairman of the CSRC (Zhou Xiaochuan) as a defendant. The first, and only, real hearing in the case occurred on 20 June 2002, and lasted for four hours. In the CSRC filings and court statements, the CSRC denied that Professor Lu qualified as an independent director (as it was revealed that he actually owned 10,000 shares of Zhengbaiwen, not to mention that the company had never made formal application/registration of his standing as an independent director). As the CSRC stated in its pleadings—confirming that that independent directors should not be held to a standard of care different from that of other directors—"Lu is just a director, and must perform the duties [a director] should perform." In the hearing, Lu protested that he *had* had comments and questions regarding the massive reorganization underlying the Zhengbaiwen fraud, but that he had been telephoned prior to the critical meeting by the company's largest shareholder and "municipal government leaders" (in many cases, the same), asking him not to make a fuss, ask any questions, or seek to impede the reorganization plan so as to "serve the interests of Zhengbaiwen's shareholders and workers." In his pleadings, Lu also said that he had never participated in board meetings where the offending public disclosure documents were discussed and approved and thus was not directly responsible for them (or the resolutions approving them); likewise, he said that he never reviewed the company's annual (financial) report, and thus had no chance to identify what aspects of the report might be false or misleading. Finally, Lu's lawyer said Professor Lu was asked to vote on plans and complex figures provided by (and signed off on by) Zhengbaiwen's accountant, and raised the question as to how a "regular" director or someone without specialist knowledge could be expected to do anything but rely completely on what had been offered to him by such experts?

According to contemporaneous media reports, a lawyer representing the CSRC countered Professor Lu's various defenses in the one hearing for the case. First, the lawyer noted that as Zhengbaiwen's unlawful activities were apparent and "clear to all," Lu Jiahao, as a sitting director of the firm, should with a minimum of diligence be deemed to have had knowledge of these problems, and should thus have direct responsibility for the unlawful activities of the company; second, Professor Lu's claims that he had not participated in meetings which reviewed and approved listing materials, and thus had not affirmatively participated in fraudulent disclosure or the ill-informed recommendation of shareholder votes, did not constitute a basis for relieving him of direct responsibility for the actions of the company.[5]

The 2001 "flower vase director" case, and the pleadings and court statements it conjured, provides an initial window into how at the margin a fiduciary duty of care was already applied in China: First, there would appear to be no special duty of care standard for "independent directors" (even those appointed to serve in such roles, unlike the confused Professor Lu): all directors will be held to the same standard of attention and diligence when acting as directors. (As described elsewhere, properly appointed independent directors may owe a modified duty of loyalty, in that they are commanded to protect the interests of non-controlling shareholders under the PRC scheme.) Second, a director must demonstrate some minimum standard of attention and diligence before *ex post* decision makers will evaluate (or defer to) the judgment supporting a specific decision or vote. A PRC director may not shirk his or her duty of care so entirely, or willfully plead ignorance of information widely known (or that he or she should have known) and offer that non-involvement or ignorance as a defense against liability or a basis for exculpation. Thus, in this case, an actor like Professor Lu will not get the benefit of any considered analysis of his actions (and their possible basis in business judgment) if he is shown to be something like *grossly negligent* in attending to his duties as a member of the board. If, as some Chinese scholars insist, there is a business-judgment rule principle implicit in China's developing corporate fiduciary duty standard (and newly introduced Article 148), then someone acting with the complete disregard evidenced by Lu will not be able to invoke it.

An interesting aspect of the case is the absence in all available media reports of any references to China's corporate or other statutory law, either purported indigenous civil law or alien Anglo-American norms, foreign-provided doctrine, or the demands of the international or domestic capital markets, in construing and enforcing the obligations of this particular director. This can be distinguished from the other cases reviewed below, where judges attempt to source fiduciary duties of care or loyalty in the 1994 Company Law, in particular Article 59, and its mention of "*loyal* performance" of duties by directors, etc. Instead, the impetus behind this particular enforcement action—and the strong articulation of directors' duty of care—comes from the appointed regulator of China's domestic capital markets, which has long been concerned about improving corporate governance to create a higher level of confidence in those markets. This confirms the strong role that the CSRC has had, and will in the short term continue to have, in enforcing and describing corporate governance norms in China (over and above the judiciary).

Duty of Care—Ye Jianmin Case (Huizhou, 2002)—Board Chairman's Approval and Operational Implementation

Jiangxi Province Higher People's Court judge Qian Weiqing—in his 2006 collection of lectures and related materials on corporate litigation—provides an interesting Guangdong Province Intermediate People's Court opinion from 2002 overturning a judgment against appellant board chairman Ye

Jianmin for damages to the company he presided over.[6] Appelant Ye was the chairman of the board of directors of a PRC limited-liability company formed from a state-owned factory, the company being the plaintiff in the original action. Ye, as the "legal representative" (*fading daibiao*) of the company, executed a contract with Shenzhen Ritai Company, pursuant to which the Shenzhen operation would source machinery (and test the same for technical conformity) on behalf of Ye's company. The machinery purchased by the Shenzhen company on behalf of Ye's firm turned out to be fake and substandard, resulting in significant losses for the plaintiff firm end-user. The court that first heard the case—the Huizhou City District People's Court—held that Ye should be responsible for the damages suffered by his company because:

> ... the defendant [Ye], in the period during which he performed his company duties, did not fully perform the responsibilities of the board chairman, and did not undertake inspection of the [machinery] purchased by the company; [moreover], the purchased machinery was entirely sub-standard, and no contract [with representations and warranties, or indemnification] was signed with the actual equipment vendor—this all resulted in serious injury to the interests of the company, for which the defendant [Ye] should bear all of the responsibility.[7]

Ye appealed the initial judgment before the Intermediate People's Court at the next higher level (the Intermediate People's Court at Huizhou City), which overturned the lower-level court's decision, and excused Ye from any responsibility for the misbegotten purchase of machinery (with costs to the original plaintiff). In doing so, the court addressed Ye's duties as a director under China's 1994 Company Law:

> With respect to the [plaintiff company's] interaction with the Shenzhen Ritai Company, there existed both approval at the board level after discussion, and the handling of payment remittances by accounting officers who were also directors, after which the purchase was handled personally by members of the supervisory board including Mr. Wang Jinsong, etc. The appellant was not the specific individual who handled the purchase of equipment. Nor did the articles of association of the company stipulate that the chairman of the board undertake inspection of purchased equipment. The appellant committed no subjective fault whatsoever, and the actions of the appellant and the "losses" of the appellee had no cause and effect relationship. ... This court holds that, in accordance with the stipulations of the [1994] Company Law, the directors, supervisory board members and managers should abide by the company's articles of association, loyally perform their tasks and protect the interests of the company, and not use their position or functions and powers in the company to seek personal gain; where in

the performance of company functions they breach law, administrative regulation or the stipulations of the company articles of association, causing injury to the company, they should bear responsibility for compensation. At the time the appellant was the chairman of the board of directors of the company, although his company and Shenzhen Ritai Company purchased machinery and equipment which was fake or sub-standard, or was without a tax receipt,[8] yet the company for which he served as legal representative had many discussions at the board level and resolutions prior to his actions, and the transaction was imple-mented by many people, constituting a collective action by the com-pany, not the individual action of the appellant. The actions of the appellant also do not present a situation involving violation of law or the company articles of association; moreover, the appellee has pre-sented no evidence to prove the fact that the appellant was seeking personal gain by his behaviour ... [9]

This finding presents a number of interesting aspects which aid in divining how a director's duty of care was construed in China before 2005:

First—and very importantly in the PRC context—the opinion reversing the lower court (and exculpating Ye for the damages suffered by the com-pany) completely ignores Ye's status as the "legal representative" and thus (under the civil law tradition) presumptive agent of the company.[10] Rather remarkably, the higher court opinion views Ye simply as a director, in fact one director of many,[11] who supports and implements corporate action which eventually brings damages to the company.

Second, the opinion attempts to draw a line as to how penetrating the duty of care inquiry should be under Chinese company law, rejecting out-right the proposition that a director of a Chinese company, even a closely held company organized as a limited liability company, should be responsible for implementing approved corporate actions, or have liability in the event such approved transactions bring injury.[12] Instead, the opinion recognizes that it is the duty of the directors to discuss, and vote on, certain kinds of deci-sions—and implicitly it is the exercise of good faith and informed judgment by the directors in such discussions and voting which provide the moment for evaluation of a duty of care. Thus, the judges have created, without any statutory authorization or reference to other similar cases, a kind of busi-ness judgment rule protection for these Chinese directors.

Third, in straining to ignore the legal representative status problem, and exculpate this legal representative *cum* chairman of the board of directors, the opinion comes close to holding that an individual director *cannot* be personally and individually responsible for the damages suffered by the legal person entity.[13] This focus on the "collective" action of the board, and the absence of "individual action" by the defendant/appellant, risks insu-lating individual directors from personal liability in the performance of their duties.

Finally, the opinion shows how Chinese judges are forced to hew very closely to the statutory text of the 1994 Company Law, and thus highlights nicely the deficiencies of that statute's narrowly drawn duties, and in turn the need for imposition of a specifically named, and far broader and flexibly applied, "duty of care." That deficiency is the assignment of liability for directors in the duty of care line (i.e., assuming no breach of duty of loyalty or self-dealing) *only* where their actions contravene positive law, regulation, or the articles of association of the company.[14] As many Chinese observers and aggrieved shareholders recognized in the early years of China's *corporatization* experiment, this structure provided for a very narrow duty of care, as directors and officers could avoid self-dealing, conform to the narrow confines of statute, regulation and the corporate articles of association, and pay little heed (or care) to the responsible management of the corporate assets.[15]

Duty of Care—Beijing University Campus Company Case (Beijing, 2004)—Exculpation of Officer's Breach?[16]

In March of 2000, the controlling shareholder of Beijing University Campus Educational Investment Company Limited (Beijing Campus) appointed Cao Jianwei to serve as the General Manager of Beijing Campus. More than a year later, Beijing Campus was approached by a state-sponsored Tianjin Development Zone company seeking a loan of RMB 3,000,000 yuan. On 2 April 2001, Cao Jianwei, without seeking the Beijing Campus board's approval or apparently going through any other corporate or transactional formalities, resolved to extend a one-year loan in the amount of RMB 3,000,000 yuan from Beijing Campus to the Tianjin borrower. The next day, Beijing Campus wired the loan principal amount to the Tianjin borrower's account, against which the borrower issued a one-page receipt. Other than the receipt, the parties did not execute any documentation or any kind of loan contract. At the end of the loan's one-year term, the borrower was able to repay only RMB 500,000 yuan of the original loan amount, defaulting on the remaining RMB 2,500,000 yuan.

Beijing Campus brought suit against the borrower in the Tianjin No. 2 Intermediate People's Court seeking payment of the remaining principal amount, and damages. The Tianjin court ruled that the borrower should repay the remaining RMB 2,500,000 yuan, and if it did not, then interest would be charged on the unpaid principal at the highest default interest rate permitted by the Chinese central bank. With attempted enforcement of this judgment against the Tianjin borrower however, it became apparent that the borrower was judgment proof: the Tianjin Development Zone Finance Bureau State Debt Service Department would not provide for (or permit) the provision of (state) assets to satisfy the judgment against the state-controlled Tianjin borrower. Accordingly, the Tianjin No. 2 Intermediate Court on 19 April 2004 declared the enforcement proceeding terminated.[17] At the same time, the court declared that the original lender, Beijing Campus, could at any time apply for enforcement of the original award against any assets of the borrower later discovered or available.[18] In the same award, the court made clear that the borrower had an unenforced judgment outstanding against it in the amount of RMB 2,627,900 yuan (principal and interest), with the formal debtors recognized to include both the original borrower but also the Tianjin Development Zone Finance Bureau State Debt Service Department.[19]

Unable to satisfy the judgment against the borrower, Beijing Campus then sued General Manager Cao Jianwei for recovery of the unpaid principal amount of the loan. The company alleged that Cao had responsibility for the damages suffered by the company and arising out of the misbegotten Tianjin loan under Article 63 of the 1994 Company Law, which reads:

> Directors, supervisory board members and managers who violate law, administrative regulation or the company articles of association in the course of performing their corporate tasks, causing injury to the company, shall be liable for compensatory [damages].[20]

The Beijing court hearing the case said that—in the normal course—it would try to determine two points: (i) had Cao acted in violation of law, and (ii) was Beijing Campus' injury caused by Cao's acts or omissions? That court, however, refused to hear Beijing Campus's suit against its General Manager Cao because the precise amount of damages resulting from the loan approved by Cao was not ascertainable (the borrower still had some ability to pay back the loan, and thus accumulate default interest obligations). Beijing Campus appealed on several grounds, primarily because (i) Cao's actions were acknowledged to be in breach of law, and (ii) these actions had brought injury to the company, thus satisfying the two prongs of Article 63 of the 1994 Company Law. Moreover, Beijing Campus urged that Cao could and should make the company whole for damages he caused by undertaking the bad loan—which injury the company asserted was distinct from the mechanics of collecting the underlying debt.

On appeal, the Beijing No. 2 Intermediate People's Court sought to determine, again per Article 63 of the 1994 Company Law, if (i) Cao had in the performance of his corporate duties violated law, administrative regulation or the articles of association of the company, and (ii) such actions had brought injury to the company. On the first inquiry, the Court found it impossible to discern from the Beijing Campus articles of association the general manager's precise authority with respect to external financial matters, and thus difficult to confirm if the loan of RMB 3,000,000 yuan he arranged by Beijing Campus to the Tianjin borrower was in contravention of the authority granted to him under those articles. At the same time, the court did determine that the actual loan by Beijing Campus—not qualified under Chinese law as a financial or banking entity—*was* in violation of China's central bank financial regulations.

Thus, the court determined, Cao's action in procuring the loan from Beijing Campus was "in violation of administrative regulation," satisfying the first prong of Article 63. On the second, injury, prong, the court analyzed the facts in two steps: first, did Beijing Campus actually suffer injury, and second, did the harm *directly result* from the unlawful actions of Cao Jianming, or did his actions and the resulting harm to the company have a direct cause and effect relationship? The court determined that because the original loan was extended in violation of China's central bank financial regulation, Beijing Campus would not be permitted to charge or collect interest on the loan extended to the Tianjin borrower. The court further decided that there was a direct connection between the non-conforming loan extended by non-financial institution Beijing Campus, procured by General Manager Cao, and the uncollectable interest. (And the appeals court agreed with the lower court in seeing the foregone interest as unquantifiable.) However, the principal loan to the Tianjin borrower was deemed enforceable (even if extended in violation of regulation), and thus something which could in theory be repaid. However, the court ruled that Beijing Campus was still unable to demonstrate for the court any direct connection between Cao's actions in extending the loan and the inability of Beijing Campus to collect the principal amount. The court took the same view with respect to other alleged damages arising from collection expenses. Thus, the higher court rejected Beijing Campus' appeal and confirmed the lower court's initial judgment, saying:

> Beijing Campus' allegations do not conform to the stipulations of Article 63 of the [1994] Company Law, and thus the lower court judgment correctly rejected Beijing Campus' suit. In view of the fact that this case has no connection whatsoever with whether or not Beijing Campus will finally be able to collect on its debt, and even if Beijing Campus is never able to collect on the loan, Cao Jianwei should have no responsibility for damages in respect of the unrecoverable amount.
>
> (Beijing Municipal Higher People's Court 2006:52)

Here we may be gratified to see two Chinese courts parsing the relevant statute extremely closely. And yet the two opinions highlight again one of the serious governance problems under China's 1994 Company Law (and a reason for the introduction of Article 148 in the 2005 Company Law). Once again, there is a strong focus on whether or not the corporate officer has acted in compliance with affirmative stipulations in law, regulation, or the corporate articles of association. In this case, the defendant officer has apparently acted in basic compliance with such positive norms; with the only item of failure on his part (procurement of an illegal loan) having no connection with the borrower's failure to perform.

A broader duty of care inquiry, as now required under Article 148 of the Company Law, would have mandated consideration of whether or not—in extending the loan to the Tianjin state borrower—the officer has acted with the requisite care in determining the creditworthiness of the borrower, and the enforceability of any future effort to collect the debt from the same party. In such case, the failure of Cao as General Manager to ensure compliance with positive law or regulation would have been only one element in an evaluation of the care he exercised with respect to Beijing Campus assets. The Beijing Municipal Higher People's Court commentator presenting these opinions bemoans the result in this case, and heralds the necessary improvements in the 2005 Company Law:

> ... analyzed in this way, no matter what actions are taken by the manager, none of these actions would directly lead to damages, and thus the meaning behind Article 63 of the [1994] Company Law has what use?
>
> (Beijing Municipal Higher People's Court 2006: 56)[21]

The answer to this lament is a separate, and broader, "duty of care"—as delivered in Article 148 of the 2005 Company Law.

Duty of Loyalty—Yantai Development Zone Huayuan Pensioners Service Company Limited Case (Yantai, 1999)—Something Beyond Contract

In April of 1999, four people in the Shandong Province municipality of Yantai joined together to form Yantai Development Zone Huayuan Pensioners Service Company Limited (Huayuan Pensioners or Huayuan).[22] Of the four, a husband-and-wife team were to provide the capital, and two other individuals—Messrs. Li Liang and Song Hongmin—were to act as General Manager and Deputy General Manager respectively of the firm. At the time of the firm's establishment, the four parties entered into a "Contracting Agreement" pursuant to which (i) the husband and wife promised to capitalize the company with RMB 2.6 million yuan by 1 June 2000 (as between the husband and wife, the wife was to contribute 70% of the initial capitalization for a 70% equity interest, and the husband 30% for a 30% interest), and (ii) the two managers promised the husband and wife (a) full return of their initial capital investment within 8 years of formation of the company, and (b) a total asset value of no less than RMB 6 million yuan on the eighth year anniversary of the firm's establishment. In the same Contracting Agreement, the managers promised not to dispose of any assets of the firm, including all fixed assets or land held by the firm.

In May of 1999, the shareholder wife and General Manager Li Liang entered into a separate "Entrustment Contract," which reduced to contractual form certain of the duties owed by the General Manager to only one of the shareholders (in this case, the 70% equity owner wife). Effective between 25 June 1999 and 25 April 2001, the Contract authorized General Manager Li to act as the proxy for the 70% equity shareholder wife in her separate role as the firm's "legal representative" (*fading daibiao*),[23] and further stated that General Manager Li would manage (vote) the 70% equity interest of the wife in the firm. While Li was given the contractual power to manage the wife's equity interest in the company, he was also contractually prohibited from selling, mortgaging, or otherwise disposing of that 70% interest. During the term of the Entrustment Contract, Li was obliged to "take all measures to protect the interests" of the wife shareholder, and forbidden from acting in his own interest or in the interest of any third party in a way detrimental to the interests of the wife, or acting affirmatively in the interest of any party other than the wife, or disclosing or using the company's commercial secrets, etc. The General Manager was to be compensated under the Entrustment Contract with a salary payment direct from the shareholder wife (and not the firm, Huayuan) of RMB 2,000 yuan per month (paid in RMB 1000 yuan monthly installments, with a bullet payment of RMB 20,000 at the end of the 20-month Entrustment Contract term if General Manager Li had not breached his various obligations under law or the Entrustment Contract). On 18 May 1999, Huayuan Pensioners was registered (and thus formally established under Chinese law), with a registered capital of RMB 260 million yuan, the registration identifying General Manager Li Liang (not the wife) as both the 70% shareholder of the firm and its "legal representative."

Just after the signature of the Entrustment Contract, and a week before the mid-May formal establishment of the Huayuan company, a transaction was commenced by the company-coming-into being, a transaction which gave rise to a too-tempting corporate opportunity for the appointed managers (and per the Entrustment Contract, agents) of Huayuan Pensioners. On 7 May 1999, Huayuan entered into a contract with a People's Liberation Army ("PLA")-affiliated company pursuant to which Huayuan would purchase land[24] from the military company, which Huayuan would use for commercial real estate development. After partial transfer of title in the land (and payment of a portion of the purchase price) to Huayuan, the Yantai military company very quickly had second thoughts, and one month later insisted that Huayuan sell the land back to the original military seller, at the original purchase price. General Manager Li agreed that he would permit Huayuan's sale of the land back to the military company on one condition: that 50% of the land went back to the original military seller and 50% to another company *designated by Huayuan* (really Li, acting "on behalf of" Huayuan). The original military seller and the company to be designated by Li were then to jointly develop the land, with the Li-designated operations' involvement obscured in all official filings and registrations. The Li-designated company ("Newco") was, somewhat predictably, a new entity established by Huayuan officers General Manager Li and Deputy General Manager Song in June 1999 to take advantage of the land development scheme under the 50/50 sell-back arrangements. Newco had the same address as Huayuan, the same business scope as Huayuan ("small district greenification"), and a registered legal representative who was none other than Li Liang. By 6 June 1999, General Manager Li (representing

Huayuan) had signed a contract pursuant to which Huayuan agreed to transfer the land back in two equal portions to the military seller and Newco, with the military company and Newco purchasers getting a credit for the remainder of the original purchase price not paid by Huayuan.

By March 2001, the husband and wife team and two original Huayuan shareholders signed an agreement with the Huayuan officers to terminate the original Contracting Agreement, depose Li and Song as officers of the firm, and re-register the 70% shareholding of the wife in the wife's name, and show her as the legal representative of the company. The military company and Li and Song's Newco did eventually develop the property, spending RMB 5.3 million yuan, for a project that was at the time of suit appraised at a commercial value of RMB 7.6 million yuan.

Huayuan, again under the control of its shareholder owners, sued former managers Li and Song and the Newco they had set up for recovery of the value of the Huayuan development opportunity taken by Newco. The court of first instance, the Yantai Development Zone People's Court, found for the plaintiff Huayuan, declaring that the officers of Huayuan had breached their duty of loyalty to Huayuan by using their privileged position as officers of Huayuan to seek a personally profitable opportunity that would not have come to them but for their corporate positions. Those two officers, having injured the company they owed a duty of loyalty to (loss of the corporate opportunity), should be responsible for the notional profits arising from such opportunistic behavior (or the RMB 2.3 million difference between the initial investment in the real estate project and the appraised value of the development at the time of the lawsuit).

The two original defendant officers rejected the lower court's finding, and brought an appeal attacking only the legality and enforceability of the various contracts the officers had entered into with the Huayuan shareholders—*or what they saw as the sole source of their legal duties.* Implicitly, then, these officers believed that they had no duty of loyalty to the Huayuan firm beyond what they had explicitly agreed to in contract, or in Li Liang's specific case pursuant to his role as agent of the 70% shareholder wife and legal representative of the firm.

These pleadings set up the question for China's corporate law rather sharply: did this corporate officer have a duty to the firm above and beyond what had been agreed in contract—whether specific contracts like the Contracting Agreement or the Entrustment Contract, or the peculiar kind of contract between shareholders that are the articles of association?

The Intermediate People's Court rejected the appellants' view of their apparent breach, and in a way that makes clear the duty of loyalty of managers (and by implication directors) in China—and the prohibition against seizing corporate opportunities—is sourced in something other than explicit contractual promises or even the 1994 Company Law. The case report summarizing the Yantai Intermediate People's Courts' rejection of the appellants' claims (almost certainly using language from the opinion) is written in a way which makes clear that the managers' legal duties have nothing whatsoever to do with the Contracting Agreement and the Entrustment Contract or the respective managers' status as agents, and everything to do with their fiduciary obligations as officers in the corporate form:

> During the period that the two appellants [General Manager Li and Deputy General Manager Song] were General Manager and Deputy General Manager of the appellee [Huayang], they took advantage of their positions to misappropriate a commercial opportunity of the appellee's; their actions in organizing their own company to cooperatively develop a real estate project infringed on the legal rights and interests of the appellee, and thus the profit arising from such cooperative development belongs to the appellee. We therefore reject the appeal and let the original judgment stand.
>
> (Wang 2005: 368)

This opinion is indeed rather remarkable: it shows a competent Chinese court actually looking beyond all available sources of law (including the 1994 Company Law and its often over-worked adverbial phrase asking that directors, officers, and supervisory board members undertake their functions "loyally"), to divine a standard corporate-opportunity doctrine from a generalized notion of fiduciary duties—and long before such generalized fiduciary duty of loyalty was explicitly written into Chinese law in late 2005.

Duty of Loyalty—Beijing Self-Dealing Case (Beijing, 2001)—Breach of Rule-based Duty of Loyalty Under 1994 Company Law

The Beijing No.1 Beijing Intermediate People's Court reports a slightly later case (Beijing No. 1 Municipal Intermediate People's Court, 4th Chamber 2005: 359–370) evidencing breach of one of the strict prohibitions against self-dealing contained in the 1994 Company Law, and not incidentally the *misjudgments* of two levels of People's Courts which heard the resulting case brought on behalf of the company and other shareholders. (The Beijing No. 1 Intermediate People's Court uses these flawed judicial responses to sensitize judges to the wider scope of loyalty subsequently mandated by the words "duty of loyalty" (*zhongshi yiwu*) in the 2005 statute, beyond those specific items listed in the 1994 Company Law.)

The facts leading up to the alleged breach of loyalty are exceedingly complex, although the breach itself is not. The company (Company)[25] was a limited-liability company established in 1999 under the 1994 Company Law. In March 2001, the Company completed a merger with, and absorption of, another enterprise (Other Company), with the resulting (continuing) Company having eight shareholders, including Parties A, B, and C. Party A was, in addition to being a shareholder, also chief financial officer of the Company until November 2000, when he became ill, retired from his officer's position, and was replaced by Party D (who does not appear to have been or become a shareholder of the Company). Party B had been a director and shareholder of the Other Company before it was merged into the Company, and was the leading shareholder and promoter of the Other Company. In the buyout-merger, Party B was appointed proxy for the Other Company's selling shareholders. With the merger and buyout (and the contemporaneous buyout of an existing shareholder of the pre-merger Company), Party B became the 15% shareholder, a director, and the General Manager of the Company. Party C was a long-time shareholder and chairman of the board of directors of the Company (he had been so since inception, and was the moving force, with Party B, behind the merger between the Company and the Other Company which created an expanded, post-merger Company).

In July 1999, before the merger with the Company, Party B (then a director and shareholder of the Other Company), contracted to purchase just under 100 square meters of real estate in Beijing (Building No. 3, Suite 305) from the Beijing XYZ Real Estate Company Limited. At that time, Party B began making installment payments on the real estate purchase price and other fees. After the merger buyout and Party B's appointment as the General Manager of the Company in March 2001, the real estate was used as the office of the Company, and Party B expressed a desire to put the property under the Company's name. On 5 March 2001, Party B used RMB 124,193.20 yuan of the *Company*'s funds to pre-pay the remaining purchase installments due to Beijing XYZ Real Estate for the office property. On 8 March 2001, Party B reported to the Company that he had used a Company check to pay off the full amount of a mortgage loan procured to finance the purchase of the property. From that date, reported Party B, the office property was "owned" by the Company. He further reported that he personally had spent RMB 487,450.82 yuan of his own funds in purchasing the office real estate, which he hoped the Company would reimburse him for. On 5 June 2001, Party B took RMB 450,000 yuan from the Company to partially reimburse himself for the expenditures he had already made in connection with the real estate purchase (presumably not including the RMB 124,000 yuan and mortgage loan pre-payments amounts which he used Company funds for).

Because the Company was never able to agree a shareholders' or board resolution ratifying the purchase of Party B's property, the complete formal transfer of ownership in the property (from the XYZ Real Estate Company, which would have continued to be the registered owner of the property as the installment payments were received)—or *guohu*—was never effected. Accordingly, on 19 September 2001, Party B informed the Company in writing that he would like to take back his ownership interest in the office real estate, and would thus return to the Company RMB 574,193.20 yuan in value expended by the Company (the aggregate of RMB 124,193.20 he had taken from the Company to fund the early payout of the installment payments, and the subsequent RMB 450,000 he had taken from the Company to reimburse his prior expenditures on the office). However, Party B alleged that he was entitled to deduct certain amounts from the funds he should return to the Company, including: RMB 450,000 yuan owed by the Company to the shareholders of the Other Company in connection with the merger buyout transaction (for whom Party B was the appointed representative); RMB 60,000 yuan of unrelated Company litigation expenses borne personally by Party B over three months prior; and 7 months of "rent" for the office space (at RMB 5,000 yuan per month) "owed" by the Company to Party B. Party B therefore urged that he should "regain" outright ownership of the office real estate (largely purchased and financed using Company funds)—still apparently registered in Party B's name—by paying over to the Company a net amount (less the deductions described above) of RMB 30,000 in cash. The board chairman of the Company (Party C), and the chief financial officer (Party D, who had replaced Party A) approved Party B's request immediately, whereupon Party D signed a Company receipt issued to Party B evidencing Company "receipt" of 574,193.20 yuan (when it had received, in cash, only 5.26% of that amount).

Party A—a continuing shareholder of the Company—thereupon sued Parties B (the self-helping General Manager, director, and shareholder of the Company) and C (the compliant chairman of the board of directors of the Company, and shareholder) "on behalf of the Company," alleging among other things that after only three months as General Manager of the Company, Party B had—without any approval from the board or the shareholders of the Company, and without any contract in place between the Company and any other party—taken advantage of his position as General Manager of the Company to lift RMB 574,193 yuan from the Company to fund payments on the installment purchase of personal real estate, which actions violated the 1994 Company Law's Articles 59, 60 and 61[26] and seriously injured the interests of the Company and its other shareholders.

In hearing the case, both the lower-level court and the appeals court wandered into somewhat murky grounds. The court first hearing the case made several interesting points, most of which departed almost entirely from any legal basis provided in PRC statute at the time:

First, the court responded to the defendants' justifiable position that China did not, at that time, allow derivative actions, i.e., that the plaintiff (Party A)—as a mere shareholder and former officer of the Company—had no power to bring the suit on *behalf of the Company* or the other allegedly injured shareholders. That lower court made one somewhat startling and other rather sensible points. Most startling, in 2001, was the statement by the lower court that, "under the [1994] Company Law's related stipulations" directors, officers, and supervisory board *should* have a "duty of loyalty" (*zhongshi yiwu*) and a "duty of care" (*zhuyi yiwu*)" (Beijing No. 1 Municipal Intermediate People's Court, 4th Chamber 2006: 362). The court seemed to divine these duties from thin air, as neither these concepts nor these terms had yet been stipulated in the national Company Law, related company law regulation, or the many governance-related CSRC regulations or pronouncements of the time. The lower court judges then make an equally startling leap by declaring that when the actions of directors, managers and other high-level management personnel injure the interests of a company, the company may bring suit against such personnel. (As noted, this concept was not at the time stipulated in the 1994 Company Law or the 1998 Securities Law; the only right of action permitted under Chinese law prior to the 2005 Company Law and Securities Law amendments was a private right to seek injunction against illegal or articles-breaching directors' or shareholders' resolutions.) Given these two fundamental conceptual leaps, it seems a small move for the same lower-level court to pull an *ad hoc* derivative suit mechanism out of the equally thin air—so that where the directors of a company frustrate the power of a company to bring suit against themselves, the shareholders have the power to bring suit *"on behalf of the company and on their own behalf."* (Beijing No. 1 Municipal Intermediate People's Court, 4th Chamber 2005: 362). (Thus, the trial court acting in 2001 fully anticipates, and in fact serves to *create,* the derivative suit mechanism established only four years later in the 2005 Company Law.) As the lower court's opinion reads:

> In the present case, because defendant Party C is the chairman of the board of directors of the Company and because by law and under the Company's articles of association he convenes the board meeting and presides over it, he should be responsible for calling a board meeting so that it can make resolutions regarding major issues that arise in the course of company operations. Party A believes that board chairman Party C and General Manager Party B have taken actions which injure the interests of the Company. In this situation, there is no way that Party C, as a conflicted party, will convene a board meeting to address his own actions, just as there is no way he can represent the company in bringing litigation [against himself]. Thus, Party A, as a shareholder of the Company, has the ability to represent the Company in appropriate litigation, with the goal behind the litigation being to protect the lawful rights and interests of the Company and its shareholders. We hold that Party A is therefore qualified to act as plaintiff in this case.
> (Beijing No. 1 Municipal Intermediate People's Court, 4th Chamber 2005: 362–363 (emphasis added))

On the direct fiduciary duty inquiry,[27] the court finds that allowance of Party B's deductions from the amounts owed to the Company by the chairman of the board of directors Party C and the chief financial officer Party D were "within the scope of authority" of such directors and officers (being a part of their normal operational and administrative duties and decision-making scope), were entirely appropriate, and *not in violation of national laws or the Company's articles of association.* (Beijing No. 1 Municipal Intermediate People's Court, 4th Chamber 2005: 362). Accordingly, the lower court rejected Party A's lawsuit (on behalf of the Company) alleging that the actions of Party B and Party C had brought any harm to the Company, and rejected the lawsuit brought by Party A on behalf of the Company. Thus, while the application of the law proved ineffective (with the court hewing close to the required breach of positive law or contract), this trial court did support—at this time with no basis in Chinese law—(i) conceptions of a two-pronged fiduciary duty and (ii) a derivative action by shareholders on behalf of the legal person enterprise against the firm's directors.

The court of second hearing took a decidedly different view from that of the lower court, and focused on the fiduciary duty-related statutory provisions in the 1994 Company Law. That court stated that the relationship between Party B and the Company with respect to the real estate first purchased by Party B and then used and purchased in part by the Company was not a "normal" contractual relationship (which might have allowed the netting out of the Company's obligations to Party B), but a purchase and sale relationship *between a company and one of its own directors or officers.* Insofar as that contract had not been approved by the shareholders of the Company, or authorized *ex ante* by the Company's articles of association, then it was on its face a breach of Article 62(2) of the 1994 Company Law (forbidding self-dealing). Under this analysis, the court said, Party B should return to the Company the funds he took from the Company for purchase of the office real estate.[28] Thus, the higher court reacted more conservatively than the court of first hearing, which was perfectly ready to pronounce the existence of so-called duties of care and loyalty and without any statutory authorization. The higher court instead ties its analysis of the problem more closely to what the 1994 Company Law actually contains—a bright-line prohibition against any kind of self-dealing (regardless of "fairness" or "fair value") and the obligation to return to the company any and all monies related to such forbidden transactions.

In an extended commentary on the case, the 4th Chamber of the Beijing No. 1 Intermediate Peoples Court's Judge Chang Jie tries to synthesize the respective broad and narrow fiduciary duty approaches of the two courts which rendered decisions in the case. Most crtically, that Beijing judge asserts that the statutory provisions contained in the 1994 Company Law are merely specific expressions of *wider* underlying duties which duties are not explicitly named in the company law, but do exist and are actionable:

> Party B, as a director and manager of the Company, has a duty of loyalty [*zhongshi yiwu*] to the Company pursuant to the relevant stipulations of China's [1994] Company Law. With respect to this so-called duty of loyalty of directors and officers, Article 59(1) of China's [1994] Company Law sets forth the basic conceptual definition of the directors'

and officers' duty of loyalty: "Directors, supervisory board members and managers should abide by the company's articles of association, loyally perform their duties, protect the interest of the company, and are not permitted to use their position or function in the company to seek personal gain." Articles 59(2)-61 of this Law then stipulate specific aspects of the directors' and officers' duty of loyalty ...

From these legal provisions, we can see that the classic duty of loyalty for directors and officers has two aspects: the duty of non-competition, and the prohibition against self-dealing. ...

So-called "self dealing" means a transaction by a director or officer with the company where he has a position for his own benefit or the benefit of another. Because of the special position of a director or officer in the company, and because the two sides in any such commercial transaction will undoubtedly have a conflict of interest, wherever a transaction occurs between the director or officer personally and the company he controls, there is the possibility that a circumstance harmful to the interests of the company will arise. Accordingly, the company law of many nations and regions contains similar laws and regulations, providing for restrictions on self-dealing by directors and officers as a legal duty. Article 61(2) of China's [1994] Company Law sets forth a basic rule with respect to self-dealing transactions between directors or officers and the company: "Except as stipulated in the company articles of association or as approved by the shareholders' meeting, directors and officers are not permitted to enter into contracts or transactions with [their] company." ...

In this case, Party B is a director and officer of the Company, and he took real estate he owned and sold it to the Company without the approval of the shareholders' meeting and without clear authorization in the Company's articles of association; this resulted in the establishment of a legal relationship for the purchase and sale of real estate between him and the Company—a legal relationship which very clearly contravenes the stipulations of China's [1994] Company Law and violates the stipulated restriction on self-dealing which is a part of the directors' and officers' duty of loyalty, and resulted in injury to the interests of the Company. Thus, Party B should return to the Company the real estate purchase funds he already took from the Company.

(Beijing No. 1 Municipal Intermediate People's Court,
4th Chamber 2005: 367–368).[29]

Shidu Department Store Trademark Case (Beijing, 2000)—Director/ Manager Self-dealing

A January 2000 Beijing Intermediate People's Court demonstrates the same easy identification, and partial sanction, of breach of duty of loyalty under the then available statutory provisions of the 1994 Company Law—and in this case notwithstanding the plaintiff's *failure to plead* a personal (director's or officer's) breach of fiduciary duties.[30] The facts are fairly simple: Mr. Hu Zhenjiang was a (the?) "managing director"[31] and general manager (or chief executive officer) of the Shidu Department Store Company (Shidu Department Store) established in September 1995. As of 12 September 1997, Shidu Department Store was the registered owner of a trademark for the business, that trademark comprising a stylized rendering of the two Chinese characters for "*shi*" and "*du*". In 1998, and at the same time as he was managing director and CEO of the Shidu Department Store, Hu formed a separate company—the Shidu [same Chinese characters] Alliance Company Limited (Shidu Alliance)—in which he invested RMB 4,000,000 yuan for a 40% equity interest (the largest equity interest in Shidu Alliance). Hu was also a managing director and the legal representative of Shidu Alliance, where he was joined by Wang Yang (supervisory board of Alliance) and Wang Qi (general manager of Alliance)—Wang Yang having worked at Shidu Department Store between September 1996 and January 1999 as planning and finance manager, and Wang Qi also at the Department Store between October 1996 and January 1999 as a floor manager. Each of Wang Yang and Wang Qi gained a 30% equity interest in Shidu Alliance. In January 1999, Hu, using his position as a managing director and CEO of Shidu Department Store, and—without informing the other shareholders of Shidu Department Store—caused it to transfer the "*Shidu*" registered trademark, *gratis*, to Shidu Alliance, the separate company in which he was a managing director, legal representative, and largest shareholder.

Shidu Department Store sued Shidu Alliance under the General Principles of the Civil Law[32] and the 1994 Company Law asking for nullification of the purported trademark transfer and return of the use of the registered trademark to Shidu Department Store. Somewhat strangely, the corporate opportunities-rich Mr. Hu was not included as a named defendant, but instead merely as a "third party" (*di san ren*). Apparently the plaintiff understood Hu's breach as something effected through the agency of the second controlled corporate entity, and not by virtue of his position as a director or officer in the first company. (This makes little sense, as the 1994 Company Law provisions underpinning the action—Articles 59 and 61—are those which focus on personal self-dealing *by directors and officers*.) Equally strange is the fact that the plaintiff did not seek damages from Hu for his apparent breach of duty of loyalty or taking of a corporate opportunity—as the plaintiff was clearly entitled to under the self-dealing related Articles 59 and 61 of the 1994 Company Law.

The Beijing Intermediate People's Court analysis starts not with the statutory duties of Hu and other "managing directors," but their acknowledged contractual duties as set forth in Shidu Department Store's Articles of Association. Those Articles contained no provision pertaining to fiduciary duties-like concepts such as care or loyalty, but instead (as was appropriate for a 1995 closely held Chinese limited liability company) focus on aspects such as the calling of shareholders' meetings, reporting to shareholders, implementing shareholders' resolutions, deciding business and investment plans, budgets, formulation of dividend distributions and loss allocations, proposals for additional financing, mergers, consolidations and liquidation, appointment or termination of senior management, etc. In addition, and consistent with the General Principles of the Civil Law and 1994 Company Law idea that certain individuals (until 2005, necessarily the chairman of the board of directors as the automatic "legal representative" of the firm) are entitled to act as agent for the company, the Articles directly empower such managing directors to sign documents on behalf of the corporate entity. Next, the court emphasizes the informational deficiencies related to keeping the first registered holder of the intellectual property asset in the dark, i.e., that the original promoters of Shidu Department Store (i) were not informed of Hu's establishment of Shidu Alliance, and (ii) were not informed beforehand of the transfer, *gratis*, of the "Shidu" trademark from Shidu Department Store to Shidu Alliance.

The court, rejecting a number of ingenious defenses offered by Shidu Alliance and Hu (as the "third party"), found for Shidu Department Store, ordering the trademark transfer arrangement void and return of the registered trademark to the department store. The basis for this finding rather awkwardly focuses on the multiple breaches of fiduciary duty of loyalty (and only fairly strained breaches of the Articles of Association) *by Hu*, not the defaults *of the named defendant* (the corporate entity controlled by Hu the breaching director/officer). After describing the importance and value of the trademark to the original registered owner, the court states:

> Hu Zhenjiang, as a managing director and the legal representative of the plaintiff, has in accordance with stipulations of law a duty to protect the interests of the company, and is not permitted to use his position or function in the company to seek personal benefits. Yet Hu, acting without the approval of the plaintiff's shareholders, irresponsibly agreed to transfer free of charge an important intangible asset of the company—the category 35 registered trademark for "Shidu"—to the defendant company, a company in which he was the largest shareholder. This transfer effected by Hu was neither authorized under the company's articles of association nor approved by the company's shareholders' meeting. This action breached the duty of loyalty [*zhong-shi yiwu*] owed by a company's managing directors and legal representative to the company, and contravened stipulations against company directors entering into self-dealing contracts or transactions with their company. These actions brought serious injury to the interests of the company.[33]

Having identified a breach by Hu, and declaring the transfer by Shidu Department Store "no expression of the real intent of" the transferor corporate entity (but instead the individual who controls it), the opinion then strains mightily[34] to reverse-apply the breach by Hu to his controlled company and the actual named defendant, Shidu Alliance. This strained jurisprudence allows the court to sanction the defendant company (for the identified breaches of the common shareholder-officer) under the General Principles of the Civil Law[35] and the almost completely unrelated general principles of the 1994 Company Law.[36]

Putting aside the rather mixed-up opinion preserved in this case—and the earnest wish that the judges had simply mandated the plaintiff company's repleading of the case (this time identifying Hu as the defendant)—there is something very noteworthy in this 2000 opinion. It is once again the invocation, by a Beijing Intermediate People's Court, of a specific "duty of loyalty" (*zhongshi yiwu*) from the 1994 Company Law, where no such duty is described in that statute. Instead, Article 59 of that Law merely says that "directors, supervisory board members and managers should ... *loyally* undertake their functions"—a phrase which in 1992–93 had to do with the full implementation of shareholders' and board instructions, not the duty of loyalty as understood under the common law tradition. As is known from subsequent developments, Chinese statute had to wait until 2005 to have an explicitly identified "duty of loyalty" in the 2005 Company Law's entirely new Article 148. And yet, here is another example of a PRC court, invoking this important corporate fiduciary duty, beyond the narrow bright-line stipulations of positive law, and in vindication of the rights of a corporate entity (and its non-self-dealing shareholders) against a corporate officer who is not even a named defendant!

Duty of Loyalty—Beijing Hua'er Case (Beijing, 2001)

Similar to the Shidu trademark case facts immediately above is a 2001 Beijing (Haidian District) controversy regarding a director-officer who left a Chinese-foreign equity joint venture to undertake a competing business.[37] This provides for yet another early invocation of corporate fiduciary duty of loyalty doctrine (also based in the two-Chinese character adverbial phrase meaning "loyally" in Article 59 of the 1994 Company Law) to trump strong defenses advocating exculpation.

From February 1999 Mr. Lin Ming was a director and deputy general manager of a Chinese-foreign equity joint venture approved one year before—Beijing Hua'er Guangdianzi Company, Limited (Beijing Hua'er). In September of 2000, Lin stopped appearing at Beijing Hua'er[38] and by January 2001 had commenced working at the Shenzhen Feilian Guangtongxin Company, Limited (Shenzhen Feilian). It is undisputed that Shenzhen Feilian was engaged in the same business, and thus in competition with, Beijing Hua'er. In 2001, Beijing Hua'er brought suit against Lin Ming, asserting that Lin's work for the second company (and his use of intellectual property and know-how gained at Beijing Hua'er, as well as his solicitation of current Beijing Hua'er employees) was in violation of law, and asked for three remedies: (i) that Lin Ming discontinue work at Shenzhen Feilian; (ii) that Lin Ming pay over to Beijing Hua'er his earnings from Shenzhen Feilian (RMB 41,660 yuan (just over US$5,000)), and (iii) that Lin Ming pay costs to Beijing Hua'er.

Many of the facts surrounding Lin Ming's leaving Beijing Hua'er and commencing work with Shenzhen Feilian in 2000–2001 were disputed by the parties. Here we focus on certain of the *legal* defenses offered by Lin Ming. First, Lin asserted that the relationship between Beijing Hua'er and Lin should be understood as only a simple employment relationship, whereby any proposed prohibition against the application of his talents elsewhere would represent an impermissible restraint on his right to work. In a related pleading, Lin pointed out that no employment contract actually existed between Beijing Hua'er and himself, and thus there was no contractual non-compete provision—i.e., if there was no contractual non-compete, there was no non-compete obligation whatsoever. Second, Lin reminded the court that Beijing Hua'er was organized as a Chinese-foreign equity joint venture, and as such was subject to the law and regulations governing such foreign-invested enterprise establishments *only*, and *not* the PRC Company Law, which governs limited liability companies and companies limited by shares.

The Beijing Haidian court's analysis rebuts the legal assertions of defendant Lin in an extremely able fashion, and clearly differentiates a *corporate* fiduciary duty of loyalty of directors and officers from the much narrower fiduciary obligations of employees at will. While noting that Beijing Hua'er's Articles of Association contained a clause—sourced in an identical article of the Equity Joint Venture Implementing Regulations[39]—forbidding general managers or deputy general managers of Chinese-foreign joint ventures from acting as general manager or deputy general manager for other "economic entities" or being involved in any competitive economic organizations, the court identifies a separate duty sourced in the underlying corporate structure itself:

> In the opinion of this court, this case should not use the Labor Law of the PRC, but instead should use *the [1994] Company Law* and the Equity Joint Venture Law. A director and deputy general manager of a company is part of the company's senior management group; their legally stipulated duty not to enter into competition with their own company is clearly set out in Beijing Hua'er's Articles of Association, *and is different from the general duty of regular employees stipulated in the Labor Law.*[40]

The court then dispenses with Lin's argument that his duties should be construed only under the 1979 Equity Joint Venture Law[41] (which has no notion of corporate fiduciary duties), by pointing out quite reasonably that the 1994 PRC Company Law was promulgated *before* the 1998 establishment of Beijing Hua'er, and that the 1994 Company Law by its terms applies to limited liability company-form firms established under the separate foreign-invested enterprise statutes (except where the issue is specifically addressed by the foreign-invested enterprise laws).[42] In sum, the court says that general legal duties sourced in the subsequent general corporate law will be applied to *all* corporate establishments in China, even those sourced in a statute dating from the late 1970s. Having determined that the Labor Law does not apply, and that general duties in the 1994 Company Law do apply, the court states:

> Article 59 of China's [1994] Company Law stipulates that directors, supervisory board members and managers should comply with the company articles of association, loyally undertake their functions and protect the interests of the company, and should not use their position or function in the company for their own profit. In accordance with this stipulation, Lin Ming, as one of the managers and operators of the company, must—at the time he has a position [in the company]—protect the interests of the company. Before the company approved his resignation, he should have continued to perform his duties as a director and deputy general manager in accordance with the good faith principle,[43] and should not take any action which harms the company. Competitive activity is a kind of behavior which brings very serious injury to the company. Because the competitive activities of directors and officers may involve the use of their position or function in the company, or their use of the technology and commercial secrets known to them, to injure the company, China's [1994] Company Law therefore provides for an absolute prohibition against directors undertaking competing activities.[44] ... Lin Ming's activities are thus at root activities which infringe upon the rights of the company. Hua'er's demand in this lawsuit that Lin Ming terminate his position at Shenzhen Feilian is therefore supported by this court.

The court found completely in favor of the plaintiff company, and ordered Lin Ming to stop working at Shenzhen Feilian (at least until such time as he has formally resigned his positions at Beijing Hua'er), and pay over to Beijing Hua'er RMB 35,000 yuan in salary earned while at Shenzhen Feilian and all of the plaintiff's costs (RMB 1,676 yuan). Here it is important to note what the 2001 Beijing court of first instance did, and what it did not do:

The court might simply have focused on contractual and specifically foreign-invested enterprise-related norms to determine that Lin Ming, personally, had acted in contravention of the Beijing Hua'er Articles of Association and the equity joint venture regulations in participating in a competing venture. (From a contractual standpoint, it might just as well have agreed with Lin in stipulating that the absence of an employment contract between the company and Lin meant an absence of any non-compete obligation (although this might have failed given Labor Law statutory sources for non-compete obligations).)

However, the court went much farther than that, and divined a duty of loyalty/corporate opportunity problem in the subsequently enacted Chinese 1994 Company Law, both for finding of the breach and assessing the money portion of the remedy. Equally important, its analysis understands the legal (but not necessarily *contractual*) rights of the corporate entity as a party in interest which has had *its* rights infringed upon. Moreover, all of this was accomplished by the court before China promulgated a national statute which specifically addresses a "duty of loyalty" or the rights and interests of the corporation and shareholders' meeting with respect to the company's officers or directors.

Notes

1 In Chinese, the statement that something is "just" a flower vase (*huaping*), means it is "for decoration" or "just for show."
2 CSRC, *Guanyu Zhengzhou Baiwen Gufenyouxian gongsi (Jituan) ji Youguanre-nyuan Weifan Zhengquanfagui Xingwei de Chufa Jueding* (Decision Regarding Sanction of the Behavior of Zhengzhou Baiwen (Group) Co., Ltd. In Violation of Securities Laws and Regulations), *Zhengjianfazi* [2001] No. 19, 27 September 2001. The details following are taken from a number of contemporaneous reports, including: *"Huaping Dongshi" Lu Jiahao Gai Fu Sha Zeren* (What Responsibility Should "Flower Vase" Director Lu Jiahao Bear?), 22 June 2002, at *zhonghuacaihuiwang* (China Finance Association Net) at www.e521.com; *Lu Jiahao: Mo Dang Huaping Dongshi* (Lu Jiahao: No Longer a Flower Vase Director), *Zhongguo Jingji Shibao* (China Economic Daily), 14 August 2002; *"Huaping Dongshi" Gao Zhengjianhui Beibohui Lu Jiaho Keneng Shangsu* ("The Flower Vase Director" Suit Against the CSRC is Denied Lu Jiahao May Appeal), *Beijing Yaole Xinbao* (Beijing Entertainment News), 13 September 2002, at www.sina.com.cn.
3 Zhengzhou Baiwen (Group) Co., Ltd. Much of the dispute, and contemporaneous writing, focused on the fact that Professor Lu thought he was an "independent" director. In fact, as the CSRC pointed out, it did not matter if Lu was a normal director or an independent director in trying to divine what his legal duties might be, and how he breached them.
4 Lu said that he had first met Zhengbaiwen Chairman Li Fuqian "socially" in late 1994, and accepted a position on the board of Zhengbaiwen in January of 1995 as a "societal director" (*shehui dongshi*). (The idea here, which it should be noted has no basis whatsoever in Chinese law, is something like an "outside" or "non-executive" director—i.e., the individual is appointed from "society" at large, and is not an officer or leader in the corporate enterprise. Apparently Chairman Li told Professor Lu that Lu would be able to monitor the company on behalf of "society" at large. Chinese law in 1995 made no distinction between directors (the "independent director" system only being implemented from 2002). Lu further stated that Chairman Li Fuqian had agreed Lu would not participate in the company's management or business, and would not be compensated by Zhengbaiwen. Professor Lu said that he thought of Zhengbaiwen as a quasi-governmental organization (dressed up as a corporate entity)—stating he could not refuse the company (government) request that he serve in the named capacity. As he said to reporters, "I was *independent* from the management level of the company, thinking

of my role as that of an honorary consultant" (indicating that Professor Lu understood his "independent" status as a signifier of his independence from responsibility for the actions of the company!)

5 The CSRC lawyer also articulated a broader rationale for the enforcement action against the hapless Lu: in court the lawyer apparently stated that the enforcement action against Professor Lu and his fellow directors was meant to get the attention of others preparing to act as directors at China's listed companies, and to force them to think hard about the liabilities they may face, and whether or not they have the capability to serve. Lu's suit ultimately was not accepted by the Beijing court, as on 12 September 2002 the court found that he had not appealed the CSRC rehearing result to the court within the 15-day time limit for appeals from administrative rehearings set forth in the Administrative Litigation Law and the Supreme People's Court Interpretative Opinion on the Administrative Litigation Law. See *"Huaping Dongshi" Gao Zhengjianhui Beibohui Lu Jiaho Keneng Shangsu* ("The Flower Vase Director" Suit Against the CSRC is Denied Lu Jiahao May Appeal), *Beijing Yaole Xinbao* (Beijing Entertainment News), 13 September 2002, at www.sina.com.cn. Lu apparently never appealed the Beijing Intermediate People's Court decision.

6 Guangdong Province, Huizhou City, Intermediate People's Court (2002) *Hui Zhong Fa Min Yi Zhong Zi* No. 322 Civil Case Judgment ("Huizhou Intermediate People's Court Judgment"), reproduced in Qian 2006: 205–207.

7 *[2002] Huicheng Fa Min Chuzi* No. 209 Civil Judgment, original opinion language quoted in Huizhou Intermediate People's Court Judgment.

8 This would indicate fraud or some similar problem to an alert buyer.

9 Huizhou Intermediate People's Court Judgment.

10 Chinese law grafts onto the shareholder-oriented corporate form established in 1992–94 certain pre-existing civil law concepts, such as the idea of a "legal representative" or "representative director" (in Chinese, *"fading daibiao"*). Under the 1994 Company Law, the chairman of the board of directors of a PRC company is automatically the "legal representative" with non-exclusive authority to bind the company at the very least in contract, and wield the firm's "chop" or seal (itself dispositive evidence of that agency power). Under the 2005 Company Law, the chairman of the board of directors is no longer automatically the firm's "legal representative" and the agency powers of the "legal representative" have been diluted.

11 "... the company for which he served as legal representative had many discussions at the board level and resolutions prior to his actions, and the transaction was implemented by many people, constituting a collective action by the company, not the individual action of the appellant."

12 "The appellant was not the specific individual who handled the purchase of equipment. Nor did the articles of association of the company stipulate that the chairman of the board undertake inspection of purchased equipment. The appellant committed no subjective fault whatsoever, and the actions of the appellant and the 'losses' of the appellee had no cause and effect relationship."

13 "... and the transaction was implemented by many people, constituting a collective action by the company, not the individual action of the appellant."

14 "... in accordance with the stipulations of the [1994] Company Law, the directors, supervisory board members and managers should abide by the company's articles of association, loyally perform their tasks and protect the interests of the company, and not use their position or functions and powers in the company to seek personal gain; where in the performance of company functions they breach law, administrative regulation or the stipulations of the company articles of association, causing injury to the company, they should bear responsibility for compensation."

15 See the same necessarily limited inquiry in the Beijing Campus case, below.

16 This case is reported in a volume of representative cases published by the Beijing Municipal Higher People's Court, with commentaries appended—see Beijing Municipal Higher People's Court 2006: 49–57 (report and analysis by Tao Jun).

17 Tianjin No. 2 Intermediate People's Court (2004) *Er Zhong Zhi Zi* No. 471.

18 Tianjin No. 2 Intermediate People's Court (2004) *Er Zhong Zhi Zi* No. 129.

19 With respect to the authority and duties of the General Manager, the Tianjin Intermediate People's Court determined as fact that the Beijing Campus articles of association required that the appointed general manager of the firm be responsible for thoroughly implementing the resolutions of the board of directors and—within the scope of authority delegated by the board—represent the company in external matters and internal administration (while being responsible for day-to-day management work).

20 This clause is similar to the general damages article for director, supervisory board, and officers' defaults that is new Article 150 of the 2005 Company Law. Compare: 1994 Company Law, Article 63: "Directors, supervisory board members and managers who violate law, administrative regulation or the company articles of association in the course of performing their corporate tasks, causing injury to the company, shall be liable for compensatory [damages]"; and 2005 Company Law, Article 150: "Directors, supervisory board members and high ranking managers who violate the stipulations of law, administrative regulation or the company articles of association in the course of performing their corporate tasks, causing injury to the company, shall be liable for compensatory [damages]."

21 The commentator proceeds to explain how, under the 2005 Company Law, the actions of Cao Jianwei are specifically prohibited, and thus actionable, under Article 149's prohibition against loans made by officers without board or shareholder approval, etc.

22 This case is reported in Wang 2005: 362–371.

23 See the discussion concerning the "legal representative" or "representative director" position under the Chinese law of enterprise legal persons in connection with the Ye Jianmin duty of care case, above at note 10.

24 Actually, land-use rights, or a long-term leasehold interest granted under contract by the owner of the land, the state.

25 The case report makes all parties anonymous. The fact that the case report by the Beijing No. 1 Intermediate People's Court does not use identifiable names, and describes serious *mistakes* by the courts that apparently heard the case, indicates that the report describes a real case, as opposed to a hypothetical formulation conceived for didactic purposes.

26 These are the Articles which specify narrow duty of care obligations and duty of loyalty prohibitions for directors, supervisory board members, and managers: see Articles 59 (obligation to abide by law and articles of association, loyally undertake tasks, protect the interests of the company, and not use position in the company for personal gain, or to procure illegal income, or misappropriate company funds); 60 (prohibition against directors and managers borrowing company funds or loaning company funds to third parties, using company funds to establish personal accounts, using company funds as security for the obligations of shareholders or other third party individuals); 61 (prohibition against directors and managers entering into competition with the company, and self-dealing (entering into contracts or other transactions with the company, unless approved by the shareholders meeting or permitted in the articles of association); and 62 (disclosure of company secrets).

27 The lower court proceeds to confirm each of the proposed deductions from the buy-back for the real estate owned by Party B to the Company. It finds no misappropriation of Company assets by Party B in either the original transaction

(transfer of the real estate to the Company by Party B) or the self-helping deductions by Party B on the buy-back payments owed by Party B to the Company.

28 The higher court then makes a detailed examination of the validity of each deduction by Party B against the amounts owed to the Company.

29 This commentary points out that in post-October 2005 China, Articles 148 and 149 of the 2005 Company Law would clearly prohibit Party B's actions, and cause the return of any monies taken from the Company in connection with the self-dealing transaction. (Beijing No. 1 Municipal Intermediate People's Court, 4th Chamber 2005: 369–370).

30 This case is reported in *Beijingshi Diyi Zhongji Fayuan Minshi Panjueshu* (No. 1 Beijing Municipal Intermediate People's Court Judgment) (2000), *yizhong zhuzi* No. 14.

31 The Shidu Opinion describes Hu as the "*zhixing dongshi*" or, literally, "managing director," a position used in China and derived from UK (and Hong Kong) practice. It is unclear whether Hu is a member of the Shidu Department Store board of directors (and what we might call in US parlance an "executive director"), as well as being a senior executive officer of the company.

32 See General Principles of Civil Law, Articles 58 and 61.

33 Shidu Opinion, 4th paragraph of judgment section.

34 "[Hu] is the major shareholder and the legal representative of Shidu Alliance. Therefore, Shidu Alliance must bear the responsibility for the actions of [Hu] in the process implementing the trademark transfer. In the process of implementing transfer of the trademark, [Hu's] subjective intent—as the legal representative [of the defendant company]—can be seen as the subjective intent of the defendant [company's] implementation of the transfer action. Thus, at the time of implementation of the transfer, the defendant should have known that the trademark transfer was undertaken by [Hu] for his own benefit using his position and without approval of the plaintiff's shareholders' meeting, and moreover that [Hu's] actions in regard of the transfer were undertaken in contravention of relevant stipulations prohibiting directors' self-dealing contracts or transactions with their own company. And the defendant [company] should have understood that its acceptance of the trademark transfer for no consideration would bring great injury to the plaintiff. In this situation, where the defendant [company] still implemented the transfer for its own inappropriate interest, then it has subjective fault, and constitutes actions harmful to the interests of the plaintiff [company] undertaken in league with [Hu's] bad intent."

35 General Principles of the Civil Law, Articles 2, 55, 58, and 96.

36 1994 Company Law, Article 4(1) (declaring that shareholders in Chinese companies shall enjoy certain rights in accordance with their equity investment).

37 *Beijing Haidian Qu Renmin Fayuan Shenli Huaer Gongsi yu Lin Ming Jingye Jinzhi Jifen An Minshi Panjue Shu*, (2001) *haijing chuzi* No. 1137, available at www.chinacourt.org/public/detail.php?id=145191.

38 One of the many items in dispute was whether or not he had formally resigned his positions as director and officer of Beijing Hua'er.

39 See *Zhonghua Renmin Gongheguo Zhongwai Hezi Jingying Qiyefa Shishi Tiaoli* (Implementing Regulations of the PRC Law on Chinese-foreign Equity Joint Ventures), 22 July 2001, CLC 2006: 1–33 (Article 37).

40 Emphasis added.

41 *Zhonghua Renmin Gongheguo Zhongwai Hezi Jingying Qiyefai* (PRC Law on Chinese-foreign Equity Joint Ventures), 1 July 1979 (as subsequently amended), CLC 2006: 1–31.

42 See 2004 Company Law, Article 18 (carried over into the 2005 Company Law at Article 218).

43 The judges here use the formulation for "good faith" under the civil law, and as declared in the General Principles of the Civil Law ("*chengshi xinyong yuanze*").

This terminology is distinct from the CSRC-inspired Chinese characters used to signify the corporate fiduciary duties, "*chengxin zeren*" or "*chengxin yiwu.*" Notwithstanding, the language in this opinion does show a nice importation of the civil law idea of good faith into the construction of corporate directors and officers' duties.

44 The opinion then continues to recite the specific prohibition against competing activities in the 1994 Company Law (at Article 61) and the above-mentioned prohibition against the same in Beijing Hua'er's Articles of Association (tracking the equity joint venture laws and regulations).

Bibliography

Bebchuk, L.A. and M. J. Roe (1999) "A Theory of Path Dependency in Corporate Ownership and Governance," *Stanford Law Review*, 52, no. 1: 127–170.

Beijing Municipal Higher People's Court (ed.) (2006) *Gongsifa Xinxing Yian Anli Panjie* [*Explanation of Difficult Case Judgments Under the New Form Company Law*], Beijing: Falu Chubanshe (Law Publishing House).

Beijing No. 1 Municipal Intermediate People's Court, 4th Chamber (ed.) (2005) *Gongsifa Shenpan Shiwu yu Dianxing Anli Pingxi* [*Company Law Hearing Guide— Critique and Analysis of Representative Cases*], Beijing: Zhonguo Jiancha Chubanshe (China Procurate Publishing House).

Black, B. and R. Kraakman (1996) "A Self-Enforcing Model of Corporate Law," *Harvard Law Review* 109, no. 8: 1911–82.

China Construction Bank (2005) "China Construction Bank Hong Kong Offering Prospectus" (October). Available at www.hkex.com.hk/listedco/listconews/sehk/20051014/LTN20051014000.htm.

Clarke, D.C. (1996) "Power and Politics in the Chinese Court System: The Enforcement of Civil Judgments," *Columbia Journal of Asian Law* 10, no. 1: 1–92.

—— (2003) "Corporate Governance in China: An Overview," *China Economic Review* 14, no. 4: 494–507.

CLC (2006) Guowuyuan Fazhibangongshi (Legislative Affairs Office of the State Council) (ed.) (2006) *Gongsi Falu Guizhang Sifa Jieshi Quanshu* [*Compendium of Company Law, Regulation and Judicial Explanations*], Beijing: Zhongguo Fazhi Chubanshe (China Legal System Publishing House).

Coffee, J.C. (1999) "The Future as History: The Prospects for Global Convergence in Corporate Governance and its Implications," *Northwestern University Law Review* 93, no. 3: 641–707.

Company Law Draft Amendment (2004) Guowuyuanfazhiban Xingzheng Mishusi (Administrative Secretariat of the Legislative Affairs Office of the State Council) "Zhonghua Renmin Gongheguo Gongsifa (Xiugai Caoan) [Company Law of the PRC (Draft Amendment)]," issued 5 July 2004.

Company Law Scholar's Draft (2004) Wang Baoshu (ed.) *Zhongguo Gongsifa Xiugai Caoan Jianyigao* [*Proposed Draft Amended PRC Company Law*], Beijing: Shehui Kexue Wenxian Chubanshe (Social Sciences Academic Press).

CSRC (2005): Zhongguo Zhengquan Jiandu Weiyuanhui (China Securities Regulatory Commission) (ed.) *Xianxing Zhengquan Qihuo Guizhang Huibian (2005 Nian Bian)* [*Compendium of Securities and Futures Regulations Currently in Effect (2005 Edition)*], Beijing: Zhongguo Jinrong Chubanshe (China Finance Publishing House).

Gilson, R.J. (2001) "Globalizing Corporate Governance: Convergence of Form or Function," *American Journal of Comparative Law* 49, no. 2: 329–357.

Hansmann, H. and R. Kraakman (2001) "The End of History for Corporate Law," *Georgetown Law Journal* 89, no. 2: 439–468.

Howson, N. C. (1997) "China's Company Law: One Step Forward Two Steps Back? A Modest Complaint," *Columbia Journal of Asian Law* 11, no. 1: 127–173.

—— (2005) "Corporate Fiduciary Duties in China—Incorporation and Extension to the Heart of China's Corporate Law Problem," paper presented at Conference: New Scholarship on Chinese Law—A Celebration in Honor of Stanley Lubman, Columbia University School of Law, New York, 15 April 2005.

Industrial and Commercial Bank of China (2006) *Industrial and Commercial Bank of China Hong Kong Offering Prospectus* (October). Available at www.hkex.com.hk/listedco/listconews/sehk/20061016/LTN20061016000.htm.

Kanda, H. and C.J. Milhaupt (2003) "Re-examining Legal Transplants: The Director's Fiduciary Duty in Japanese Corporate Law," *The American Journal of Comparative Law* 51, no. 4: 887–901.

La Porta, R., F. Lopez-de-Silanes, A. Schliefer, and R.W. Vishny (1997) "Legal Determinants of External Finance," *Journal of Finance* 52, no. 3: 1131–1150.

Lieberthal, Kenneth (1995) *Governing China: From Revolution Through Reform*, New York: W.W. Norton.

Liu, J.H. (1998) *Gufenyouxiangongsi Gudongquanyi de Baohu* [*The Protection of Shareholders' Rights in Companies Limited by Shares*], Beijing: Falu Chubanshe (Law Publishing House).

Liu, L.S. (2003) "Global Markets and Parochial Institutions: The Transformation of Taiwan's Corporate Law System," in C.J. Milhaupt (ed.), *Global Markets, Domestic Institutions: Corporate Law and Governance in a New Era of Cross-border Deals*, New York: Columbia University Press, 400–434.

Liu, S.D. (2006) "Beyond Convergence: Conflicts of Legitimacy in a Chinese Lower Court," *Law and Social Inquiry* 31, no. 1: 75–106.

Luo, P.X. (2006) "Judicial Plights in The Context of the New Company Law of China," paper presented at The Third Asian Law Institute (ASLI) Conference, Shanghai, PRC, 25–6 May 2006.

Milhaupt, C.J. (ed.) (2003) *Global Markets, Domestic Institutions: Corporate Law and Governance in a New Era of Cross-border Deals*, New York: Columbia University Press.

——(2005) "In the Shadow of Delaware? The Rise of Hostile Takeovers in Japan," *Columbia Law Review* 105, no. 7: 2171–2216.

Peerenboom, R. (2002) *China's Long March Toward Rule of Law*, New York: Cambridge University Press.

Pistor, K. and C. Xu (2003) "Fiduciary Duty in Transitional Civil Law Jurisdictions: Lessons from the Incomplete Law Theory," in C.J. Milhaupt (ed.), *Global Markets, Domestic Institutions: Corporate Law and Governance in a New Era of Cross-border Deals*, New York: Columbia University Press, 77–106.

Qian, W.Q. (ed.) (2006) *Gongsi Susong* [*Corporate Litigation*], Beijing: Renmin Fayuan Chubanshe (People's Court Publishing House).

Shanghai Stock Exchange (2004) Shanghai Zhengquan Jiaoyisuo (ed.) *2004 Shichang Ziliao* [*2004 Market Data*], Shanghai: Shanghai Stock Exchange.

Share System Collection (1994) Guojia Guoyou Zichan Guanliju Qiyesi (National State-owned Assets Bureau Enterprise Department) (ed.) *Gufenzhi Fagui Zhidu*

Wenjian Huibian [*Share System—Collection of Laws and Regulations, System, Documents*], Beijing: Neibu Ciliao (Internal Publication).

Story, J. (1874) *Commentaries on the Law of Agency*, 8th edn. rev., Boston: Little, Brown & Co.

Stout, L.A. (2003) "On the Export of U.S.-Style Corporate Fiduciary Duties to Other Cultures: Can a Transplant Take?" in C.J. Milhaupt (ed.), *Global Markets, Domestic Institutions: Corporate Law and Governance in a New Era of Cross-border Deals*, New York: Columbia University. Press, 46–76.

Tenev, S., C. Zhang, and L. Brefort (2002) *Corporate Governance and Enterprise Reform in China: Building the Institutions of Modern Markets*, Washington, DC: World Bank and the International Finance Corporation.

Wang, B.S. (1994) "Gufenyouxiangongsi de Dongshi he Dongshihui [Directors and the Board of Directors at Companies Limited by Shares]," *Waiguofaxue Shiiping* [*Foreign Legal Studies Commentary and Explanation*] 1: 5–18.

Wang, L.M. (2004) *Zhongguo Minfadian Caoan Jianyigao Ji Shuoming* [*Proposal Draft and Explanation of Draft Chinese Civil Code*], Beijing: Zhongguo Fazhi Chubanshe (China Legal System Publishing House).

Wang, S.Q. (ed.) (2005) *Xingongsifa—Dianxing Anli Pingxi* [*The New Company Law—Critiques and Analysis of Representative Cases*], Beijing: Zhongguo Gong-shang Chubanshe (China Industrial and Commercial Publishing House).

West, M.D. (2001) "The Puzzling Divergence of Corporate Law: Evidence and Explanations from Japan and the United States," *University of Pennsylvania Law Review* 150, no. 2: 527–601.

Xi, X.M. and W. Jia (2003) "Zhengquan Shichang Xujia Chenshu Minshi Peichang Zhidu [The Civil Compensation System for Misrepresentation in Securities Markets]," *Zhengquan Falu Pinglun (Securities Law Review)* 3: 33–75.

Xin, C.Y. (2003) "What Kind of Judicial Power Does China Need?" *International Journal of Constitutional Law* 1, no. 1: 58–78.

Zhao, X.D. (ed.) (2004) *Shangshi Gongsi Dongshi Zeren yu Chufa* [*Responsibilities and Sanctions for Directors of Listed Companies*], Beijing: Zhongguo Fazhi Chu-banshe (China Law System Publisher).

—— (2005) *Xinjiu Gongsifa Bijiao Fenxi* [*Comparative Analysis of the New and Old Company Laws*], Beijing: Renmin Fayuan Chubanshe (People's Court Publishing House).

10 The politics of corporate governance in Taiwan

*Lawrence S. Liu**

Introduction: the political economy

Domination by politics

In election-intensive and diplomatically isolated Taiwan today, domestic politics dominates everything. Since the late 1980s, its vigorous political reform has taken precedence over goals for economic growth, creating a feisty, precocious democracy but leaving a polarized society marred by subethnic alienation and controversies over reunification with or separation from China. Cut-throat competition among political parties such as the KMT, DPP, PFP, and TSU since 2000, while no party had a majority, has turned the political scene into a killing field. Corporate governance in Taiwan has fallen prey to this phenomenon.[1] Lackluster corporate and regulatory governance in the government-dominated financial sector, for example, is a very relevant factor in Taiwan's indigenous "financial crisis" of 1998, the government-coerced moratorium of foreclosures in 1998–99 and the cleanup of non-performing loans (NPL) since the 2000s. While President Chen's family and in-laws faced prosecutions in 2006–2007 for corruption and insider trading, for example, faction politics within the DPP led to a very harsh law-enforcement campaign against the business community so as to regain popular support and ensure a public image of distancing from Chen.

Meanwhile, cross-Strait politics as played in Taiwan has arguably reduced the competitiveness of Taiwanese firms, and circumvention of China-related investment rules has aggravated their corporate governance problems. For two decades, Taiwan's industries have migrated massively into China despite these rules. One such rule, which was borrowed from a Company Law provision soon after its repeal, is an investment quota for listed companies capped at 40 percent of their net worth. Other rules impose industry-specific restrictions such as those for banking and high-tech manufacturing. One foreign securities analyst estimated that this kind of investment restriction puts a 10 percent "regulatory discount" (amounting to US$60 billion, based on the market capitalization of US$600 billion at the end of 2006) on the value of Taiwan's capital market.[2]

Although illegal, circumvention of investment rules motivated by perceived political consideration is viewed by some in Taiwan's business community as legitimate. However, evasion of law clearly worsens the corporate governance challenge because, to avoid government attention and enforcement, listed companies would try to be as opaque as possible in regard to China-bound investment. One such example is the alleged non-compliant, gratuitous transfer of technology and business by United Microelectronics Technology (UMC), a Taiwan-based leader in the semiconductor foundry business, to a similar business called Hoqien that was set up by former senior UMC employees in China and run as a strategic affiliate. The government soon launched a prosecution for alleged breach of trust despite a later gesture by Hoqien to "donate" 15 percent of its interest to UMC through a gratuitous share offering.

Foreign firms have arbitraged this introverted policy and profited handsomely from restrictions forcing Taiwanese firms to forego assured revenues and strategic growth in China. For example, in 2006 Standard Chartered Bank bought Hinchu International Commercial Bank (HICC) because, according to HICC's founders, the Taiwan bank was barred from serving its customers in China and had no future unless it became a part of a foreign bank to unshackle itself from restrictions imposed by Taiwan's government. Also in 2006, American private equity fund Carlyle announced intentions to work with controlling owner-managers to launch a tender offer for ASE, a Taiwan-based leader in packaging and testing semiconductor chips, and if successful, to delist it. Rumored to avoid the 40 percent China-investment cap, ASE attracted the attention of Taiwan's top political leaders from all parties, and soon pledged massive investment in Taiwan. The buyout deal eventually failed, ostensibly for lack of agreement on the buyout prices, but not before the government had publicized its displeasure with foreign private equity funds openly testing China-related investment rules and even planning to borrow locally to finance such reflagging deals.

Ambivalent government–business relationship

With its martial-law past and industrial policy inclination to create economic success so as to legitimize the regime, Taiwan has had an ambivalent government–business relationship. Through elaborate laws and rules affording the government wide discretion, it guides, cajoles, regulates, and competes with private businesses. Despite democratization, the government is still an entrenched owner-regulator in key sectors such as financial services, transportation, energy, and telecommunications. After martial law was lifted in 1987, many previous grievances resurfaced and were handled politically rather than judicially, giving elected politicians who do not have much respect for the law an angle to meddle in these matters, including individual cases such as mergers and acquisitions in the financial market. Politicians and regulators generally have more faith in government actions than in market forces, and see corporate governance as a social-justice issue against Taiwan's business community. On the other hand, the government has failed to set a good example by demanding high corporate governance standards at state-owned enterprises (SOEs). Instead, for example, the government intensified its intervention in SOEs and the many partially privatized listed companies, ignoring their boards and other stakeholders. For example, it forced corporate name changes upon some SOEs for ideological reasons, and bureaucrats sitting as directors for the majority (that is, the government itself) excluded labor directors from the decision-making process leading to these changes. The government controls about half of the assets in the banking sector to ensure enough control not only to maintain "stability" in the market, but perhaps also to achieve political goals. For example, senior executives of SOEs and government-linked banks have publicly signed pledges of support, a highly political act, before major elections. Also, financial regulators even issued directives requiring banks to waive conflicts of interest at the board level, so that government-supported directors in private banks in which the government or government-linked financial institutions also own shares would not be held liable for competing with the banks they serve.

Until the establishment of the Financial Supervisory Commission in 2004, the Ministry of Finance (MOF) and related ministries were both the regulator and the owner of government-linked listed companies and financial institutions. Even today, retired or seconded senior government officials often head up these firms. Beginning with the cross-Strait crisis in 1996, both the KMT and the DPP governments mobilized various public and centralized private pension funds, including a National Stabilization Fund, to stabilize the stock market in plain disregard of the fiduciary duty of the trustees to preserve and enhance fund assets. With insufficient funding at its Central Deposit Insurance Company (similar to but far weaker than its American counterpart) or the Financial Restructuring Fund (set up following the American Resolution Trust Corporation model), the government has used state-owned financial institutions to bail out failing banks.

This essay shows, in detail, how politics has informed major corporate governance issues in Taiwan. The following section examines major issues regarding "juridical directors" and the transplant of the independent directors system. The next two sections look at how employees are treated as stakeholders, and review the concept and enforcement of fiduciary duty. This is followed by an examination of important accounting and disclosure issues. The next section assesses the market for corporate control in Taiwan, and M&A deals and issues, and is followed with illustration of how Taiwan enforces corporate laws. The final section is a conclusion.

Configuring the board of directors

The problem with juridical directors

A major corporate governance problem in Taiwan is juridical directors allowed by Article 27 of the Company Law. Originated in pre-1949, KMT-controlled China as a handy tool to control SOEs, this rule allows corporate and government (but not individual) shareholders to appoint natural persons as their representatives so as to be elected as directors and supervisors. Therefore, the government uses this power to redesignate representatives whenever convenient, without re-election. Appointees may be academics, serving or retired regulators, cronies, and politicians. This rule also aggravates the dysfunction of supervisors under Taiwan's binary board structure, and intensifies the conflict of serving two masters.

The remedy for this problem seems easy: abolish Article 27 altogether. But politics would not allow it because repeal would be against the self-interest of the government; politicians want to remain grabby, and regulators are deeply concerned with losing control over partially privatized SOEs. As a result, the Securities and Exchange Law was amended in 2006 to set forth an illusory prohibition: directors and supervisors may not be appointed by the same shareholder. But circumvention is easy by using different holding entities. Bureaucrats knew about this loophole before they drew up this amendment. This hypocrisy was made known when the long-rumored Rebar Group corporate scandal finally broke in 2006–2007, in which the family patriarch Mr. Wang and his fourth wife disappeared, but not before the family had siphoned funds from group companies for years by using shell companies to enter into multiple related-party transactions approved by seemingly unrelated juridical directors. Regulators dealing with this crisis, again, first made a big fanfare about the sins of juridical directorship and swore to repeal it, only to quietly drop this idea after a review meeting with senior politicians in the cabinet.

Gradual migration to unitary board

Against this background came Taiwan's gradual migration to the unitary board system. Despite the binary board model in Taiwan, in 2002 it followed some foreign (including Japanese) experience and began to require that companies applying for initial public offerings install at least two independent directors and one "independent supervisor" (thereby implicitly admitting that supervisors in fact have not been independent).[3] Further, in 2006 a Securities and Exchange Law amendment for the first time provided for the legal basis for opting into a unitary, Anglo-American style of board of directors, with an audit committee in lieu of supervisors.[4] The same amendment also for the first time sets forth the legal authority for mandating independent directors at financial holding companies, banks, large securities firms, and large-cap listed industrial corporations. This mixed menu of optional and mandatory rules transplanted Anglo-American rules (including the American Sarbanes-Oxley Act) and is overlaid upon the existing rules of more civil law origin.

Gradual migration to the unitary board with an audit committee will remain controversial in Taiwan for some time. Traditionalists certainly prefer the old regime. Some academics have forcefully argued that the binary system could work just as well as the unitary system. Again, politics has had much to do with this reform. Taiwanese regulators pushed for this migration largely because this is the perceived global trend (that is, formal convergence). Already suffering from diplomatic isolation, Taiwan does not want to appear to be under-performing in the corporate-governance ratings, including in informal reviews at corporate-governance roundtables with other Asian economies annually organized by the Organization for Economic Co-operation and Development (OECD), one of the rare opportunities for Taiwan to attend international conferences organized by government entities. More important, Taiwan's regulators could not abolish the juridical directorship system. The requirement of having one-fifth of board members as independent directors (but with a minimum of two) serving individually rather than as representatives hopefully will increase board accountability.

The new regime also reflects a political perception of saints (independent directors, especially those who are academics) and sinners (incumbent management, especially "family-run" companies and controlling persons). The new amendment took its final drafting form in mid-2004, when the Procomp securities fraud scandal exploded right before the formation of the new Financial Supervisory Commission (FSC), forcing the new agency to start its work in the shadow of major corporate scandals. In the aftermath of another corporate scandal involving the Rebar Group in 2006–2007, senior FSC officials have been threatened with prosecutions for failing their public duty to enforce corporate laws and their neglect in forcing failing banks to fold. Distrusting and sometimes demonizing family control, Taiwanese regulators therefore wanted independent directors and audit committees to alleviate their supervisory burden. This is why under the 2006 amendment only independent directors or the audit committee (if one is set up) have the power to approve important corporate matters and internal systems. Tipping the accountability balance, and despite ownership concentration in Taiwan, this new rule virtually grants independent directors, who typically do not own (and are discouraged from owning) shares in their companies, a veto over important corporate matters. Signaling more draconian regulatory measures ahead, beginning in 2007, a rule now requires listed companies to videotape or audiotape board meetings, compliance with which is enforced by requiring external auditors to comment on it in their opinions. These tapes will be convenient for law-enforcement authorities, who in recent years have developed a keen interest in investigating business crimes such as the breach of trust offense discussed below.

Labor as stakeholder

Enterprise law

While American corporate law is largely devoid of employee concerns, European corporate law follows the "enterprise law" approach and stresses these concerns much more, as exemplified by co-determination statutes in Germany, the Netherlands and some Scandinavian countries. In this regard, Taiwan follows Europe more closely, even though it has not yet gone to the extreme of co-determination.[5] Taiwan's Company Law codifies a number of employee-oriented policies. For example, the articles of incorporation of a Taiwan company must provide that a minimum percentage of net after-tax profits shall be awarded to employees as bonuses, and employees in companies other than SOEs enjoy a pre-emptive right to subscribe for 10–15 percent of any offering of new shares for cash.[6] These socialist rules were designed to ameliorate the perceived sharp edges of hard-core capitalism.[7] But they can lead to perverse consequences.

Employee bonus shares

Take mandatory employee bonuses as an example. Embedded in traditional Chinese business culture and used as political tool to co-opt workers, the ideal is simple: when a business is profitable, its owners should pay bonuses (out of net profits after tax).[8] In fact, however, employees already customarily receive performance-based bonuses (usually measured by multiples of monthly wages) on a pre-tax, expensing basis. In other words, they actually receive two "bonuses," the first dictated by labor market conditions, and the second by the employee-welfare provisions in the Company Law. Historically, the minimum profit-sharing provision in the corporate charter has been set very low so as to achieve token compliance. But this percentage increased substantially, sometimes to the 5–10 percent range for high-tech companies, after Taiwan's capital market became more mature and new listings increased in the late 1980s.

But the most perverse result relates to the "bonus shares" awarded to employees pursuant to this rule. It is the product of politics blended with two quirky rules in Taiwan's Company Law. First, the Company Law permits employees to receive shares in lieu of cash as mandatory after-tax bonuses.[9] Second, the Company Law has followed a very traditional and rigid concept of legal capital, which means in part that shares must have a par value, and that registration of paid-in capital is mandatory. From an accounting perspective, shares awarded to employees as bonuses are valued on the basis of the par value, which is nominal (and usually NT$10 per share) and bears no relation to net worth or market value. As a result, employees may receive listed shares whose market value is substantially more than accounting value or par value, with very weak vesting or similar lock-up mechanisms. Moreover, employees pay personal income tax on the basis of the nominal amount par value.[10] Since this is mandatory sharing of after-tax profits, the company cannot expense the bonuses.

The Taiwan high-tech sector, with its strong growth potential and the desire to reward and retain talent through non-cash compensation, took significant advantage of these rules during the bull market of the 1990s, despite claims by some Western competitors such as Micron that this amounted to dumping their products on the export market (as the failure to expense reduced labor cost, which in turn reduced selling cost). The rule's use of par value created a Frankenstein: arbitraging the rule eroded the government's tax base, aggravating Taiwan's budgetary deficit. Also, as the Company Law does not dictate how such bonuses (and new shares reserved under the pre-emptive employee subscription right for new shares) are to be allocated among the employees, it is safe to assume that senior management reaped a good share of the windfall.[11] Without meaningful vesting or lock-up rules for the bonus shares, the system does not necessarily reduce employee turnover. Yet shareholders suffer significant dilution because of the award of such cheap stock.

Reforming the bonus shares scheme

Reforming the bonus shares scheme is desirable, except that it will also be politically painful. The reform could cause a stock market decline, as expensive salaries significantly reduce corporate earnings. The tech sector epitomizes Taiwan's competitiveness and wields significant lobbying power. Hopeful of market stability and prosperity, regulators and politicians pursued delaying tactics out of concern over the after-effect of any reform. It was not until both foreign institutional investors and grass-root investors made increasingly vocal complaints that a moderate change in the dividend policy of Taiwan companies was made. Finally, during the mid-2000s, Taiwan's budget deficit and concern about nonconformity with the global trend toward expensing options began to force a change (to begin in 2008) towards expensing bonus shares.

Labor in the state sector

Other than the bonus shares and pre-emptive subscription right, Taiwan's mild socialism has not favored employees as stakeholders. Unionization and labor movements in Taiwan's vibrant private sector were suppressed during the martial law era, and still do not have much following. However, since the change in government in 2000 some form of co-determination has emerged in the state-owned sector, largely the result of party competition and populist politicking in Taiwan. At government-linked industrial companies and financial institutions, workers are much more organized than in the private sector. For job security reasons, they are generally opposed to privatization, including divestiture of government-held shares or the issuance of additional issues to dilute the government's ownership. Where government-linked companies are multi-product, multi-division firms, they also oppose the breakup and sell-off of operating units.

Union-appointed labor directors in the state sector

In 2000, the Law Governing the Management of State-owned Enterprises was amended to require that SOEs have one-fifth of the board of directors be representatives of the union. This is a transplant of the *Aufsicherat* system from the German co-determination statute, albeit a heavily diluted version. This rule came about first as the collateral damage of a reform initiative by the Taiwan government in the mid-1990s to separate the business arm (later known as Chung Hua Telecom, or CHT) from the regulatory arm of the Directorate General of Telecommunication (DGT), so as to corporatize and then gradually privatize it.[12] To placate the 36,000 or so DGT employees who would eventually lose their civil servant status as the employees of a private company, a special statute governing CHT's status was adopted. The CHT statute guarantees that at least one-fifth of its board of directors should be "experts." In enacting this statute, Taiwan's Legislative Yuan adopted a concurrent resolution ensuring that such experts should first be drawn from CHT's unionized employees. Although not legally binding, this resolution is so powerful that it would have been political suicide for officials in the executive branch to ignore it. Hence, the seed of co-determination in Taiwan's state sector was sown.

State-sector unions resisting full privatization

With increasing unionization in the state sector, privatization came to a halt by the mid-1990s. Privatization under Taiwan laws means only reducing government ownership below 50 percent so as to free SOEs from direct budget, personnel, and procurement controls by the Legislative Yuan. Privatization is "achieved" by SOEs making initial public offerings (IPOs) and subsequent secondary offerings, which generated additional revenues for the government but changed little at these companies after the IPO. Partially privatized SOEs remain under the control of the government, which typically controls the board of directors. The Ministry of Finance, for example, has become the *über*-board of government-linked listed banks, overriding the real board of directors. Increasingly, the chairman at these partially privatized SOEs is hand picked by senior politicians on the basis of loyalty rather than merit. Where it is politically fashionable to show Taiwan-consciousness, senior politicians directed that some SOEs change their corporate name by substituting "Taiwan" for "China." The government-controlled boards at these SOEs then hurried to get this done, locking out labor directors from the board meeting and ignoring the costs of a sudden change of the corporate name in board discussions. In the heavily govern-ment-controlled financial sector, unions at government-controlled banks view further privatization, particularly mergers with privately held banks, as a sell-out to big business and have fought bitterly against such initiatives.

Fiduciary duty

Traditional codes and concept

A 2001 amendment to the Company Law made the first explicit mention of "fiduciary duty" in Taiwan. But fiduciary duty as a concept had long exis-ted in Taiwan. For decades, Taiwan's Company Law and Securities and Exchange Law have maintained provisions that are functional equivalents of fiduciary duty rules, such as provisions requiring non-competition by directors, conflicts avoidance, and informed consent of related-party trans-actions at arms' length. More important, Taiwan's Criminal Code makes "breach of trust," which includes breaching a duty of due care resulting in benefits to others, a criminal offense. Borrowed from Germany, this rule can lead to the same perverse results as the German Federal Supreme Court is ruling in the *Mannesmann* case, in which the award of a bonus to executives of an acquired company for obtaining a higher acquisition price became a crime.[13] The real issue lies not in the concept of fiduciary duty but in the challenge and side effects of enforcing fiduciary duty in Taiwan's highly politicized environment by prosecutors and private plaintiffs, under increasing goading by politicians after a long neglect of law enforcement.

Fiduciary duty and "fit and proper" test

An emerging issue for administering the "fit and proper" test for directors, supervisors and officers of Taiwan's financial institutions is a new façade to examine the fiduciary duty. For example, in 2005–2006 Taiwan's Financial Supervisory Commission began to take a more expansive view of "fiduciary duty" by including reactions to "public image" as an important component of the fiduciary duty of directors and supervisors of Taiwan's financial institutions. Along the same line, actions "lacking in good faith," a loose standard that incorporates societal impressions and not necessarily invol-ving "moral turpitude," can be deemed a violation of such duty. Violations of this sort would make persons unfit to serve in financial institutions, which provides the government with convenient political leverage over the financial sector.

Business judgment rule

There is no Taiwanese equivalent to the American business judgment rule. A 2005 district court decision, perhaps the very first of its kind, applied convoluted logic to interpret the concept of fiduciary duty found in the Company Law as amended in 2001, while also attempting to explicitly transplant this American rule.[14] Taiwanese prosecutors and courts are not concerned with the potential chilling effects of second-guessing the business judgment of the board and management in hindsight. This can be draconian because, with the offense of criminal breach of trust, there can be over-deterrence of perceived inadequate care by corporate agents. Judges in Taiwan are trained as civil servants, and typically begin serving on the bench at the tender age of mid to late twenties. They do not have much social experience, and they rarely understand the dynamic challenges faced by directors and managers in the business community. Therefore, where sufficient dissatisfaction with a board action leads to a law suit against directors for breaching the duty of due care, judicial exculpation is politically incorrect and practically impossible.

Accounting and disclosure

The challenge of meaningful disclosure

Taiwan's corporate law system requires extensive disclosure from listed and public reporting companies. Quantitatively, the system is elaborate and, among Asian economies, well above average. Qualitatively, however, form often trumps substance. Politically, the securities regulators want to be perceived as looking after the interests of small investors through rigorous mandatory disclosure and merit review of offerings. Small investors account for the overwhelming (albeit gradually decreasing) majority of securities trading in Taiwan.

The real challenge is to ensure meaningful disclosure. For example, for almost two decades, Taiwan has required public companies to provide auditor-reviewed quarterly reports. However, the Company Law applies on the basis of individual companies. Stand-alone (instead of consolidated) financial statements of listed companies, therefore, became the principal financial statements. Regulators knew this did not make sense, but did not want to antagonize industrialists by increasing the cost of disclosure and audit. With listed companies making more investment overseas and becoming more like holding companies, inadequate transparency became a bigger problem over time. The ACT Initiative of the cabinet in 2003 called for substituting consolidated financial statements for stand-alone financial statements, and relevant measures began to be implemented over 2005–2006. Also, until the early 2000s, disclosures of public companies focused only on the parent company. Therefore, even though many "land mine companies" in the indigenous financial crisis around 1998–99 used wholly owned subsidiaries to engage in secretive stock repurchases so as to "stabilize" stock prices, no disclosure of this round-about share buy-back was explicitly required. These buy-backs were done so that the "stabilized" stock price would support the valuation of shares pledged by insiders. The securities regulators at the time took the politically convenient enforcement position that they had jurisdiction only over the parent company, not the unlisted wholly owned subsidiaries!

Regulatory zeal to be popular with retail investors also led to mandatory forward-looking statements. Intended to provide better visibility of future earnings, this rule could be abused by insiders to manage earnings or to defraud investors, as shown in the Procomp case of 2001–2002. Soon thereafter, Taiwanese regulators discovered that they had created a monster, because under a merit review system retail investors regarded forecasts as performance guarantees. The rules were finally amended in the mid-2000s to allow voluntary forward-looking statements.

Faustian deal: weakening accounting rules to whitewash NPLs

Despite significant efforts to improve accounting and auditing practice, the government has also manipulated accounting rules to suit its own political purposes. A case in point is Article 15 of the Financial Institutions Mergers Act of 2000, which allows financial institutions disposing of non-performing loans (NPLs) to amortize losses arising from such dispositions over five years, instead of a one-time charge as required by good accountancy. Adopted soon after Taiwan's first change in government, this rule allows banks to smooth their losses. Banks are simply too important politically to be allowed to fail. In the end, the government's credibility suffered for bending rules to allow banks to cook their books. More important, banks with asset-quality problems still failed, as evidenced by the politically well-connected Rebar Group/Chinese Commercial Bank scandal in 2006–2007. The political cost was high: a run on this bank forced the resignation of an FSC chairman (who said the bank had positive net worth and there was no need for receivership, just a few hours before the bank run). At the trial of some defendants in 2007, the judge scolded former ministers of the MOF and senior FSC officials for dereliction of regulatory duties.

Premature M&A disclosure

Another disclosure problem relates to merger and acquisition (M&A) activities. A company's decision to make an acquisition is highly proprietary and confidential; yet the result is uncertain because the market is beyond the control of the acquiring firm. In Taiwan, however, regulators err on the side of premature disclosure (for example, even taking the position that disclosure of non-binding letters of intent without price terms should be made shortly after signing). The reason is that the regulators know enforcement against insider trading is weak. Yet enforcement is also uneven. For example, in the early 2000s some senior officials at the MOF (which was both owner and regulator at that time) wanted to broker the merger of partially privatized, government-linked banks to show the government's achievements in financial reform. They proceeded to cajole a few banks to sign letters of intent, even though they knew that the proposals would not succeed, due to union opposition and weak synergies. Still, these crude matching-making attempts led to many publicized signing ceremonies and the euphoria of achieving financial reform. However, premature disclosure of these sketchy deals led to active trading followed by a decline in share prices when it was clear there would be no follow-through. Investors trading during this market hype suffered, but no enforcement actions ever took place.

Mergers and acquisitions

Ambivalent government policy

Corporate takeovers played no part in Taiwan's economic development and did not register as a policy tool in the minds of its policymakers. To be sure, a market for corporate control can improve corporate governance. But even ostensibly neutral rules can be adverse to M&A transactions, such as the three-year term (instead of the common one-year term in the Anglo-American regime) for electing directors and supervisors under the Company Law.[15] Moreover, political consideration has adversely affected, for example, the consolidation of the fragmented financial services industry in Taiwan. Foreign analysts rated Taiwan's M&A policies as "restrictive," and noted that

> [The] Taiwanese government seems to be favoring populist, vote-winning policies ahead of effective industry consolidation, and the media is sensationalizing public resistance and worries of the government selling assets cheaply to the private sector.[16]

For example, despite a freeze in awarding new licenses for financial institutions and the need to consolidate its financial market, hostile takeovers are viewed with great suspicion by financial regulators for being culturally "un-Taiwanese" (as it could dethrone founders) and politically troublesome (as the government would be clueless as to which tycoons to support, as they can be raiders or incumbents). As a measure of this animosity, the term "hostile" takeover is often (mis)translated into Chinese as "malicious" or "evil" takeover by legislators, regulators, and academics alike. Taiwan's Legislative Yuan almost adopted a resolution to require government-appointed directors in all government-linked companies to oppose any hostile takeover. Indeed, until early 2002, Taiwan's Securities and Exchange Law prohibited tender offers without prior government approval. The review for granting such approvals required the government to look into the "social and economic conditions" surrounding the proposed tender offer. Therefore, there were only one or two tender offers between 1988 and 2002.

Also, in addition to a mandatory-bid rule, Taiwan has taken the extraordinary step of criminalizing noncompliance with the rule. On the other hand, regulators knew they could not demand full compliance with the rules so they added a loophole: any purchases accumulating no more than a 20 percent block during any 50-day period would not trigger a mandatory bid. Enforcement in this new area of the law has been a morass.

This ambivalence reflects Taiwan's long-held political ideology and industrial policy that building something is better than acquiring it from others. The financial service sector was suppressed and heavily controlled by the government for political reasons, obviating for decades the need to develop sophisticated M&A expertise. Corporate, exchange control, and financial laws in Taiwan were too inadequate and restrictive for sophisticated M&A transactions.

Control of proxies

Taiwan's corporate law heavily regulates proxy solicitation, and the Securities and Exchange Law even uses unusual (perhaps even unique) language to "eradicate" proxies.[17] In general, Taiwan's proxy rules stand corporate governance goals on their head and have a perversely anti-takeover impact. This can only be explained by political considerations. Controlling shareholders and incumbent management are viewed as industrialists who have helped to build up a strong national economy. Therefore, regulators and the public in Taiwan traditionally favored them rather than "corporate gadflies" (known as "professional shareholders" in Taiwan, they are similar to *sokaiya* in Japan). Proxies can be and are "sold" in Taiwan so as to ensure a quorum and maintain control by the incumbents. To be sure, naked selling of proxies is illegal. However, proxy rules permit listed companies to provide small gifts at shareholders' meetings as "souvenirs," thereby legalizing the collection of proxies while delivering souvenirs.

To suppress proxy solicitation, generally a person acting as the proxy of a shareholder having 3 percent of the voting power can not act as the proxy for other shareholders. In order to openly and proactively solicit proxies (known in regulatory practice as "limited solicitation"), shareholders have to own a significant stake, currently 800,000 shares, continuously for six months. The right to solicit proxies without limitation requires a 10 percent block held continuously for a year. With increasing concerns over takeovers in the financial sector (many of which involved government-linked banks), the FSC in 2006 increased the holding threshold for proxies involving financial institutions to 12 percent. This measure was adopted in tandem with an MOF proposal to condition the minimum level of private-sector ownership block before the government would divest their remaining holdings in financial institutions. The proposal has the air of regulators helping government owners in change-in-control transactions. Yet in 2004 the government had intervened even more directly. The government, announcing its intention to ensure integrity in proxy solicitations and maintain orderly market conditions, mobilized all leading securities firms, including stock exchanges and clearing companies in which the government holds substantial ownership, to form the Taiwan Integrated Shareholder Service Company (TISSC), a de facto state-run proxy solicitation company. The government effectively controls TISSC, and a former career regulator runs its daily business.

M&A deals and issues

Taiwan's M&A experience in the last ten years has been schizophrenic: Taiwanese firms have no problems doing M&A deals outside Taiwan (such as Acer's acquisition of Gateway), but face far more restrictions in the home market for similar activities. Takeovers involving financial firms are extremely difficult, and hostile takeovers are frowned upon, indicating heavy government regulation and political intervention of the financial sector in the name of "stability," "market order," and "corporate governance." Indeed, after a few widely publicized cases around 2003–2005, the regulators began to use moral persuasion to forbid insurance companies (including insurance subsidiaries of financial holding companies) from buying, through market purchases and without prior approval, an initial block of the shares of target banks or securities firms. Such purchases are commonly used in the West as a precursor to subsequent acquisitions of the entire firm. Indifferent to more permissive M&A practices abroad, the regulators oddly claimed this way of "using other people's money" violates corporate governance principles. In 2007 this policy culminated in the passage of an Insurance Law amendment that even seeks to limit how insurance companies can vote such initial blocks.

In 2002, essentially through mergers, 14 financial holding companies were formed as a result of the Financial Holding Company Law. But thereafter the government stopped issuing further financial holding company licenses in disregard of public criticisms and industry anxiety. In addition, the Taiwan government disallowed existing banks from setting up new branches or relocating existing branches, except when acquiring failing banks, so as to arrest the market trend toward further fragmentation. The government's inability to replenish its Financial Restructuring Fund, a scheme based on the Resolution Trust Corporation (RTC) model of the U.S. for bank bailouts, is the main reason why competition was suppressed, so that the weaker firms could have some prolonged breathing space. Politicians therefore could avoid (or at least delay) problems arising from bank failures. But with entry barriers under this "convoy" system, exit could not be forced upon weaker financial firms or their shareholders, and they actually have bargained for higher selling prices.

As a result, most such takeover transactions, especially those involving a government-linked bank, could not proceed successfully without the definitive blessing of regulators and politicians in the executive and legislative branches of the government. Indeed, when the government announced a plan in 2004 generally known as Financial Reform Round II, it set up goals such as reducing both the number of government-linked banks and the number of financial holding companies by half within two years. But neither goal was reached. Senior politicians and regulators lacked the political will to withstand pressure and union opposition to fully privatize government-owned banks. Haphazard deals with the government's hand visible and deeply involved raised criticisms of favoritism, inconsistent policies, and botched executions. These deals involved government-controlled financial institutions such as First Financial Holding,[18] Chang-Hua Commercial Bank,[19] Mega Financial Holding.[20] Private-sector M&A deals also became highly controversial because of government intervention. They include companies such as Waterland Financial Holding[21] and China Development Financial Holding's acquisition of Taiwan International Securities.[22]

Stock exchange integration

In the course of developing its capital market, Taiwan has established stock exchanges and clearing and centralized facilities through companies financed by SOEs and financial institutions, with the exception of GreTai Securities Market (GTSM), which in form is a nonprofit organization. These entities are all tightly controlled by the government and heavily regulated by the FSC and its predecessor. They are usually headed by former senior government officials at the FSC or other agencies, and their appointment is usually approved by top leaders. In Taiwan's bureaucracy, regulators have regarded such appointments as a natural path after retirement. In recent years, global trading and the trend for bourses around the world to consolidate, corporatize, and become listed have also led Taiwan's policymakers to think about consolidating its centralized trading market.

Despite this realization and a sense of urgency, Taiwanese policymakers have not been able to adopt a clear policy on how to consolidate. Again, politics was a major factor. Regulatory constraints have been so heavy that merging these entities into a new holding company would require an amendment to the securities law. But regulators appear to procrastinate because of difficulties in getting legislation, even bills with only a few provisions, through the wildly politicized Legislative Yuan in Taiwan. Bureaucratic politics was another factor. Even though it is possible to structure around some legal issues affecting consolidation by having one of the entities become the parent company, the apparent but unspoken concerns about job security of the senior management of these companies would have stalled the consolidation plan. With high turnover among FSC chairmen there is no real leadership or desire to push for stock exchange integration in light of these perceived difficulties.

Corporate law enforcement

Politics matters immensely to corporate law enforcement in Taiwan. It explains the laxity or fervor of enforcement activities. First, financial rules and regulations are detailed and elaborate, providing regulators with wide discretion. Regulators want to be perceived as protecting individual investors and holding big business at bay. Second, pervasive criminalization permeates corporate, securities, and banking laws, reflecting a strong belief in the coercive power of the state and the willingness to second-guess business decisions. For example, offenses including "breach of trust" in the Criminal Code and related laws are typically vague. Third, senior politicians in the executive and legislative branches of the government, usually less interested and unsophisticated in economic and financial policy, can be pivotal. They can stand aside or demand swift and draconian justice when public opinion so demands. Fourth, Taiwan's fragmented and vibrant press will irresponsibly fuel public opinion so long as sensationalist journalism sells. Fifth, courts are largely ineffective, usually deferring to regulatory agencies, and justice is often delayed. In sum, corporate law enforcement in Taiwan has mostly been weak and sporadic, but is at times massive and frantic. Over-regulation coexisting with under-enforcement leads to unpredictable law enforcement, except it is certain that populism reigns.

Administrative enforcement

As the dominant enforcers in Taiwan, regulators used to mete out mild and token sanctions. However, since 2005 there have been heavier fines and non-monetary sanctions—at least strong populist sentiments supporting such actions. Still, over- and under- attention by politicians has reduced the predictability of regulatory enforcement and skewed the proportionality of the sanctions. Regulators often resort to informal sanctions such as forcing resignations and stalling applications. Enforcement information is often made public (formally or otherwise), leading to trials in the court of public opinion.

Taiwan's Code of Administrative Procedure requires agency adjudications to be fair, well informed and proportionate to the harm caused by an alleged violation. A hearing is to precede such adjudications if they will lead to deprivations of the rights of citizens. Where informal pressure is used, regulators tend to pay lip service to these rules. In addition, even though the law allows citizens to resist "administrative guidance" (that is, moral persuasion), out of fear of retaliation, regulated entities rarely challenge it seriously. Also, unlike in common law jurisdictions, regulators in Taiwan can issue sanctions without having to sue in court first; it is the regulated entities that have to sue so as to challenge agency action. Regulated entities are virtually bound to lose the first round, because it involves an administrative appeal against a supervising agency. They will face an uphill battle in judicial review because of high deference to regulatory discretion. More seriously, regulators can defer to or even favor the state as owner. Examples include seeking conflicts waivers where there are government ownership or government-appointed directors in private-sector financial institutions.

Regulators everywhere are subject to capture and bureaucratic forbearance. The worst of such conduct in Taiwan took the form of coercing banks into moratoriums against foreclosing their loans and failing to take over effectively defunct banks around the turn of the new century, when Taiwan went through intensive elections and shifts in political power. Insufficient government budget for an RTC-type financial rescue and concerns with panicky depositors were the main reason for not throwing problem banks, whose owners were often politically connected, into receivership. Delayed bank failure follows a pattern: siphoning value from banks or other firms in the same group through related-party transactions when firm value is dissipating. Financial regulators usually knew about these problems through routine or special examinations but did nothing of significance. As of this writing, courts in Taiwan are just beginning to look into this history, using perfect hindsight because of the receivership of the Chinese Commercial Bank in late 2006 and the scandals related to the controlling Wang family that also controlled the Rebar Group. Called in 2007 as witnesses in the prosecution of the Wang family and managerial cohorts for breach of trust and related offenses arising from this scandal, former ministers of finance (MOF being the regulator until 2004) and current senior officials of the FSC were shocked when prosecutors and even the judges in court second-guessed their past forbearance to the point of threatening indictment for dereliction of public duties.

Criminal enforcement

The judiciary and the criminal justice system have been under tight political control in post-war Taiwan, even after the lifting of martial law in 1987. Criminal investigation authorities also collect security-related intelligence. Although more independent now, Taiwanese prosecutors and investigators have been a part of the civil service and are susceptible to similar bureaucratic problems. For lack of expertise in economic and financial matters and constraints in allocating crime-fighting resources, in the past they rarely initiated white-collar crime cases on their own, and often waited for regulators to "refer" the matter to them. But populist politics has been fervent since the late 1990s. As enforcement activities against business crimes in the 2005–2007 period suggest, these phenomena can leave much room for political leverage, including who, and when to prosecute (or not).

Also, in stark contrast to the business-judgment rule in some jurisdictions, crimes such as the loosely framed "breach of trust" allow officials to second-guess business decisions in hindsight. Public outcry against massive securities fraud, criminal breach of trust, or insider trading now demands swift and cogent justice, while ensuring due process of law when getting justice done is less of a concern. So law enforcement officials can abuse their power, and suspected questionable practices include coercive tactics, leaking information so as to work up public support, and (as found by a district court in an ethics case involving a presidential contender in 2007) even editorializing testimony by witnesses taken in pre-trial proceedings. If called only as a witness, a citizen may not seek counsel during interrogations, soon after which he is often formally charged. Even if counsel is present when he is interrogated as a suspect, he may only observe quietly.[23]

Civil enforcement[24]

Taiwan's plaintiff-unfriendly civil justice system has likewise weakened civil enforcement of corporate laws. Implicit in this system is an age-old political bias against civil society in general, and against causing private disputes, including litigation, in particular. For example, filing tort claims under a "loser pays" system for court fees requires the plaintiff to post a prepaid bond on an amount-based sliding scale of about 0.7 percent (formerly 1 percent) of the claim. This can be a major hurdle in making mass tort claims. Other barriers include the lack of discovery and high information costs. Political control and doctrinal training in the past have molded judges into civil servants who syllogistically apply black-letter rules of law. Taiwanese lawyers have been a cartel (currently about five thousand in a land of 23 million people), in part because the government regarded them as trouble makers. For example, many leaders in the opposition movement since the 1970s are lawyers. Accordingly, the government has imposed restrictive bar admission rates, with the post-war average being about 1–2 percent. While contingency fees exist, lawyers have no risk appetite for financing mass tort litigation. Collective action problems for group litigation also aggravate the plight of small investors. The general rule for derivative actions is a paper tiger because of stringent shareholding requirements, such as 3 percent continuous ownership for a year. The 3 percent hurdle was reduced, through a Company Law amendment proposed by the Ministry of Economic Affairs (MOEA), from 5 percent in 2001 as a token gesture to improve corporate governance. However, the MOEA is also responsible for industrial development and trade enhancement. So it felt that removing this hurdle would hurt its constituencies. According to official judicial statistics, suits against directors and supervisors in each of the last ten years can be counted on a few fingers, and perhaps they do not even involve listed companies because of this high hurdle.

Innovative derivative action for profit disgorgement

Gradual democratization increased demand for more access to civil justice, including redress of major corporate mischief. Taiwan's Securities and Futures

Bureau (SFB, known then as the SEC) came up with a brilliant innovation in the early 1980s. It asked organizations regulated by it such as the Taiwan Stock Exchange (TwSE), and the Taiwan Securities Firm Association to contribute seed funding to set up a nonprofit foundation, the Securities and Futures Institute (SFI). A training and outreach body staffed by retired or former SFB officials who are trusted by the SFB, the SFI in the political sense is "owned" by the SFB. It buys 1,000 shares (the minimum trading unit) of each public company so that it can assert derivative claims. The Securities and Exchange Law was amended to install the American strict-liability, short-swing profit disgorgement rule. Unlike the Company Law, the securities law allows any shareholders to sue, without requiring any continuous and significant holdings. If the company fails to seek disgorgement, its directors and supervisors will be jointly and severally liable.[25] The SFI's Investors Protection Center obtained short-swing trading information from the market surveillance task force of the stock exchanges such as TwSE and GTSM. Although it is unclear how much disgorgement actually has been made, this initiative is probably the most successful securities law enforcement program in Taiwan.

Piggyback class actions

Taiwan experienced a series of indigenous "land mine company" scandals in the late 1990s, even though it avoided the Asian financial crisis. In reaction to public demand for justice, the SFI's Investor Protection Center (IPC) innovated further. It solicited claims from investors, and filed "piggyback" civil litigation alongside the criminal prosecution tried by the same judge, following a rule borrowed from the German code of criminal procedure to enhance judicial economy. This strategy allows it to piggyback on prosecutors' investigative power to overcome information costs. The judge's power to waive hefty court fees as serving the public interest reduces the financial cost. A civil judgment still depends essentially on a finding of criminal liability. The benefits of the action can be outweighed by substantial delays in the criminal proceedings, and these piggyback proceedings were often continued pending criminal convictions. In the end, many culprits either fled the country or became judgment proof. Nonetheless, it was a way to alleviate political pressure and create the perception that justice was being done against the perpetrators. This became the genesis of Taiwanese-style de facto securities class actions under the Securities and Futures Investors Protection Law of 2003, discussed next.

Direct investor protection suits

Inspired by the representative litigation model in the Consumer Protection Law, a nonprofit foundation called the Securities and Futures Investors Protection Center was set up by spinning off the IPC from the SFI. Its funding came from a "toll charge" assessed against stock exchanges and securities firms associations, and ultimately borne by the trading public. A special provision caps the prepaid court fees regardless of the amount of the actual claims. The Securities and Futures Investor Protection Center (SFIPC) can sue if authorized by at least 20 aggrieved investors, and it files an independent civil suit without piggybacking on the criminal prosecution, thereby potentially saving more time.

This kind of "opt-in" securities litigation is likewise a political relief, and constitutes an alternative to the "opt-out," lawyer-financed class action model in America. Retired SFB officials and former senior executives from government-linked banks conveniently head up SFIPC's senior management, and the SFIPC is answerable to the regulators. The SFIPC is also directed by the SFB on what cases to initiate and what parties to pursue, and will let this be known to their opposing parties in settlement discussions. Despite these political constraints, the SFIPC has recruited good litigators who view their work as a sort of emerging practice in public-interest law.

By the mid 2000s, the SFIPC had developed a rigorous enforcement program. In the Procomp case filed in late 2004, it claimed about US$182 million on behalf of over 10,000 investors. In the Infodisc case filed in early 2005, it acted for more than 10,000 plaintiffs to seek about US$95 million of damages. In the Summit case filed in early 2006, the SFIPC claimed about US$11 million for 1,590 plaintiffs. As of late 2006, the SFC has filed 41 civil cases and acted for a total of more than 57,000 plaintiffs, claiming a total amount of about US$738 million. The largest case involved Pacific Wire and Cable, in which the SFIPC acted for more than 25,000 investors claiming about US$250 million.

Faced with principal defendants who are often judgment proof or in hiding, the SFIPC in recent years has aggressively pursued a "deep pocket" strategy to target underwriters and external auditors serving the companies. The SFIPC alleges aiding in fraud so as to seek settlement from the secondary players. Information about the progress of the SFIPC's settlement negotiations and the total settlement amount (but not the amount of individual settlements) is made known to the public, so that there will be societal pressure on and reputation risks to these firms. Perhaps more successful than the principal law suit against the ring leaders, this strategy has been effective in collecting real settlement monies from underwriters and the Taiwanese affiliates of the big four global accounting firms, which collectively control about 80 percent of the audit market for listed companies in Taiwan. In the Procomp case, four underwriters settled with the SFIPC for about US$2.4 million, and two audit firms settled with the SFIPC for about US$2.8 million, both records for Taiwan. However, the financial community has argued that these settlements may have had a chilling effect as well. It has argued that the scope of firms included in the settlement was too broad because there was no plausible evidence that some firms aided and abetted the fraud, or that they were negligent during the relevant period when they served these "land mine" companies. Compounded by other factors, such as the new system at the SFB since 2005 to place more responsibility on underwriters sponsoring securities offerings, competition from Hong Kong, and the industrial hollowing-out effect, Taiwan in 2006 saw the lowest number of IPOs of recent years.

Conclusions

Taiwan has made recognizable progress on corporate governance development. For example, its acceptance of the independent director and audit committee regime, properly understood, is a first step towards changing the problematic juridical director system of the past. Warts and all, it also has found innovative ways to enhance investor protection in a weak civil justice system, such as the investor-protection, class-action litigation sponsored by a government-supported foundation as a public good. The most salient and saddening feature of the corporate governance story in Taiwan, however, is that it now runs the risk of being hijacked by politics. After decades of economic development along free-market principles, Taiwan has become more introverted and corporatist, and is gradually manifesting socialist tendencies. With the manufacturing sector moving out (often to China), the cross-Strait investment restrictions pose significant corporate governance challenges. The service sector has become the driving force of the Taiwanese economy. But many service industries, financial services in particular, have been heavily regulated, and significant government ownership still pervades in these sectors. Regulatory governance and the governance of government-linked listed companies, including the government's policy towards and its role in takeover transactions, are critical issues for corporate governance as well as Taiwan's competitiveness. Worst of all, Taiwan's press and politicians see corporate governance as an issue involving "distributive justice," and have politicized and sensationalized the enforcement of corporate law rules such as the vague "breach of trust," criminalizing not only fraud but also honest business mistakes, and chilling the business community. Despite the global credit crisis arising from the American sub-prime mortgage market turmoil in 2007, Taiwan probably will not experience a financial crisis of the kind that sent shock waves through Asia in 1997. But the cantankerous political environment is sapping it of the energy from reforms, which could otherwise improve corporate governance and overall competitiveness.

Notes

* The author was involved in some policy initiatives, law drafting and transactions described herein. The usual disclaimers apply.
1 For an earlier account of corporate governance in Taiwan, see Liu (2002).
2 Kurtz (2006).
3 Taiwan's board structure is closer to the dual-board mode of Japan (with directors and supervisors, or statutory auditors, both being elected by shareholders)

than the German two-tiered model. Also, there was no employee co-determination or representation on the board until the late 1990s, after politics made its way into government-linked, unionized listed companies.

4 This optional approach was the position of the ACT Initiative 2003 of Taiwan's cabinet in 2003. ACT stands for "Accountability for Companies in Taiwan." The author was chief consultant for this project.

5 Examples of very intrusive and rigid labor legislation include the Labor Standards Law enacted in 1984 largely for manufacturing companies but made applicable to all private-sector companies over the last 20 years. It sets minimum employment, severance, and retirement terms and essentially invalidates terminable-at-will contracts. Another example is Massive Layoff Law, which transplants plant closure laws from some Western industrial countries. The Labor Union Law and Collective Bargaining Law were very sleepy until democratization since the late 1980s led to more active unionization, collective bargaining and strikes.

6 Articles 235, 267. There are some exemptions for foreign-owned and -controlled companies.

7 This reflects the influence of Chinese thinkers and revolutionaries like Dr. Sun Yat-sen, the founding father of the Republic of China. Dr. Sun visited England in the late 1800s and was very receptive to Fabianism, understood in China at the time as a form of mild socialism.

8 Perhaps reflecting this cultural background, the term "dividend" under Taiwan's Company Law consists of two components: interest on the shares and bonuses. Article 232.

9 Article 240.

10 As a result of high-tech sector lobbying, Taiwan's Statute for Upgrading Industries codified the rule of taxing bonus shares at par value. The root issue is whether it makes sense for Taiwan to tax stock dividends (although employees do not receive bonus shares as "dividends" and they are not treated as shareholders for purposes of such distribution).

11 A related issue is whether the chairman of the board is an employee and therefore qualified for such bonus shares. A no-brainer in Western industrial countries, this issue arose in Taiwan because its highly formalistic Civil Code maintains a detailed classification of contract types, and this classification treats a director as a "mandate" (under the Roman Law concept of *mandat*), that is, someone retained to render services. As such, he is not an employee simply because he is chairman. Therefore, Taiwanese companies will make sure their full-time chairmen take on additional corporate chores so as to qualify them to receive salary and compensation essentially as *employees*.

12 The definitive title of this initiative is "Asia-Pacific Regional Operations Center" (APROC), and it is intended to improve Taiwan's competitiveness by deregulation. See Liu (1996).

13 See Gevurtz (2007).

14 Civil Judgment No. 93-Chung-Su-144 (20 April 2005, Taipei District Court).

15 They can be removed with or without cause. Therefore, the three-year term is not absolute.

16 See Cheng (2006) on Chinatrust Financial Holdings in Taiwan.

17 SEL, article 25.

18 Forced resignation of its chairman for improper execution of a GDR placement, and forced resignation of its president for inappropriate statements in an emotional outburst while answering questions in the Legislative Yuan.

19 Issuance of convertible preferred shares containing unusual terms through a little-publicized bid with the government's promise, without receiving additional consideration like control premium, to support the highest bidder in the next board election and ignoring a subsequent open proposal by Temasek of Singapore,

having lost the bid for the preferred shares, to acquire a majority of all issued shares.

20 FSC-approved unsolicited bid by Chinatrust Financial Holding to invest a significant block in the government-controlled Mega as a precursor to proxy contest, and surprising turn-around in policies, including forcing a former vice premier who was elected as independent director to resign so as to maintain a majority of government-friendly directors on the board.

21 Proxy contest, where other government-linked banks are minority shareholders.

22 Hostile takeover and tender offers frowned on by politicians.

23 For similar views about the criminalization of American corporate law, see Lerner (2007).

24 See, also Liu (2000 and 2007).

25 This could include "deemed" profit, as the Enforcement Rules to the Securities and Exchange Law, which were drafted with input from American trained academics, codifies the *in terrorem* American case law for computing actual or deemed profits.

Bibliography

Cheng, Sophia (2006) "Company Update: Government limits future expansion: near-term negative," *Merrill Lynch (Taiwan) Equity Research* (28 June), 2–3, quoted in Kathrin Hille, "Labouring under the heavy weight of expectation: Taiwan's next finance minister will have his work cut rescuing the government's privatization and consolidation agenda," *Financial Times*, 16 (4 July).

Gevurtz, Franklin (2007) *"Disney* in a Comparative Light," http://ssrn.com./abstract=965596 (26 February).

Kurtz, Michael (2006) "The Price of Playing Politics," *Asian Wall Street Journal* (13 December), 13.

Lerner, Craig and Moin A. Yahya (2007) "'Left Behind' after Sarbane-Oxley," *American Criminal Law Review* 44. Available at http:ssrn.com/abstract=981064.

Liu, Lawrence S. (1996) "Aspiring to Excel—The Uneasy Case of Implementing Taiwan's Asia-Pacific Regional Operations Center Plan," *Columbia Journal of Asia Law* 10: 199–243.

—— (2002) "Global Markets and Parochial Institutions: The Transformation of Taiwan's Corporate Law System," in Curtis J. Milhaupt (ed.), *Global Markets and Domestic Institutions*, New York: Columbia University Press, 400.

—— (2000) "Simulating Securities Class Actions: The Case in Taiwan," *Corporate Governance International* (December).

—— (2007) "The Merits of Shareholder Collective Actions (Class Action Suits) in Chinese Taipei" (ch. 1); "Procomp: A Case in Chinese Taipei" (ch. 2), in OECD, *Enforcement of Corporate Governance in Asia: The Unfinished Agenda*, Paris: OECD.

11 An analytical framework for controlling minority shareholders and its application to Taiwan

Wallace Wen-Yeu Wang and Carol Yuan-Chi Pang

Introduction

Controlling shareholder structures are prevalent in both Europe and East Asia (see, e.g., Claessens *et al.* 2000: 81; Faccio and Lang 2002: 365; La Porta *et al.* 1999: 471), and entail agency costs of expropriation by the controlling shareholder. This not only impacts the corporation through expropriation and mismanagement; unfettered expropriation could lead to disinclination to invest and result in poorly developed capital markets.

Empirical studies have shown that Taiwan suffers from controlling shareholder structures accompanied by a sharp separation of control and cash flow rights (controlling minority structure) that characterize much of East Asia. The myriad of influences (including U.S., German, and Japanese) to which Taiwanese corporate law has been subjected, coupled with a gradual long-term prospect for corporate reform, causes Taiwanese corporate law to display parallels with East Asian countries and its own distinctive features. Taiwan provides an interesting model for observation and analysis.

This essay begins by providing an analytical framework for controlling shareholders. This is followed by presentation of the current situation of Taiwan, a country characterized by controlling-minority shareholder structures and poor shareholder protection. It highlights the novel approach of Taiwanese law in seeking to deal with the issue by mandatory ownership concentration. The next part discusses the possible avenues of regulation derived from our analytical framework, and the essay ends with the conclusion.

The controlling shareholder structure

The costs and benefits of the controlling shareholder structure

Theory suggests the incentives of the controlling shareholder to expropriate decrease with cash flow rights and increase with the deviation between cash flow rights and control rights. Theory has been confirmed in empirical research (see, e.g., Claessens *et al.* 2002: 2755–2756; La Porta *et al.* 2002: 1147; Lemmon and Lins 2003: 1445). Conditional on maintaining control, the deviation between ownership and control has been dubbed the controlling minority structure (Bebchuk *et al.* 2000: 445).

This structure poses the most severe challenge to the protection of minority shareholders. First, the structure of control in the hands of those who hold a small ownership stake in itself distorts the incentives of the controlling shareholders in relation to economic decisions for the company, notwithstanding the absence of diversion ("tunneling") or outright theft of company resources (Morck *et al.* 2004: 21–22). Second, the controlling shareholder typically controls the board, management, and shareholder meetings owing to the number of votes, insulating it from traditional corporate governance mechanisms such as the market for corporate control. Thus, non-electoral mechanisms for shareholder protection play a critical role.

However, it is important to note that, despite the possible increased extraction of private benefits of control, controlling (minority) shareholder structures could potentially be beneficial to public shareholders, and efficient depending on the tradeoff between the benefits of heightened monitoring of managers and the increased extraction of private benefits of control (Gilson and Gordon 2003: 785; Gilson 2006: 1650–1652; Demsetz and Lehn 1985: 1159). Additionally, the structure could have other beneficial aspects. For example, controlling shareholders could be well suited to overcome weak enforcement of property rights in weak legal and institutional environments (Claessens and Fan 2002: 75). The controlling shareholder's reputation could also facilitate external financing. If the controlling shareholder also controls other firms, this could lead to better firm performance by pooling resources and information as well as by reducing transaction costs (Morck *et al.* 2004: 17–18; Khanna and Palepu 2000: 867).

Determinants of ownership structure

Extensive empirical evidence in law and finance literature demonstrates the positive association of controlling shareholder structures with poor legal minority shareholder protection. This literature argues that ownership concentration is a result of poor legal protection of minority shareholders and the consequent high level of private benefits of control (La Porta *et al.* 1999: 511; La Porta *et al.* 2000: 13–15; Dyck and Zingales 2004: 537–538). The reason is that in weak legal regimes high private benefits of control encourage control and prevent the dissipation of control once acquired, due to fear of exploitation and loss of private benefits of control (Bebchuk *et al.* 2000: 473–474; La Porta *et al.* 1999: 473; Zingales 1995: 425; Bebchuk 1999:1). Additionally, controlling shareholders who amass control over vast resources would in turn have the incentives and ability to lobby politicians more effectively to serve their interests, thus locking in the state of poor protection (Morck *et al.* 2004: 37–47).

Further research has demonstrated, however, the existence of controlling shareholder structures in countries with good shareholder protection, most notably Sweden, and dramatically differing levels of private benefits of control among controlling shareholder structures (Dyck and Zingales 2004: 537; Nenova 2003: 325). Thus, the ultimate empirical finding seems to be that countries with poor minority shareholder protection and corresponding high levels of private benefit extraction are invariably characterized by the prevalence of controlling shareholder structures, but not vice versa. Good shareholder protection, on the other hand, gives rise to both controlling and diffused ownership structures, most notably Sweden and the United States respectively.

This dichotomy exists because, with poor legal protection, benefits from expropriation are extremely large and lead inevitably to the assembling and maintenance of control; conversely, under good legal protection of minority shareholders, there is no such overriding factor, allowing for a variety of ownership structures to arise.

We can infer from the above that, conditional on good shareholder protection, controlling shareholder structures are not undesirable or economically inefficient in themselves (Gilson 2006: 1652–1660). Correspondingly, empirical research of U.S. firms does not indicate a link between ownership structure (diffused or concentrated) and firm performance (Demsetz and Lehn 1985: 1179; Morck *et al.* 2004: 15). The relevant dichotomy is between sound and poor shareholder protection, i.e., low and high levels of expropriation.

Analytical framework for regulation

The above analysis leads to the conclusion that while controlling shareholder structures could arise both in countries that provide good protection and those providing bad protection for minority shareholders, there is a crucial distinction: in the former, the most economically efficient ownership structure prevails; in the latter, controlling shareholder structures would *always* prevail, regardless of the impact on the company and the economy.

It thus follows that only when the level of private benefits of control is lowered can market forces operate to select the most value-enhancing ownership structure. Moreover, the deviation of control and cash flow rights affects the incentive to extract private benefits of control. The prominent role of such deviation in distorting and preventing the efficient choice of ownership structures has been documented (Bebchuk 1999: 1; Song 2002: 233–236).

The most straightforward and uncontroversial approach would be to lower the private benefits of control that arise from expropriation of minority shareholders and the company through heightened monitoring and enforcement. Not only would this encourage competition among ownership structures, it would also protect corporate value and minority shareholders. On the other hand, private benefits of control that arise from other sources, such as the political context, social standing, and synergies with existing businesses should not be regulated. This is primarily because the amount of such benefits is not likely to be large and will often not prevail against substantial efficiency concerns, making their regulation unnecessary. Moreover, their value is also highly subjective and abstract, making them nearly impossible to regulate coherently.

Another possible approach is to regulate the ability to leverage cash flow rights into incommensurate control. However this approach is problematic because it assumes that the benefits of controlling minority shareholder structures are always outweighed by the costs. As noted above, however, while controlling minority structures inherently pose serious incentive issues, they can also have economic benefits, especially when corporate governance mechanisms are adequate.

Despite these concerns, we argue that the ability to leverage cash flow rights into incommensurate control should be limited. In most countries beyond the initial stage of economic development, the benefits of controlling minority structures are in fact likely to be outweighed by their drawbacks. The extent and intensity of regulation—for example the choice between prohibition and incentives or the threshold triggering regulation—ultimately involve the legislator's balancing of benefits and drawbacks based on each country's situation.

The case of Taiwan

Controlling minority structure and poor protection of minority shareholders

Extensive financial research has indicated that the ownership structures of Taiwanese firms are characterized by the widespread presence of controlling shareholders and separation of ownership and control (see, e.g., Claessens *et al.* 2000: 81; Claessens *et al.* 2002: 2755–2756; Yeh *et al.* 2001: 21). Seventy percent of 251 Taiwanese listed companies in 1998 had controlling shareholders and 58.2 percent of listed firms were controlled by families (Yeh 2005b: 315). Deviation of cash flow rights and control rights is common and especially severe under family control (Yeh 2003: 92–96). The means of enhancing control are primarily pyramidal structures, cross-holdings, and participation in management or the board (Claessens *et al.* 2000: 92; Yeh 2003: 93–97; Yeh 2005b: 317). The latter two mechanisms are associated with discounts on corporate value (Yeh 2005b: 322).

Thus, Taiwanese firms exemplify the controlling minority structure. Is this structure largely formed and chosen by market forces for economic efficiency reasons or by poor protection of minority shareholders with its attendant high private benefits of control? We believe the answer lies in whether Taiwan provides good minority shareholder protection. If so, controlling minority structures are shaped by forces beyond incentives to expropriate, and are therefore not a result of the corporate law.

As noted earlier, empirical studies and theory suggest that a high prevalence of controlling minority structures over widely held firms often correlates with poor shareholder protections. Another piece of intriguing evidence is that Taiwanese family-controlled firms that have low levels of excess control have lower relative performance than both family-controlled firms with high levels of excess control and widely held firms (Yeh *et al.* 2001: 37, 46). Family firms also exhibit economically significant incentive effects of cash flow ownership and entrenchment effects of deviation of voting from cash flow rights, as indicated by firm valuation (Yeh 2005b: 318–322; Yeh 2003: 99). This is consistent with the fact that controlling shareholders can and do significantly expropriate from minority shareholders when it serves their own interests. This empirical pattern clearly signals the existence of poor minority shareholder protection (La Porta *et al.* 2002: 1163).

The above evidence, coupled with our assessment of current law and jurisprudence, suggests that Taiwan suffers from poor minority shareholder protection. This results in the predominance of controlling minority structures in Taiwan by encouraging the formation of control blocs and preventing their break-up.

Current Taiwanese approach—mandatory ownership concentration

Although the overall stance of Taiwan's legal system on ownership structure and the separation of ownership and control is somewhat ambiguous,[1] Article 26 of the Securities and Exchange Act, which provides that directors and supervisors of publicly listed firms must collectively hold a fixed percentage of the company's shares, is clear in mandating a minimum degree of integration between ownership and control. The fixed percentage varies with the amount of capitalization, but otherwise seems to lack clear basis. The assumption underlying this provision is that a minimum degree of ownership concentration in the hands of the controller is beneficial to all companies. This mandatory minimum level of ownership concentration is novel in that it intervenes directly in the ownership structure of companies and warrants several considerations.

First, we can examine the empirical evidence on the relationship between firm performance and shareholdings of controlling shareholders. A study of Taiwanese firms finds that firm performance increases with family ownership when it is below a firm's critical control level, but then decreases with family ownership when it crosses the "critical" control level until the degree of control becomes high (Yeh *et al.* 2001: 37).[2] This suggests that, once control is established, excess holdings are necessary to align the interests of the controller and the firm. Accordingly, it seems that holdings just below insulation or greatly in excess of control would be most effective in limiting expropriation by the controller. It is questionable, however, whether Article 26 contributes to this aim. Since the critical control level of each individual firm varies, the optimal holdings for a given firm will vary and cannot be mandated across all firms.

The second consideration arises from a broader efficiency perspective and concerns the fundamental issue of the choice between ownership structures.

Article 26 expressly requires a degree of ownership concentration in the hands of the controller. This sits uneasily with the point made earlier, that whether diffuse ownership is preferable to the controlling shareholder structure depends primarily on the tradeoff between heightened monitoring and extraction of private benefits of control, which varies with the circumstances of each company and industry. Each ownership structure has its attendant costs and benefits, and individual companies could efficiently make different choices. A specific company could prefer more diffuse ownership when the market for corporate control, product market competition, and alignment of incentives are sufficient to counteract the separation of ownership and control, making increased holdings of those in control unnecessary or inefficient. Article 26 precludes the option of diffusion beyond its fixed percentage of controller holdings.

From the above analysis we can conclude that, at best, Article 26 is ineffective, and at worst, inefficient and detracts from firm performance. It is also problematic to interfere with the freedom of citizens to hold or dispose of property without adequate regulatory basis. If poor minority shareholder protection and the prevalence of controlling shareholder structures are taken as given, however, decreasing the deviation of control from ownership will directly lower the incentive to expropriate, and could be useful before fundamental reform. Yet, ultimately, choice of ownership structure should be left to individual companies.

Article 26 also gives rise to enforcement problems (Lai 2005: 95–101). The first issue is that when the total holdings of directors or supervisors fall below the mandated level, all directors or all supervisors, regardless of whether their actions contributed to the decrease in holdings, are under the obligation to make up for the shortfall. This unreasonable outcome is exacerbated in the event that the amount of shares sold by a director exceeds half of his holdings at the time of his election. In such event his automatic discharge under Article 197 of the Company Law effectively exempts the director from the obligation to contribute to the shortfall and from possible fines.

Another problem involves the election of representatives—"juridical shareholders"—as directors or supervisors. As described in detail below, Article 27 of the Company Law permits juridical shareholders such as corporate or government entities to appoint natural-person representatives to be elected in their own capacity. The Rules and Review Procedures for Director and Supervisor Share Ownership Ratios at Public Companies, affirmed by the Highest Administrative Court, provide that, in this situation, the elected representative is the proper subject of the fines. However, this is unfair, as the juridical shareholder remains free to replace its representatives, and consequently retains control over the exercise of the directors' or supervisors' duties. It is the alteration of the holdings of the juridical shareholder that is relevant to the regulatory goal. The elected representative is not responsible for the alteration in holdings of the juridical shareholder.

Consequently, the imposition of fines on the elected representative instead of the juridical shareholder is problematic and unfair.

Current regulation and prospects for reform in Taiwan

Overview of the corporate legal system

Under Taiwanese Company Law, the company limited by shares is the standard model for large companies with a large number of shareholders. Companies limited by shares are also the only ones that may publicly issue securities. Correspondingly, the bulk of the Company Law and securities laws are devoted to its regulation. The discussion of this essay also focuses on this subset of corporations.

The organizational structure of a company limited by shares consists of three organs: the shareholders' meeting, the board of directors, and the supervisor. The current directors/supervisors system can be categorized as a type of binary system, where supervisors serve to monitor the performance of the board of directors externally on an *ex post* basis.

Concerning the delineation between the shareholders' meeting and the board of directors, the latter is charged with carrying out business operations, with management as an auxiliary, when not explicitly otherwise provided for in the Company Law or company charter.[3] The law provides that certain important issues must be passed by shareholders' meeting resolution, but in practice the shareholders' meeting has failed to play an active role. This is in part due to collective action problems and inactive institutional ownership. Moreover, prior to a 2005 amendment, shareholders could not raise proposals for the shareholders' meeting and were restricted to voting "yes" or "no" to proposals made by the board of directors.

The dominance of the board is further reinforced by the weak supervisor system. Supervisors are elected by the same method as directors, and thus must have the support of the large shareholders who also elect the directors. This election system, coupled with the paucity of eligibility qualifications and clear authority, has unsurprisingly caused the failure of the supervisor as a monitoring mechanism.

At the same time, the board is also extremely vulnerable to the influence of large shareholders. This vulnerability is caused by large shareholders entrenching themselves through deviation of voting rights and cash flow rights and collective action problems—prior to the 2005 amendment, only the board could nominate candidates for director or supervisor positions. This permitted a self-perpetuating cycle of incumbents and their supporters to monopolize their positions indefinitely. Additionally, Article 27 of the Company Law permits a juridical shareholder to exert absolute control (mainly through the unilateral power of replacement) over multiple director and supervisor seats. This potentially allows a controlling shareholder to wield significant power over both the executive and supervisory organs, increasing the vulnerability of the board.

Review of current regulatory measures and future prospects

Against this general introduction of the Taiwanese corporate system, we now seek to highlight possible avenues for reform.

Disclosure rules and the concept of beneficial ownership

Ownership structure affects agency costs and should be of interest to investors. Thus, the capital market can potentially play a significant monitoring role. Market forces raise the capital costs of controlling shareholder structures without adequate internal control mechanisms, and this would correspondingly factor in the equation of the benefits and drawbacks of maintaining a controlling position.

An important precondition for the capital market to monitor the ownership structure of a company is the disclosure of the shareholdings of those in control and ultimate shareholders. Under Article 25 of the Securities and Exchange Law, directors, supervisors, officers, and large shareholders in possession of more than 10 percent of the shares of a publicly issued company must disclose their holdings and any changes in ownership. The calculation of shares held by shareholders includes those shares held under the names of their spouses, minor children, and those held for them under the name of other parties. In the event that a juridical shareholder and its authorized representatives are directors or supervisors under Article 27, the shares held by them are included in the calculation.

To further facilitate the identification of the ultimate shareholders, publicly listed companies must list in the prospectus their ten largest shareholders as well as shareholders with over 5 percent of the total shares.[4] Furthermore, in the case that directors or supervisors are juridical shareholders or their representatives, the juridical shareholder must disclose its ownership structure.[5] Mandatory disclosure to the public stops at the first level of oversight, regardless of whether the primary shareholders are also juridical persons. In practice, companies also voluntarily disclose the ownership structure of all juridical shareholders.

There are two problematic issues in the above framework. First, the level of disclosure of ultimate controlling shareholders is incomplete and may stop at the level of a juridical person, which could impart little information about the ultimate controller. Second, the criteria for calculating share ownership are too inflexible and narrow. Taiwan has not adopted the comprehensive and broad definition of the concept of beneficial ownership under American law. To take an example, the shares owned by a holding company would not be attributed to its controlling shareholder for purposes of disclosure.

Cross-holdings

OVERVIEW

Generally speaking, cross-holdings are structures in which firms own blocks of each other's stock. In discussing cross-holdings and their effect on control, however, relevant financial literature has been narrower in scope, and cross-holdings are defined as when the firm both has an ultimate owner and owns shares in its ultimate owner or in a firm that belongs to its chain of control (La Porta *et al.* 1999: 471; Yeh 2003: 92–93). This kind of cross-holding easily allows controlling shareholders to magnify control in relation to equity investment, which can result in large deviations between ownership and control. Empirical studies indicate that controlling shareholders in Taiwan commonly utilize this cross-holding mechanism to enhance their company control rights.[6]

However, cross-holdings falling outside this narrow scope can also enhance control to a certain extent, as insiders in otherwise unrelated corporations tend to vote for the incumbents. Therefore, both the narrower and more general forms of cross-holding are important to constructing and maintaining a controlling minority ownership structure.

Cross-holdings have various recognized beneficial and detrimental effects. However, their negative effects, such as entrenchment and tunneling, are exacerbated in the case of subsidiaries holding the shares of the controlling company or other companies along the chain of control. Conversely, the benefits of cementing strategic alliances and risk dispersal seem muted in this situation. A controlled company performs no new positive function by owning the shares of its controller: It is already at the disposal of its controller. Thus the balance of benefits and drawbacks is different in the two situations, and should be regulated separately.

LEGISLATIVE DEVELOPMENT

Prior to 2001, only a single article, Article 369-10 of the Company Law, dealt with inter-corporate cross-holdings. Article 369-10 regulates only cases of mutual investment—where two companies have invested in each other to the extent that one-third or more of the total number of the voting shares or the total amount of the capital stock of each company is held or contributed by the other. When those criteria are met, the requirements are twofold: notification to the target company and disclosure of holdings once they reach the one-third threshold, and the limitation of voting power to one-third of all votes. This alleviates the entrenchment of control.

However as noted, cross-holdings between companies along the chain of control should be subject to enhanced regulatory scrutiny. The case for regulatory scrutiny is even more strengthened by the fact that, under Article 167I, subject to limited exceptions, a company is prohibited from buying back its own shares. To be consistent, a company should at the same time be prohibited from engaging in such conduct through the conduit of its subsidiaries. Yet Article 369-10 only regulated cross-holdings, and thus when the subsidiary's holding of shares of the controlling company did not reach one-third, cross-holdings between companies along the chain of control would fall outside its scope entirely.

This deficiency prompted the 2001 enactment of Article 167III and IV, which explicitly prohibits subsidiaries from purchasing or accepting as a security in pledge, shares of the controlling company and shares of companies along the chain of control. This Article was not retroactive and previous purchases by the subsidiaries were still valid. This was a cause for concern because many subsidiaries had already completed purchases of the controlling company or companies along the chain of control before the amendment. This was further dealt with by the 2005 amendment of Article 179, which stripped such shares of their voting rights. Article 167III and Article 179 override Article 369-10 in the event of overlap.

Thus, Taiwanese law now rightly provides for separate frameworks for regulating cross-holdings along a chain of control and otherwise. An important remaining loophole is that the concept of "control" under Article 167 and Article 179 is still determined by the formalistic criteria of majority of the total number of outstanding voting shares or of the total amount of the capital stock, which allows entrenchment through companies that are effectively controlled subsidiaries.[7] Nevertheless, these amendments have made it more difficult to magnify control through cross-holdings and will rein in the most flagrant abuses.[8]

Incorporating the concept of control

PRESENT FRAMEWORK

Prior to the 1997 enactment of the Chapter on Affiliated Enterprises, only those holding an official position within the company could be legally liable under Taiwanese corporate law. While controlling shareholders could theoretically be civilly liable under tort law for intentional injury done in a manner against the rules of morals, the abstract concepts of tort law were difficult to prove in practice.

One possible reason for this gap was that Article 178 of the Company Law already prohibits the voting of interested shareholders that may impair the company's interests. Yet this Article does not apply to the election of directors and supervisors, so controlling shareholders can still exert their influence through other organs.

Article 369-4[9] under the Chapter of Affiliated Enterprises is the only article under Taiwanese law that deals specifically with the responsibility of controlling shareholders outside of their official capacity. The definition of control in this Chapter is quite comprehensive and covers the concept of substantive control. A few observations should be highlighted.

The scope of Article 369-4 is limited to the case where both the controller and subordinate entity are companies. While the responsible person of the controlling company may be jointly liable with the controlling company, it is still extremely easy to evade, as the ultimate controller would only have to avoid an official position in the controlling company. The original draft sought to regulate to some extent the control of non-corporate entities (e.g., head coordinating office) but this was deleted from the final version.

The second significant feature of Article 369-4 is that rights toward the controlling company belong to the subordinate company, not to the minority shareholders or creditors; minority shareholders or creditors may only bring derivative suits on behalf of the subordinate company. Third, this Article is significant in that it attempts for the first time to delimit the duty of the controlling shareholder. As seen, the controlling company does owe a duty, albeit exclusively to the subordinate company.

The determination of the detrimental nature of a business or transaction is made by reference to the standard of an independent company (Faung 2000: 303). This makes clear that Taiwanese law holds inter-group arrangements to the same standard as business between unrelated companies. The only leeway granted to controlled/subordinate companies is that appropriate compensation at year end may preclude liability, and represents an acknowledgment by Taiwanese corporate law of the existence and importance of affiliated enterprises as an economic entity, a departure from the traditional viewpoint of individual companies as the regulatory unit. The content of this duty merits discussion.

First, as noted above, actions that are carried out for the interest of the corporate group would still fall under the term "contrary to normal business practice" and the only leeway allowed is that appropriate compensation can preclude liability. This regime is extremely hard to implement in practice, as demonstrated by the German experience (Hertig and Kanda 2004: 124–126). Difficulties such as determining and quantifying detrimental transactions aside, an important difficulty concerns the artificial projection of autonomous interests of the subordinate company in the context of comprehensive corporate group strategy (Antunes 1994: 350–358). This gives rise to the fundamental issue of the content of the duty of controlling shareholders, which permeates the entire corporate governance framework. It is worth rethinking, under the integrated operation of a corporate group, whether a member company may appropriately pursue the benefit of the group as a whole rather than the individual company's benefit.[10]

Second, the purpose of granting the reprieve of year-end appropriate compensation was to accommodate intra-group arrangements economically beneficial to the corporate group as a whole. Yet this Article, on its face, permits the utilization of this mechanism for any arrangements regardless of their purpose. It remains a question under Taiwanese law whether a transaction improperly arranged for the personal benefit of the controller of the controlling company is covered by this Article. If so, it would run counter to the objective of facilitating economically beneficial intra-corporate groups arrangements and accord too much discretion to controlling shareholders. Moreover, in that case, the Article could, paradoxically, create a lower standard for the controlling company under tort law than under the Company Law (Faung 2000: 295). The Article adds failing to pay appropriate compensation at the year end as a prerequisite of liability, which is not required under tort law.

It seems that this Article should be correctly interpreted as applying only to arrangements carried out for the economic benefit of the corporate group as a whole. However, this interpretation would mean that the sole article dealing with the liability of controlling shareholders does not impose any further responsibility, but only seeks to accommodate the economic reality of corporate groups (Faung 2000: 295). Its ultimate result is only to clarify the ambiguity concerning whether actions carried out for the benefit of the corporate group as a whole could be legitimate.

Moreover, this Article is difficult to enforce, as minority shareholders or creditors still bear the burden of proving general and abstract terms. Controlled/subordinate companies' business may be highly interconnected, with innumerable transactions among themselves. Pinpointing the disadvantage of specific transactions is extremely difficult. Coupled with the high enforcement costs and litigation risks of the derivative suit, the enforcement mechanism under Article 369-4 is extremely weak.

Third, the wording of Article 369-4 is ambiguous on whether the company would be liable for negligence toward the subordinate company (Huang 2001: 111–118). As both controlling companies and directors exert control and should be held accountable, it is arguable that their duty toward the subordinate company should be the same as that of directors and include, *inter alia*, the duty of care.

FUTURE REFORM

When seeking to regulate the responsibility of controlling shareholders, the guiding principle should be the overlap of control and accountability. Many countries, such as the United Kingdom and Korea, have sought to resolve the issue of control and accountability by introducing the concept of "shadow director" or "de facto director." The extent of the application of the concept of substantive control can vary. For example, under the Korean version, the de facto director does not assume the duty of directors for the purposes of applying the provisions on self-dealing (Kim and Jeong 2000: 164).

Article 369-4 takes another approach by separately regulating conflicted shareholder transactions. However, most aspects of a controlling shareholder's duty remain governed solely by tort law. A simpler and more comprehensive approach would be perhaps to adopt the concept of shadow director and provide that those who directly or indirectly exert control over a company's personnel, financial, or operational matters assume the same duties as the company's directors. This would encompass the ultimate controller regardless of its form and automatically extend the duty of directors to the company or third parties.

Nevertheless, the rights accrue to the subordinate company under this approach. Therefore, the problems of high enforcement costs and derivative suits remain. A possible resolution would be to confer direct rights on creditors and minority shareholders toward the controlling shareholder and a shift in the burden of proof to the defendant. Another lingering issue is the precise content of the controller's or director's fiduciary duty in the context of the pursuit of benefit to the corporate group as a whole.

Related-party transactions

Controlling shareholders expropriate resources through their control of company organs, primarily the board. Thus, besides regulating the controlling shareholders directly, expropriation could also be limited through procedural protections and liability imposed on directors of the controlled company.

PRESENT LEGAL FRAMEWORK

As discussed earlier, only Article 369-4 covers potential responsibility of the controlling shareholder without regard to his official position. Other laws on related-party transactions all hinge on the official position of the actor.

The departure point of the Company Law is the generally applicable Article 206, which applies the provisions of Article 178 on interested shareholders, *mutatis mutandis*, prohibiting interested directors from voting, or voting on behalf of other directors, on the matter in question if the company's interests may be impaired. This provision seems on its face quite restrictive, as the concept of "interested" seems broad, and the transaction must in theory be approved by disinterested directors. However, the interpretation of Article 178 has been extremely restrictive to date.[11] However, the framers of the Company Law presumably considered this mechanism adequate in most conflict of interest situations. Consequently, they only provided for further protection under Article 223 in very limited circumstances.

Article 223 of the Company Law provides that where a director conducts any legal act with the company on his own account or for any other person, the supervisor (not the directors, as is usual) should act as the representative of the company. To further combat the prevalence of related-party transactions, Article 171 of the Securities and Exchange Act was amended in 2004. It imposes criminal liability on directors, supervisors, managers, and employees of publicly listed companies who directly or indirectly cause the company to undertake disadvantageous and abnormal transactions to the significant detriment of the company, and directors, supervisors, and managers who, with intent to procure a benefit for themselves or for a third person, act contrary to their duties or misappropriate company assets.

ANALYSIS OF PRESENT LEGAL FRAMEWORK

Article 223 is the only article that deals specifically with self-dealing by directors, but its ambit is limited to when a director is the other party to the transaction or its representative. Thus, it seems that the regulation of most related-party transactions depends on how the board reaches its decisions. Article 206 regulates this matter but has proved ineffective. The reasons include the lack of rules mandating disclosure of interest and the time and ability constraints of most directors. Also, most directors are reluctant to give offense to their colleagues in the absence of flagrant conflict of interest. Another critical reason is that the interpretation of "interested" is unclear. If the above-mentioned interpretation of Article 178 is followed, it seems that the ambit of Article 206 would be too limited. For example, in a case where the director is elected in the capacity of a representative of a juridical shareholder and the transaction involves the controlling shareholder of the juridical shareholder, no legal rights are gained nor legal obligations incurred for the director. Moreover, despite the fact that such a juridical shareholder of a publicly listed company would normally disclose its ownership structure, the level of disclosure can stop at the first layer of holdings. This contributes to the opaqueness and difficulty of determining conflict of interest.

Compliance with Articles 223 and 206 exempts transactions from judicial review of their validity on account of conflict of interest. The only recourse remaining is a damages remedy, which is limited to the general provisions of fiduciary duty and civil law torts. The vague terms are ill-suited to the complexities of related-party transactions and the situation is further exacerbated by the placing of the burden of proof on the plaintiff.

Article 171 of the Securities and Exchange Act seeks to address the issue through the imposition of criminal liability, but as provisions of criminal liability are strictly interpreted to ensure foreseeability, liability is difficult to establish in practice (Wang 2003: 52). Moreover, related-party transactions concern monetary damages and the imposition of civil liability should arguably be the preferable way to compensate the company. In reality, however, related-party transactions are mostly resolved through criminal proceedings, due to the weakness of the civil liability framework.

The most fundamental and effective way to regulate related-party transactions is to establish effective procedural mechanisms that enable disclosure, and independent and impartial parties to review the transaction. The most pressing issue, currently, is perhaps to establish a truly impartial organ within the corporate governance structure, which could take the form of either independent directors or improved supervisors.

Moreover, regardless of whether the procedural safeguards are followed, it should remain possible for the company to claim damages from the directors in question and prove that the transaction was manifestly unfair to the corporation, to enable the courts to revoke the transaction. Absent procedural compliance, the legal effect of the transaction should depend on the company's (independent director or supervisor) ratification. Another worthy reform would be to place the burden of proof on the alleged interested directors engaging in related-party transactions who have better access to relevant information and evidence. This would encourage the company or shareholders on its behalf to bring suit.

Independent directors

Findings have indicated that boards of Taiwanese corporations are populated with insiders. Studies show that the largest shareholders in listed companies provide less than 20 percent of the capital but hold more than half of the board seats (Yeh 2005a: 252). Moreover, board affiliation with controlling shareholders is higher when controlling-shareholder voting rights substantially exceed cash flow rights of the firms. As controlling owners' cash flow rights increase, however, the likelihood of family members on boards decreases, suggesting that the insider dominant board structure is attributable to agency problems from separation between control and cash flow rights (Claessens and Fan 2002: 82; Yeh and Woidtke 2005: 1858; Yeh 2003: 99). In the presence of family control, a positive valuation effect exists when controlling families hold less than 50 percent of board seats (Yeh *et al.* 2001: 40–42).

The above suggests that boards are used to establish the control of a controlling minority shareholder, and that board composition plays an important role in corporate governance in Taiwan.

CURRENT LEGAL FRAMEWORK

The concurrent regulation of independent directors and independent supervisors applies at the stage of application for public issuance of shares.[12] However, these rules only apply to companies applying initially for listing or trading on the over-the-counter market and take the form of a contract entered into by the Stock Exchange or the GreTai (over-the counter) market with the issuing company. As a result, the Stock Exchange and the GreTai have had trouble with companies that do not re-elect independent directors after successful public issuances. The only other avenue open to the regulatory authorities is administrative guidance.

The independence of independent directors from the controlling shareholder, and the minimum number of reserved seats (two), are still inadequate. Furthermore, the minimum seats requirement may give rise to concerns of constitutionality, due to insufficient delegation of authority.

Because this requirement affects the fundamental rights of natural and juridical persons, it should be based on express authorization from the legislative branch, rather than unauthorized administrative rules. Another important issue is the fact that the regulations stipulate the simultaneous existence of independent supervisors and independent directors. The layering of monitoring mechanisms could negatively impact delineation of powers and accountability. This is further exacerbated by the fact that independent directors have no clear authority or powers by law.

REFORM

The amendment to the Securities Exchange Law effective in January 2007 provides companies with three possible frameworks: The first is a company that does not elect independent directors and relies solely on the supervisor system. The second is a company that elects independent directors but does not establish an auditing committee. In that case, independent directors and supervisors would exist simultaneously, but the former's function would be limited to reviewing specific resolutions of the board of directors and a record of its opposition. The third scenario is where a company both elects independent directors and establishes an auditing committee in the place of the supervisor.

The audit committee must be composed entirely of independent directors, and laws concerning supervisors are to be applied *mutatis mutandis*. Except for resolutions concerning financial reports, the board can still pass the same resolution by special majority but the opposition of the auditing committee must be recorded. When a company opts for the binary structure of the board of directors and supervisors, however, the mechanism is that opposition or reservations of independent directors to board resolutions concerning certain important issues must be recorded.

The amendments are a step forward but seem inadequate to provide for effective monitoring. First, the amendment leaves open the possibility of structures with only supervisors or both independent directors and supervisors. The former is problematic as the supervisor system in Taiwan is still extremely weak. The latter confers too little authority on independent directors and could also bring potential overlapping and unclear power delineation between independent directors and supervisors. Second, the blurred delineation of the powers of the board, executive board, and management makes it difficult to clearly outline the duties and responsibility of independent directors, and this ambiguity could hamper effective monitoring on their part.

In theory, under a well-conceived design, both supervisors and independent directors should be able to monitor effectively. While, as compared to supervisors, independent directors have the advantage of actively contributing to and participating in board decisions and policing on a more real-time basis,[13] the realization of these benefits could arguably be left to an individual company's choice. Furthermore, as Taiwanese companies have already become accustomed to the binary system, the supervisor organ should not be abruptly abolished without overriding policy concerns. A preferable regulating framework would follow the Japanese example and allow for a choice between a binary system of directors and supervisors and a unitary system with the establishment of nomination, auditing, and remuneration committees composed primarily of independent directors under the board of directors. Companies which provide explanations should be free to choose to maintain the binary system of supervisors. It should be emphasized that these two alternatives should be separate, comprehensive, and avoid intermingling. Independent directors and supervisors should not coexist, to avoid confusion over supervisory functions and powers, and the committees should be an integral part of the unitary system. The unitary system additionally necessitates the adjustment of the division of power between the board and management. The board should be recast as an organ in charge of monitoring the management and setting broad policy, rather than carrying out business activities as it is currently positioned.

This framework would avoid the inevitable confusion following from the coexistence of both supervisors and independent directors. Moreover, the structural flexibility would prompt a beneficial competition between organizational structures. It follows that a company's choice of whether to adopt an independent director system would ultimately be subject to capital market inspection and provide an additional avenue for competition among companies.

Rules on numerous details concerning the operation of the independent directors system still await issuance by the securities authorities. The prerequisites of effective monitoring include a nomination and election process insulated, to an extent, from those that control directors, strict qualifications for monitors, sufficient compensation, and sufficient authority.

Juridical shareholders and their representatives as directors

Article 27 permits juridical shareholders or their authorized representatives to be elected directors or supervisors. In the former case, the juridical shareholder (director) assigns a natural-person representative to carry out the duties. In Taiwan, many controlling shareholders of group companies elect the investment companies they control as juridical directors of subsidiaries. In the latter, the authorized representatives are elected as individuals, but are under the control of the juridical shareholder. Many government agencies, such as the Ministry of Economic Affairs and the Ministry of Finance, have put in place representative directors in the corporations they control. The juridical shareholder may replace its authorized representative at will, unilaterally displacing the original wishes of other shareholders. Additionally, more than one authorized representatives of the same juridical shareholder may be elected, and it is permitted for the same juridical shareholder to have representatives respectively elected for directors and supervisors.

Article 27 most likely arose from a formalistic analogy of juridical persons to natural persons. The problems Article 27 gives rise to are many. First, juridical shareholders and their stand-ins may occupy more than one position, as opposed to one for natural-person shareholders. Second, the juridical shareholder maintains complete control over its authorized representative through the unilateral power of discharge. It is thus unlikely that such directors and supervisors would have the incentive or ability to carry out their duties effectively. Not only are they deprived of term protection, they also owe possibly conflicting duties to both the company and the juridical shareholder. Third, the fact that authorized representatives of the same juridical shareholders may simultaneously be elected directors and supervisors undermines the basic corporate governance mechanism that supervisors monitor the board. On this last point, the amendment of the Securities and Exchange Law promulgated in January 2007 prohibited juridical shareholders of publicly issued companies or their representatives to be simultaneously elected as directors and supervisors. Fourth, the subject of directorial liability is unclear under Article 27. Jurisprudence is as yet inconclusive, but the current inclination is to hold the natural-person representatives liable. If so, there is a disconnect between liability and the real actor, and the juridical shareholder and its controlling shareholders can easily evade liability.

All of the above increase the ease of expropriation. From another perspective, Article 27 also enhances the control of controlling shareholders and its opacity. The assumption of these posts by juridical shareholders or their representatives increases the difficulty of discerning the identity of the natural person or corporate group ultimately in control and allows complete control over plural board seats.

Article 27 remains popular among corporations and the government, due to its usefulness in establishing comprehensive control. The government in particular relies on it to exert control over companies in which it has substantial investment. These factors have prevented an overhaul of this Article.

Conclusion

In this essay, we first noted that ownership structure can be assessed from an efficiency perspective, and efficiency concerns should play a role in deciding the ultimate ownership structure of each company. We then pointed out the distorting factors of high value of control and deviation between control and cash flow rights. Under these two avenues, the essay sought to discuss the reforms and prospects of Taiwan, a system characterized by controlling minority structures and poor shareholder protection. The reforms put forward in this essay would provide minority shareholders with better protection. Whether they can be implemented depends a great deal upon the joint efforts of lawmakers, regulators, and shareholders in Taiwan.

Notes

1 See Article 192–216 versus 197–227 of the Company Law.
2 (Yeh *et al.* 2001: 29) states that ownership concentration affects the critical level of control and changes over time.
3 The 2005 addition of shareholder proposal rights raises the issue of the extent of the proposal right, specifically the precise delineation of the power of the board of directors and the shareholder meeting.
4 Criteria Governing Information to be Published in Public Offering and Issuance Prospectuses, Article 11.
5 Criteria Governing Information to be Published in Public Offering and Issuance Prospectuses, Article 10(1) iv.
6 Yeh (2003: 93) finds that 40.1 percent of companies in the sample utilized the cross-holding mechanism.
7 This differs from the Chapter on Affiliated Enterprises, which adopts a substantive concept of control.
8 Another similar concern is whether the one-third threshold for mutual investment is set too high, because one-third of shares are normally sufficient to exercise control.
9 Article 369-4 of the Company Law: "In case a controlling company has caused its subordinate company to conduct any business which is contrary to normal business practice or not profitable, but fails to pay an appropriate compensation upon the end of the fiscal year involved, and thus causes the subordinate company to suffer damages, the controlling company shall be liable for such damages."
10 See Hertig and Kanda (2004: 125) discussing the well-known French *Rozenblum* case, which held that a French corporate parent may legitimately divert value from one of its subsidiaries if three conditions are met: the structure of the group is stable, the parent is implementing a coherent group policy, and there is an equitable intra-group distribution of costs and revenues overall.
11 Current jurisprudence limits "interested" to when the shareholder's rights or obligations would be affected immediately by the resolution.
12 See Taiwan Stock Exchange Corporation Criteria for Review of Securities Listings, ROC Over-the-Counter Securities Exchange Criteria Governing Review of Securities Traded on Over-the-Counter Markets, and their ancillary rules.
13 Klein (1998: 275) finds a positive impact for inside directors on finance and investment committees, probably due to informational advantages; we consider that independent directors also have such advantages compared to supervisors, and thus contribute to firm performance.

Bibliography

Antunes, J.E. (1994) *Liability of Corporate Groups, Autonomy and Control in Parent-Subsidiary Relationships in US, German and EU Law: An International and Comparative Perspective*, Boston: Kluwer Law and Taxation Publishers.

Bebchuk, L.A. (1999) *A Rent Protection Theory of Corporate Ownership and Control.* Available at http://ssrn.com/abstract=168990 (accessed 30 July 2007).

Bebchuk, L.A., R. Kraakman, and G. Triantis (2000) "Stock Pyramids, Cross-Ownership and Dual Class Equity: the mechanisms and agency costs of separating control from cash flow rights," in Randall Morck (ed.) *Concentrated Corporate Ownership*, Chicago: University of Chicago Press.

Claessens, S. and J.P.H. Fan (2002) "Corporate Governance in Asia: a survey," *International Review of Finance* 3: 71–103.

Claessens, S., S. Djankov and L.H.P. Lang, (2000) "The Separation of Ownership and Control in East Asian Corporations," *Journal of Financial Economics* 58: 81–112.

Claessens, S., S. Djankov, J.P.H. Fan and L.H.P. Lang (2002) "Disentangling the Incentive and Entrenchment Effects of Large Shareholdings," *The Journal of Finance* 57: 2741–2771.

Demsetz, H. and K. Lehn (1985) "The Structure of Corporate Ownership: causes and consequences," *Journal of Political Economy* 93: 1155–1177.

Dyck, A. and L. Zingales (2004) "Private Benefits of Control: an international comparison," *The Journal of Finance* 59: 537–600.

Faccio M. and L.H.P. Lang (2002) "The Ultimate Ownership of Western European Corporations," *Journal of Financial Economics* 65: 365–395.

Faung, K.L (2000) "Legal Issues on the Regulation of the Chapter of Affiliated Enterprises of Abuse of Control Part I," *Chengchi Law Review* 63: 271–321.

Gilson, R.J. (2006) "Controlling Shareholders and Corporate Governance: complicating the comparative taxonomy," *Harvard Law Review* 119: 1641–1679.

Gilson, R.J. and J.N. Gordon (2003) "Controlling Controlling Shareholders," *University of Pennsylvania Law Review* 152: 785–843.

Hertig, G. and H. Kanda (2004) "Related Party Transactions," in R.H. Kraakman *et al.*, *The Anatomy of Corporate Law, A Comparative and Functional Approach*, New York: Oxford University Press.

Huang, M.J. (2001) *Legal Framework for Publicly Issuing Companies and Corporate Governance*, Taipei: Angle Publishing.

Khanna, T. and K. Palepu (2000) "Is Group Affiliation Profitable in Emerging Markets? An analysis of diversified Indian business groups," *The Journal of Finance* 55: 867–891.

Kim, K.S. and S.W. Jeong (2000) "Controlling the Controlling Shareholders: Conduct, Structure, and Market," in D.K. Yoon (ed.), *Recent Transformations in Korean Law and Society*, Korea: Seoul National University Press.

Klein, A. (1998) "Firm Performance and Board Committee Structure," *The Journal of Law and Economics* 41: 275–303.

Lai, I.J. (2005) "Is Risk to Investors Lower with Higher Shareholdings of Directors and Supervisors?" *Review of Financial Risk Management* 1: 87–101.

La Porta R., F. Lopez-De-Silanes, and A. Shleifer (1999) "Corporate Ownership Around the World," *The Journal of Finance* 54: 471–517.

La Porta R., F. Lopez-De-Silanes, and A. Shleifer and R. Vishny (2000) "Investor Protection and Corporate Governance," *Journal of Financial Economics* 58: 3–27.

—— (2002) "Investor Protection and Corporate Valuation," *The Journal of Finance* 57: 1147–1170.

Lemmon, M.L. and K.V. Lins (2003) "Ownership Structure, Corporate Governance and Firm Value: evidence from the east asian financial crisis," *The Journal of Finance* 58: 1445–1468.

Morck, R., D. Wolfenzon, and B. Yeung (2004) *Corporate Governance, Economic Entrenchment and Growth*. Available at www.nber.org/papers/W10692 (accessed 30 July 2007).

Nenova, T. (2003) "The Value of Corporate Voting Rights and Control: a cross-country analysis," *Journal of Financial Economics* 68: 325–351.

Song, O.R. (2002) "The Legacy of Controlling Minority Structure: a kaleidoscope of corporate governance reform in Korean chaebol," *Law and Policy in International Business* 34: 183–245.

Wang, W.W.Y. (2003) "The Delineation of Civil, Commercial and Criminal Law: From the Perspective of Illegal Corporate Actions," *The Taiwan Law Review* 103: 49–60.

Yeh, Y.H. (2003) "Corporate Ownership and Control: New Evidence From Taiwan," *Corporate Ownership & Control* 1: 87–101.

—— (2005a) *The Disappearing Stock King-preemptive discovery of landmines*, Taipei: Sunbright Press.

—— (2005b) "Do Controlling Shareholders Enhance Corporate Value?" *Corporate Governance: An International Review* 13: 313–325.

Yeh, Y.H. and T. Woidtke (2005) "Commitment or Entrenchment? controlling shareholders and board composition," *Journal of Banking and Finance* 29: 1857–1885.

Yeh, Y.H., T.S. Lee, and T. Woidtke (2001) "Family Control and Corporate Governance: evidence from Taiwan," *International Review of Finance* 2: 21–48.

Zingales, L. (1995) "Insider Ownership and the Decision to Go Public," *Review of Economic Studies* 62: 425–448.

IV
Analysis and commentary

12 Controlling-family shareholders in Asia

Anchoring relational exchange

Ronald J. Gilson[*]

In recent years, corporate governance scholarship has begun to focus on the most common distribution of public corporation ownership: outside of the United States and the United Kingdom, publicly owned corporations often have a controlling shareholder (Gilson 2006: 1641; Enriques and Volpin 2007: 117). The presence of a controlling shareholder is especially prevalent in developing countries. In Asia, for example, some two-thirds of public corporations have one, and they mostly represent family ownership (Claessens *et al.* 2000: 92–93; 2002: 2741). The law and finance literature, exemplified by a series of articles by combinations of Rafael La Porta, Florencio Lopez-de-Silanes, Andrei Shliefer, Robert Vishny and others, treats the prevalence of controlling shareholders as the result of bad law (La Porta *et al.* 1999: 471; 1997: 1131; 1998: 113; 2000: 3); more specifically, controlling shareholders are ubiquitous in countries that do not adequately protect minority shareholders from the extraction of private benefits of control by dominant shareholders. The logic is straightforward. Controlling shareholders will not part with control because that will expose them to exploitation by a new controlling shareholder who acquires a controlling position in the market.

The law and finance account of the distribution of ownership, while compelling as far as it goes, is at best partial. I have argued elsewhere that the syllogism is too simple to explain all controlling shareholder systems, because we find significant numbers of controlling shareholders in countries with good law (Gilson 2006: 1641). If jurisdictions that adequately protect minority shareholders have a significant number of companies with a controlling shareholder, something other than bad law is at work. And while the link between shareholder protection and distribution of shareholdings remains persuasive with respect to countries with poor shareholder protection—minority shares change hands at a significant discount to controlling shares in such jurisdictions (Dyck and Zingales 2004: 537; Nenova 2003: 325)[1]—it still leaves important parts of even this landscape unexplained. It does not, for example, explain why in Asian countries controlling shareholders are likely to be families. And it does not explain, given poor shareholder protection, why we observe minority shareholders at all. Since the law and finance account does not posit the existence of observable limits on how much of a minority shareholder's investment the controlling share-holder can extract, why is not the value of minority shares in such jurisdictions and, it follows, the number of minority shareholders, zero?

In this article, I want to continue the effort to complicate the controlling shareholder taxonomy by looking at the impact of bad law in a very different sense than contemplated by the law and finance literature. In particular, I want to address the effect on the distribution of shareholdings when a jurisdiction provides not only poor minority shareholder protection, but poor commercial law generally.[2] Put differently, the goal is to play out the implications for the distribution of shareholders when the focus is not on conditions in the capital market, where poor shareholder protection has figured so prominently, but on conditions in the product market, where the driving legal influence is the quality of commercial law that supports the corporation's actual business activities. Can bad commercial law help explain shareholder distribution?

In an important sense, the law and finance literature's sharp focus on minority shareholder protection treats the shareholder distribution as independent of what the company actually does. In Miller-Modigliani terms, the distribution of shareholdings is irrelevant to the company's actual activities. Just as the division of capital between debt and equity on the right side of the balance sheet does not, under the irrelevancy propositions, affect the value of real assets on the left side of the balance sheet (Ross *et al.* 2005: 407–409), the line that separates the two sides of the balance sheet also isolates the distribution of equity among shareholders from the value of the corporation's assets. My hypothesis is that bad commercial law, as opposed to just poor minority shareholder protection as contemplated by the law and finance literature, breaks down the separation between equity distribution and firm value. I posit that the presence of a controlling shareholder and, in particular, a family controlling shareholder, allows the corporation to better conduct its business, but in a way quite different than the potential for a controlling shareholder to more effectively police the agency conflict between management and shareholders, the productive advantage typically ascribed to a controlling shareholder structure (Gilson 2006: 1650–1652).

Broadening the concept of "bad law" to take into account not only the quality of minority shareholder protection, but also the quality of commercial law more generally, frames the problem. In an environment of bad commercial law, a corporation's basic business depends on its capacity to engage in self-enforcing exchange—that is, commercial transactions where the parties perform their contractual obligations because it is in their self-interest to perform, not because of the threat of legal sanction. With bad commercial law, exchange must be self-enforcing because there are neither authoritative rules, nor an effective judicial system to enforce those obligations.[3] Transactions in this circumstance take place in a reputation market, which substitutes for law (or its shadow) as a means to assure that parties perform their contractual obligations.

Framing the problem as one of commercial contracting in a bad law environment suggests a very different function for shareholder distribution than contemplated by the law and finance literature. When commerce must take place in a reputation market, in which a corporation's business must be effected through self-enforcing transactions, the distribution of share-holdings, and particularly the presence of family ownership, facilitate the development and maintenance of the reputation necessary for a corporation's commercial success.[4] More speculatively, the role of reputation in the product market may help explain why we observe publicly held minority shares in the capital market even though poor shareholder protection does not impose a formal limit on the amount of private benefits that a controlling shareholder can extract. If bad behavior toward minority shareholders can affect the corporation's reputation in the product market as well as the capital market, then self-imposed limits on controlling shareholders' extraction of private benefits may derive from their concern over success in the product market. Indeed, the corporation may have minority share-holders at all, despite the high price of equity capital in the face of poor minority protection, as a kind of hostage to support its reputation in the product market.

My ambition here is to offer a working hypothesis, an account neither formal in method, nor deeply grounded in the history and structure of particular jurisdictions.[5] What happens when we turn the capital market-oriented bad law account of concentrated ownership on its head, and focus instead on how product market-oriented bad law influences the distribution of equity? The value of so minimalist an approach lies in framing the issue clean of the complications inevitably associated with particular jurisdictions, with the hope that, if the account proves intriguing, it then will be of assistance in the real task—that of understanding the development of particular national markets, and one of the foundations of economic development more generally.

The first part of this essay sets out the basic problem of commercial exchange in a jurisdiction without effective commercial law. The following part develops how conducting business through a corporation can facilitate reputation formation and maintenance. Next, I examine how family ownership can improve a corporation's capacity to act as a reputation bearer in the product market, and this is followed by speculation on why a controlling family shareholder might voluntarily limit the amount of private benefit extraction from minority shareholders, not because the treatment of minority shareholders affects the controlled corporation's ability to raise additional equity capital, but because bad behavior will degrade its reputation in the product market. The penultimate part addresses a final speculation, now about the dynamic character of controlling shareholder systems in developing countries. The role of shareholder distribution described here is one that supports reputation-based product markets. Such markets are limited in scale so that further economic development requires a transition to institutions that support anonymous product markets—a rule of law-based commercial system with effective formal enforcement. The transition, however, will be impeded both by the particular characteristics of existing institutions—what Paul Milgrom and John Roberts call "supermodularity[6]—and by the political influence of those who have large investments that are specific to a reputation-based product market. The concluding part frames the question with which we are left: how does the necessary transition take place in the face of structural and political barriers?[7] More specifically, does the answer relate to the recent historical pattern of economically benevolent dictators observed during the transition period in many countries that have successfully developed?

The structure of reputation markets

In its most simple form, a self-enforcing commercial arrangement can be based only on the expectation of a long horizon of future transactions. Where two parties expect to engage in repeated transactions, neither will have an incentive to misbehave in a particular transaction because bad behavior by one party in a transaction will be punished by the counterparty, whether by retaliating in future transactions, changing the terms of future transactions or refusing to engage in future transactions at all (Dixit 2004: 16). This simple reciprocity model has significant limitations. First, it requires the expectation of a lengthy relationship to avoid the incentive to cheat. In the absence of future dealings, one party has no reason not to cheat on the current exchange. And even the expectation of future rounds may be insufficient to assure self-enforcement if the number of rounds and their present value is small compared to the payoffs from cheating (Dixit 2004: 61; Fudenberg and Maskin 1986: 533). Second, and for my purpose more important, the requirement of long-lasting bilateral exchange to support a self-enforcing transaction severely limits the size of the economy. Individuals are limited in the number of long-term trading partners they can directly support.

To increase the number of parties with whom one can trade requires adding the concept of reputation. If one party will trade with others in the future, but may not trade with any single party repeatedly—that is, if trade will be multilateral rather than bilateral—self-enforcement will still work if the party's behavior in one exchange becomes known to future counterparties. In other words, to support multilateral exchange the party must become known beyond its current trading partners—it must develop a reputation.

Self-enforcing commercial exchanges when individual parties do not necessarily expect to transact with each other in the future—reputation-based markets—require a number of supporting factors. First, parties must expect to engage in similar transactions in the future, even if not with the same trading partner; this creates the potential for punishing bad behavior.

Second, performance or breach must be observable, in the sense that there is a shared understanding among potential future trading partners of what constitutes good or bad behavior. Third, a party's behavior in one exchange also must be observable in a different sense; the party's actual performance—whether the party behaved badly or whether it performed as anticipated—must be observable by potential future trading partners.[8]

These factors have implications that limit the kind of market that can be supported by reputation-based exchange, all of which will restrict the level of commercial activity in that market. Professor Avinash Dixit, in his model of relation-based exchange, uses the concept of "distance" to express the limiting impact of these factors (Dixit 2004: 67–71). The choice of the term invokes the language of physical distance as a metaphor for the investment in information necessary to establish and maintain a reputation for contractual performance. Physical distance makes information costly to transmit in the absence of advanced technology.

Similarly, both a shared understanding of what constitutes performance and the observability of breach depend, in the end, on the cost of information transmission. The common values that underlie a shared understanding of performance under differing circumstances must be transmitted among future trading partners; as conditions change and values evolve, new information must be transmitted. Communicating this information is a function of distance: it is more costly and less successful to communicate both with traders who are physically distant from the core of market participants, and with traders who are socially distant from the core, whether by culture, language, or class.[9]

Correspondingly, it is more costly to communicate the necessary information to sustain reputation-based transactions that are new or complicated: the concept of performance that must be shared requires more information and more new information, and lacks the shared understandings that define adequate performance in the traditional markets. The result is straightforward. "[C]heating becomes more attractive the more distant the partner" (Dixit 2004: 68).

The scope and scale of a reputation-supported market is thus defined by a tradeoff between the gains from trading with more distant partners, who may offer different skills and goods and at least additional volume, and the increased costs associated with transmitting information to them. These costs increase in the distance to the marginal trader, while the accuracy of a trader's reputation decreases in that distance. The implication is that the size of the market depends on information technology: the better the technology, the lower the cost of transmitting shared values and performance information and, therefore, the less distant potential trading partners are from each other and the larger the size of the market that can be supported by reputation. This relationship between information costs and the size and diversity of a reputation-based market creates the role for corporations to reduce the costs of establishing and sustaining such a market.[10]

Corporations as long-lived repositories of reputation

David Kreps, in a well-known essay on the economics of corporate culture, argues that a corporation can play a special role in a reputation-based market because of its superior capacity to establish and maintain a reputation (Kreps 1990: 91). Recall that the stability of a reputation market depends on a party's assessment that there will a sufficiently long series of transactions with an existing trading partner, or with future trading partners with access to the party's prior performance, to prevent anticipation of a rollback cascade from subverting contractual performance in the first place. As discussed in the previous part, the length of anticipated dealings prevents an equilibrium of voluntary performance of obligations from unraveling into cheating in the current round, once it can be expected that there will be a final round in which it will be in a party's interest to cheat.[11] In contrast to individuals who die or retire, corporations have an infinite life; they will not necessarily have a final period that triggers a cascade into current non-performance. As a result, corporations will invest more in establishing a reputation and be more diligent about protecting one. As Kreps puts it, "The firm is a wholly intangible object in this theory—a reputation bearer" (Kreps 1990: 111).

One additional step is necessary to enable the corporation to function as a long-lived reputation bearer. As a formal matter, a corporation is just a long-lived piece of paper on which appears the corporation's charter. The corporation's decisions—in our context, to perform its contractual obligations or not—are made by individuals with finite professional lives. It may be in the corporation's interest—that is, in the interest of future owners of the corporation—for it to invest in establishing a reputation and then invest in sustaining it by performing its obligations to trading partners, because those investments will pay off over the corporation's infinite life. But the investment will not be made unless it is also to the advantage of the short-lived individuals who actually make the corporation's decisions. For example, if all profits are currently paid out and the decision makers have no way to benefit from the value of the corporation's reputation when they retire, then the corporation, in effect, will have a final period determined not by the corporation's infinite life, but by its current owners' mortality.

Kreps's solution to the problem of causing short-lived individuals to think like a long-lived corporation is to allow the current generation of decision makers to sell their position (equity) to the next generation of decision makers. By allowing the current generation to secure a payment based on the discounted value of future corporate earnings, they then have an incentive to value the corporation's future dealings beyond the length of their own careers, and therefore to make efficient current investments in the corporation's reputation, because what they will receive for their positions is a function of the value of the corporation's future trading (Kreps 1990: 108–110).[12]

The value of a long-lived reputation bearer in a jurisdiction with bad commercial law now should be apparent. Developing long-lived bearers of reputations as trading partners reduces the costs of building reputations—one reputation lasts a long time—and, by reducing the number of participants over time, reduces the costs a trading partner must incur to learn the reputation of potential trading partners. The resulting reduction in information costs decreases the distance between traders and therefore increases the range of parties with whom any single trader can contract. In turn, this increases the size, scale, and diversity of the market that reputation-based trading can support and, in the end, increases productivity and economic growth.

The family as a more efficient reputation bearer

In fact, the strategy of reducing information costs through trading partners organizing production in long-lived corporations, and thereby increasing the size and scale of reputation-supported product markets, is more complicated than the discussion thus far has acknowledged. As we saw above, Kreps gives current corporate decision makers the incentive to invest in long-term reputation by organizing the corporation so that the decision makers can sell their stake in the corporation before retiring. This eliminates the problem of the decision makers' facing a final period, even if the corporation does not. But this temporal arbitrage does not quite work.

In Kreps's account, the arrangement that creates the incentive for the decision makers to cause the corporation to invest in reputation that will pay off after their careers end, and which makes that reputation credible to potential trading partners, is part of the corporation's internal governance structure. This structure is not readily observable by potential outside trading partners; the information costs of learning about the corporation's internal characteristics, which are central to a trading partner relying on the corporation's reputation, are very high. At this point, poor shareholder protection law (in addition to poor commercial law) enters the analysis. An effective corporate disclosure regime will require the corporation to make public the structure of its owners' and managers' incentives, thereby reducing the costs of acquiring this information not only by the capital market, but by potential trading partners as well. Without the ready availability of such information, the corporation may not succeed as a long-lived reputation bearer, because trading partners will have no credible reason to believe that the relevant reputation is that of the corporation rather than the short-lived decision maker.

Recent corporate governance debates demonstrate that the problem of high information costs concerning the incentives of corporate decision makers, and the difficulty of evaluating them even if disclosed, are hardly theoretical. Not long ago, criticism of the U.S. corporate governance system claimed that the incentive structures of U.S. corporations resulted in myopic planning, with too high a discount rate being applied in the capital budgeting process. German and Japanese corporations, in contrast, were said to be long-term oriented because their decision makers faced a different, more patient, incentive structure. Not many years later, the direction of the debate had switched, with the U.S. system lauded as providing incentives to innovate that were not present in the more conservative German and Japanese governance systems (Gilson 2001: 329; 1996: 327). Even more recently, the argument has shifted again. Executive compensation scandals, concerning both the absolute amounts paid and the integrity of the process by which stock options were granted, at least raise questions concerning the incentive structure that had been said to support innovation, as well as doubts concerning the observability of managerial incentives even in the United States—the jurisdiction with what is likely the best shareholder protection (Aggarwal *et al.* 2006).

My point is not to extend this continually shifting debate, but only to note that it is very hard to get the corporation's internal incentives right even when you are trying.[13] And the harder it is to get it right, the higher the information costs associated with an outside potential trading partner trying to assess whether the corporate decision makers have the right incentives to cause the corporation to make investments in its long-term reputation for performing its contractual obligations with trading partners. The harder it is to evaluate internal incentives, the more assessment of a particular company matters, and the more a particular trading partner has to know to assess the corporation's reputation. Of course, this company-specific information is costly, especially in a jurisdiction with weak shareholder protection, and the resulting impact on a reputation-based commercial market should be clear. The increased cost of assessing reputation increases the distance between potential traders, and reduces the size and scale of commercial activity that can be supported. Kreps's conception of the corporation as a bearer of reputation thus, in part, founders on the barriers to transmitting the information on which the corporation's reputation depends.

Here, finally, is where family ownership comes into the account. When the corporation is owned by a family, the internal incentives become much more transparent. The problem with Kreps's model is the need for an intergenerational transfer between the current and the next generation of corporate decision makers, so that current decisions will take long-term reputation creation into account. In turn, the transfer mechanism has to be observable to potential future traders, a communication process that can be expected to be costly when the mechanism and its underlying incentive structure has to be set out in an explicit contract. In contrast, family ownership solves the intergenerational transfer process rather elegantly. Because of intra-family inheritance and family ties, the current generation of decision makers, at least in functional family businesses, treats the next generation's utility as the equivalent of its own, so there is no temporal distortion of incentives to invest in reputation.

The critical point is that family ownership substitutes for internal incentive and transfer mechanisms as an assurance of the corporation's commitment to long-term reputation, but with one important difference. Family ownership is much more easily observed by potential trading partners; so long as cultural values concerning family support the belief that current decision makers are committed to intergenerational utility equivalence,[14] information concerning the corporation's commitment to contractual performance is cheaper to transmit.

By this point, it is apparent where the argument is going. The combination of Kreps's insight that, because of its infinite life, the corporation can be an effective bearer of a long-term reputation for contractual performance, with the fact that family ownership can be a low-cost way of communicating to potential trading partners that the corporation values future trading, increases the size and scale of the reputation-based trading market. If the corporation is the bearer of reputation, family substitutes for internal contract as the corporation's DNA. In an environment of bad law—both commercial and shareholder protection—controlling family corporations will have an evolutionary advantage.[15]

While it is beyond my ambition to fully explore the implications of this conclusion here, I will address one such implication to provide an example of what is possible. It is commonplace in developing countries that family-controlled companies are conglomerates, operating in a range of different industries that do not share production economies of any type, whether scale, scope, or vertical integration. The two most familiar explanations for conglomerate organization in this setting are financial. First, in the absence of an efficient external capital market, an internal capital market in which project funding is determined not by the market, but by the corporation's internal capital budgeting process, may well be more effective. Of course, this explanation is consistent with the capital market-oriented bad law argument: poor shareholder protection means poor disclosure, which in turn means an informationally inefficient capital market. Thus, a conglomerate serves to internalize the capital allocation process (Khanna and Palepu 2000: 868). Second, a controlling shareholder bears the cost of non-diversification, especially where a weak local capital market makes laying off risk costly. A conglomerate strategy allows diversification at the company level, where it benefits the controlling shareholder (Gilson and Black 1995: 332–357).

A third explanation for conglomerate organization in developing countries, building on the role of family ownership developed here, is product-market rather than capital-market focused. The conjecture is that family control combines with Kreps's conception of the corporation as a reputation bearer to reduce the information costs associated with maintaining a reputation. Because in a country with bad commercial law all transactions are reputation based, investment in reputation produces an asset subject to economies of both scale and scope. Once family ownership is established, the marginal cost of transmitting that fact, and thereby providing a foundation for reputation-based trading, is decreasing with scale. And the same forces that create reputational scale economies within a single industry also create reputational scope economies across industries, because reputation for contractual performance need not be industry specific where the performance uncertainty is integrity, not capacity. To be sure, the cost of information transmission may be initially higher when the corporation enters a new industry, so that potential traders in that industry are at a greater functional distance from the corporation; nevertheless, family ownership remains a less costly fact to convey.

Why minority shareholders?

We now move to a more speculative but also more narrowly defined question of how the product market influences the distribution of shareholders in the capital market. The role of family ownership in supporting self-enforcing corporate commercial exchange explains family control of corporations in developing countries, but it does not itself explain public ownership of a minority stake in the family-controlled corporation, also a familiar element of shareholder distribution in developing countries.[16] Thus far in the analysis, the product-market explanation for family ownership shares this gap with the law and finance explanation of concentrated ownership. As discussed in the introduction, a bad shareholder-protection explanation for the prevalence of controlling shareholders does not explain why we observe any minority shareholders. If investors know that there is an effective upper bound on the amount of private benefits that a controlling shareholder can divert, then they will pay a fair price for the earnings that remain and earn a fair return on their investment, even if the trading price for minority shares is significantly below that for controlling shares to reflect the diversion. The problem is that the literature does not reveal the source of that upper bound.[17]

One could imagine that the need for controlling shareholders to return to the capital market to raise equity in the future could support an upper bound—an expected decrease in the price paid in the next offering would decrease the incentive to divert following the first. There is, however, reason to be skeptical of this explanation. As a factual matter, such companies do not frequently return to the capital market for equity, sharing that characteristic with public corporations in developed countries. The explanation may be simply a bad shareholder-protection variant of a pecking-order theory of capital structure (Brealey *et al.* 2006: 490–496; Ross *et al.* 2005: 450–453). This theory posits that a company's choice of what securities to issue turns on the informational asymmetry between the company and prospective investors, and that the asymmetry is more significant the riskier the security. As a result, a company will use retained earnings to finance its activities when it can, with debt the second choice (less risky than equity because debt has priority), and equity (whose value is dependent on the most risky part of the company's future earnings) as the last resort. Because the difficulty of securing credible information about future corporate performance—which underlies valuation of an equity offering—is much greater in a bad shareholder-protection jurisdiction, information asymmetry and the place of equity at the bottom of the pecking order are reinforced. Thus, the cost difference between bank financing or internal financing on the one hand, and equity financing on the other, should be substantially greater than in a good shareholder-protection jurisdiction.

The need to return to the equity market is therefore not a likely source of an upper bound for controlling shareholder private-benefit extraction in bad shareholder-protection jurisdictions; cost considerations make equity capital an even less attractive source of financing in these jurisdictions than in those with good shareholder protection. Indeed, it is a two-sided puzzle, with the possibility of a lemon's market on both sides: why do companies choose to pay the very high price for equity, given the bad shareholder-protection discount and the availability of cheaper alternatives; and why do minority shareholders purchase any shares at all in the absence of an observable ceiling on private benefit extraction? Without more, both issuers and investors should shun this segment of the capital market.[18]

An attractively more straightforward, but still troublesomely vague, source for a ceiling on private benefit extraction is the intuition that even in a bad shareholder-protection jurisdiction, the courts or regulators (or someone in authority) will act if a controlling shareholder is too greedy or too blatant in his exploitation of the minority. Perhaps even other controlling shareholders will support action against behavior that, because of the extremity of its revealed avarice, calls attention to the more measured diversion of others, something of an honor among thieves argument (or, less judgmentally, a private-ordering solution to enforcement) (Greif 2005: 732–735; Richman 2004: 2338–2348). But here the problem is how the market knows what the self- or collectively imposed ceiling is. Even if the market is informationally efficient, in the sense that it is an unbiased estimate of the ceiling's height, the estimate is likely to vary widely around the unobservable true value. Because all companies with a controlling shareholder will present the risk of uncertainty in the height of the ceiling, which cannot be diversified away in the national market, the minority share discount will be driven even higher.

If, instead, we approach the problem of locating a ceiling on private benefit extraction from a product-market perspective rather than a capital-market perspective, an alternative explanation is possible, although it shares a troublesome vagueness with the unofficial ceiling-on-diversion explanation just considered. In this product market-based explanation, minority shareholders may play an important reputation role in jurisdictions with both bad shareholder protection and bad commercial law. As we saw in the first part of this essay, the cost of transmitting performance information is critical to the scale of the reputation-based product market that can be supported. Suppose that the treatment of minority shareholders is visible to a company's potential trading partners at a low cost, perhaps because such exploitation is covered by the local newspapers.[19] Fair treatment of minority shareholders then serves as evidence of the corporation's integrity, including its commitment to performing its contractual obligations, a signal that is credible because it is costly—some extraction of private benefits of control must be given up. If the family-controlled corporation does not cheat in easy (because of poor shareholder protection) ways by exploiting minority shareholders, the reasoning goes, the controlling-family shareholder also will not cheat its customers.[20]

The decision to have minority shareholders, then, can be explained not by the need for capital at the time of the initial public offering or in the future, but as a way of developing reputation that will be valuable in the product market (and which may justify the higher cost of capital for a one-time issuance of minority shares). From this perspective, minority shareholders play the role of reputational canaries, whose value is that they help to credibly convey to potential traders that the corporation is an honest trading partner. The analysis is akin to Klein and Leffler's argument that reputation for product quality is supported by sellers investing in long-lived assets unrelated to product quality (like expensive offices for public accounting firms) whose value drops sharply if the company fails as a result of providing poor-quality goods or services (Klein and Leffler 1981: 615). More generally, think of corporate investment in image advertising; its principal value is demonstrating something about corporate character, which is believed to influence potential customers' assessment of the corporation's product or service. In our context, the investment (or image advertising) is foregoing poor treatment of minority shareholders, which requires having minority shareholders in the first place.

To be sure, this preliminary account of a product market-based role of minority shareholders is far from complete. The most significant gap that remains is how potential trading partners know what the acceptable level of diversion is, so they that can know when the canary is gasping. In this respect, the account suffers from the same problem as does the explanation that there is an unofficial ceiling on diversion that is both observable by minority shareholders and observed by controlling shareholders. As developed in the first part of this essay, any reputation-based account of exchange—here the account is cross-market with reputation in the capital market supporting exchange in the product market—requires a shared understanding of what constitutes appropriate performance, now with respect to treatment of minority shareholders.

While it is beyond my ambition here to fully develop the product market-based account, the shape of a hypothesis does take form. The gap in an informal ceiling-on-diversion explanation for the presence of minority shareholders is that one still is left without an explanation for why one wants minority shareholders in the first place, given less costly alternatives of bank financing or internally generated funds. The product market-based account provides an answer to why the family corporation might want minority shareholders—because of the impact of their treatment on the corporation's reputation in the product market—but still requires a mechanism by which fair treatment is visible to the family corporation's customers. An important difference between the two accounts, however, is that the product market-based explanation of minority shareholders as a signal of commitment to contractual performance at least provides an enforcement mechanism. In the product-market account, mistreatment of minority shareholders will be punished in the product market. In a setting in which the corporation need not return to the equity market, the informal-enforcement explanation does not explain how mistreatment of minority shareholders in excess of the norm is punished at all; rather, like the economist's joke about being stranded on a desert island, it simply assumes unspecified informal enforcement through an unidentified actor.

Turning now to the observability problem with a product market-based explanation of minority shareholders, the product-market account starts with two advantages. First, the controlling-family shareholder in the product market-based account has a clear incentive to make its treatment of minority shareholders observable to product-market customers; without that disclosure, there is no reason to have the minority shareholders at all. Second, the observability of minority shareholder treatment need not be perfect. Rather, the signal of fair treatment of minority shareholders need only add information to the direct information the corporation's customers receive concerning the quality of its contractual performance. Here the point is not merely whether the product market-based explanation for the existence of minority shareholders is better than an informal enforcement explanation—even if better, both explanations could be wrong—but whether, net of its cost, it adds anything to the operation of the product market's direct transmission of information concerning product quality.

There is good reason to think that the capital-market signal of product quality sent by the treatment of minority shareholders adds to a customer's information set concerning product quality. Here the idea is that assessing product quality is difficult in a jurisdiction with poor commercial law. The experience of an individual customer may be a noisy measure of overall producer quality, even to the particular customer—did the customer receive a bad lot or was the seller simply a poor producer? Given the barriers to actual observation in a jurisdiction with poor commercial law—for example, where techniques such as warranties are not viable—room exists for a signal of quality that supplements a customer's direct observation. Additionally, the minority-shareholder signal may have a cost advantage over further direct observation of product quality. The minority-shareholder signal is given by the family-controlled corporation; additional direct information concerning product quality in a bad commercial law jurisdiction requires aggregation of information from many parties, the institutions for which may be expensive to create and which require significant collective action.

This analysis still leaves a gap: how does the controlling-family share-holder make its signal of fair treatment of the minority credible? But this is an acceptable place to stop in describing what, in the end, is meant only to be a hypothesis. Signals have to be understood in a context, and their development is dynamic: a signaler changes its signal as it better under-stands the recipients' response. For now, it is enough that a hypothesis of a product market-based explanation of the existence of minority shareholders in family-controlled corporations is plausible. It is more completely speci-fied than an informal enforcement explanation and it need not be a better signal of quality than producers' direct provision of information—it need only add to the total information the customer receives. My claim is that the product market-based account is worth our thinking about.

Of course, a product-market/reputation account and an informal enfor-cement ceiling are not mutually exclusive, nor are they the only approaches to explaining why family-controlled companies in developing markets have minority shareholders. Yet another account places the motive for the exis-tence of minority shareholders in the realm of political economy. In many emerging market countries, having a stock market is like having a national airline—a badge of modernity that does not demand an economic justifica-tion. The government wants a stock market; the company goes along by issuing equity and paying the higher cost of capital—a tax of sorts—and the individual investors buy equity for the same reason that Americans buy state lottery tickets, or because few alternative investments are available. This account also lacks a ceiling on private-benefit extraction, but one can imagine that if the government wants to have a stock market, it may have the capacity to enforce, however informally, a particular ceiling.[21] In any event, elements of a product-market/reputation account, an informal ceiling account, and a vanity stock market account for minority shareholders all may be operative; and the relative importance of each may differ, depending on the context of a particular national market. The key is understanding the range of explanations that may be at work.

The dynamics of reputation-based exchange

This brings us to the final element of our assessment of family-controlled cor-porations in developing markets. To this point, the analysis has been largely static, with attention focused on the conditions necessary for reputationally based self-enforcing exchange, and the complementary shareholder distribution in jurisdictions with bad commercial law. I want to close with a preliminary consideration of the dynamics of such markets, to the end of framing a central question about national economic development: How does a nation make the leap from reputationally based to anonymous, rule of law-based commercial relationships that is necessary to sustain economic growth?

A reputation-based commercial system can grow quickly (Dixit 2004: 82; Li 2003: 651). However, such a system runs into an upper bound. For example, the distance-limited size of the market for a particular product discussed in the preceding part forces a corporation to expand into unrelated businesses to achieve economies of scale and scope associated with its reputation. This strategy comes, however, with a cost: production of unrelated products with which the corporation has no experience will be less efficient. As with any expansion, decreasing returns on reputation will set in at the margin as sales extend to trading partners at a greater "distance." At the same time, marginal costs will increase with "distance" as a result of expanding into new geographical markets, and expanding into unrelated but geographically proximate businesses, both from lack of experience and from the difficulty of managing the growing number of different industries in which the now-conglomerate corporation participates. Because both the number of potential traders within a feasible reputation distance from the corporation, and the number of industries in which the firm can successfully operate, have finite limits, sooner or later economic growth in reputation-based product markets slows down.

At this point, the jurisdiction has to transform its commercial law to a system that provides effective formal enforcement of contractual obligations in order to extend the reach of its producers to buyers too distant to rely entirely on reputation-based self-enforcement.[22] However, this process is unlikely to be linear, and ultimately may not succeed. As Dixit reasons,

> [t]he fixed costs of rule-based governance are a public investment; therefore society must solve a collective action problem to put such a system in place. This is not automatic; there are the usual problems of free-riding, underestimation of the benefits to future generations in today's political process, and the veto power of those who stand to lose from the change.
>
> (Dixit 2004: 80)

The potential for those who have been most successful in the relation-based economy to resist transition to a rule of law-based system is a matter of particular concern. Precisely those families whom the existing relation-based system most advantages, and who therefore have the greatest system-specific investment in reputation, have the most to lose from the reduction in entry barriers caused by a system transition to rule of law-based formal enforcement,[23] and who likely also have the most political influence. As Mancur Olson has argued, these families will have both the incentive and the resources to make more difficult, or to block, the development of new formal institutions that devalue the families' investment in relation-supporting institutions.[24]

As a result, economic growth may falter or turn negative in this transition period, when existing relation-based institutions are becoming less efficient and their replacement by rule of law-based commercial institutions is not yet complete. The same institutions that made the economy grow so quickly during its early development period then operate as a barrier to effective transition, a phenomenon that Paul Milgrom and John Roberts call "supermodularity" (Milgrom and Roberts 1994: 12). As they put it, "(e)ven if a coordinate adjustment on all relevant dimensions might yield an improvement in performance, it may be that until all the features of the new pattern have been implemented, the performance of the system may be much worse than in the original position" (Milgrom and Roberts 1994: 12). Indeed, John Shuhe Li ascribes the shift between the "East Asian Miracle" and the "East Asian Financial Crisis" to just such a phenomenon: "The dismantling of too many existing relationship-specific mechanisms in so short a period can damage the future potential of economies at an early stage of development to catch up; i.e., before reaching the turning point where relation-based governance is still more cost-effective than rule-based governance . . . ." (Li 2003: 669).

Conclusion: how is the transition to rule-of-law enforcement accomplished?

The function of shareholder distribution looks quite different when approached from the product-market side than from the capital-market side. While the absence of effective minority shareholder protection may in some circumstances explain the absence of corporations whose shares are widely held,[25] it does not explain why we observe minority holdings at all, nor the special role of controlling-family shareholders in many countries. From the perspective of the product market, shareholder distribution, including family control, may play a role in facilitating the corporation's operation as a reputation bearer in markets where commercial exchange is supported by reputation rather than by formal enforcement.

A focus on shareholder distribution from a product-market perspective also highlights the importance of a dynamic account of the institutions necessary for economic growth. For developing economies, reputation-based markets can develop more easily and grow more quickly than markets that support anonymous trading, because the institutional structure of a system based on formal enforcement is both more expensive and more difficult to develop. Formal enforcement requires the rule of law, and a well-functioning government (Damm 2006).

The problem is transition. The institutions that supported relation-based exchange, and in which the families that have been most successful have large investments, ultimately become barriers to further development; a public-choice analysis suggests that those who have succeeded in a relation-based economy will resist the transition to formal enforcement. The politics of transition, then, are driven by the size of one's piece, rather than the size of the pie. If this analysis is plausible, we are left with a task and a conjecture. The task is to develop a dynamic account: what breaks the transition log-jam—how does a country overcome the political barriers to shifting the character of its product markets by supplementing reputation with rule of law-based formal enforcement?[26] The problem is made especially interesting because dictators as a class do not foster faster economic growth (Rodrik 2000: 3); only certain dictators appear to have accomplished that. The conjecture, which I am pursuing in work with Curtis Milhaupt, is that, in countries that in recent years have successfully made the switch, the architects of the institutional and market transition were what we term "economically benevolent dictators," whose political power allowed the imposition of their individual utility function—continued economic growth even at the expense of (or by buying off) influential families[27] If this conjecture turns out to explain some of the variance in development between different nations, the task is not to find more dictators—economically benevolent dictators, even if one could find them, have not been benevolent along other important dimensions—but instead to understand the function the unusual dictators played and then to design less oppressive substitutes.

Notes

* For helpful comments on an earlier draft of this essay, I am grateful to Patrick Bolton, Luca Enriques, Victor Goldberg, Jeffrey Gordon, Zohar Goshen, Kon Sik Kim, Michael Klausner, Curtis Milhaupt, Alan Schwartz, Robert Scott, and to the participants at a conference on "A Decade After Crisis: The Transformation of Corporate Governance in East Asia," 29–30 September 2006, Tokyo, Japan, sponsored by the Center of Excellence Program in Soft Law at the University of Tokyo, The Center on Financial Law at Seoul National University, and the Center for Japanese Legal Studies at Columbia Law School. An earlier version of this work previously appeared in the Standford Law Review – 60 Stan. L. Rev. 633 (2007).
1 The price difference between controlling and non-controlling shares, however measured, is dramatically smaller in countries with good shareholder protection.
2 I should be clear at the outset that my shorthand terms "poor" or "bad" commercial law encompass two different sources of failure: (1) substantively bad law—i.e., inefficient rules—regardless of the quality of enforcement; and (2) substantively good law but with poor enforcement. Thus, a wonderful civil code in a system without effective courts would fall within my terms.
3 John Shuhe Li states that: "[I]n catching up economies, there is generally not rule-based [formal enforcement] governance; hence relation-based governance is the only available mechanism to enforce agreements" (Li 2003: 658); Klein and Leffler (1981); Tesler (1981).
4 Interesting recent work has sought to link elements of corporate governance other than shareholder distribution to conditions in the product market. See, e.g., Cremers et al. (2006; Perez-Gonzales and Guadalupe (2005).
5 There is a very interesting literature addressing the institutions necessary to support trade that is both formally sophisticated and historically grounded. The work of Avner Greif on the organization of the Maghribi traders and of Avner Greif, Paul Milgrom and Barry Weingast on medieval European trade, are examples of this work. See Greif (1993); Greif et al. (1994).
6 Milgrom and Roberts (1994).
7 Here I anticipate ongoing work with Curtis Milhaupt. See text accompanying note 27 below.

8 I develop similar conditions to reputation-based contracting in the venture capital market in R. J. Gilson, "Engineering a Venture Capital Market: Lessons from the American Experience," *Stanford Law Review* 55 (2003): 1067. Douglas North states the conditions in terms of the barriers they present: Exchange "is difficult to sustain when the game is not repeated (or there is an end game), when information on the other players is lacking, and when there are large numbers of players" (North 1990: 12). The discussion in the text assumes the condition that MacLeod and Malcomson specify as necessary before the game is worth the candle: "The fundamental requirement for an implicit contract to be self-enforcing is that there exist sufficient economic surplus from continuing it over what the parties can jointly get if it is terminated" (MacCleod and Malcomson, 1989: 448).

9 "Cultural beliefs and behavioral norms coordinate expectations and provide a shared understanding of the meaning of various actions" (Greif 2005). See Mobius and Szeidl (2007) (modeling a decrease in trust among trading partners in a reputation market as heterogeneity of potential trading partners increases).

10 This account assumes that misbehavior is punished only by individuals—the injured trading partner and those who learn of the misbehavior—who decline to trade with the misbehaving trader. However, reputation markets can develop institutions that facilitate the market's operation by collectivizing information acquisition and sharing, and expanding the breadth of responsive sanctions. See Greif (2005: 733–734); Richman (2004). Because of the path dependency of institutional characteristics in particular jurisdictions, an account of their development requires a rich historical context (Greif, 1993). My argument does not depend on the simplified presentation in the text; however, its application to a particular country will require developing the context, including the institutional structure of the reputation market.

11 The unraveling reasoning is that a potential trading partner will also know that the party will not perform in the final round, so it will anticipate that behavior and not perform in the next-to-last round, which will be anticipated by the first party, and so on back to non-performance in the current round.

12 Other techniques also can be used to bond future reputation, such as making observable investments in assets that will be valuable only if the corporation is successful. See Klein and Leffler (1981). However, all strategies require confronting the time preferences of the corporation's short-lived decision makers.

13 Compare Bebchuk and Fried (2004) (criticizing the design on U.S. executive compensation), with Murphy (2002) (rebutting criticism), and Holmstrom (2005) (assessing criticisms and defenses).

14 Cultural values concerning the importance of family and the tradeoff between intra-family loyalty and individual self-interest will differ among countries. See Gilson (2006: 1641, 1673) (cultural value of family control in Asia). Once the commitment to maximizing family wealth, as opposed to that of individual family members, breaks down—whether through cultural change as a result of modernization or because of what I have called the "gravity of generations" Gilson (2006: 1668)—then inside conflict over distributional issues will result in decreased commitment to reputation and reduced productivity generally. This, in turn, will undermine the support family ownership provides to reputation-based product market exchanges. Mueller and Warneryd argue that public ownership responds to such internal distributional competition by forcing inside managers to unite against the outside owners' demand for resources. While Mueller and Warneryd do not have family ownership in mind, the intuition seems applicable: dysfunctional family ownership leads to a public offering. Their model, however, assumes that the public's investors have the power through legal rules to assert themselves, a circumstance that is likely not present in developing countries (Mueller and Warneryd 2001). For a striking example of the disintegration of

intra-family loyalty within a very successful U.S. family-controlled business, see Andrews (2003) (internal conflicts within Pritzker family lead to breakup of family fortune).

15 Steven Tadelis develops a model of reputation formation that, in contrast to Kreps's focus on moral hazard (one party cheating in a future round), is based on adverse selection (future buyers are uncertain about whether future owners will be talented or trustworthy) (Tadelis 1999). Tadelis' model assumes that shifts in ownership of a business are not observable by customers of the business—hence the adverse-selection problem that drives the model. Family ownership, by making ownership shifts to non-family transparent to future clients, therefore reduces the barriers to the operation of a reputation market in an adverse selection driven model, just as it does in Kreps's moral hazard approach. To be fair, Tadelis does briefly consider the possibility that family ownership might address the adverse-selection problem, but dismisses the fact of family ownership as providing too little information to support a separation between good and bad service providers: "Clearly, businesses that have signs claiming that they have owned by the same family for 75 years convey little information about the quality of the current owner, let alone of the key employees" (Tadelis 1999: 560). In settings where family ownership powerfully predicts individual family-member preferences for business success, Tadelis dismisses the impact of family ownership too quickly. His point might be better understood as a prediction of regression to the mean in talent as control shifts from the business's founder to her heirs. There is some empirical evidence that supports this inference. Gilson (2006: 1668–1669) (reviewing studies).

16 A number of explanations have been advanced for why a controlling shareholder would want to establish public minority shareholders, whether in an initial public offering or in a spin-out public sale of a minority interest in a previously wholly owned subsidiary. These include the evaluative information provided by the pricing of an efficient stock market and the availability of publicly traded shares as an incentive compensation vehicle. See Gilson and Gordon (2003: 791); Schipper and Smith (1986: 153, 182). Such information-based explanations, however, require an efficient stock market, a condition that is not consistent with poor shareholder-protection law.

17 Almeida and Wolfenzon (2006) provide a good example. In Almeida and Wolfeszon's model, the extent to which the controlling shareholder can divert assets is expressed as the "pledgebility" parameter; the model then yields different results depending on the extent to which returns can be effectively committed to minority investors. However, there is no discussion of the institutional structure that allows an effective commitment not to divert more than a particular value of the parameter. Shleifer and Wolfenzon (2002) use a similar modeling technique to parametize the level of diversion.

18 Gilson (2006: 1674–1678), addresses possible responses to these adverse selection problems.

19 Dyck and Zingales (2004: 582–586) (treating newspapers as a corporate governance constraint). Luca Enriques has pointed out that the role of the financial press may be limited to a handful of developed countries where there is a widespread confidence in the newspapers' journalistic integrity. Absent that confidence, they cannot play the contemplated "shaming" role. Private correspondence with the author.

20 I recognize that I am at this point glossing over a serious problem—why is a controlling shareholder's treatment of minority shareholders more observable than the quality of the products or services it provides? Or, setting the bar at a realistically lower level, is the controlling shareholder's treatment of minority shareholders sufficiently observable that it adds something to the customer's

assessment of the corporation's reputation based only on the products or services it provides? I will return to this concern after describing the product market explanation for minority shareholders in family controlled corporations.

21 The enforcement of a Japanese main bank's obligation to undertake a rescue of its clients has been said to operate in this informal way. While a main bank had no formal legal obligation to undertake a rescue, the Ministry of Finance had to approve applications to open new bank branches, a decision that was left entirely in the Ministry of Finance's discretion. The failure to discharge the informal rescue obligation would be punished by the denial of branch applications. See Aoki *et al.* (1994: 27–32).

22 Both Dixit (2004: 80–82) and Li (2003: 659–661) stress this point. Douglass North has stated that "the inability of societies to develop effective, low-cost enforcement of contracts is the most important source of both historical stagnation and contemporary underdevelopment in the Third World" (North 1990: 54).

23 For example, in a system with good commercial law, contractual commitments such as warranties can provide new entrants a substitute for difficult-to-acquire reputation. When KIA, a Korean automobile manufacturer entered the U.S. market, it offered a substantially longer warranty than its established competitors.

24 Olsen (1982). Almeida and Wolfezon (2006) make the same point about conglomerates in developing countries. Once conglomerates become a large enough part of the economy, they may impose a negative externality by causing the overall capital market to operate inefficiently, even if the conglomerates' internal capital markets operate efficiently as a result of a kind of crowding-out phenomenon. In this setting, government intervention may be necessary to reduce the conglomerates' role.

25 Recent scholarship suggests that in some countries causation may run in the opposite direction. Franks *et al.* (2005) and Cheffins (2004: 591) argue that U.K. shareholding patterns arose from informal relations of trust and confidence that encouraged equity investment by investors geographically proximate to the issuer. Here the influence is from product market to capital market. This diversity in actual history among jurisdictions is consistent with Avner Greif's conclusion that the structure of reputation markets in individual countries will be path dependent. Because "cultural beliefs and behavioral norms will coordinate expectations and provide a shared understanding of the meaning of various actions. *Ceteris paribus*, initial social structures and cultural features therefore influence which, among the many possible organic [reputation market structures] will emerge … " (Greif 2005:762). See sources in note 12 above (discussing path dependency of corporate governance institutions).

26 Avner Greif and David Laitin provide an analytic road map for developing a dynamic account of system change, noting that a game theoretic account explains an equilibrium, not what causes a system to shift to a new equilibrium (Greif and Laitin 2004: 633). A shift resulting from changed external conditions is easy enough to explain—the rules of the game have changed. The harder question is to explain how systems change as a result of internal forces. Given the equilibrium analysis, "[e]ndongenous institutional change appears, then, to be a contradiction in terms" (Greif and Laitin 2004: 633).

27 Fareed Zakaria makes a related claim whose point is to explain the development of democratic government rather than economic development. He argues that the success of democracy is a function of per capita GDP. In his view, the first step toward representative government is economic development, which may require a dictator, but which also then creates the middle class that will bring the dictator down (Zakaria 2004: 69–73). Played through Greif and Laitin's model, above note 26, this would be an example of an equilibrium whose circumstances undermine its stability.

References

Aggarwal, R., I. Erel, R. Stulz, and R. Wiliamson (2006) "Do U.S. Firms Have the Best Corporate Governance? A Cross-country Examination of the Relation Between Corporate Governance and Shareholder Wealth," working paper, available at http://ssrn.com/abstract=954165.

Almeida, H. and D. Wolfenzon (2006) "Should Business Groups Be Dismantled? The Equilibrium Costs of Efficient Internal Capital Markets," *Journal of Financial Economics* 79: 99.

Andrews, S. (2003) "Shattered Dynasty," *Vanity Fair*, May.

Aoki, M., H. Patrick, and P. Sheard (1994) "The Japanese Main Bank System: An Introductory Overview," in M. Aoki and H. Patrick (eds.), *The Japanese Main Bank System*, New York, NY: Oxford University Press, 3.

Bebchuk, L. and J. Fried (2004) *Pay Without Performance: The Unfulfilled Promise of Executive Compensation*, Cambridge, MA: Harvard University Press.

Brealey, R.A., S.C. Myers, and F. Allen (2006) *Principles of Corporate Finance*, 8th edn., Boston, MA: McGraw-Hill/Irwin.

Cheffins, B.R. (2004) "Are Good Managers Required For a Separation of Ownership and Control?" *Industrial and Corporate Change* 13: 591.

Claessens, S., S. Djankov, and L. Lang (2000) "The Separation of Ownership and Control in East Asia Corporations," *Journal of Financial Economics* 58: 81.

Claessens, S., S. Djankov, J. Fan, and L. Lang (2002) "Disentangling the Incentive and Entrenchment Effects of Large Shareholdings," *Journal of Finance* 57: 2741.

Cremers, K.J.M., V.B. Nair, and U. Peyer (2006) "Weak Shareholder Rights: A Products Market Rationale," Yale ICF Working Paper No. 06-29, available at http://ssrn.com/abstract=890570.

Damm, K. (2006) "Legal Institutions, Legal Origins, and Governance," John M. Olin Law and Economics Working Paper Series, 2nd edn., No. 303, available at http://ssrn.com/abstract_id=932694.

Dixit, A. (2004) *Lawlessness and Economics: Alternative Modes of Governance*, Princeton, NJ: Princeton University Press.

Dyck, A. and L. Zingales (2004) "Private Benefits of Control: An International Comparison," *Journal of Finance* 59: 537.

Enriques, L. and P. Volpin (2007) "Corporate Governance Reforms in Continental Europe," *Journal of Economic Perspectives* 21: 117.

Franks, J., C. Mayer, and S. Rossi (2005) "Spending Less Time With Family: The Decline of Family Ownership in the U.K.," in R. Morck, (ed.), *The History of Corporate Governance Around the World: Family Business Groups to Professional Managers* Chicago, IL: University of Chicago Press.

Fudenberg, D. and E. Maskin (1986) "The Folk Theorem in Repeated Games With Discounting or With Incomplete Information," *Econometrica* 54: 533.

Gilson, R.J. (1996) "Corporate Governance and Economic Efficiency: When Do Institutions Matter?" *Washington University Law Quarterly* 74: 327.

—— (2001) "Globalizing of Corporate Governance: Convergence of Form or Substance," *American Journal of Comparative Law* 49: 329.

—— (2003) "Engineering a Venture Capital Market: Lessons From the American Experience," *Stanford Law Review* 55: 1067.

—— (2006) "Controlling Shareholders and Corporate Governance: Complicating the Comparative Taxonomy," *Harvard Law Review* 119: 1641.

Gilson, R.J. and B.S. Black (1995) *The Law and Finance of Corporate Acquisitions*, 2nd edn., Westbury, NY: The Foundation Press.

Gilson, R.J. and J.N. Gordon (2003) "Controlling Controlling Shareholders," *University of Pennsylvania Law Review* 152: 785.

Greif, A. (1993) "Contract Enforceability and Economic Institutions in Early Trade: the Maghribi Traders' Coalition," *American Economics Review* 83: 525.

—— (2005) "Commitment, Coercion and Markets: the Nature and Dynamics of Institutions Supporting Exchange," in C. Menard and M. Shirley (eds.), *Handbook of New Institutional Economics*, Dordrecht: Springer, 727.

Greif, A. and D. Laitin (2004) "A Theory of Endogenous Institutional Change," *American Political Science Review* 98: 633.

Greif, A., P.R. Milgrom, and B.R. Weingast (1994) "Coordination, Commitment and Enforcement: the Case of the Merchant Guild," *Journal of Political Economics* 102: 745.

Holstrom, B. (2005) "Pay Without Performance and the Managerial Power Hypothesis: A Comment," *Journal of Corporation Law* 30: 703.

Khanna, T. and K. Palepu (2000) "An Analysis of Diversified Indian Business Groups," *Journal of Finance* 55: 868.

Klein, B. and K.B. Leffler (1981) "The Role of Market Forces in Assuring Contractual Performance," *Journal of Political Economics* 89: 615.

Kreps, D.M. (1990) "Corporate Culture and Economic Theory" in J.E. Alt and K. A. Shepsle (eds.), *Perspectives on Positive Political Economy*, New York, NY: Cambridge University Press.

La Porta, R. (1998) "Law and Finance," *Journal of Political Economics* 106: 113.

La Porta, R., F. Lopez-de-Silanes, and A. Shleifer (1999) "Corporate Ownership Around the World," *Journal of Finance* 54: 471.

La Porta, R., F. Lopez-de-Silanes, and A. Shleifer and R. Vishny (1997) "Legal Determinants of Finance," *Journal of Finance* 52: 1131.

—— (2000) "Investor Protection and Corporate Governance," *Journal of Financial Economics* 58: 3.

Li, J.S. (2003) "Relation-based Versus Rule-based Governance: an Explanation of the East Asian miracle and East Asian Crisis," *Review of International Economics* 11: 651.

MacLeod, W.B. and J.M. Malcomson (1989) "Implicit Contracts, Incentive Compatability, and Involuntary Unemployment," *Econometrica* 57: 447.

Milgrom, P. and J. Roberts (1994) "Complementarities and Systems: Understanding Japanese Economic Organization," *Estudios Economicos* 9: 3.

Mobius, M. and A. Szeidl (2007) "Trust and Social Collateral," NBER Working Paper No. 13126.

Mueller, H.M. and K. Warneryd (2001) "Inside Versus Outside Ownership: a Political Theory of the Firm," *Rand Journal of Economics* 32: 527.

Murphy, K.J. (2002) "Explaining Executive Compensation: Managerial Power Versus the Perceived Cost of Stock Options," *University of Chicago Law Review* 69: 847.

Nenova, T. (2003) "The Value of Corporate Voting Rights and Control: a Cross-country Analysis," *Journal of Financial Economics* 68: 325.

North, D.C. (1990) *Institutions, Institutional Change and Economic Performance*, New York, NY: Cambridge University Press.

Olsen, M. (1982) *The Rise and Decline of Nations*, United States: Courier Companies.

Perez-Gonzales, F. and M. Guadalupe (2005) "The Impact of Product Market Competition on Private Benefits of Control," Working Paper, available at http://ssrn.com/abstract=890814.

Richman, B.D. (2004) "Firms, Courts and Reputation Mechanisms: Towards a Positive Theory of Private Ordering," *Columbia Law Review* 104: 2328.

Rodrik, D. (2000) "Institutions for High-quality Growth: What They Are and How to Acquire Them," *Studies in Comparative International Development* 35: 3.

Ross, S.A., R.W. Westerfield, and J. Jaffe (2005) *Corporate Finance*, 7th edn., Boston: McGraw-Hill/Irwin.

Schipper, K. and A. Smith (1986) "A Comparison of Equity Carve-outs and Seasoned Equity Offerings: Share Price Effects and Corporate Restructuring," *Journal of Financial Economics* 15: 153–186.

Shleifer, A. and D. Wolfenzon (2002) "Investor Protection and Equity Markets," *Journal of Financial Economics* 66: 3–27.

Tadelis, S. (1999) "What's in a Name? Reputation as a Tradeable Asset," *American Economic Review* 89: 548.

Tesler, L. (1981) "A Theory of Self-enforcing Agreements," *Journal of Business* 53: 27.

Zakaria, F. (2004) *The Future of Freedom* New York, NY: W.W. Norton and Company.

13 The uncertain value of shareholder suits in Asian corporate governance

Michael Klausner

Introduction

As chapters of this book detail, one element of corporate governance reform in Asia has been the introduction of two types of shareholder lawsuits: derivative suits and securities class actions. These suits are imports from the United States. Experience with these suits in the U.S., however, has been problematic. Among the problems is the fact that the executives responsible for misconduct rarely bear personal out-of-pocket liability.[1] Instead, shareholders pay, either through directors' and officers' liability insurance, purchased by the corporation, or through settlements paid directly by the corporation. It is unclear whether these suits deter misconduct, while it is clear that they do not provide meaningful compensation. It may well be that directors and officers should be protected from liability in these cases because non-meritorious cases are too common and the amount at stake if a director or officer is held liable is too great. But that raises the question whether the suits should exist in the first place. Further, as transplants in Asia, where controlling shareholders are prevalent, these types of suits may not address the corporate governance problems that companies experience.

Shareholder suits in the U.S.

Shareholder suits in the U.S. are plagued by a dilemma. Their objective is to deter misconduct and to compensate victims. In other settings, a simple suit for damages accomplishes this dual goal. Not so in the context of a shareholder suit. Because corporate officers and directors have responsibility for enormous amounts of shareholder wealth, their misconduct can cause massive losses. In many cases, the officers and directors of a company do not have the personal wealth to cover those losses. Moreover, due to the possibility of judicial error and abusive lawsuits, it would be bad policy to expose officers and directors to bankrupting liability risk. One solution might be a cap on liability, but that would introduce another problem: Lawyers would not bring a suit without the prospect of collecting sufficient fees. Consequently, an additional source of funds is needed. In the U.S. that source is the shareholder of the company that has experienced the alleged misconduct. Through director and officer (D&O) liability insurance, indemnification, and direct payments by the corporation to the plaintiffs to settle a case, the shareholders of the company that has suffered from the misconduct pay on behalf of the executives alleged to have engaged in the misconduct. Thus, in the aggregate, at least, shareholders pay themselves. The dynamics of settlement are such that individual officers and directors themselves rarely pay a penny. Compensation is not accomplished, and there is reason to doubt that deterrence is achieved.

The problem is clearest in class actions for violation of the securities laws. In these suits, the corporation itself is a defendant. The corporation's officers and directors can be defendants as well, but the corporation is fully liable and, in the vast majority of cases, the corporation settles the suit and, along with its D&O insurer, pays the full amount agreed to. If the corporation is bankrupt, its D&O policy typically covers the amount for which the plaintiffs have settled.

In a derivative suit, the defendants are the corporation's officers and directors. Nonetheless, it is rare that they pay. They are covered by a D&O policy—again, paid for by the corporation—and nearly all suits settle for amounts no greater than the policy limit.

Whether settlements are paid by the corporation or the D&O insurer, the source of funds is the shareholder on the defendants' side of the case. These suits result in large amounts of cash flowing from defendants' shareholders to plaintiff shareholders, with plaintiffs and defense lawyers taking a large slice in the process. The same shareholders are often on the paying and receiving sides of settlement, with moving money from one pocket to the other. But even if they are not, the cycle of cash is a net loss to shareholders in the aggregate. Perhaps there is some deterrence purchased. There may be reputational costs to pay for officers and directors involved in these suits, and there certainly is a cost in terms of time and aggravation. There is also a remote chance of an out-of-pocket payment, especially for officers. It is impossible to measure the extent of deterrence created by the threat of these suits. But there is reason to wonder whether the deterrence purchased is worth the cost.

Shareholder suits in Asia

Two questions arise with respect to the importation of American-style shareholder suits into Asia. First, will the experience be different? Second, how well tailored are these suits to corporate governance problems in Asia?

Will shareholder suits in Asia be different?

In Japan, the courtroom door was opened to derivative suits in 1993, when the filing fee for these suits was reduced. As Professor Fujita explains, the incidence of derivative actions increased from near zero to an average of over 150 suits per year. Because these suits were rare prior to 1993, Japanese law lacked protections similar to those available to officers and directors in the U.S.—such as the business judgment rule and procedural rules for dismissal. Officers and directors of Japanese companies, therefore, were at risk and in at least two cases they paid damages. Political and economic forces responded, however, by establishing protections for management. Courts created a business judgment rule and required plaintiffs to post bonds. The legislature gave management the authority to seek dismissal of a suit and gave shareholders and the board authority to place a cap on officers' and directors' liability.[2] In addition, a D&O insurance market has developed since the 1990s. As of the end of the 1990s, 70 percent to 80 percent of Japanese companies had purchased D&O insurance.[3] Thus, it appears that a new, post-1993 equilibrium has been reached in which, again, officers and directors do not face significant liability risk. But unlike the pre-1993 regime, there will be shareholder suits, and shareholders will bear their cost.

Korea has imported both derivative suits and class actions from the U.S. In 1998 the Korean legislature reduced the minimum shareholding requirement for plaintiffs from 5 percent to 1 percent for small companies and to 0.05 percent to 0.01 percent for large companies, with the goal being to make the threat of these suits a meaningful element of the corporate governance system. Few derivative suits have been filed, however, and those that have been filed have been filed by the People's Solidarity for a Participatory Democracy (PSPD), a nonprofit corporate governance advocate funded by donations rather than by shareholders motivated by the economics of the lawsuit. In 2004, the Korean legislature enacted legislation authorizing securities class actions. No class actions have been filed, however.

As Professor Song has explained in this book, the economics of derivative suits and class actions deter shareholders from bringing these suits. Plaintiffs pay their own costs unless they win, and even if they win, they may not be fully reimbursed for their litigation costs. In addition, Korea has a "loser-pays" rule under which a plaintiff who loses a shareholder suit must pay the defendants' costs.

Professor Song advocates the elimination of these barriers and the facilitation of a "lawyer-driven" litigation system in Korea similar to that of the U.S.[4] But why would the result be different from what occurs in the U.S.: A flow of cash from shareholders on the defendant side to shareholder plaintiffs, with much of the cash making a round trip and lawyers taking a substantial portion off the top? D&O insurance is prevalent in Korea. Why won't the insurers fund settlements in both derivative suits and class actions, and charge commensurate premiums? And since corporations are defendants in Korean class actions, what is there to stop them from paying whatever settlement amounts are not covered by insurance?[5] Again, I am not necessarily arguing for greater exposure to personal liability in private class actions. If non-meritorious actions cannot be filtered out, then protecting officers and directors may be the best course. But the question this raises is whether anything is gained from instituting these suits in the first place.

In Taiwan, the Investor Protection Center, a government-sanctioned non-profit organization, is authorized to bring class actions for violation of the securities laws. As Professor Wang explains in this volume, this arrangement may result in the filing of more meritorious lawsuits. But the defendant in these class actions is still the company.[6] It remains to be seen whether the Center will succeed in extracting payments from officers or directors who have engaged in misconduct.

Finally, in mainland China, derivative suits are permitted but the shareholding threshold is prohibitively high, and class actions are not authorized. Consequently, shareholder suits do not exist. In this book, Professor Tang argues that derivative suit rules should be eased to encourage lawsuits and that class actions should be authorized. Professor Tang does not, however, address the issue of who should be the defendants in these suits and how to avoid having shareholders pay for a system whose cost may be greater than its benefits.

In sum, the shareholder suits already authorized in Korea, Japan, and Taiwan, and the reforms advocated in this volume for those jurisdictions and for mainland China follow the models of U.S. derivative suits and securities class actions. It seems reasonable to expect that these suits will encounter the problems experienced in the U.S.—namely, a lack of compensation and ambiguous deterrence, with public shareholders paying the bill. It may be that the benefits of these suits nonetheless outweigh the costs; some degree of shareholder litigation may be better than none. But the U.S. system should not be imported without an awareness of the drawbacks and a judgment that they are a price worth paying. Furthermore, as discussed in the next section, there may be an alternative, or perhaps additional, approach—also with precedent in the U.S.—that is better tailored to a corporate governance regime with controlling shareholders.

Shareholder suits and controlling shareholders

In the U.S., controlling shareholders have fiduciary duties to minority shareholders, and minority shareholders can bring a class action against a controlling shareholder to enforce those duties. Any action by a company that disproportionately favors the controlling shareholder can give rise to such a suit. Leaving political feasibility aside, this is a more promising approach than either the derivative suit or the securities class action for companies with a controlling shareholder. Ideally, the controlling shareholder targeted would be a real person or group of people.

Consider the advantages of a class action by minority shareholders against a controlling shareholder (where a controlling shareholder is present). First, the controlling shareholder has assets that can satisfy a judgment. Even if other assets can be hidden, the controlling shareholder's shares in the company can be transferred to minority shareholders in payment of damages. Consequently, minority shareholders will be compensated for their losses.

Second, class actions by minority shareholders against controlling shareholders would create deterrence. The controlling shareholder would be forced to internalize costs that it imposes on minority shareholders. To the extent management is responsible for misconduct unrelated to that of the controlling shareholder, the controlling shareholder will have incentives to put controls in place. In addition, if management is independently responsible for the conduct that led to a damage payment by the controlling shareholder to the minority shareholders, the controlling shareholder should have a cause of action against management.

Third, there would be no problem of over-deterrence, as there may be when officers or directors bear liability risk. Excessive caution is less a concern for parties such as controlling shareholders, who are not involved in day-to-day management. In contrast to executives, controlling shareholders stand to gain a substantial portion of the upside potential in any business decision.

In contrast, consider a derivative suit or a class action against officers or directors of a company with a controlling shareholder. In a derivative suit, the controlling shareholder indirectly gets a pro rata share of the payment to the company (assuming the controlling shareholder is not also an officer). If a class action is brought against a company and the company pays damages, the controlling shareholder is on both sides of the transaction (unless he is excluded from the class).[7]

There are surely complications with this proposal. A cause of action against a controlling shareholder may confront formalistic jurisprudential objections based the fact that the controlling shareholder has no role in management. Or there may be pressure to require proof that the controlling shareholder was directly involved in the misconduct, which would probably render the cause of action useless as a practical matter. Controlling shareholders may also be difficult to identify. Their assets may be hidden or otherwise invulnerable to legal process; and their stock may be pledged to banks for financing. Or their assets may be insufficient to compensate shareholders, especially if their financial interest in the company is less than 50 percent. In addition, the suit would have to be brought against the controlling shareholder alone. If the company's officers or directors are defendants as well, the defendants could conspire among themselves to have the officers and directors accept responsibility to the extent necessary to have the D&O insurance policy pay.[8] Finally, for a cause of action against controlling shareholders to be effective, shareholders and their lawyers would need incentives to bring suits. Thus, the reforms discussed by the authors in this volume would remain important. Despite the challenges entailed in creating an effective cause of action against controlling shareholders, aiming reform in this direction may be at least as fruitful as relying on derivative suits and securities class actions.

Notes

1 Outside directors bear out-of-pocket liability in less than one half of one percent of cases (Black *et al.* 2006). My ongoing research indicates that officers make personal payments in approximately 5 percent of cases.
2 Tomotaka Fujita, Chapter 1 in this volume.
3 Cheffins and Black (2006: 1461–1462).
4 Ok-Rial Song, Chapter 5 in this volume.
5 For a more detailed analysis, see Black *et al.* (2005).
6 Wallace Wen-Yeu Wang and Chen Jian-Lin, "Reforming China's Securities Civil Actions: Lessons from US's PSLRA Reform and Taiwan'ts Government Sanctioned Non-profit Organization," forthcoming *Columbia Journal of Asian Law*, Spring 2008.
7 A question for those advocating class actions in Asia is therefore whether controlling shareholders would be excluded from the class. My understanding is that this issue has not been addressed.
8 If the controlling shareholder had insurance as well, presumably it would pay for the policy rather than having the company pay, and the insurer would price the policy according to the risk posed by the controlling shareholder. Therefore, even with insurance, the controlling shareholder would internalize the cost of its behavior.

References

Black, Bernard, Brian Cheffins and Michael Klausner (2005) "Shareholder Suits and Outside Director Liability: The Case of Korea in Youngjae Lim, Corporate Governance and the Capital Market in Korea." Available at http://papers.ssrn.com/abstract=628223.
—— (2006) "Outside Director Liability," *Stanford Law Review* 58: 1055–1159.
Cheffins, Brian and Bernard Black (2006) "Outside Director Liability Across Countries," *Texas Law Review* 84: 1385–1480.

Index